ARMAMENT OF BRITISH AIRCRAFT
1909–1939

Prototype Hawker Hector: a tribute to the pilots of the Aeroplane and Armament Experimental Establishment, Martlesham Heath, and to the art of *Flight* photographer John Yoxall, who will not be seeing this book, though he helped to make it. The author was in the Hector's rear cockpit when this picture was taken, and his recollection that the Lewis gun of this particular Hart variant was on an unusual gun-mounting is confirmed in later pages. (*Flight International.*)

ARMAMENT OF
BRITISH AIRCRAFT
1909–1939

H. F. KING
M.B.E.

Formerly Editor of 'Flight International'
and 'Air-Cushion Vehicles'

PUTNAM
LONDON

By the same author

AEROMARINE ORIGINS
THE WORLD'S BOMBERS
THE WORLD'S FIGHTERS

© H. F. King 1971
ISBN 0 370 00057 9
*No part of this book may be photocopied without written
permission from the publishers*
Printed and bound in Great Britain for
Putnam & Company Limited
9 Bow Street, London, WC2E 7AL
by Richard Clay (The Chaucer Press) Ltd
Bungay, Suffolk
Set in Monotype Times
First published in 1971

'Afterwards, just for safety's sake, I always carried a carbine with me in the air.'

Lieut W. S. Douglas (Lord Douglas of Kirtleside),
describing a 1914 encounter

'The Norman sight for the Lewis seems to be awfully good . . . many a Boche diving on the tail of a Bristol has been badly stung . . .'

Maj Vere Bettington, C.O. of No. 48 Sqn., to
Capt Louis Strange, 13 May, 1917

'. . . orders were issued for four Handley Pages, each carrying one 1,650 lb bomb, to attack Kaiserslautern . . .'

'The War in the Air,' Vol. VI—Independent
Force Operations, 1918

'Oh, I just gave him a squirt.'

Battle of Britain pilot

CONTENTS

Foreword	ix
Admiralty Air Department	1
Aircraft Disposal Company	3
Airspeed	3
Alcock	4
Armstrong Whitworth	5
Arrow	26
Austin	26
Avro	27
Beardmore	42
Blackburn	44
Boulton & Paul (later Boulton Paul)	73
Bristol	89
British Aerial Transport	122
de Havilland	123
Dyott	146
Fairey	147
Felixstowe	180
Gloster	183
Grahame-White	201
Handley Page	202
Hawker	226
Kennedy	264
Mann, Egerton	265
Mann & Grimmer	265
Martin-Baker	265
Martinsyde	267
Miles	270
Nieuport	271
Parnall	272
Pemberton-Billing	276
Phoenix (English Electric)	276
Port Victoria	277
Robey	278

Royal Aircraft Factory	280
Sage	298
Saunders	299
Saunders-Roe (formerly S. E. Saunders)	299
Short	306
Siddeley	319
Sopwith	320
Sunbeam	355
Supermarine	356
Tarrant	373
Norman Thompson	373
Vickers	373
Westland	424
White & Thompson	451
Wight	451
Index	453

FOREWORD

Excruciating spasms of classifying, sub-classifying, reclassifying and de-classifying were my lot before I found the first elaborate schemes for this work to be wholly unrealistic. So simplicity prevailed, for it was clear that rigid specialisation, whether in classes of aeroplanes or weapons, has seldom proved enduring. Attempts to formulate, and rigidly to designate, have proved both arbitrary and unacceptable. A first volume devoted to aircraft, and grouped according to maker rather than class, and a second dealing with weapons, became desirable not only for reasons of bulk but because the aircraft descriptions could then be related directly to other volumes in the Putnam aeronautical series.

Avoidance of rigid classification by type is now widely endorsed by other writers, to whose diligent researches immediate and grateful acknowledgement is rendered, in the pleasant reassurance of their own declared indebtedness to *Flight* and my own work for that journal. There is, too, the added satisfaction that their names appear today with prominence and frequency over the Putnam imprint.

Handbooks and makers' descriptions are drawn on without stint or shame, for these are rarities indeed, and as well as lending authenticity have lightened a sometimes weighty task with such diverting renderings (and this comes instantly to mind) as 'cartridge case' for 'ammunition box'. With delight, moreover, the frequent appellation 'gun shoots' has been noted for case and link chutes ('shoots' were sportingly prescribed for the Pup); and though the S.E.5a is accorded its flawless complement of 'Constantinesco gear, Vickers gun mount, ammunition box and Foster mount for Lewis gun', one discovers—strayed no doubt from the 'howdah' positions on the Felixstowe F.2A—indubitable 'gun bearers' on the 'de Havilland No. 4'. The pulse-rate is further quickened by a solemn, public, official assurance (and I hold the evidence) that the Blenheim had an armament of 'four fixed pom-pom guns, arranged in pairs in the engine nacelles, firing through the airscrew discs . . .' This revelation was vouchsafed by a national museum; and in all solemnity an institution hardly less august advised that a low-drag mounting by de Havilland embodied a 'gun carriage', and that a mounting produced contemporaneously by Avro had a device for releasing locking-bolts from 'holes in the runway'. One ponders the progress of de Havilland's gun carriage along Avro's runway.

Airship armament is hardly touched upon, although it offers rewards for specialised research; nor is a place accorded to foreign equipment in British service, except to mark a trend. Aircraft type numbers and sub-type suffixes are shunned where names are adequate, and specification numbers are cited only where these are helpful. In quoting from documents designations are rendered without alteration, thereby preserving both authenticity and a certain picturesqueness.

Respecting both aeroplanes and weapons, facts hitherto unrecorded are set down, and these may sometimes be at variance with the contentions of other writers. But one sticks to one's guns.

In respect of text this volume is as complete as I can make it, and the pictures show trends of design and development, often in directly comparable views. It is pleasing that many of these pictures are new or show new detail; also that such a number have an interest not only in the context of armament but as studies in aeronautical architecture. The original print showing the nose of the Avro Bison can be scrutinised for long and rewarding periods through a magnifying glass; and to remark that in many of the Sopwith originals individual blades of grass are clearly visible to the naked eye is far from an exaggeration. That pictures such as these will bring joy to readers of this book as they do to its author is my confident hope. I hope also to present more such pictures in the second volume, for, although called *British Aircraft Weapons*, it will be very much a book of aeroplanes, as well as of guns, bombs and torpedoes.

Perhaps this present volume may have an added usefulness as a compendium of British military aeroplane types up to the year 1939—those at least that bore arms or with which armament may reasonably be associated; and that their number totals well over 500 bespeaks a national achievement of impressive magnitude. Most of these types are illustrated, to the extent of 443 photographs and drawings. A number of exotic weapon installations are absent; but these are already familiar in standard works, and I am content that they should remain there in tribute to the diligence of their discoverers. It is pleasing that a great many of the pictures in this volume are entirely new. Graphically, then, the gathering is an exclusive one and textually an inclusive one.

Surveying the product of many years it must be remarked that by no means all that is chronicled in these volumes gives cause for satisfaction, and least of all the sterility of the years immediately after 1918. Yet this very sterility was in large degree born of austerity, and a very great deal may be placed to Britain's credit. One may instance:

Early recognition (too early it might be judged) of the potential of heavy guns in aircraft, as manifest in experiments before the 1914–18 war. Some of the earliest of these experiments were conducted from a Sopwith pusher seaplane, now first identified as No.127. Trials with this aircraft are shown to have antedated those made with the historic Short No.126.

Repeated attempts throughout the 1914–18 War to adapt large-calibre guns to aircraft, and in particular the recoilless American Davis gun, the 37-mm Coventry Ordnance Works gun and Vickers Pom-poms. Also the fitting of the Vickers 'rocket gun' (to be described and ascribed, for the first time it seems, in Volume 2) on at least two types of anti-airship fighter, and more likely three or four, it is later suggested. Design of a special Vickers mounting for a 1-pounder gun, as described and illustrated in the context of the Vickers F.B.24E. This type, and the Martinsyde F.1 are two 'mystery' aeroplanes, the true purpose of which may now be first established. Then, following the First World War, repeated, if unsuccessful, attempts to revive the philosophy of heavy guns for fighters, involving considerable ingenuity of design, as instanced by such developments as the massive Westland 'ammunition dispenser'.

Design, during the 1914–18 War, of a power-operated mounting by Constantinesco. This mounting will be shown to have had astonishingly close links with the power-driven gun turrets of the Second World War.

Development of ingenious systems allowing machine-guns to be fired through the airscrew arc, notably the Constantinesco hydraulic gear. Design of electrical systems, by Martinsyde and others, and of a type of rotary deflector by Vickers.

The inventiveness of serving personnel in producing much-needed items of armament equipment suitable for general adoption, notably the Scarff ring-mounting for the Lewis gun and the Norman, Neame and Hutton sights for the same weapon.

Development of special fighter armament for Home Defence at night, taking the form of explosive darts, explosive/incendiary ammunition, novel gun installations and sights, gun heaters and flash eliminators.

Provision of a wide range of high explosive and incendiary bombs, with bombs of 1,650 lb and 3,300 lb available at the Armistice.

Perfection, especially in 1918, of advanced forms of bombsights (notably Wimperis course-setting). Early experiments with gyro-stabilised sights.

Imaginative and successful development of torpedo-dropping aircraft, leading to the Sopwith Cuckoo of 1918 and the Bristol Beaufort available in 1940.

Ambitious, if inconclusive, development of specially armed and armoured aircraft for low-flying attacks, and in particular the Sopwith Salamander of 1918.

Early recognition of the need for enclosed gun turrets, instanced by Bristol, Boulton Paul and Westland designs, and the extensive employment of such turrets (power-driven) by 1940.

Construction during 1939/40 of an experimental fighter, the Gloster F.9/37, which, on evidence now first presented, appears to have been the most heavily armed fighter in the world, though the fact would certainly not have been publicised at the time.

Finally, Britain's entry into the war of 1939 armed with eight-gun fighters; for though the guns were American in origin (being descended, as will be shown, from a gun experimentally installed on an RAF Bristol Fighter in 1918) the Hurricanes and Spitfire were Britain's own.

So, too, was the gyro gunsight being fashioned at Farnborough as the battle raged in 1940.

As for my own competence to put these volumes together, I quickly and stoutly disclaim any close acquaintanceship with ballistics or explosives; nor am I intimate with trail-angles, vectors or wind-speed bars. Weapons as artifacts have always lured me. Between the wars I spent some cherished seconds at the public's expense depleting Vickers belts and Lewis drums at sand-filled butts, but may be deemed to have discharged my debt by discharging a 9-mm Luger pistol at a low-flying Me 109 in 1940. Once, in a breathless dive, I savoured cordite from the Vickers gun of an Audax, bracing myself the while against the Hawker ring-mounting for Gun, Lewis, ·303in, Aircraft Mk.III; and with zestful frequency I plotted, as much for my personal gratification as for John Yoxall's camera, hell- and hair-raising dive-bombing peel-offs. The conniving squadron commanders might well have known better; but they were always first off the stack. Seemlier ways were impressed upon me while curled like a winkle behind a Blenheim's armour, benighted over Africa. The turret Brownings, the gunner advised, were jammed with sand. And mercifully so: their flash might have proved illuminating to the fighter groping with tracer astern. I never discovered what it was.

Further respecting turrets, I once propelled myself around in Armstrong Whitworth's birdcage on the first of all Ansons, with a Hart obliging as target; and it was in the Turret Demon prototype (J9933, of such fond memory) that I gyrated in Nash and Thompson's lobsterian device. Somehow, too, I contrived to break with costly sound a four-gun Boulton Paul installation atop a Roc. The manner in which this came to pass I fail to recollect, never daring at the time to put the facts on paper. Certain it is that any such acquaintanceship with so secret a fighter might have gained me free entry to The Tower. Certain too, the date was more or less coincident with a Contractor's Dinner at Martlesham Heath.

One day off Martlesham's neighbouring establishment at Felixstowe I was well-nigh strangled in the tail-gun position of a Perth—not by the Scarff ring-mounting but by my old-school scarf, taughtened in a Buzzard's slipstream. In the prow was an emplacement for a 37-mm C.O.W. gun, though that fearsome piece of ordnance had not been shipped. To these impressive un-credentials may be annexed a most highly privileged flight in the Wellesley prototype—with dummy bomb nacelles, doubtless for dummy bombs. Likewise the release from a Shark (actual) of a Torpedo, Aircraft, Mk.VIII (Practice). I even observed the track of that torpedo all the way to HMS *Dunedin*—only to see it disappear under the hull, as pre-ordained. Nor did any more spectacular results attend torpedo-drops from a Swordfish and a Vildebeest; and when I found myself flat on the floor of a Hart, tense at the bomb-aimer's panel, with target in sight and switch to hand, it was the pilot who pulled-off the bombs. Even when I took seat in a Vincent the sole rear armament was my 0·45-in Smith &

Wesson revolver (Lend Lease), and this I deemed it prudent to sit upon, lest the out-of-work Me 109 pilot I was conducting to Heliopolis should seek to requisition it. When this hapless airman enquired concerning the edifice called Vincent, which he appeared to view as some wondrous Eastern antiquity, I had to tell him that it was one of Britain's Stukas. Which was true.

And yet I find new heart, having once been described, in a broadcast of 1939, as a well-known authority on aircraft armament. (Though still I find myself reflecting that B.B.C. correspondent and comrade-in-arms Charles Gardner was merely disarming me, having made a barefaced crib of one of my articles in *Flight*.)

In extremis I may adduce what may constitute a bullet-proof credential, conferred by Cobber Kain just after I had watched him bring a Do 17 to a swift and smoky end in France. Woefully vague were Cobber's answers to my questions (the Dornier wasn't stopping, he explained); so he proposed resorting to the I.O.'s office to see what had been promulgated on armament and such. Covertly he opened a secret folder—guarding another of my *Flight* reviews.

I never heard the Brownings on that day, for Cobber had started work at 27,000 feet; and months went by before I saw another Hurricane dealing with a Dornier, this time low above Canterbury. No silence then, nor even 'a rattle of machine-gun fire'. There were instead what sounded like some quick explosions, and within the hour I was raking over the smouldering product of their work. There came to mind at that moment, as at this, pre-1940 chats with Sydney Camm on fighters and their guns; and this, in turn, recalls an occasion when, playing gunner in one of three Battles, I found myself at the wrong end of 48 Brownings, brought to bear by two flights of Hurricanes. Uncocked; but a shuddery experience. I wrote afterwards: 'With 48 guns against three it was difficult not to regard it all as rather a waste of time.'

It may well be that some of those very Brownings were soon to be fired in anger, and perhaps I even came across them in France, when the ground-crew were doping fabric over the gun-ports of Cobber's Hurricane.

I make no formal dedication of these volumes; but had I sought to do so I think I might have aimed them at the armourers—the men behind the men behind the guns. Or perhaps it might have been the men behind the armourers—men like Aldis, Brock, Buckingham, Challenger, Clark-Hall, Colley, Constantinesco, Dibovsky, Frazer-Nash, Hale, Hazelton, Hyde-Thomson, Lewis, Longmore, L'Estrange Malone, Maxim, Norman, North, Pomeroy, Ranken, Samson, Scarff, Sorley, Strange, Sueter, Vickers and Wimperis—to list a few alphabetically, and not in sequence of chronology or merit.

May these books help to keep their names in memory.

London 1971   H. F. K.

Admiralty Air Department

A.D. Scout (Sparrow)   This aeroplane must be considered a curiosity not only in respect of design and construction but of armament and propulsion also; for if, as stated on the best authority, the intended weapon was a Davis recoilless gun, and if this was to lie on the floor of the nacelle, as indicated by drawings, then the engine and airscrew must have been of singular construction to withstand the blast of the rearward charge, even if this propelled a dose of Epsom salts, as it is known to have done on one occasion at least. In any case, the A.D. Scout is a notable machine in aeronautical history, for even if the gun was a Lewis machine-gun, as suggested by one drawing, and if this was fixed, as indicated by other evidence, the 'Admiralty Scout' (designed 1915) may well have been Britain's first fixed-gun fighter. Whether armament of any kind was actually installed is not known, but there is photographic and other proof of a sturdy pillar at the front of the nacelle, the tip of the pillar lying at the level of the pilot's eyes. This pillar may well have been associated with a sight.

A.D. Type 1000   Although this very large three-engined floatplane of 1915/16 was intended to carry one or more torpedoes or a load of bombs it appears never to have been armed, and as a flying machine it was not successful. Armament must have influenced the design greatly, leading to the adoption of twin fuselages and twin independent floats beneath them.

Although not itself successful, the A.D. Type 1000 was a very notable early example of how armament could influence the design of aircraft. The two floats were independently mounted, one beneath each fuselage, allowing a clear drop for the torpedo or bomb load. In this picture no engines are installed.

This arrangement would allow the projectiles, especially the torpedo or torpedoes, to fall freely. In terms of pilot view for sighting a torpedo, the type was probably never rivalled by any subsequent aircraft, for the frontal portion of the central structure housing the crew was glazed.

It has been stated that one intended weapon was a 12-pounder gun, for use against airships. The Navy did indeed have such a gun in their armoury, known as the '12 pdr 12 cwt'. If, then, a 12-pounder was indeed intended, it must be hoped for the crew's sake that this was to be of the Davis recoilless type.

A.D. Flying Boat A free Lewis gun pillar-mounted in the bow cockpit and a light bomb load (two 65-lb?) was the armament of this patrol and reconnaissance machine of 1916. (See also Supermarine Channel.)

A.D. Navyplane Built in 1916 for the same duties as the A.D. Flying Boat, the Navyplane twin-float seaplane had a pillar-mounted Lewis gun in the nose of the nacelle and provision for a small bomb load. In later years Maj T. M. Barlow, who was well acquainted with this aircraft, with gun-mounting development generally, and with the Fairey 'High-Speed' mounting in particular, said that the mounting was of 'movable, pivoted, traversing' type and was the 'forerunner of certain modern types'.

The A.D.C.1 inherited its very neat gun installation from the Martinsyde F.4 Buzzard.

Aircraft Disposal Company

A.D.C.1 On 11 November, 1924, exactly six years after the Armistice, the Aircraft Disposal Company Ltd flew a version of the Martinsyde F.4 Buzzard, having the foregoing designation and powered with an Armstrong Siddeley Jaguar engine. The installation of the two Vickers guns (1,200 rounds) remained unchanged. The weight of the two Vickers guns was scheduled as 66 lb and of the ammunition as 86 lb. It was stated:

'Two sliding doors in the deck fairing, ahead of the windscreen, give access to the gun mechanism, and the high deck fairing, with its tumble-home sides, affords ample room for mounting the guns without crowding. Steel guards are fitted between the guns and the petrol tank.'

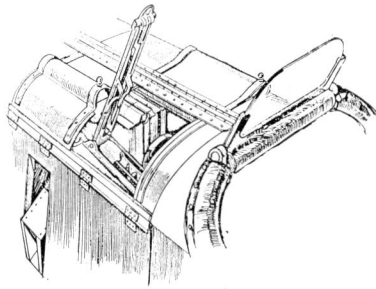

Complementary views of the A.D.C.1 gun installation. The sketch shows how sliding doors gave access to the locks of the guns. The rear cover, or lid, of one gun is seen raised.

Airspeed

Convertible Envoy During 1936 Airspeed (1934) Ltd delivered to the South African Air Force three Series III Convertible Envoys having a single Lewis gun in a manually operated Armstrong Whitworth dorsal turret, a fixed Vickers gun (nose, starboard), with ring-and-bead sight, and provision under the fuselage for three 100-lb or sixteen 20-lb bombs. Four other similar aircraft without military equipment, but capable of conversion in four hours, went to South African Airways.

Oxford I The original (Mk.I) version of the Oxford twin-engined advanced trainer (1937) was laid out for training in bombing (including high-level, with oxygen supply) and air-gunnery. For bombing there was a

Airspeed Oxford I, showing Armstrong Whitworth manually operated turret with guard-rail and bomb-aimer's window in nose.

prone position in the nose, and for gunnery an Armstrong Whitworth manually operated dorsal turret above the entrance door, with a guard-rail behind it to protect the tail surfaces The turret was at first a mock-up. In July 1937 it was reported: 'So far no bomb doors have been fixed. When the practice bombs are in position, half their diameter is exposed below the fuselage.' The bombs, sixteen of $8\frac{1}{2}$ or $11\frac{1}{2}$ lb, were stowed in the centre-section. There were two release switches, one for the pilot and one at the bomb-aimer's station. The pilot controlled selection and jettisoning. The following weights were quoted for armament items: four Light Series bomb-carriers, 50 lb; course-setting bombsight, 15 lb; Lewis gun, sight and accessories, 27 lb; ammunition drums, 18 lb. During the war an emergency installation of eight 20-lb bombs was made.

Alcock

Alcock A-1 Named by 'Jack' Alcock the Sopwith Mouse (being built largely of Sopwith components), this most private of private-venture aircraft (1917) had a single fixed Vickers gun on the centre line of the fuselage, á la Pup and Triplane.

Armstrong Whitworth

F.K. 3   Unlike the B.E.2c, the duties of which it shared, the 'Little Ack' of 1915 had built-in provision for armament. This was a Lewis gun attached to a spigot which moved along what was officially described as a 'gun rail', in the form of a U-shaped track round the rear of what in a more conventional aircraft would have been the aft cockpit. In fact pilot and observer/gunner shared the same cockpit, as an illustration shows. In addition to its operational functions as an artillery co-operation, 'contact patrol' and bombing machine, the F.K. 3 rendered service as a trainer, and for instruction in air-gunnery was fitted with a Hythe camera gun. As a single-seat bomber the type is known to have carried bombs of 16, 100 and 112 lb weight. 'Military load' of the two-seater was given as 80 lb and 'human load' as 440 lb.

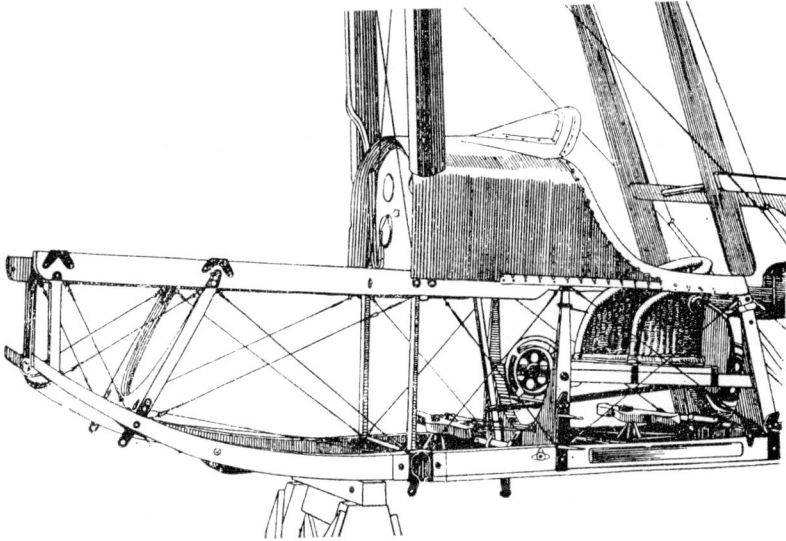

Official drawing of Armstrong Whitworth F.K.3, showing the communal cockpit with the 'gun rail' at the rear.

F.K. 8   Superior to the F.K. 3 in power and armament, the F.K. 8 of 1916 was used not only for the duties named for the earlier type but for Home Defence work as a fighter. The pilot had a Vickers gun mounted under the cowling and firing through a port in the nose. This was synchronised by Constantinesco gear, a fact that was proclaimed by the 'box' type generator projecting from the cowling of late-production aircraft. The generator was bracketed to the crankcase so that a gear wheel, fastened to the generator coupling flange, could be driven at twice airscrew speed, by a gear ring bolted to the rear face of the airscrew boss. The rear Lewis gun was on a

Scarff ring-mounting, set considerably below the top decking of the fuselage. A twin-gun installation has been identified. Bombs included 20-lb H.E. and 40-lb Phosphorus types.

Just as the much-maligned B.Es achieved the destruction of Zeppelins, so was the 'Big Ack' credited with bringing down a Gotha. (In the sea off the North Foreland. Crew, 2nd-Lieuts F. A. D. Grace and G. Murray.)

F.K. 10 Several examples of this two-seat 'fighter-reconnaissance' quadruplane were built during 1916/17. The pilot's fixed Vickers gun was on the centre line, with faired breech casing, and the observer's Lewis gun was generally on a rocking-pillar mounting, though at least one specimen of the F.K. 10 had a Scarff ring-mounting.

F.K. 12 There were Sopwith and Vickers counterparts of this 1916 three-seat escort and anti-airship fighter triplane, all three having unconventional armament layouts to give a clear field of fire. The middle wing was attached to the top of the fuselage and carried two manned nacelles, each probably intended to have a Lewis gun on a pillar mounting. The guns would have commanded a wide field of fire in the forward hemisphere, being sited forward of the airscrew. Originally the gun-nacelles were above the middle wing; later they were underslung and of different form.

Armadillo Competitor of the Sopwith Snipe, Austin Osprey, Boulton & Paul Bobolink and Nieuport B.N.1, the Armadillo (1918) had two widely spaced synchronised Vickers guns in a remarkable installation, completely enclosed in an angular cowling and firing through tunnels. Provision was made in the early design stages for a Lewis gun on the upper-starboard wing root, but the gun was not fitted.

Ara Designed in 1918, like its rivals the Snark, Snapper and Siskin, the Ara (completed 1919) had another unusual armament installation, the two Vickers guns (500 rpg) again being internal, but mounted very low in the fuselage. There were two holes in tandem in the fuselage sides in the area where the breech casings of the guns were probably located. Being round rather than rectangular these may have been associated with the ventilation of fumes from the guns rather than ejection.

Sinaia The Sinaia twin-engined bomber was completed in 1921, at about which time the Siddeley Deasy Motor Car Co Ltd was absorbed by a new joint holding called Sir W. G. Armstrong Whitworth Ltd. As with the Siskin, the name of the aircraft was originally prefixed by 'Siddeley'. One official document called it the 'Siddeley Deasy bomber'. The armament scheme was remarkable. Provision was made in the nose for a 37-mm Coventry Ordnance Works gun, and in the tail of each of the two very elongated engine nacelles, mounted on the lower wings, was a Scarff ring-mounting for one or two Lewis guns. Bomb-stowage was apparently internal.

Provision for a 37-mm Coventry Ordnance Works gun in the fuselage nose and Scarff ring-mountings for Lewis guns in the tails of the elongated nacelles were features of the Armstrong Whitworth Sinaia bomber.

Awana Although it carried 25 armed men, this twin-engined troop-carrier of 1923 had itself no apparent provision for armament.

Wolf Originally produced, like the Hawker Duiker and Short Springbok, as a corps reconnaissance aircraft, though later used for training, the Wolf (1924) had a Scarff ring-mounting for two Lewis guns and a fixed Vickers gun on the port upper cowling. The Vickers gun installation was similar to that on the early Siskins. Provision for light bombs was probably intended.

Siskin Prominence will be given in Volume 2 to the views of Maj F. M. Green concerning fighter armament. In expressing these views he mentions a fighter in which it had been found possible to increase the ammunition supply to 'rather over 2,000 rounds'. This fighter was the 'Siddeley Siskin', or Siskin I, designed by Maj Green himself and first flown in 1919. A contemporary statement declared in respect of the later metal version: 'The two main guns can be carried directly over the steel-tube longerons of the frame. A belt box can be fixed between the two guns with sufficient capacity to take up to 2,000 rounds of ·303 ammunition. An additional gun can be carried on the top plane.' This last feature is of particular interest because Maj Green had been closely concerned with the S.E.5, which had a similar installation, and was also largely responsible for the Royal Aircraft Factory design which formed the basis of the Siskin. It will be noted later that other fighters of the late-war period, including the Snipe, originally had provision for a third gun. This feature, however, was not perpetuated in the Siskin series, and neither was the increased ammunition supply.

As originally flown, with Dragonfly engine, the Siskin had two Vickers guns (still with the large-diameter cooling jackets of the war years), disposed externally, forward of the cockpit sides, with case chutes and link

7

The original Siddeley Siskin (*top*) had Vickers guns of war-time pattern (Class C), but the Rumanian Siskin V, shown for comparison, had Class E guns.

8

chutes immediately below them. The trigger motors for the C.C. gear, with their associated piping, were prominent. With the fitting of the Jaguar engine no obvious changes were made, though the aircraft appears to have been tested without the guns in place.

The next Siskin variant calling for comment was the Mk.V, as supplied to Rumania and having a basically similar airframe configuration. The entire forward portion, however, was redesigned, and the guns (now of the E Class, having the small-diameter perforated cooling jackets) were on a new type of external bracket mounting. Though differing again in fuselage form, the Siskin III—the first of the breed to be adopted by the RAF (1923)—retained a similar installation. The ring sight and the front bracket for the Aldis sight were attached not to the fuselage but to the upper wing (likewise on the Rumanian Siskin V). Four 20-lb bombs could be carried under the fuselage, and a Hythe camera gun over the top wing. The most startling of the early Siskins was the experimental Mk.III of 1925, which had its Jaguar engine almost entirely enclosed, with small holes for the cooling air round the frontal periphery. There is some indication that an effort was made to fair the guns on this example.

It may be noted here that in 1923 the point was made by Armstrong Whitworth that, although the Siskin was manoeuvrable, it was stable at 'ordinary flying speeds', so that it could be 'left to itself' in the event of the pilot needing to clear a gun-stoppage.

By far the most common of all the Siskins was the IIIA, first flown in 1925 and remaining in RAF service into the 1930s, when it was replaced by the Bristol Bulldog. In this mark the guns were internal. An official account stated:

'The two Vickers ·303 in., Mk.II air-cooled guns are mounted on a common braced tubular superstructure fitted to the front frame forward of the cockpit. Each gun is supported by two U-shaped fittings to which it is fixed by transverse pins at the front and rear ends of the breech casing. The rear supports may pivot about their vertical axes but are otherwise fixed, whilst the front supports are capable of vertical adjustment. The front fixing pins allow lateral adjustment to be made.'

Of 'Belt boxes and chutes' it was remarked:

'Each box has a capacity of 600 rounds. The boxes are carried between two tubular bearers fitted between the top longerons. The mouth of each box is closed by a hinged lid which is fixed by two spring-loaded plungers. The case and link chutes have a common outlet at each side, these being made integral with the detachable portions of the top fairing forming the doors which give access to the belt-box filling orifices.'

The account continued:

'Aldis and ring-and-bead sights are provided, the usual position of the latter being on the fuselage centre line, the Aldis sight being mounted

9

8 in. to starboard, but the positions are interchangeable. If the Aldis sight is fitted centrally, a modified windscreen, having an aperture for the eye-piece, must be fitted. The mountings are secured to wood bases which are built into the plywood fairing of the cockpit.'

Although the official account makes no mention of the fact, the bead sight was mounted, in one type of installation at least, on a substantial pylon structure over the engine, immediately behind the airscrew. To resume the official account:

'The installation of the twin C.C. gear is standard in all respects. The 11 ft. 6 in. primary and secondary pipe lines from the roller-and-cam type generators are taken along the bottom of the front frame at their respective sides, to the third cross member and then up to their corresponding trigger motors. The air release valves are fitted to a small panel mounted under the fairing in a central position, forward of the main instrument board.' The mounting of the reservoir was then described—'the handle just clearing the lower edge of the main instrument board.'

And later:

'Fittings are provided for the mounting of a type G.III camera gun

Perched above the Jaguar engine of this Siskin IIIA is the bead for the ring-and-bead sight. The Aldis sight is also seen. (*Flight International.*)

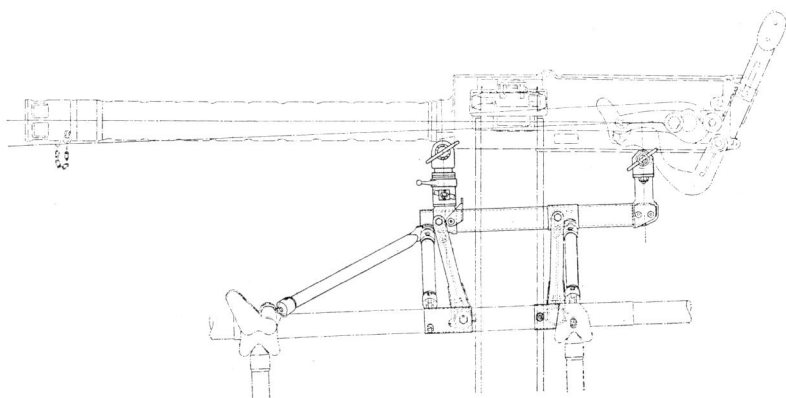

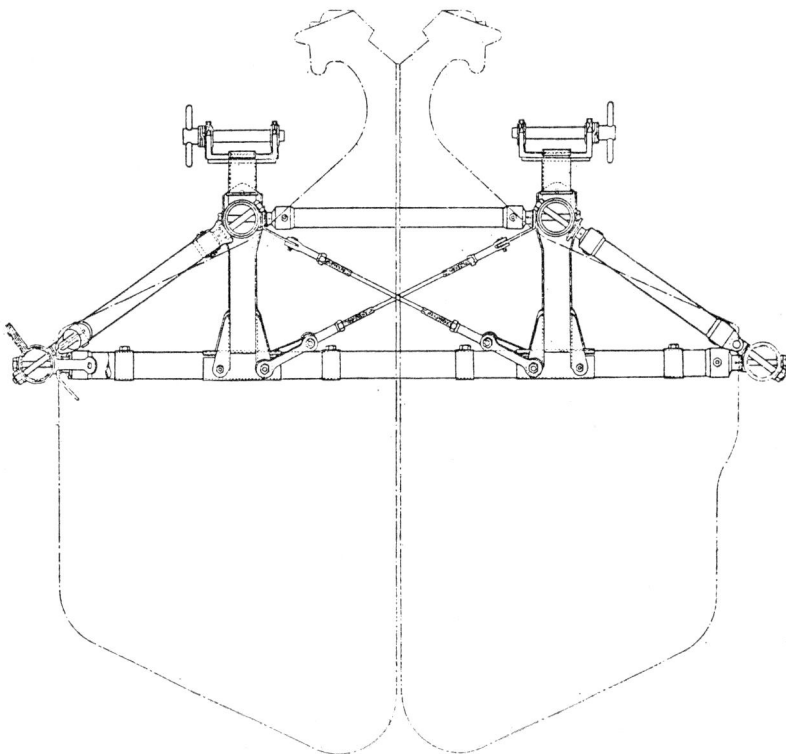

Mounting of Vickers Mk.II gun on Armstrong Whitworth Siskin IIIA. In the lower view the belt boxes are shown in outline. The drawings are not to the same scale.

Like several other RAF fighters, the Siskin IIIA was eventually fitted with collector boxes for the 'empties'. The nearest machine has a Light Series bomb-carrier under the cockpit and the other two have G.3 camera guns inverted on the top wing. (*Flight International.*)

above the spar joints of the top planes. The front support is pivotal, whilst at the rear provision is made for vertical and lateral adjustment.'

Of bomb-release gear:

'The Light Series Mk.II release quadrant is mounted on a wood platform fixed to the rear end of the port footboard, at the side of the seat. This type of quadrant permits release of the bombs separately or simultaneously. The Light Series carrier is attached to an arrangement of tubular bearers fitted within the bottom of the front frame, below the floor boards. The release cable is led through a nipple at the rear end of the quadrant and thence over two pulleys to the pulley at the port side of the bomb carrier.'

In the introductory portion of the account quoted, the ammunition is described as 'ball' and the bombs as 20-lb H.E. (Aircraft).

It remains to be noted that in later years RAF Siskin IIIA aircraft were fitted with external collector boxes to retain the cartridge cases and links aboard.

There was no change in armament on the experimental Siskin IIIB.

Ajax   The Ajax two-seater was built in 1925 as a companion type to the Siskin, with fighting as a primary duty. Armament does not appear to have been installed, but a point of special interest is that the tailplane was built without external bracing in order to allow the fullest possible rearward field of fire.

Atlas   Developed during 1926 from the Ajax, the Atlas was adopted by the RAF as the standard army co-operation two-seater to succeed the Bristol Fighter, the basic armament of which was retained. The 'Atlas A.C. Mk.I' or 'Atlas A.C.' (to quote two designations officially used for this version) had a Vickers Mk.II gun for the pilot, mounted internally on the centre

Armstrong Whitworth Atlas A.C. Mk.I, displaying eight 20-lb bombs, G.3 camera gun on starboard lower wing, Aldis and ring sight, Scarff ring-mounting with Lewis gun, and bombsight on side of rear cockpit.

Left, installation of Vickers gun and belt box on Armstrong Whitworth Atlas I.
Right, Avro ring-mounting on Atlas II.

line (as on the Bristol Fighter) and firing over the Jaguar engine through a
deep trough. The gun was mounted on a fore-and-aft member carried on
inverted-V struts attached to the top longerons. The ammunition box held
600 rounds, and Type C synchronising gear was fitted. There were both
1·8-in Aldis and 4½-in ring-and-bead sights, the bead being braced from
the front inverted-V struts. A No.7 Scarff ring-mounting was fitted over
the rear cockpit, immediately behind the pilot, and carried a Mk.III
Lewis gun with Norman sight and five Mk.II No.2 magazines. Under each
lower wing was a Light Series Mk.I carrier for H.E. 20-lb Mk.I bombs, for
which a Sight, Bomb, High Altitude Mk.IA could be fitted on the star-

Armstrong Whitworth Atlas II with tubular bomb-carriers under wings and Lewis
gun on Avro ring-mounting. Note installation of pilot's bead sight above exhaust
collector-ring.

14

board side of the fuselage. The bombs could be released from either cockpit.

There was a general-purpose version of the same aeroplane (1927) with added tankage and heavier bomb load (e.g. four 112-lb), but this was not adopted.

The Atlas II private-venture light bomber and multi-purpose aircraft of 1931 was re-engined (Panther, later Tiger) and extensively redesigned. Though the Vickers gun installation remained unaltered the Scarff ring-mounting was superseded by one of Avro type (see Avro Antelope). The main bomb load was four 112-lb or two 250-lb, and four 20-lb bombs were carried outboard on the port side. The crude external bomb-sighting arrangement of the Atlas I—a relic of the war—was succeeded by a prone position for the bomb-aimer/air-gunner, who had his own instrument panel, course-setting sight and bomb-release controls, though the 20-lb bombs could be released from either cockpit. The two gunsights were stated to be in the standard RAF position and could be interchanged if desired.

Starling The Starling I and II single-seat fighters differed greatly from the Siskin, though retaining distinct 'A.W.' characteristics; and the two marks differed greatly from each other. The first appeared in 1927 and had a twin Vickers gun installation very much resembling that of the Siskin IIIA, with prominent ejection chutes high in the fuselage flanks. In the Starling II, however, these chutes were not in evidence, betokening internal collection of the 'empties', or, more probably, disposal below the fuselage. Nor did these chutes appear on any of the succeeding Armstrong Whitworth fighters. (See under Scimitar.)

Aries The Aries (1932) was an easy-maintenance development of the Atlas I, equipped for army co-operation and armed as the Atlas I.

A.W. XVI First produced in 1930, this single-seat fighter successor to the Siskin and Starling, and progenitor of the Scimitar, was quite extensively altered during development (it appeared in both 'Fleet fighter' and land-based day and night fighter versions); but the armament of two Vickers guns remained throughout. These were installed with quite exceptional neatness, their presence being manifested by two ports (later two troughs) in the top cowling and, of course, by the Aldis and ring-and-bead sights. A carrier for four 20-lb bombs was fitted well outboard under the port lower wing.

A.W.19 A 'removable cradle for an 18 in torpedo' is a salient item in a makers' description of this general purpose/torpedo-carrying aircraft of 1934. The torpedo was a Mk.VIII or Type K, for which a heating system was provided. Bombs up to 1,000 lb in weight (typically two 500-lb or four 250-lb) were disposed under the wings and had electrical release. The pilot's Vickers gun was mounted to starboard, the bead sight being

The Armstrong Whitworth Starling I (*top*) had a gun installation generally resembling that of the Siskin IIIA. On the Starling II (*lower*) the ejection chutes had disappeared. (Upper picture, *Flight International*.)

Twin ports behind the engine, together with the Aldis sight, alone proclaim the presence of guns aboard the A.W.XVI (*top*). On the Scimitar (*lower*) the guns were largely housed in a 'hump'. (Lower picture, *Flight International*.)

immediately forward of the windscreen on the centre line, with the ring a short distance ahead of it. An Avro ring-mounting (one Lewis gun) was fitted aft of the top wing, tilted forwards below the top line of the fuselage as on the Hawker Demon.

In connection with this aeroplane, Armstrong Whitworth made some interesting and valuable comments on the specification to which it was built (G.4/31) and also on design requirements with particular reference to the torpedo case. Having commented on 'G.P.' requirements generally, they went on: 'In the latest specification the duty of torpedo carrying has been added, which has still further increased the complexity of the requirements.' Of the aircraft itself: 'The fuselage is of such internal dimensions that the observer can move about freely inside to take up the appropriate stations for bomb aiming, torpedo adjustment, navigation and generally attending to the equipment. The roots of the lower main planes are swept upwards at the fuselage junctions to provide the necessary ground clearance for the torpedo and at the same time permit an adequate gap between the planes without an undue depth of fuselage.'

The pilot's cockpit was immediately ahead of, and on a level with, the top wing, and the fuselage decking dropped sharply away to the top line of the engine cowling. The excellent view afforded was also related to armament, and in particular to the dive-bombing requirement and to 'accurate torpedo direction and launching'. Figures available for the A.W.19 afford an excellent illustration of the effect of armament on performance. Maximum speed and climb figures were: G.P. without bombs, 172 mph, 15,000 ft in 12·5 min; G.P. with bombs, 165 mph, 15,000 ft in 14 min; torpedo aircraft, 160 mph, 15,000 ft in 23 min.

Scimitar   A Camel-type hump forward of the cockpit, housing the two Vickers guns entirely (except for the muzzles and small lengths of the cooling jackets, which projected from the forward end) was the most striking characteristic of this 1934 single-seat fighter. A makers' brochure lists the guns as Vickers 'Mk.E' and another A.W. document gives these particulars of armament and explains the absence of the time-honoured ejection chutes in the fuselage sides:

'The guns are mounted on top of the fuselage below the decking and are arranged in such a manner that the usual stoppages may be dealt with by the pilot when in flight. The ammunition is carried in containers situated alongside each gun, each having a capacity of 600 rounds. Access for loading is obtained by removable panels on either side of the fuselage. Spent cartridges and links pass down chutes and are jettisoned below the fuselage. Either a ring-and-bead or an Aldis tube sight may be fitted. The attachment fittings provide the necessary adjustment to enable the sights to be harmonised with the guns. Twin Constantinesco interrupter gear is fitted. The generator is driven from the back of the engine and is accessible for timing purposes. The reservoir is conveniently situated on the right-hand side of the cockpit. One carrier for four

A peep beneath the Scimitar's hump. The rear brackets for the two Vickers guns are seen, but the guns are not installed; nor are the firing levers present on the control column.

20-lb bombs can be fitted below the lower left-hand plane.' Another company description declared that the bombs were carried 'on the starboard lower main plane'.

It was remarked at the outset that the Scimitar had a Camel-type hump forward of the cockpit, but the affinities between these 1917 and 1934 fighters were far more basic. Except in detail and quantity of ammunition, the armament was identical. Moreover, the RAF had yet to take into service the Gloster Gauntlet, armed to the same basic formula. These facts, however, detract in no wise from the Scimitar's excellence as a gun platform.

A.W.23 Built in 1935 as a bomber transport, this twin-Tiger monoplane was the basis of the Whitley bomber, and like the first Whitley had an Armstrong Whitworth manually operated turret at nose and tail (one Lewis gun in each). Internal provision was made for bombs up to some 5,000 lb in weight.

A.W.29 A counterpart of the Fairey Battle, this Tiger-engined monoplane of 1936 had a generally similar bomb-stowage arrangement, namely cells in the wing outboard of the retractable undercarriage. In the design of these cells, dive-bombing was a prime consideration. On one occasion the makers named torpedo dropping as one of the duties of the A.W.29,

B   19

though there appears to be no confirmation of torpedo gear having been fitted. According to the special bomb-dropping schemes mentioned, the bomb doors were held closed by a spring, but could be opened either positively by a crew member or by the weight of the falling bomb. The positive opening was to be used 'if time permitted', for it was recognised that inaccuracy might result from the impact of the bomb on the doors. With this same scheme was associated ejector gear, taking the form of two radius rods engaging the bomb externally near its centre of mass to direct it clear of the airscrew. The rods engaged with trunnions, secured by an external strap, and the forked ends of the radius rods were pivotally mounted well forward of the bomb. When the rods had turned through about 90 degrees, the trunnions slipped from the forked ends. The radius rods were then retracted by return springs, assisted by air pressure. There was a later scheme for opening the bomb doors first, to prevent the radius rods from fouling the edges of the doors, so preventing the doors from shutting. The rods operated a cam mechanism for opening the doors before the bomb could hit them and for holding them open during and after release until the radius rods were retracted into the bomb bay.

The maximum bomb load of the A.W.29 as constructed was probably six 250-lb plus four 20-lb. There was an Armstrong Whitworth manually operated turret for a Lewis gun over the trailing edge, and the pilot had a wing-mounted Vickers gun (starboard).

The Armstrong Whitworth manually operated turret as applied to a single-engined and a twin-engined bomber: *top*, A.W.29; *lower*, Whitley prototype.

Whitley It was the defensive armament of the Whitley (first flown 1936) that was most significant in the development of the type; specifically, the advance from one manually trained Lewis gun in the tail to four Browning guns in a power-operated turret. The prototypes and early-production aircraft had an Armstrong Whitworth manual turret, of the type described in connection with the Avro Anson, in nose and tail. A single Lewis or Vickers G.O. (Class K) gun was mounted in each. After the S.B.A.C. Display in June 1937 *Flight* remarked: 'The Whitley's front and rear turrets had been deleted and the positions covered in by appropriate fairings. It is said that Nash and Thompson turrets are awaited.' It was, in fact, in the Mk.III version of the aircraft (1938) that the first Nash and Thompson installation made its appearance, this taking the form of a nose turret mounting a single Vickers G.O. (Class K) gun. The rear A.W. turret was retained, but another innovation on this mark was a retractable ventral Nash and Thompson turret having a 360-degree traverse. This mounted two Browning guns and was installed only on Whitley IIIs. A revised bomb installation (provision for two 2,000-lb) was another feature of this mark. With the Whitley IV a truly massive advance was registered, for though the ventral installation was deleted, the tail turret was now of Nash and Thompson type, housing four Browning guns. This development may well be compared in its technical significance with the introduction of the British eight-gun fighters. Another improvement in the Whitley IV was the fitting of a Plexiglass 'chin' in the nose for the bomb-aimer. The Whitley V had a slightly lengthened fuselage which extended the field of fire from the tail turret.

The following description was written in the summer of 1937, after inspection of a Whitley II:

'Entrance is through a door in the port side behind the wing . . . Aft of the door the catwalk leads back to the tail gun turret. A trap-door through the floor leads to a compartment reserved for flares and practice bombs. Forward of this comes the bottom gun turret. The doors of the bomb compartments are opened by the weight of the bombs. They are wooden-framed and metal-covered and are very stiff for their great length. They are closed by elastic ropes. The bow gunner can reach the turret through a well below the dashboard on the right-hand side.'

It would have been more accurate to state that the bomb-doors *could* be opened by the falling bombs, for, as noted in connection with the A.W.29, inaccuracy could result from the impact of the bombs on the doors. As indicated below, positive hydraulic opening was normal.

As already intimated, the Whitley's four-gun tail turret was of great historical significance, and the density of fire obtained was acknowledged by the Germans. Having examined a specimen, however, (and possibly primed with other information) a German expert remarked:

'Hitting results depend very much on the aircraft being kept stable, in view of the considerable distance separating the turret from the

LIMIT OF DOWNWARD FIRE

LIMIT OF UPWARD FIRE

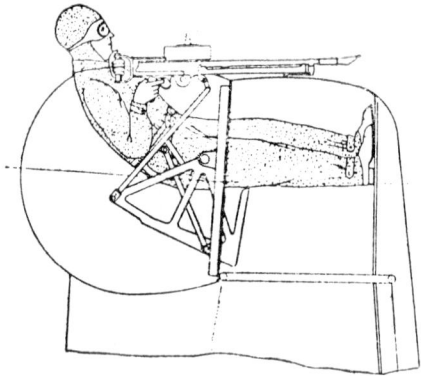

TURRET STRUCTURE ATTACHED
TO ROTATABLE RING

RHOMBOID PANELS

PLUNGER OPERATED BY
LEVER ON GUN ARM
SEAT PIVOT ATTACHED
TO ROTATABLE RING

ROTATABLE RING

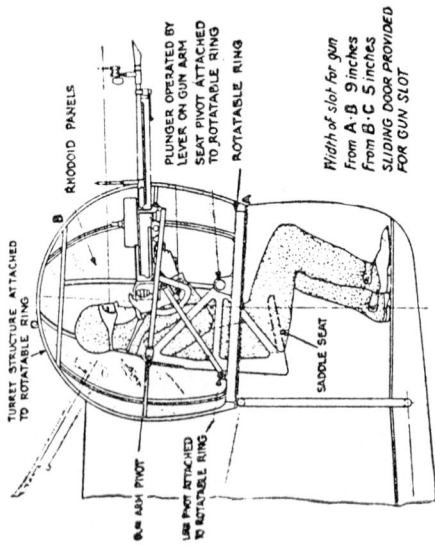

Width of slot for gun
From A·B 9 inches
From B·C 5 inches
SLIDING DOOR PROVIDED
FOR GUN SLOT

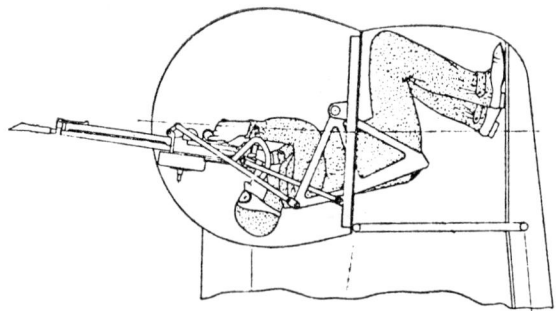

GUN ARM PIVOT

ARM PIVOT ATTACHED
TO ROTATABLE RING

SADDLE SEAT

Makers' drawings of Armstrong Whitworth manually operated turret.

22

Armstrong Whitworth manually operated turret, with one Lewis gun, in tail of
A.W.23 bomber transport. The Whitley I bomber had a similar installation.

centre of gravity. Gusty weather or evading manoeuvres place a heavy
physical strain on the gunner as the result of accelerations, and considerably reduce the efficiency of defensive fire.'

The earlier Armstrong Whitworth turret, for which seven drums of
ammunition were provided, had also come in for German criticism. It was
remarked that the 'angles of aiming' were not as wide as the 'angles of
fire', as the former depended on the height of the gunner. 'Field of sight'
was described as 'principally good, but impaired by 'the curves of the
transparent plastic'.

There were two separate bomb bays in the fuselage and fourteen cells
for smaller bombs in the inner portions of the wings, both inboard and
outboard of the engine nacelles. Two 2,000-lb bombs could be taken,
and two 500-lb + twelve 250-lb was a possible load. Typical for a trip to
Germany was two 500-lb + six 250-lb. The bombs were loaded from trol-

23

leys by means of hand-operated winches. Carriers for eight practice bombs could be fitted externally under the forward bomb bay.

Whereas the Hampden and Wellington were employed (with severe losses) on daylight operations in the early phases of the war, the Whitley was always a night bomber, and many were the aircrew of the later four-engined 'heavies' who served in, or trained in, Whitleys. An early publication describing the work of Bomber Command conveys the operating environment as experienced by a tail gunner and a bomb-aimer:

'The striking thing about a tail turret is the sense of detachment it gives you. You're out beyond the tail and you can see nothing at all of the aircraft unless you turn sideways. It has all the effects of being suspended in space. It sounds, perhaps, a little terrifying, but actually it is fascinating. The effect it has on me is to make me feel that I am in a different machine from the others . . .'

Nash and Thompson hydraulically operated power-driven turret with four Browning guns in tail of Whitley V. (*Flight International.*)

'When about to turn in for the run the pilot will say "Opening bomb doors". This is done hydraulically. As soon as they are open the navigator takes charge. He brings the aircraft on to the target by instructing the pilot how to steer. If he wishes him to turn to the left he will say "Left, left", repeating the word. If, however, he wishes him to go to the right he will say "Right" once only. The reason for this is that there is often a considerable amount of crackling on the "inter-comm." which

A tractor arrives with a trailer-load of 500-lb G.P. bombs to bomb-up a Whitley V. Note also the Nash and Thompson power-driven turret, with single Vickers G.O. (Class K) gun and the bomb-aimer's Plexiglass 'chin'. (*Flight International.*)

makes it difficult to distinguish the actual words spoken . . . Presently the navigator will say "Steady", and the pilot will then hold the aircraft on its course until he hears the navigator say "Bombs gone". All the time the navigator has been gazing through the bomb-sight. Conveniently at hand are a number of switches by which he can control the manner in which the bombs are dropped. These may fall in a "close" or an "open"

Hand-winching 500-lb G.P. bombs into the fuselage bay of a Whitley V.
(*Flight International.*)

stick . . . The bomb-sight is so constructed that it can be automatically set to make allowance for the ground speed of the aircraft and the force and direction of the wind. If necessary the bombs can be released automatically when the aircraft has reached a certain position indicated on the bomb-sight. They are also released by hand pressure on a button. As soon as they have fallen the navigator reports "Bombs gone".'

Arrow

Active   The tiny Arrow Active sesquiplane (Mk.II, 1934) was certainly intended for, if not physically adapted for, military applications. Describing themselves as 'Specialists in aircraft armaments, internal combustion engines, general engineering designs and constructions', the makers declared:

> 'Up to the present the Arrow Active is the only example among British aircraft to embody all the characteristics of a modern metal fighter in compact and economic form . . . A feature of the aircraft is its ready adaptability to the purpose of high-speed practice bombing. Provision for a series of nine to twelve $8\frac{1}{2}$-lb practice bombs may be readily effected on the underside of the centre structure . . .'

Austin

Austin-Ball A.F.B. 1   Apparently at the suggestion of Capt Albert Ball, VC, DSO, MC, this single-seater of 1917 had a Lewis gun on a special mounting for upward firing only (a form of attack which Ball favoured), and, of greater interest, a second Lewis gun lying between the cylinder blocks of the Hispano-Suiza engine and firing through the airscrew shaft. An existing photograph shows the external Lewis gun, which was mounted at an angle and pointed through the airscrew arc when at its lowest position, with the 'single' (47-round) drum.

Osprey   In addition to two synchronised Vickers guns on the fuselage decking forward of the cockpit, and having ejection chutes in the fuselage sides, the single-seat Osprey (1917/18) had provision, as had competitive fighters, for a Lewis gun with a limited arc of movement. The aircraft being a triplane, this was mounted on the rear spar of the 'centre centre-section'. The actual installation was in dummy form only (land-service type, with 'single' drum).

26

Greyhound   Designed in 1918, like its competitors the Bristol Badger and Westland Weasel, this intended Bristol Fighter replacement had two close-set, internally mounted synchronised Vickers guns firing through ports in the nose and a Lewis gun on a Scarff ring-mounting almost flush with the decking atop a narrow fuselage, which allowed an extensive field of fire. Fighting effectiveness was enhanced by the closeness of pilot and gunner. The reported ammunition supply of 1,700 rounds may indicate 500 rounds per gun for the pilot and seven double drums for the gunner.

Avro

503 (Type H)   There is reason to suppose that a seaplane of this type, which appeared in 1913, made a bombing attack on Zeebrugge early in the war, but the load is not known.

508   This pusher biplane is given precedence over the armed 504s by reason of the fact that it was built before the outbreak of war specifically to carry a gun. To quote from the catalogue of the Aero and Marine Exhibition held at Olympia in March 1914:

> 'The 1914 Type Two-seater Gun-carrying Push Machine (*sic*) is a new model and embodies many novel features and advanced ideas . . . The observer or gunner is seated in the front of the machine, thus giving him a clear range of vision.'

504   'Each machine was fitted to carry four 20 lb T.N.T. bombs and four petrol incendiary bombs. No dummy bombs were available for testing, and the carriers were actually tested with live bombs.' So ran an Avro account of the historic and greatly daring raid on the Zeppelin installations at Lake Constance by four Avro 504s of the RNAS on 21 November, 1914. The H.E. bombs concerned were of Hales type; the incendiaries, with which the name of Wg Cdr F. A. Brock has been associated, were never carried. The bombs were hung two under each side of the fuselage on carriers devised by the Avro company. They were held in position by split-pins and were released by the pilot pulling on four wires. An elementary system of sighting by means of pins attached to the fuselage was installed. Thus armed, the 504, of enduring memory as a trainer beyond compare, and first flown in 1913 as an aeroplane with no specific application, answered its call to arms with the highest distinction. Nor was the Friedrichshafen raid the only occasion when 504s carried bombs with dramatic, if not always such telling, effect. An early raid (14 December, 1914) was made, for example, on the Bruges–Ostend railway line, on this occasion with four 16-lb bombs. In a single night (17 May, 1915) a 504 attempted to engage L.Z.38 with two grenades and two incendiary bombs, but was thwarted by the Zeppelin's rapid climb, and a similar machine dropped bombs on the stern of L.Z.39, causing damage, though the bombs passed clean through without exploding. For Home Defence some 504s carried four 20-lb bombs. A box of Ranken Darts was another anti-Zeppelin load.

As for gunnery, in early 504 two-seaters the pilot sometimes had a pistol and the observer a rifle, a frustrating scheme, for the observer sat under the centre-section. Yet, concerning Avro No.398, the following account has been rendered by 2nd-Lieut (later Lieut-Col) C. W. Wilson:

> '. . . . a Taube was seen coming from the south. Major Higgins instantly gave the order: "There you are Wilson. Go and take his number." I was off the mark at once, but Rabagliatti scrambled on board 398 before me, with a rifle and ammunition. We headed north, climbing, Rabagliatti kneeling on his seat in front and steering me till we got into position ahead and below as we had always meant to do. He then began firing and ejecting his empties into my face, cursing at the lack of result. Suddenly his face lit up, and waving his rifle in the air he pointed to the ground. . . . We were credited with the *first* German machine in the official history of the RFC.'

This feat of British marksmanship was performed on 25 August, 1914.

As for machine-gun mountings, one of the most historic of all times was associated with Avro No.383 and with the names of 2nd-Lieut L. A. Strange and Capt L. de C. Penn-Gaskell. Both these officers made contributions of note to the development of air armament. The mounting on the Avro consisted of a metal tube from a defunct Henri Farman and a length of rope to hoist the gun from the fuselage decking, the gun itself retaining a stock as on land-service guns for firing from the shoulder. This mounting was plied effectively on 22 November, 1914, when Lieut F. G. Small forced down an Aviatik after firing one full 47-round drum and 25 rounds from a second drum. Later, single-seater 504s (sub-types C,D,F and converted K) were occasionally and variously armed with Lewis guns, the C being specifically intended for anti-Zeppelin work and having to this end the gun mounted to fire upwards at 45 degrees through the centre-section. The most refined installation was probably on the K night-fighter conversion, which had a Lewis gun on a Foster mounting in association with a Hutton illuminated sight. A fixed synchronised Vickers gun, as well as a Lewis gun on a Scarff ring-mounting, is ascribed to the 504G, and a number of other 504s are known to have had synchronised guns.

Although, as might be expected, no reference to armament appears in official publications concerning the 504, the following note is to be found in *Erecting and Aligning 80 h.p. Avro Biplanes Type 504*, issued by A. V. Roe and Co Ltd in 1915 ('with a view to instructing our clients') and including 'classes 504, 504a, b, c, and d':

> 'Although normally the tail is parallel to the top body-rail, peculiari-

ties of the machine, or special requirements in the way of weight carry-ing, may necessitate an alteration in the angle of the tail.'

Avro 504Ks, fitted with Hythe camera guns were used at Dymchurch for training cadets.

510 During 1915 a few two-seater floatplanes of this type were used by the RNAS for coastal patrol, but there appears to be no record of any armament which may have been carried.

519 Though evidently intended for military use, the intended functions of this 1916 biplane two-seater cannot be determined. Defensive armament could not have been employed effectively because of fuselage form, but it may be significant that the Avro company have mentioned 'several large single-engined bombers' built by them before March 1916.

521 Designed in 1915 as a two-seat 'fighting scout', the 521 (completed 1916) was intended to have a rear-mounted Lewis gun, though this does not appear to have materialised.

Pike Bearing the type number 523, the Pike was built in 1916 as a formid-able fighter, stoutly armed, of long endurance, and capable of bringing heavy fire power to bear upon airships. Lights were also installed to this end. Only later does the type appear to have been developed for bombing. The nose was designed to take, and actually had installed on at least one occasion, a large-calibre quick-firing gun, apparently of Hotchkiss type. In a second Pike this gun was replaced by a Lewis gun on a ring-mounting, but in both examples the rear gunner had a Lewis gun, likewise ring-mounted. Bombs could certainly be carried on the Pike, and A.V. Roe himself is said to have designed the horizontal tier-stowage.

527 This Sunbeam-engined 504 development of 1915/16 was a last attempt to develop the type as a fighter. The pilot was not armed, but the gunner had a Lewis gun on a pillar mounting, apparently operating conjointly with a guide-ring.

528 A mystery aeroplane, which seems to have existed (1916), and which may well have had bomb nacelles mounted on the lower wing. If this fact could be substantiated the 528 might be considered as the Wellesley of its time.

529 and 529A These aeroplanes, of 1916/17, were specifically long-range bombers. Located between the lower wing spars, the bomb compartment was of three-ply and could take twenty 50-lb bombs, suspended by their noses. A bombsight and release gear were installed in the nose, and on the 529A at least the bomb-aimer appears to have assumed a prone position in a jutting structure. He communicated with the pilot by speaking tube. Scarff ring-mountings, with one Lewis gun each, were fitted at the nose and dorsal positions, but the gunner who manned the dorsal ring was also responsible for a third Lewis gun which fired through the floor. A contemporary document stated:

> 'A special seat is made in the floor through the rear cockpit and a long hole is arranged in the floor through which a good view downward and backward is obtained. When it is not required to use this opening it is covered by a sliding door.'

The same account listed the following weights: guns, 70 lb; ammunition, 100 lb; bombs, 1,080 lb.

530 Quite rightly this two-seater fighter of 1917 has been compared with the Bristol Fighter, but its advanced design has not, perhaps, been sufficiently stressed, especially in respect of armament provisions. Avro made reference to a 'turret-like structure' having a wing secured to it and housing a gun firing through an opening and allowing vertical adjustment. A fixed gun firing through the airscrew boss was also mentioned, and the rear gun was said to be 'raised clear of the top plane'. As it materialised, the 530 had a single synchronised Vickers gun in the pylon, or 'turret' structure, with ejection chutes projecting from the fuselage sides, and the gunner had a Lewis gun on his high-set Scarff ring-mounting.

Spider Although a contemporary drawing shows two Vickers guns on this 1918 'wireless scout' (the 'wireless' signifying rigid wing bracing) only one gun was actually fitted, though this had more than the normal amount of ammunition. The gun was mounted slightly to starboard of the centre line and was largely internal. One contemporary specification listed these items: 'gun, 70 lb; mounting and ammunition box, 20 lb; belt and 800 rounds, 60 lb; Very pistol with cartridges, 8 lb.' Like the later single-gun Hawker Hornbill, the Spider carried more than the usual quantity of ammunition for a Vickers gun.

Manchester The Manchester twin-engined bomber of 1918 was comparable with the Boulton & Paul Bourges. Bombs up to some 880 lb in weight were stowed internally and were aimed and released from the nose position, where there was a hinged window, as on the Bourges, and a Scarff ring-mounting. There was a similar defensive gun installation in the dorsal position aft of the wings. Twin guns were apparently intended for both mountings.

Aldershot Produced in 1922, the Aldershot, with Rolls-Royce Condor engine and two-wheel split-axle undercarriage, saw limited RAF service as a day and night bomber. It was a massive aeroplane, despite its single engine, and had a two-deck fuselage, with the pilot and navigator forward (though behind the wings) together with the gunner on the top deck, and a bombing position and facilities for navigation and wireless on a lower deck. Notwithstanding the Aldershot's size (span nearly 70 ft) the pilot had a fixed Vickers gun, and even an Aldis sight in addition to a ring-and-bead

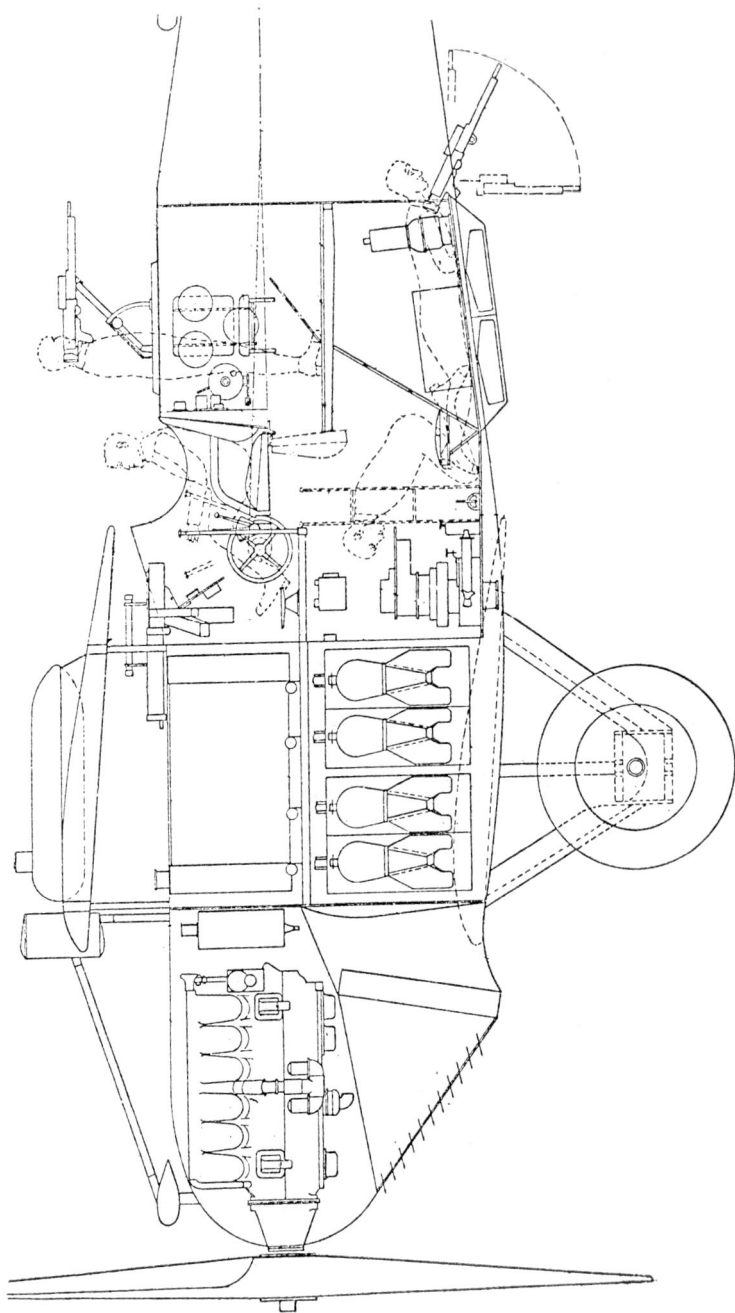

Makers' drawing of Avro Aldershot, showing vertical stowage for bombs; pilot's Vickers gun, with case and link chutes, belt box and Aldis sight; dorsal gun station, with firing platform, spare ammunition drums and Scarff ring-mounting; and ventral gun station. The draughtsman was apparently unacquainted with the functions of the spade grip and pistol grip on the Lewis gun.

sight. The gun was mounted largely externally, high on the fuselage to port, and the rear gunner had a Scarff ring-mounting for a Lewis gun. It is not, apparently, the pilot's gun alone which has eluded historians, but the ventral gun also. This was originally associated with a kind of 'bathtub' understructure, apparently to accommodate the prone bomb-aimer, but Aldershots in service had a simple gun-arm of U-form carrying a circular attachment for a Lewis gun.

It will be gathered from the drawing on page 31 that the Aldershot was a highly integrated 'weapon system'. In laying out this aeroplane Avro were at pains to concentrate the heavy and varied military load as near as possible to the centre of gravity. Crew members could move quite freely around to perform their duties at various stations and (as will be observed) in an interesting variety of postures. Photographic work, as depicted in progress, required genuflection; bomb-sighting and firing below the tail demanded prostration. Likewise in evidence is the internal stowage for 250-lb bombs. Heavier bombs (loadings of two or three 520/550-lb bombs have been identified) were carried externally inboard of the undercarriage assemblies, together with four 20-lb sighter bombs. It has been stated that the Aldershot could carry 2,000 lb of bombs, but the makers gave this figure as 'disposable load of bombs and armament'.

Avro Aldershot, showing external carriers for 520/550-lb bombs, ventral gun arm and Scarff ring-mounting.

While showing features enumerated in the foregoing caption, this view of an Aldershot also discloses the Vickers gun installation.

Bison Though apparently completed late in 1921, the Bison did not appear on the Open List until late in 1925, when it was officially described as a '4-seat gunnery spotter'. The type was remarkable for its capaciousness (crew members could stand in the cabin), but the usual armament of a fixed Vickers gun for the pilot and a Lewis gun on a Scarff ring-mounting in the dorsal position was carried. The Vickers gun was mounted externally on brackets to port, in line with the cockpit, and had Aldis and ring-and-bead sights supported on a structure of great sturdiness and prominence ahead of the windscreen. The sights themselves were actually above the level of the windscreen. There were stations for bomb-carriers beneath the wings (apparently four 112-lb or two 230/250-lb + eight 20-lb) and fuselage (four 20-lb). The 20-lb carriers could be used to drop marine markers.*

Ava The twin-Condor Ava (1923) was a counterpart of the single-engined Blackburn Cubaroo, being intended for coastal defence and carrying externally beneath the fuselage either an Admiralty Whitehead 21-in torpedo weighing some 2,800 lb or a bomb load of 2,000 lb or more. Two examples were built, and the torpedo cradle was fitted to both, the second machine at least actually having the projectile loaded on. This machine also had some form of sight forward of the cockpit. There were Scarff ring-mountings for Lewis guns in the nose and dorsal positions and an unusual type of ventral gun position which was aptly likened to a deck chair. This was immediately below the dorsal position.*

* The Bison and Ava are illustrated on page 34.

Avenger Lion-engined and monocoque-built in wood for the highest performance, and designed moreover for alternative sets of wings, the Avenger single-seat fighter of 1926 underwent considerable modification, though the armament remained as two Vickers guns. These were disposed with their breech casings very low, and well aft, in the cockpit sides, the ejection chutes being let in to large access panels and the barrels projecting into troughs.

The dummy torpedo shown here on the Avro Buffalo is of the Mk.IX pattern. Also seen is the trough for the Vickers gun and the recessed installation of the Scarff ring-mounting.

Buffalo The private-venture Buffalo I and II deck-landing torpedo-bombers dated from 1927 and were identically armed: an 18-in Mk.VIII or Mk.IX torpedo in a tubular-steel cradle beneath the fuselage; a fixed Vickers gun for the pilot, very neatly installed at upper port, and firing through a trough; and a rear Scarff ring-mounting. Twin Lewis guns for the latter were mentioned in a makers' description, and the mounting was attached well below the level of the fuselage decking, this, presumably, being aerodynamically advantageous, if restrictive, in fighting efficiency. Under-wing bombs were doubtless intended, and windows below the pilot's cockpit suggest a prone bombing position. On each side of the pilot's windscreen was a pyramid mounting for a torpedo ring-sight.

◄ Avro Ava, showing nose, dorsal and ventral gun positions. Under the fuselage, in line with the propeller, is the pistol stop for the torpedo.

Except that no bombs are in place on the Light Series carrier under the lower wing, the armament of this Avro Avocet appears to be complete.

Avocet Like the Vickers Vireo, the Avocet of 1927 was a Lynx-engined light naval fighter. The fuselage was of very small cross-section, and there were bulges over the breech casings of the two Vickers guns, mounted just below shoulder-level in the cockpit sides and having separate case and link chutes. The Aldis sight was offset to port, the ring-and-bead sight to starboard. Between the undercarriage radius rods, under the lower wing, was a carrier for four 20-lb bombs.

Antelope Like its sleek competitors for day bomber orders as the 1920s ended—the Hawker Hart, Fairey Fox II and (in some degree) de Havilland Hound—the Antelope had a special low-drag rotatable gun mounting of its makers' own design. This mounting was developed during 1928, in which year the aircraft first flew. Fine achievement though it was, the Antelope won no orders, though the gun mounting gained a measure of success. In 1928 Avro said of the mounting that:

'The pivotal attachments of the elevating arm to the trainable ring project beyond the circumferential edge of the ring, thereby permitting the arm to be turned down to a position vertically below the pivots.'

36

In this connection it should be mentioned that the Antelope's fuselage was of notably small cross-section. It was further stated:

'The pivots form part of a hollow tube containing a longitudinally sliding rod operating a wire from a lever on the elevating arm. This rod has cones for releasing the elevating locking bolts from a toothed sector, and arms for afterwards releasing the training locking-bolts from holes in the runway.'

As originally installed in the Antelope, the Avro ring-mounting does not appear to have embodied the compression-spring housing on top of the ring opposite the gun arm. This housing is clearly visible in the illustrations of the Armstrong Whitworth Atlas II and also in those on later pages showing the Avro 637. The mounting will be described in more detail in Volume 2 of this work.

Avro Antelope, showing trough and chutes for Vickers gun and Avro ring-mounting with Lewis gun.

The Antelope's main bomb load of four 112-lb or two 230/250-lb was carried under the wings, and there was a Light Series carrier (four 20-lb bombs) beneath the fuselage. The pilot's Vickers gun was on the port side, the blast trough running immediately below the exhaust stubs of the Rolls-Royce F (Kestrel) engine.

626 A 1930 development of the Tutor trainer, the Type 626 was intended for 'the complete instruction of all military flying personnel'. It was claimed:

'Not only can all branches of pilotage instruction from elementary flying training to advanced aerobatics be undertaken, but, by the use of alternative equipment, the aircraft may be employed for the instruction of pilots and observers in all branches of applied flying training, such as offensive and defensive gunnery, bombing, wireless, photography etc.'

Although a two-seater, the 626 had a third cockpit to take the Avro ring-mounting for a Lewis or Vickers Class F gun with one spare magazine. The pilot had a fixed Vickers gun, centrally mounted (alternative to the rear gun) and there was provision for two Light Series carriers (four 20-lb bombs each) under the wings. The fixed gun had 100 rounds.

The 626 was a most useful aircraft not only for instructional work but as an economical general-purpose type also and was quite extensively exported. It was, however, the Type 637 which was considered as the true 'G.P' type in the Avro Tutor family.

637 Developed during 1932/33, this type was described by Avro as a 'medium-duty general-purpose aircraft fitted with the normal armament and equipment appropriate to this class of aircraft'. It had a Cheetah engine and several other differences compared with the 626. The fixed Vickers gun was set in the fuselage immediately in front of the pilot, the portion from the trigger motor aft, together with the greater part of the

Avro 637, showing installation of Vickers gun and Aldis sight, and Lewis gun on Avro ring-mounting.

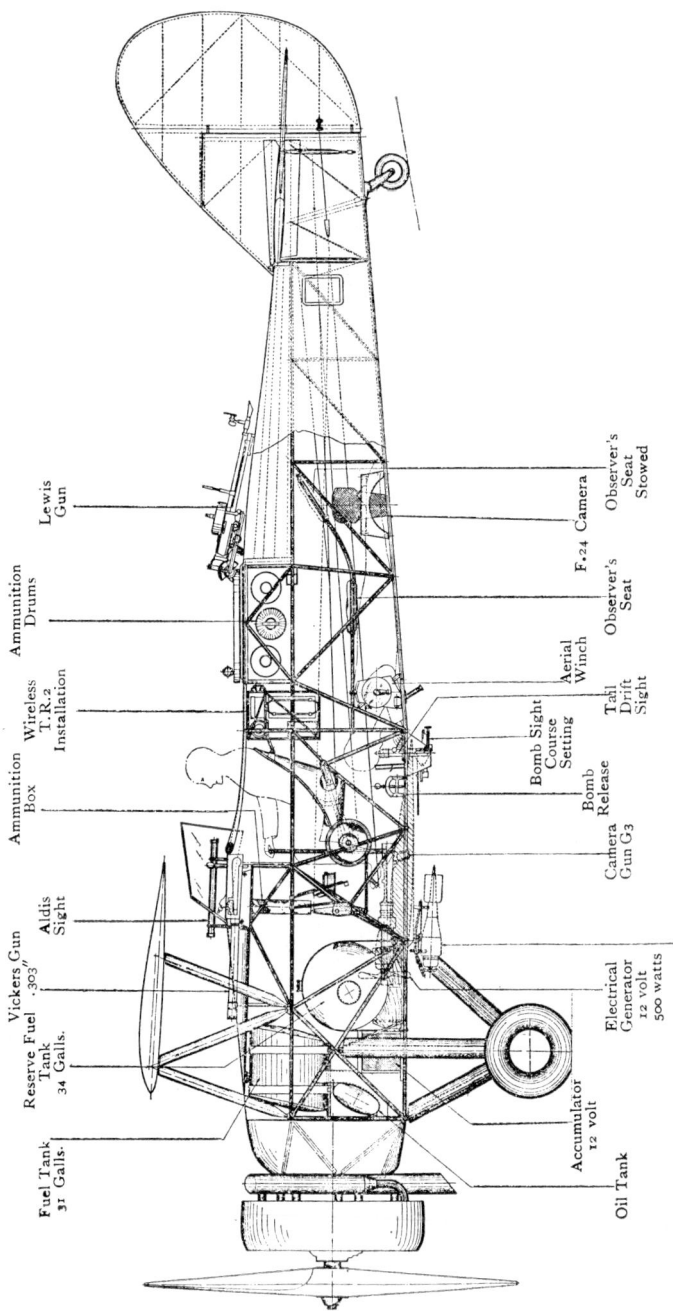

Fuel Tank
31 Galls.

Reserve Fuel
Tank
34 Galls.

Vickers Gun
.303″

Aldis
Sight

Ammunition
Box

Wireless
T.R.2
Installation

Ammunition
Drums

Lewis
Gun

Accumulator
12 volt

Electrical
Generator
12 volt
500 watts

Bomb 20 lb.
and carrier
(Light Series)

Camera
Gun G3

Bomb
Release

Bomb Sight
Course
Setting

Aerial
Winch

Tail
Drift
Sight

Observer's
Seat

F.24 Camera

Observer's
Seat
Stowed

Oil Tank

Avro drawing of Type 637 'economy bombing and fighting aeroplane', showing
distribution of military equipment.

39

Aldis sight, being housed within an unusual box-form windscreen. A ring-and-bead sight was an alternative to the Aldis. The Lewis, or Vickers Class F, gun was on an Avro ring-mounting. Other armament items were listed as: 'Two Light Series carriers for four 20-lb bombs or four dummy practice bombs each; bomb-release controls for either observer or pilot; Wimperis course-setting bomb-sight.'

636 Built in 1935, this type could be regarded either as a fighter-trainer or as a fighter/trainer, for it could be used for training fighter pilots or as a fighter converted from the training configuration. The mounting of the two Vickers guns in an abrupt hump forward of the front cockpit was one of several features which bespoke the makers' new Hawker Siddeley affiliations. (See Armstrong Whitworth Scimitar.) Aldis and ring-and-bead sights were carried on braced tubular members.

Anson I   The Anson prototype (Avro 652A) was matched against the D.H.89M during 1935 for a lucrative contract. These two general reconnaissance aeroplanes underwent their Service trials with the Coast Defence Development Unit at Gosport, and it must have been on almost the very day that the Anson was finally selected (May 1935) that the present writer was permitted to fly in this new monoplane and to occupy the Armstrong Whitworth manually operated turret. The Anson was matched in mock combat against a Hart, and this was the report:

'The writer was fortunate enough to be allowed to act as "gunner" in the Avro. In the nose there is a bomber's compartment, with the pilot's cabin, navigator's compartment and W/T compartment behind. To the rear of the W/T compartment is a gun turret, or "parrot cage", of the Armstrong Whitworth type, half of which protrudes above the fuselage

Early-production Avro Ansons with and without Armstrong Whitworth turret. The turret served not only for defence but as a look-out for reconnaissance, additional to the already generous fenestration. (*Flight International.*)

decking. No gun was fitted to the mounting, details of which must perforce remain undescribed. Certainly the 652 is an aircraft fit for gentlemen to fight from; except in very tight turns, when g took a hand, one could just sit and shoot or be shot at as the case might be.'

The Armstrong Whitworth manually operated gun turret was patented in November 1933. The weight of the gunner upon his seat was balanced against that of the gun. There was a link motion whereby his line of vision remained in the same relationship to the gunsight throughout the entire range of elevation. Armstrong Whitworth claimed that the balancing of the mechanism completely overcame the effect of acceleration during manoeuvres, and one's personal recollection of g taking a hand may be attributed to the fact that no gun was fitted. To fire vertically downward the gunner stood, and the weight of the gun was taken directly on the mounting.

The turret rotated on rollers in a vertical track, rotation being effected by reaction of the gunner's feet on the rubber-covered cockpit floor. There was a mechanical lock to enable the turret to be secured at any desired angle of traverse. Merely leaning backward or forward was sufficient to alter elevation, and, in practice, it was claimed this movement was quite natural, demanding no mental effort by the gunner. Although independent locks were provided for both the rotational and elevating movements, the gun could be fired with the entire mechanism free, no ill effects being experienced from recoil. It was possible, therefore, to follow a target continuously. The only external unbalanced force was caused by the protrusion of the gun barrel. Firing aft, and through a traverse of 60 degrees on each side, it was claimed, no inconvenience was experienced at any speed. When firing broadside, however, the gun barrel created a rotational force which had to be resisted by the gunner.

Substantially of spherical formation, the turret casing consisted of a metal framework and formed Rhodoid panels. The slot for the barrel had an articulated sliding cover, allowing the turret to be completely sealed when not in use. The turret weighed about 97 lb. Five 97-round ammunition drums were provided. When not in use the gun lay in a recess in the fuselage decking.

The pilot had a single fixed Vickers gun mounted to his left and firing through the nose fairing. The bomb-aimer's station was on the right of the nose, and there was a sliding door in the floor for the course-setting bombsight. An adjustable windscreen prevented entry of air through the aperture. On the bomb-aimer's right were release controls for the bombs. Release was electrical and fusing mechanical. The bombs—two 100-lb and four or eight 20-lb—were carried in the wing roots. Flares or floats were alternatives to the small bombs.

Later armament developments than those mentioned (two extra guns at the side windows, a 20-mm gun in the fuselage bottom, Bristol turret for training) do not come within the compass of this review.

Manchester   Although the Manchester twin-engined heavy bomber was first flown during 1939, and therefore commands some notice here, this particular machine carried no armament, though the second, which flew in 1940, did. Detailed study of the Manchester's armament is most fittingly linked with that of the Lancaster's, and left for another occasion. For convenience it may be recorded that the Manchester had power-driven turrets in the nose, ventral and tail positions (F.N.5, F.N.21A and F.N.4A or F.N.20). The nose and ventral turrets had two Browning guns each, the tail turret four. In service the F.N.21A was deleted, and a dorsal turret (modified F.N.7, of Botha type) was fitted instead. Initially the bomb load was eight 1,000-lb bombs, but modifications accommodated 4,000-lb bombs.

Beardmore

W.B. I   Glide-bombing was the mode of attack intended for this two-seat biplane bomber (1916/17) by the RNAS. The bomb load has been given as six 110-lb, but no such bomb appears to have been used by the RNAS and it is reasonable to suppose that the bombs were of the H.E.R.L. 100-lb pattern. These bombs were intended specifically for anti-submarine work and were horizontally stowed. The observer was stationed far aft and sighted the bombs through a hatch in the floor, passing his instructions to the pilot by means of a special visual system. Provision was made for a free Lewis gun at the observer's station.

W.B. II   As was becoming to a company having Beardmore's standing in the fields of naval architecture and gunnery, the W.B. II two-seat fighter (also suitable for reconnaissance and patrol) exhibited originality in armament. The first machine (1917) had a fixed Vickers gun and a Lewis gun on a simple ring-mounting. The second was higher powered, and— even more interesting than its twin-Vickers-gun installation—its Lewis gun was on a Beardmore–Richards mounting, designed by G. Tilghman-Richards and nicknamed 'The Witch's Broomstick'. The central member of this mounting was a pillar mounted on a 'universal footstep bearing' at its lower end and supported by, and guided upon, a coaxial annular guide ring round which it could be traversed. This arm carried at its upper end a gun-arm, one end of which was mounted on a pivot pin carried by the pillar, the other end being fitted with a pivoted block carrying the stem of a fork to which the gun was secured. The pillar could be locked in any position round the guide ring and the gun-arm could be locked in any position relative to the pillar. The locking was effected by spring-actuated bolts carried by the pillar and operated by levers, like-wise on the pillar. The pillar was further fitted with a seat, capable of

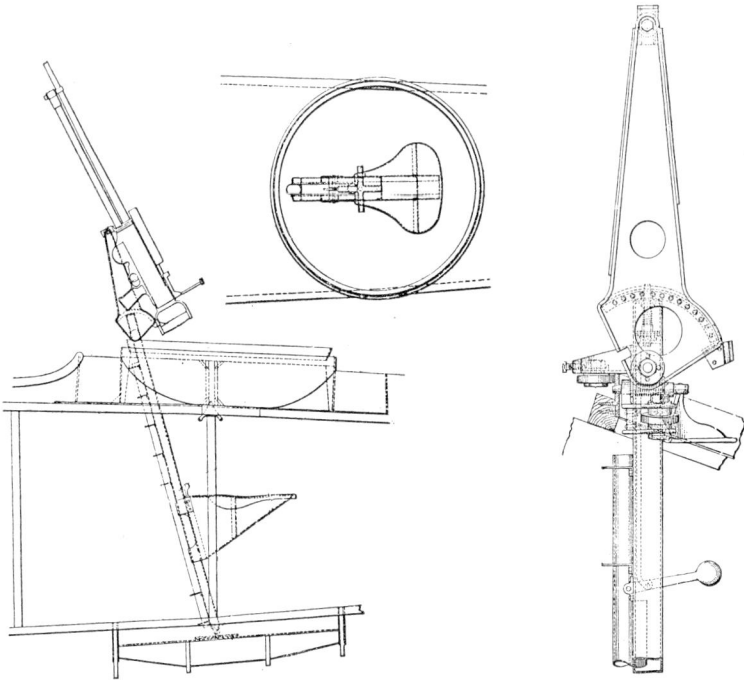

Secrets of 'The Witch's Broomstick'—the Tilghman-Richards gun mounting for the Beardmore W.B.II—seen in original makers' drawings. The detail view shows the locking arrangements for the gun arm.

being locked at any desired height. With the pillar displaced laterally to its full extent the line of fire could extend to 15 degrees past the centre line of the aircraft.

During the course of W.B. II development the guide ring was built up from the fuselage to enhance the gun's effectiveness and the gunner's comfort.

W.B. III Dating from 1916/17, this very extensively modified Sopwith Pup, for shipboard service, had a single Lewis gun, for which three ammunition drums were provided (one on the gun). Photographs show single (47-round) drums, but a contemporary account mentioned '300 rounds', suggesting that double (97-round) drums were intended. The gun was at first carried on a tripod mounting, apparently designed at the Grain experimental station, installed forward of the cockpit, so that the gun fired through a hole in the centre-section. Later the gun was mounted slightly to starboard above the centre-section, firing a little upwards over the airscrew.

W.B. IV Of wholly original design, this single-seat 'ship's aeroplane' of 1917 was remarkable in having the pilot in front of the wings, the Hispano-Suiza engine being mounted in the fuselage over the centre of gravity and driving the airscrew through an extension shaft (compare Westland F.7/30). A fixed synchronised Vickers gun fired out through the nose immediately behind the airscrew on the port side, the breech casing being in the fuselage. The installation was very neat and there were separate case and link chutes. Forward of the watertight cockpit was a sturdy tripod for a Lewis gun.

W.B. V This contemporary of the W.B. IV had an armament of even greater—indeed exceptional—interest, though the airframe/engine layout was conventional. It was specifically designed for the French Hispano-Suiza/*canon* Puteaux installation, of the type that became generically known as *moteur canon*. Although a 37-mm gun was actually installed in the first W.B. V, it found no acceptance among pilots, who were as cramped by its presence in the cockpit as they were disconcerted by the possibility of malfunctioning. French pilots using a similar installation in SPADs were said to become bemused by the explosive fumes. A fixed Vickers gun was therefore substituted, this being mounted on top of the fuselage with the breech casing faired. As secondary armament there was a free Lewis gun on a pylon mounting ahead of the cockpit and firing through an aperture in the centre-section.

W.B. 26 It was claimed for this two-seat fighter of 1925 (designed for the Latvian Government) that it was exceptionally difficult to cripple with machine-gun fire, and indeed it was an exceptional aeroplane in several respects, not least in armament. The pilot had two Beardmore–Farquhar guns, synchronised by C.C. gear, and the gunner had one gun of the same type on a Scarff wind-balanced mounting. It was declared:

> 'The rear gun is so mounted in relation to the wings and fuselage that it can be operated almost throughout the entire upper hemisphere, while, in a downward direction, owing to the fact that the gunner's cockpit is aft of the trailing edge of the lower plane, the gun can be fired almost vertically, an angle of 10 degrees only beyond the vertical being obstructed by the fuselage. In order to improve the field of fire aft the vertical fin is of the cantilever type, to which the tailplane is braced by one strut on each side.'

Blackburn

Seaplane Type L During 1915 this aircraft is said to have been armed with a machine-gun (presumed Lewis) for service with the RNAS, and an early Blackburn document states that it was originally designed to meet the requirements of a coastal-patrol seaplane, with an observer/gunner forward and the pilot behind. The same document mentions a load of two

'165-lb' bombs (presumed 65-lb), though it is doubtful if these were ever carried.

T.B. Ranken Darts formed the sole recorded armament of this anti-airship seaplane of 1915. The figure of 70 lb quoted by the makers for 'military load' doubtless included the weight of the canisters and associated gear.

Triplane The layout of this single-seat 'scout' of 1915/16 was much along the lines of the A.D. Scout, and concerning the supposed intended armament of a Davis recoilless gun the same remarks apply. A nacelle-mounted Lewis-gun installation was certainly schemed, this being intended (according to a Blackburn document) to give 'an exceptional arc of fire'. A makers' drawing, dated June 1916, shows this triplane armed with a single land-service Lewis gun, apparently having freedom of movement only in elevation, mounted on the nacelle with the 47-round ammunition drum and entire breech casing housed in a 'hump' fairing immediately ahead of the cockpit. 'Military load' was stated by Blackburn to be a mere 50 lb.

G.P. and S.P. These floatplane forerunners of the Kangaroo (1916/17) had nose and dorsal Scarff ring-mountings, with a Lewis gun each (one Blackburn document mentioned twin guns) installed on the top longerons, with the coaming built up fore and aft. They were designed to carry four 230-lb bombs under the wings or a 14-in torpedo under the fuselage. The bombsight was fixed to the starboard side of the front cockpit.

Kangaroo Built in 1917 as a landplane development of the G.P. and S.P., the Kangaroo had Scarff ring-mountings in the nose and dorsal positions and was at one time intended to have a prone position also. This was to be arranged below the fuselage in conjunction with an extended tail skid. There was also a scheme involving what Blackburn termed an 'open-ended casing', housing a gun at each end. This was dated October 1917. 'Military load' of the Kangaroo was quoted by the makers as 1,220 lb, but this was inclusive of guns and fittings, and another Blackburn document gave the bomb load as 1,040 lb (equivalent to two 520-lb bombs). The recorded four 230-lb or one 520-lb internal loads (bombs vertical, noses up) were probably not usable in addition to external carriers. A photograph shows a Kangaroo with two 230-lb flat-nosed anti-submarine bombs side by side under the lower longerons. The bombs were sighted from the nose (RNAS Mk.IIA Low Altitude sight). A 520-lb bomb was dropped to good effect on at least one occasion, falling very close to a submarine, which was despatched by depth-charges from HMS *Ouse*.

The Kangaroo's crew numbered three; the front gunner acted as bomb-aimer/observer and the rear gunner as wireless operator. The first machine had, in the first instance, a low-set forward gun-ring as on the S.P. and G.P., but on production aircraft the ring was carried high above the top longerons, on a higher level even than the pilot's cockpit. The field of fire was thus broadened. The rear mounting was protected in some degree by building up the coaming ahead of it, and additionally there was a wind-screen for the gunner. Fields of fire benefited from the very narrow cross-section of the fuselage, but there was official criticism that the gunner was prevented from firing astern by the 'box' tail. The official general-arrangement drawing shows Lewis guns with 'land-service' cooling jackets and with 'single' (47-round) drums. One Blackburn document mentioned twin guns.

Blackburd   Like its counterpart the Short Shirl, the Blackburd was a single-seat deck-landing torpedo-carrier (not 'torpedo-bomber', for that requirement came later), designed for the 18-in Mk.VIII torpedo weighing 1,423 lb. (The 18-in Mk.IX, as carried by the Blackburn-built Sopwith Cuckoo, weighed about 1,000 lb.) A makers' description mentioned con-trols in the cockpit to adjust the mechanism of the torpedo in the air and the weight of the 'torpedo gear' was listed as 50 lb. The torpedo was carried parallel to the fuselage centre line; and the centre line was parallel to the top and bottom lines. 'It was like a flying box,' recalled G. E. Petty, who was responsible for several Blackburn torpedo aircraft, but he saw fit to add: 'The only excuse was that by then production was of primary importance, and Harris Booth eliminated all trimming.'

That the Blackburd was a more remarkable aeroplane than has hitherto been apparent, and not respecting armament alone, is evident from the following contemporary account, which affords a classic example of how a new form of armament and a new technique of operation could influence aircraft design:

'As the run on a ship is necessarily very limited, the machine must be capable of getting off at a comparatively low speed, or, in other words, the lift component of the reaction on the wing section must be a maxi-mum. In the "Blackburd" aeroplane this is obtained by the use of wing flaps, which are pulled down before flight, and consequently alter the

Recorded in the text are new facts concerning the remarkable Blackburn Blackburd, the frontal portion of which is shown at left and the torpedo installation at right.

46

The two sets of torpedo crutches on the Blackburd are seen at left. The second picture shows the lever near the pilot's wicker seat. This singular device performed a plurality of functions, as described in the text.

wing section to one of deep camber and high maximum lifting capacity. When once off the deck the flaps are released and automatically resume their normal position. To prevent any instability, which might be caused by a too sudden change of section, a specially-constructed oil dashpot is used, which allows the flaps to assume the neutral position gradually. In practice the time taken for this operation is about 43 seconds.

'For getting off the deck wheels are fitted, but when once off, these, together with their axle, are dropped by means of a lever which also actuates the dashpot. By releasing the wheels, two long skeleton steel skids are left clear for use in case of landing again on the deck, and if it is inevitable that the machine should alight on the water, these skids have not the "tripping" effect that wheels possess. Once in the water, the machine is kept afloat by means of air bags fitted inside the fuselage and in the bottom of the engine cowl. Another interesting feature of this skid chassis is the arrangement of the springing gear. This consists of two vertical telescopic compression struts, which, when compressed, cause the skid to move slightly forward, with the result that when landing, the machine appears to creep forward, first on one skid and then on the other. Attached to the front tubes of the chassis are timber hydrovanes, one above the other, and the reaction of the water on these when alighting keeps the nose of the machine up and counteracts any tripping effect.

'The torpedo is held in position by means of two sets of crutches and one adjustable tension strap round the torpedo itself. In order to prevent the torpedo from moving fore and aft, a raised stop on the top of the torpedo fits into a fixed steel block on the under side of the fuselage. The control for dropping the torpedo is very ingenious, and at the same time fool proof. A long-handled wooden lever is pulled into the rear position before flight and fixed there by means of spring plungers. Immediately after rising, the pilot pushes the lever forward and releases, by this one operation, both the wheels and axle, and the wing flaps

47

previously mentioned. Now suppose the pilot wishes to drop the torpedo, he pulls back the lever into its original position and, by doing so, releases the two ends of the torpedo strap simultaneously, and starts the motor in the torpedo itself. When one considers that each control usually means a separate lever, and that the average torpedo-plane pilot has at least 15 different controls to operate, it is evidently a great boon to have four worked by one lever. Another advantage of this gear is that the torpedo cannot be released until the wheels and axle have been dropped clear.'

The Blackburd carried no guns.

Swift Built in 1920, the Swift was a single-seat torpedo-dropper like the Cuckoo and Blackburd, but incorporated many advances, of which those affecting armament have a particular interest. In its developed form it was adopted by the RAF as the Dart, which will be dealt with separately. As on the Blackburd, the torpedo was the 18-in Mk.VIII, with the lighter Mk.IX as an alternative. The pilot still had no gun, doubtless in the interests of weight-saving, for the Dart was quite handy in the air. A split-axle undercarriage was fitted to permit torpedo stowage and this was originally designed to be jettisonable, as on the Blackburd. To take the loads imposed by the torpedo, the entire central portion, including the

Blackburn Swift with incomplete or dummy torpedo (probably Mk.VIII).

48

engine mounting, the middle part of the fuselage, undercarriage, and centre-sections of top and bottom wings were made of steel.

The second volume of this work will instance the very strenuous efforts put forth by the Blackburn company in the early 1920s to develop and promote the torpedo-dropping aircraft, in the realisation not only of the operational potential of the class but of their own need for survival. The Swift was the chosen instrument, and in 1920, when the prototype appeared at Olympia during July in partly mocked-up form, it was stated that the torpedo was not shown in place as 'the gear for slinging and dropping it, etc., is of such a nature that the authorities do not wish details published'. After the passage of years these details can now be given in three company descriptions dating from the early part of 1920. One description related to:

'The provision of a vertically depending leg having a tine (a spiked fitting) which extends into or beyond the plane of rotation of the vane-wheel at the nose of the torpedo, whereby the vane-wheel is held against rotation after the usual safety pin is removed until the torpedo is dropped. A fork fitted to the end of the leg embraces the nozzle between the vane-wheel and the torpedo body. The leg is hinged to a bracket secured beneath the radiator of the aircraft, and is connected by a flexible member to a spring which normally holds the leg against the

Blackburn Dart with Mk.IX torpedo. The pistol stop is seen in position.

49

nose of the torpedo and causes the leg to fold up against a stop when the torpedo is dropped.'

This device, which prevented the vane-wheel (which armed the torpedo, or rendered it live) from rotating before release, was officially known as a 'pistol stop'.

Another Blackburn description concerned exhaust silencers, and in this connection it must be explained that the element of surprise was considered of great importance in the developing technique of air-torpedo warfare. For the Napier Lion engine of the Swift, in fact, a Blackburn silencer was produced, having an expansion chamber about three feet long.

The third of the descriptions mentioned was of exceptional interest because it concerned the mechanism for setting the depth-regulating device of the torpedo. It was explained:

'The mechanism comprises an operating shaft with hand wheel mounted in bearings near the aviator and geared by a worm and worm wheel to an indicator dial movable opposite a pointer. The shaft is provided with a sprocket wheel connected by a chain to a sprocket wheel on an adjusting shaft mounted in a ball bearing. An extension is telescopically mounted in the shaft by means of a slot and pin connection which compels the extension to rotate with the shaft but allows small longitudinal displacements of the extension against the compression spring. The extension carries by means of a universal joint a key adapted to fit the setting stud of the depth-regulating device of the torpedo.'

These developments respecting armament were instrumental in establishing Blackburn as a world leader in the development of torpedo aircraft. Together with other technical advances to be detailed in this and the coming volume, they may be judged to merit a higher opinion of Blackburn achievements than is frequently expressed.

On the later Swifts at least there was a sighting bar running continuously between the inner pairs of interplane struts, being further supported by the front pair of centre-section struts. This bar was associated with two small-diameter rings bracketed to the fuselage decking just outside the side panels of the windscreen. These rings were features of Blackburn torpedo aircraft as late as the Shark prototype.

As intimated earlier, the Swift was intended to make silent, gliding approaches to the target, and in this connection a speed of 120 knots was mentioned.

Dart The original Swift was bought by the Air Ministry in 1920 and was developed into the RAF (Fleet Air Arm) type built in quantity as the Dart. As an alternative to the torpedo (Mk.VIII or the smaller Mk.IX) a bomb load could be carried under the inner wings, the normal load being two 520-lb. In service, a carrier for four practice bombs or marine markers was attached well aft under the fuselage. No guns were fitted, but a Dart pilot could use his slow-flying capability as a protective measure.

It was the Dart which marked the introduction into Fleet Air Arm service of the 'torpedo-bomber' class of aircraft, a fact which was not relished by designers who already had perplexing problems concerning aerodynamic and structural design, further aggravated by deck-landing and stowage requirements. With the Dart, however, the tactics of torpedo attack were developed to a high degree, and were of many kinds, depending upon weather, type of target and sometimes personal initiative. B. J. Hurren had first-hand knowledge of this work and gives a breezy account in his book *Perchance* (Nicholson & Watson, 1949), alluding, incidentally, to the surprisingly large formations which were massed for secret exercises. Of tactics he relates:

'The star position for dropping was ahead of the target ship, bearing about 45 degrees from that ship and distance 1,100 yards. In the flurry of the dive to attack, clearly only one pilot could jockey to the optimum position, as the torpedoes were launched if possible simultaneously, or nearly so. There were thus good reasons for seeking other methods of attack, and many ingenious ideas were evolved.'

Sighting arrangements were identical with those on the Swift.

Blackburn A companion type to the Dart, the Blackburn was a four-seat deck-landing fleet spotter of imposing bulk. These facts notwithstanding,

Blackburn Blackburn, showing brackets for gunsights, Vickers gun with case and link chutes, and Scarff ring-mounting.

the pilot was allowed the customary fixed Vickers gun, with 500 rounds. This was mounted externally on the port side of the cockpit, and a prerequisite among Blackburn armourers was a head for heights, for the gun was atop a lofty access ladder. Even the loading handle was external, and latterly there was a short ejection chute for cases and links. Aldis and ring-and-bead sights were variously fitted, but the Aldis alone, centrally mounted, was the common Service installation. Aft of the top-wing trailing edge was a cavernous cockpit, cut away below the top fuselage level, and behind this was emplaced a Scarff ring-mounting for a Lewis gun. It might seem merciful to add that a bomb load was not demanded in addition (the engine being a Lion of a mere 450 hp), but indeed it was demanded, and there were tubular carriers for two 112-lb or 230/250-lb bombs below the inner sections of the lower wings. A Light Series carrier was attached beneath the fuselage.

The Blackburn was adapted to carry glider targets (16-ft) for anti-aircraft practice.

Cubaroo   Strongly suggestive of a 'mightier yet' Blackburn, the Cubaroo (so named because of its Cub engine and the fact that it was intended for coast-defence, like the Kangaroo) appeared in 1924. The most scrupulous search by the present writer among photographs and documents has (somewhat disappointingly) disclosed no evidence of a fixed gun. The free-gun armament, however, was distinctly interesting. Abaft the upper wing was a Scarff ring-mounting for a Lewis gun, and in this vicinity the fuselage assumed a diamond section, the gunner's command of the upper hemisphere being thus extended. But this was not the sole rear armament:

Blackburn Cubaroo, showing torpedo crutches and bomb-carriers under the fuselage and the commanding emplacement of the Scarff ring-mounting at the rear. Note abrupt change in fuselage section to ensure maximum field of fire from this position.

a contemporary description mentions 'doors through which a machine-gunner can shoot under the tail on either side, this opening being made easier by the fact that aft of the cabin the fuselage is triangular in section so that the guns can shoot on either side of the keel.' It seems, in fact, that there was a single prone position for the manning of a gun or guns firing through ports, which could be covered by sliding doors, above the lower wing roots. This is borne out by a contemporary description which states:

> 'Behind the central portion the fuselage is arranged in three storeys, wherein are provided chart and wireless rooms, an upper and lower gun position and a bombing look-out, etc.'

Concerning the unusual form of fuselage mentioned, *Flight* remarked primly:

> 'There are, we believe, several reasons for this form of body, but into these it would be imprudent to delve too far, and we leave it to our readers to draw their own conclusions.'

The torpedo carried by the Cubaroo was of the Admiralty Whitehead 21-in type, weighing, according to contemporary accounts, $1\frac{1}{2}$ tons. A Blackburn document has given the weight as 3,000 lb, but this may have included some 200 lb for associated gear. The steel torpedo crutch was flanked by carriers for, apparently, four 520/550-lb bombs.

Airedale Tested during 1926, the Airedale was a high-wing monoplane deck-landing fleet spotter. A three-seater, its crew dispositions were similar to those of the Blackburn. Aldis and ring-and-bead sights betokened the

The pilot's Vickers gun on the Blackburn Airedale was carried on the starboard side, but this view shows the sight mountings, with Aldis sight in place, bomb-carriers under fuselage, and Scarff ring-mounting at rear of large aft cockpit.

fitting of a fixed Vickers gun, which was mounted very far forward on the starboard side of the fuselage, firing past the cylinders of the Jaguar engine. The brackets carrying the gun were fore and aft of the crank which operated the elevator cables. The Scarff ring-mounting carried a single Lewis gun. Two Light Series carriers were fitted in tandem under the fuselage.

Greek Blackburn Velos seaplane, showing characteristic built-up emplacement for Scarff ring-mounting.

Velos   Developed during 1925 for export, the Velos was in essence a two-seater Dart with twin-float undercarriage, this being designed to permit the dropping of an 18-in torpedo. Tubular carriers could alternatively be fitted for bombs up to two 520-lb (landplane) or two 230-lb (floatplane). Bomb selectors were fitted in the rear cockpit and a 'sighting slot' was said to be provided near the starboard side. The pilot had no gun, but immediately behind his cockpit was a Scarff ring-mounting for a Lewis gun (or, according to one Blackburn statement, twin guns). On production aircraft built in Greece the ring was very noticeably built up from the fuselage to improve the field of fire. As a torpedo-carrier the Velos was intended to be flown as a single-seater. Sighting arrangements were as on the Swift and Dart.

Ripon   Although there were many developments and variants of the Ripon two-seat torpedo-bomber (1926), the basic armament of torpedo or bombs plus fixed and free guns remained unaltered. The pilot's Vickers gun was mounted beneath the top-port fuselage decking with its breech casing inside the cockpit and the cooling jacket exposed in a shallow trough. The case chute was considerably below the link chute. On the Ripon I, and initially the Ripon II also, the rear Lewis gun was on a Scarff ring-mounting, but thereafter the Fairey 'High-Speed' mounting was standardised, the gun lying in a recess when stowed, with only the sights and ammunition drum protruding above the fuselage top-line.

The torpedo-carrier was of steel tubular construction, with the usual two crutches, and in later machines this was modified to give the torpedo a nose-down attitude. Dropping height was of the 25-ft order. Sighting bars were attached between the front and rear centre-section struts. On the

Three stages in the development of the Blackburn Ripon: *top*, Ripon II with Scarff ring-mounting and torpedo in line of flight; *second*, Ripon II with Fairey 'High-Speed' mounting and torpedo at nose-down angle: *third*, Ripon III with torpedo in line of flight. Later the torpedo on this aircraft was carried nose-down.

Ripon I the bead for the gunsight was attached to the top centre-section, but later aircraft had the bead attached to the fuselage just forward of the windscreen and the ring a little distance ahead, or, in the final arrangement, just behind the engine. The massive bracket was one of many accumulated excrescences. Design provision was made for six 230/250-lb bombs or three of 520/550 lb, but these loadings would include bombs under the fuselage, of which there is no known instance. In the lower wings were strong-points for four main bomb-carriers, latterly of Universal type, with a Light Series carrier outboard under the port and/or starboard wing. There was a prone bombing station beneath the pilot, with sight and fusing and release controls. In place of the torpedo an 1,100-lb smoke container, or 120-gal auxiliary petrol tank, with wind-driven pump, could be slung in the crutches.

In Volume 2 the name of Lieut R. H. Clark-Hall, RN, will be mentioned more than once for its association with the development of Naval aircraft armament, and in particular gunnery. In connection with the Ripon, and in token of the continuity of direction from which British Service aviation has more than once benefited, one may remark that the Ripon's torpedo installation was explained to visiting Dominion Premiers during 1930 by this same officer. He was then AVM Clark-Hall, Director of Equipment, Air Ministry.

In the context of the Sopwith Cuckoo, many aircraft of which type were built by Blackburn, mention is made of a restriction on diving, and another restriction may be recorded in connection with the Ripon II. During 1934 the Air Ministry issued an order that this aircraft must never be dived without the pilot having first adjusted and locked the tail incidence, so that it would be necessary to hold the aircraft in the dive.

Iris The first of several marks of the Iris three-engined flying-boat appeared in 1926. This had a Scarff ring-mounting in the bow for a single Lewis gun and a similar installation on the hull abaft the wings. Two additional Lewis guns could be manned at sliding hatches in the hull, external

Blackburn Iris prototype, showing gun positions and bomb-carrier under wing.

fittings being provided for the purpose. Tubular bomb-carriers were secured to the lower wings at the attachments of the hull/wing bracing struts. Two 520/550-lb or four 230/250-lb bombs were standard loads. In a later form (Iris II) the original Iris had a modified stern, incorporating a third gun position with Scarff ring-mounting aft of the tail. The tail unit was modified accordingly, the centre rudder being deleted in favour of a forward-mounted servo unit. The Iris V had a considerably modified nose, with provision for the Scarff ring-mounting to be slid fore and aft to facilitate mooring. One Iris (S1593) had special provision in the bow for a 37-mm C.O.W. gun, but the bow section of this boat was different from that of the later Perth and the Vickers-Westland mounting does not appear to have been initially installed.

Vickers gun and ring-and-bead sight installation on Lincock III.

Lincock   The Lincock private-venture light fighter was first produced in 1927. Armament, fitted only to Mk.III aircraft (1930), was two fixed Vickers guns, mounted about mid-way down the fuselage sides and firing through troughs. There were the usual case and link chutes and a 'teardrop' fairing to allow access to the loading handle of the starboard gun. The Chinese Lincocks had ring-and-bead sights. The ammunition boxes were between the seat and the rudder bar, and could be loaded in position or readily removed. The Lincock was also offered with one gun only, in which case electrical or wireless equipment could be carried.

Turcock No armament was installed on the Turcock fighter of 1927, but design provision was made for two Vickers guns with 1,000 rounds of ammunition.

Beagle Built to the same difficult specification as were the Hawker Harrier and Handley Page Hare, the Beagle (1928) suffered from the same lack of power. But it got to Martlesham, and ultimately served at the Torpedo Development Unit, Gosport. High-altitude day bombing being the envisaged alternative duty to torpedo-bombing, the bomb-aimer had a prone position below the pilot's seat, with sight, altimeter, A.S.I., inclinometer and auxiliary rudder control. The pilot's Vickers gun was mounted

Blackburn Beagle, showing torpedo installation and Lewis gun on Scarff ring-mounting.

low and externally to port; the observer/bomb-aimer's Lewis gun was on a wind-balanced Scarff ring-mounting. Eight 112-lb bombs were apparently carried on Martlesham trials, and these were alternatives to four 230-lb. They were attached in tandem pairs. The torpedo was carried in a tubular cradle, and, according to the makers, could weigh up to about 2,000 lb. The torpedo-carrier was a massive tubular frame. Arming and release controls were fitted in the pilot's cockpit and sighting bars were carried transversely between the front interplane struts and fore and aft between the front struts and the cross-bar of the lateral N struts.

Beagle with 112-lb bombs in tandem and showing also the installation of the Vickers gun.

Nautilus Succumbing though it did in competition to the Hawker Osprey, the Nautilus fleet fighter reconnaissance biplane (1929) exhibited uncommon features. The armament of one Vickers and one Lewis gun was, of course, officially prescribed, together with four 20-lb bombs. The Vickers gun fired through a deep trough, the upper edge of which was virtually a fairing for the port cylinder bank of the 'F' Type (Kestrel) engine. Aldis and ring-and-bead sights were fitted. The rim of the gunner's cockpit was a little countersunk below the fuselage top-line and the mounting intended may have been of the type designed by the Blackburn company in 1927. This revolved within the cockpit on upper and lower parallel roller-tracks which could conform in plan to any convenient shape, e.g. circular, elliptical or horseshoe. Even parallel straight tracks could be used. The elevating arm, which supported the gun on a universal joint, was pivoted to the mounting and counterbalanced by tension springs.

The Light Series carrier on the Nautilus was under the lower centre-section.

Sydney Built in 1930, the Sydney was a monoplane development of the Iris and had Scarff ring-mountings for single Lewis guns in the bow, dorsal and tail positions. Bomb-carriers do not appear to have been fitted, but a possible load of about 1,000 lb was mentioned for the type and

Mooring operations in flying-boats were rendered the more difficult by the presence of a Scarff ring-mounting, as will be gathered from this picture of the Blackburn Sydney. In later types the ring was made to slide rearwards. Note also the dorsal ring-mounting; there was a third mounting in the extreme stern.

intended loads were four 230/250-lb or two 520/550-lb. The second pilot sighted and released the bombs.

M.1/30 and M.1/30A These two Buzzard-engined torpedo-bomber prototypes of 1932/33 differed in structure and wing cellule. Armament was the same. The pilot had a Vickers gun firing through a trough in the port fuselage decking, the ejection chute being built in to the rear centre-section strut fairing. The rear Lewis gun was on a Fairey 'High-Speed' mounting, as formerly on the Ripon and latterly on the Shark. A ring-sight was fitted ahead of the windscreen and a pillar-mounted bead in the plane of the front centre-section struts. A sighting bar for the torpedo appears to have been carried transversely on the rear centre-section struts and to have been continued a short distance aft on each side. Provision was made for four to eight Universal bomb-carriers and for the usual Light Series carriers to be fitted under the wings. Possible main loads were apparently four 500/520/550-lb or eight 250-lb bombs. There was a prone bomb-aiming position beneath the floor of the pilot's cockpit. Torpedo stowage was not inhibited by an underslung radiator, as on the Vickers M.1/30, but as aircraft speeds were rising, Blackburn were becoming increasingly aware of the necessity of reconciling optimum launching angle of the missile with minimum drag in the air. Accordingly they developed in 1930 a two-position scheme for carrying and launching, though, as will be seen, this was not adopted for the Shark, which followed the M.1/30s, and was not, in fact, revived until the coming of the Firebrand in the late war years.

In describing the new carrier Blackburn mentioned a frame or spreader with front and rear crutches and slings. By hingeing the frame at the rear

60

For the experimental M.1/30 and M.1/30A Blackburn developed a two-position torpedo-carrier, of a type which did not come into general service until the adoption of the Firebrand late in the Second World War.

the front crutch could be guided up and down by members on the aircraft, the middle part of the frame being connected to the piston rod of an hydraulic jack, controlled through a by-pass and valves by a lever. Thus, for launching, the frame was swung down before the drop.

3MR4 Although otherwise called (possibly as a cover-name) 'Reconnaissance J' or even 'Ripon (Hispano-Suiza)', this aeroplane has been termed by G. E. Petty, who was largely responsible for its design, a 'torpedo bomber'. It was built in 1929 for Japan and was heavily armed. There was a synchronised Vickers gun in the port side of the fuselage with the breech casing in a prominent 'tear-drop' fairing, one or twin Lewis guns on a Scarff ring-mounting, and design provision for another Lewis gun firing downward through the floor. The aperture provided served alternatively for the course-setting bombsight, and the gun was on rails so that it could be stowed internally. With reduced fuel load, and without the third crew-member forward of the gun-ring, it was possible to carry a torpedo of about 1,800 lb. Alternatively bombs could be carried under the fuselage, fusing and release controls being installed in the rear cockpit.

B-2 The B-2 trainer of 1931 was designed with armament training much in mind. An early makers' brochure declares:

'Provision is made for two 20-lb bombs on a carrier below each bottom plane near the root, with a bomb release control between the two seats and a camera gun on the port side of the cockpit with Aldis sight on the coaming in front of the port seat.'

A camera gun was actually installed on the second production aircraft.

61

Perth The ultimate development of the Iris family of flying-boats, the Perth appeared in 1933. Respecting armament, the most notable innovation was provision for a 37-mm Coventry Ordnance Works gun on a manually operated mounting in the bow. This installation was the subject of much publicity, for there was little awareness at the time of much earlier installations of the same weapon, the wider use of which Vickers were promoting. Thus the Perth has always been associated with its 'big gun'. The mounting for this gun was of the Vickers-Westland type, as originally developed by Westland for the Westbury. A Scarff ring-mounting for a Lewis gun could be fitted in the bow position as an alternative installation, this being slidable fore-and-aft on rails. The makers described crew and armament installations as follows:

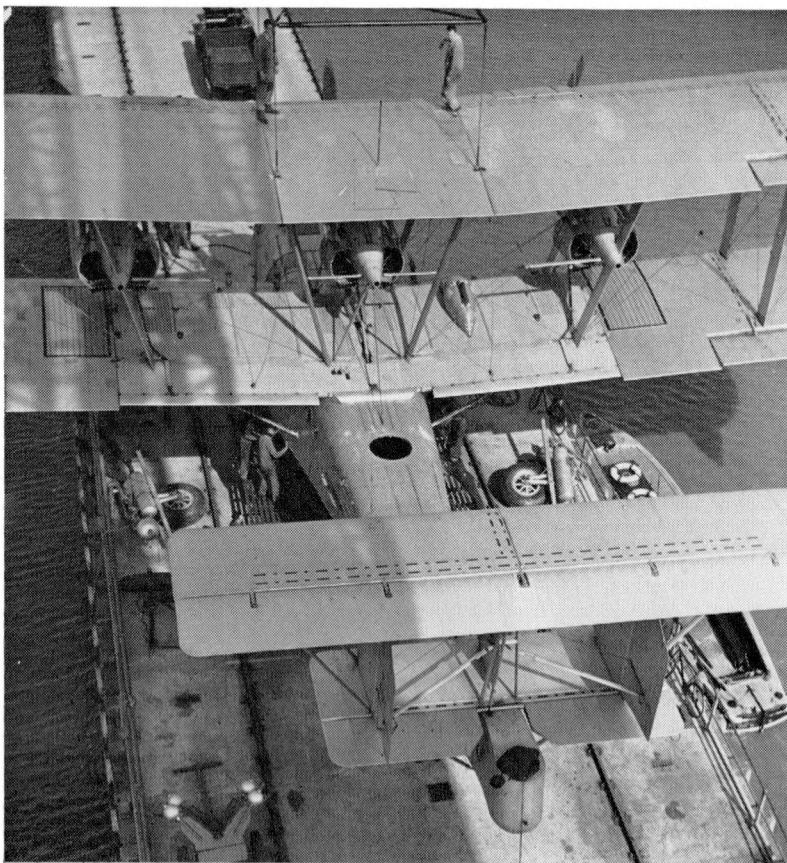

The crane at the Marine Aircraft Experimental Establishment, Felixstowe, afforded a vantage point for viewing the rear armament provisions on the Blackburn Perth. The Scarff ring-mountings and Lewis guns are not fitted, but fields of fire may be gauged. (*Flight International.*)

This view of a Blackburn Iris leaves no doubt that the 37-mm Coventry Ordnance Works gun was actually installed in the bow emplacement.

'Crew of five, consisting of a pilot, a navigator, who also acts as gunner or second pilot, a wireless operator, an engineer/gunner, and an additional gunner. Stations are arranged as follows: bow cockpit with 37-mm automatic gun or machine-gun; cockpit with dual controls; navigator's station; officers' quarters; men's sleeping quarters; enclosed wireless cabin and galley; rear gun cockpit; lavatory; and tail-defence cockpit.'

Bombs—four 500-lb or eight 250-lb—could be carried beneath the inner wings, the fusing and release controls being in the bow cockpit. Light Series carriers for marine markers or 20-lb bombs were fitted close in to the hull. There was a bomb-loading winch in the men's quarters.

Baffin The Baffin was a Pegasus-engined development of the Ripon for the Fleet Air Arm and was taken into service during 1934. Armament was generally similar to that of the Ripon, and Universal bomb-carriers were standard. Four were fitted, No.2 carriers (50/550-lb) inboard and No.1 carriers (50/250-lb) outboard. There were side windows to light the prone bombing station. The torpedo was invariably carried nose-down. A collector box for the pilot's gun was sometimes fitted.

F.7/30 This fascinating, if wholly unsuccessful, fighter, built to the specification which spawned the other four-gun machines of its period, was completed in 1934. Gun troughs immediately above the exhaust manifolds of the Goshawk engine proclaim in photographs the location of two of the guns, but the other pair are less readily detectable. The greatly thickened upper wing roots give the clue, for the guns were housed within them and the ports can be seen in a frontal view. Ring-and-bead sights were mounted on prominent posts above the steeply sloping nose, the ring being immediately ahead of the windscreen.

The elusive positions of the four Vickers guns on the Blackburn F.7/30 are here apparent—two in the upper wing roots and two firing through troughs above the exhaust manifolds. The two lower apertures are supercharger air intakes.

There were attachments for a four 20-lb bomb-carrier under the starboard wing.

Shark The prototype of the Shark torpedo-spotter-reconnaissance two/three-seater carrier-borne biplane flew in 1933. Essentially it was related to the M.1/30A, but, apart from very numerous differences in structure, power plant and equipment, it incorporated a new type of Blackburn torpedo-carrier with which production Sharks (Mks. I, II and III) went into service with the Fleet Air Arm. This carrier consisted of a central beam of narrow box section and two double-V crutches of streamline tube. Together with the suspension gear (comprising release cables, winches and release slips) these were the only external parts. The main central beam was tapered in side elevation, with maximum depth forward, and its upper side was shaped to conform to the underside of the fuselage. The nose of the beam was an Alclad fairing, and the tail was a channel bracket, to which were attached the air-release spring and cable. Attachment was at two points. Housed in the nose fairing was a spring-loaded earthing contactor, and behind the contactor was a leather-faced aluminium casting forming the central support of the front crutch and adjustable to two positions for different types of torpedoes. Further aft of the suspension gear in the plane was a spring-loaded stop-plate, with which the stop on the torpedo engaged. At the rear crutch position was a second leather-faced casting,

The Universal type of bomb-carrier, adopted by the RAF in succession to types dating from the First World War, was developed by the Blackburn company. Six of these carriers are seen on a Shark, each with a 250-lb bomb. In the port outer position is a Light Series carrier.

which was not adjustable. The housing for the torpedo's depth-adjusting gear was formed by the rear portion of the beam. This gear consisted of a main operating spindle, just behind the rear crutch, and two vertical domed spindles in brass bearings further aft. The spindles were interconnected by sprockets and chains and rotated simultaneously. Each had a spring-loaded and universally jointed key, which connected with the appropriate plug on the particular pattern of torpedo, the key not in use being hinged up at its universal joint clear of the projectile. The crutches each consisted of two V-shaped members, the inner extremities of which were bolted to brackets on the central beam, with the outer ends attached by thumbscrews into sockets on the fuselage. At the apex of each V was an adjustable foot, which screwed down on to the torpedo. The actual suspension gear was attached by two thumbscrews to two brackets on the fuselage—in the case of the Shark to the rear undercarriage joints—and consisted of a release slip and a small winch on each side and two release cables. The electrical heating system comprised a generator, voltage regulator, wiring and plugs, and the depth-adjusting gear was worked by the pilot by means of a small dashboard handle which turned an indicator showing a depth setting and operated the depth-adjusting gear in the torpedo beam through a flexible drive. Mechanical or electrical release controls could be fitted. In the Shark II the torpedo was set at a less nose-down angle.

Like the Fairey Swordfish, the Shark carried a formidable bomb load, and a fully bombed-up Shark was a sight to be remembered. The six Universal carriers for the heavy bombs were of necessity well outboard beneath the wings in order that the bombs might clear the floats of the seaplane version. The most impressive load of all was six 250-lb plus four 20-lb, the Light Series carrier for the small bombs covering part of the wing-tip roundel. When 500-lb bombs were loaded, these were on the inner carriers; four could be lifted. Asymmetric loading was possible, and one recalls a lively performance by a Portuguese Shark with a 500- and a 250-pounder under the starboard wing and three 250-pounders to port. The bombs could be fused and released from either cockpit and there was the usual prone aiming position, with course-setting sight over the bombing hatch. A notable advantage was that the wings could be folded with bombs in place.

The pilot's fixed Vickers gun fired through a deep trough in the port-upper position; the gunner had a Lewis (or Vickers G.O.) gun on a Fairey 'High-Speed' mounting, this being very far aft, when stowed, owing to the length of the rear cockpit. The Sharks supplied to Portugal had a Vickers-Berthier gun on the same type of mounting. For this gun there were ten drums of ammunition. Ahead of the rear cockpit was an embryonic protective hood. Further protection was afforded on the Shark III by a cockpit canopy.

The following is a makers' description of crew and armament installations:

'Pilot's cockpit situated behind and below cutout of top centre-plane. Equipment includes torpedo controls, bomb controls, fixed machine-gun, arrester-gear control, cockpit heating, wheel-brake control, engine-starting gear. Pilot's parachute seat is adjustable. Rear cockpit arranged for 1 or 2 members of crew according to duties of aircraft. Crew protected by special hinged metal hoods. Forward portion of cockpit arranged for navigation, bombing and photography; rear portion for machine-gunnery and wireless communication.'

There were some interesting variations in the arrangement of sights. On the prototype and early production aircraft the sighting bars for the torpedo were supported by the rear centre-section struts and a vertical strut between the top centre-section and the fuselage. The two small rings flanking the windscreen, a characteristic of Blackburn torpedo aircraft dating back to the Swift, were present on the prototype but are not identified on production aircraft. A ring-sight was fitted ahead of the windscreen and a pillar-mounted bead in line with the front centre-section struts. On the prototype the bead was further forward. Later Sharks had sighting bars running between each pair of centre-section struts in side elevation and between the front pair as seen from the front. Brackets for an Aldis sight were fixed to the fuselage ahead of the windscreen, slightly offset to port.

The wings of the Shark could be folded with bombs in place. Also shown here is the sighting bar for the torpedo.

67

(*Left*) Features seen in this Shark close-up are the torpedo sighting bar, running between the centre-section struts, and the trough for the Vickers gun (port side). (*Right*) The Blackburn company itself developed the new type of torpedo-carrier used on the Shark, seen here in close-up and described in the text.

The present writer once took part in a practice torpedo-attack in a Shark of the Torpedo Training Unit at Gosport (one of two elements of the Coast Defence Development Flight, the other being the Training Squadron), and set down these impressions:

'The take-off, complete with the massive "fish", is something to marvel at; there is no suggestion of staggering into the air as with some of the earlier types. We are six, the leading ones in each flight of three bearing instructors who will note the shortcomings of their charges. Their machines do not carry a torpedo.

'Some miles out to sea is the cruiser *Dunedin*. Her job in life is to steam back and forth offering herself as a target. She also helps to pick up the torpedoes, which are set to run beneath her. Even so, their wake is ample to permit accuracy to be assessed.

'The obliging *Dunedin* sighted, we whistle down one by one towards the inhospitable white-flecked water. As we level off, the waves stream past in alarming proximity. Precise judgement of height over water requires a good deal of experience. *Dunedin* crosses the torpedo sights about a mile ahead, and as her hull grows larger we lift into a climbing turn. Facing aft, we see our "fish" burrowing under the waves, and despite the depth at which it is running can follow its track right up to the ship.

'One by one the big biplanes sweep just above the white horses and drop their torpedoes with varying success. A special camera on each records accuracy, We circle the *Dunedin* and regain formation, except for two of our number, who stay behind to point out the torpedoes to the salvage crews.'

B-7 Produced in 1935, this private-venture general-purpose aircraft was very closely related to, though by no means identical with, the Shark. The Vickers gun installation remained unaltered, but the rear cockpit was revised and the gun mounting moved forward. There were strong points for four Universal carriers under each wing.

Skua The Skua was a two-seat carrier-based fighter/dive-bomber, first flown in 1937. It was the first specialised dive-bomber to enter British service and has been accorded (the present writer feels) less than its deserved acclaim. In his Fifth Sir George Cayley Memorial Lecture during 1958 the Skua's designer, G. E. Petty, made this modest declaration:

'It had very effective dive-brakes. It was in full production at the beginning of the war and, in fact, had the distinction of shooting down the first enemy aircraft (Do 18) during an operation from the *Ark Royal*. This was followed by the sinking of the German cruiser *Königsberg* by two squadrons of Skuas which scored three direct hits . . . Our only regret was that we were not allowed to go ahead with a simplified version with fixed undercarriage as a first-class dive bomber for the Air Force as an answer to the German "Stukas."'

69

It may be added, concerning the *Königsberg* operation, that Mr Churchill was able to announce in the Commons afterwards that 'only a streak of oil a mile long' was to be seen; 'as if', he concluded, 'the desired result had been achieved'.

The Skua's basic armament is described in an early Blackburn specification thus:

'As a two-seat fighter, the Skua has provision for four fixed machine guns mounted in the leading edge of the main planes, firing forward outside the airscrew arc, and one movable machine gun on a special mounting in the rear cockpit. The fixed guns are arranged for pneumatic control from the pilot's cockpit. For practice or training purposes a camera gun may be mounted on the starboard side of the centre plane and the same pneumatic control as for the machine guns may be used. For dive-bombing, provision is made for carrying one large bomb in a recess under the fuselage. Two Light Series carriers, each capable of carrying four small bombs, practice bombs or flares, may be mounted, one under each main plane. Provision is made for electrical fusing and release.'

There is another relevant extract:

'The observer-gunner is situated well aft of the wings and is provided with a fixed seat mounted on the raised end of the bomb compartment for wireless operation. A hinged hood encloses the rear end of the cockpit and a well in the fuselage decking houses the machine gun when not in use. The cabin enclosure has sliding side panels, which, when opened, operate wind deflectors preventing the slipsteam entering the cockpit. The pilot's windscreen is specially strengthened . . .'

Military load of the dive-bomber (Case A) was quoted as 1,836 lb; of the two-seat fighter (Case B) as 1,321 lb; and of the drogue target aircraft (Case C) as 1,381 lb.

Specifically, the fixed guns were of Browning Mk.II pattern; the free gun a Lewis Mk.IIIE or a Vickers G.O.; and the 'one large bomb' a 500-lb S.A.P., provided with ejector arms to swing it clear of the airscrew arc in a diving attack. The Browning guns were almost entirely buried within the wings, with only the flash eliminators visible, and were very widely spaced, one on each side of a landing light. The pilot had a reflector sight. The 'special' gun mounting at the rear was of the Fairey pillar type, as fitted to the Fairey Battle and Westland Lysander.

Mr Petty's allusion to the effectiveness of the Skua's dive-brakes was well merited, for apart from facilitating take-off and landing they limited the speed in the bombing dive to some 220 knots. They may thus be regarded as an item of armament equipment. Each was operated by an hydraulic jack mounted between the inner flap runners in the mainplanes. A flow-control valve was introduced into the system to form an hydraulic lock for any position of the flaps, which could therefore be set at any angle and the main system relieved of the high pressure set up by the flaps in the down position at high speeds. The effectiveness of these flaps was experienced by the present writer early in 1939 on a test flight with Blackburn test pilot 'Bill' Bailey. A report in *Flight* related:

'Aerobatics were ruled out as we had no harness or "dog chain", though there was a useful bar across the fuselage. This was appreciated, particularly when Bailey throttled back and tipped the Skua straight over on to her nose, leaving us, to all intents and purposes, swimming in air and defying all the laws of gravity and rational behaviour. We did three dives at between 80 and 90 degrees. By the third I was deriving genuine pleasure from floating about in the Alclad confines like an aerobatic goldfish in a jar, watching the horizon tilting at right angles, dropping steadily towards the Yorkshire fields and grey Humber and waiting for the pull-out.'

Showing the action of the retractable fairing abaft the Boulton Paul four-gun turret on the Blackburn Roc.

Roc   The first Roc was flown in 1938. The type was a 'turret fighter', intended as a counterpart of the RAF Defiant, but even the respectable, if inadequate, performance of the Boulton Paul machine was lacking in the Naval Blackburn machine by reason of peculiarly naval requirements and the relatively low-powered air-cooled engine. With its four Browning guns (600 rounds per gun) the Boulton Paul Type A Mk.II turret was mounted some distance aft of the pilot, and largely aft of the wing trailing edge. The automatically retractable fairing behind the turret left an unbecoming hump above the sharply tapered fuselage. Four light bombs

71

could be carried beneath each wing and some Rocs were adapted to take two Universal carriers in addition, these being fitted inboard of the light carriers. Bombs of 100, 112, or 120 lb could be loaded, in addition to bombs of 20 or 40 lb.

Botha   The prototype of the Botha GR Mk.I was first flown in 1939. In addition to its general reconnaissance duties the type was required to operate as a torpedo-bomber. The pilot was seated to port and the navigator/bomb-aimer had a prone position in the nose to starboard. To the rear were a radio operator and a gunner. All crew stations were interconnected by a gangway along the starboard side. The pilot had a fixed Browning gun, there were twin Browning guns in the dorsal F.N.7 turret, and there was internal stowage for the 18-in torpedo (Mk.XII or Mk.XIV) or bomb load (four 250-lb or two 500-lb or one 500-lb + two 250-lb or one 2,000-lb). The hydraulically operated bomb doors were removed when the torpedo or the 2,000-lb bomb was carried. One aircraft was used for mine-laying experiments. Strong-points were provided for additional bomb-carriers under the wings outboard of the nacelles.

Looking back on the Botha its designer once declared:

'The original specification was intended for comparatively short-range operation. The collapse of France made this short range inadequate and its role was changed to an operational trainer for bomber crews. As a fully equipped operational aircraft it was very suitable for this work . . .'

Bothas did, in fact, serve with Air Navigation and Air Gunnery Schools until 1944.

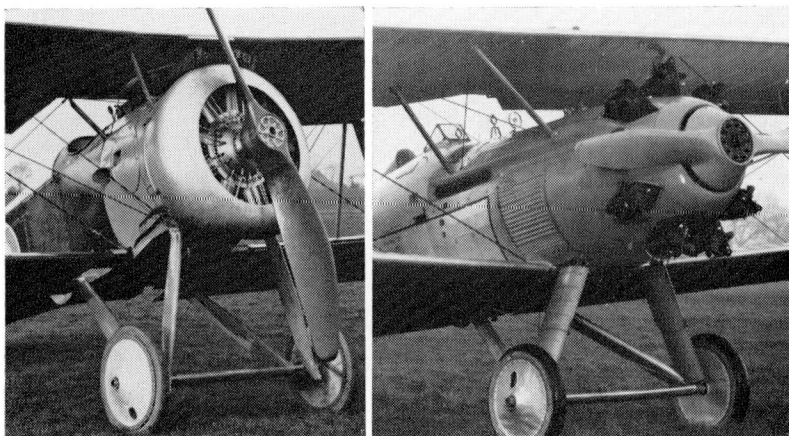

Fashions in fighter armament: *left*, Boulton & Paul Bobolink of 1918, with twin Vickers guns over cowling; *right*, Partridge of ten years later, with twin Vickers guns in bulged fuselage. The ring sight and brackets for Aldis sight are seen.

Boulton & Paul (later Boulton Paul)

Bobolink This 1918 rival (unsuccessful) of the Sopwith Snipe had its two Vickers guns mounted externally forward of the cockpit. Ejection chutes were in the fuselage flanks. Design provision was made for a pivot-mounted Lewis gun on the starboard centre-section, giving a restricted field of fire.

Bourges The Bourges twin-engined bomber of 1918/19 was not only the progenitor of a remarkable family of generally similar 'fighting bombers', which culminated in the Overstrand, but itself displayed unusual armament features. Nose and dorsal gun positions, internal bomb-stowage, and bomb-aimer's station in the nose were features retained throughout development, but one departure, made in the interests of armament, was both structural and aerodynamic. This involved the 'gulling' of the inner sections of the top wing into the fuselage to extend the fields of fire, or, as Boulton & Paul preferred to put it, to give the pilot and gunner an unrestricted view fore and aft.

In the original Bourges the two gun mountings were of the well-known Scarff ring type, with a trunnion device for twin Lewis guns. Fuselage width was almost exactly that of the gun-ring diameters; the nose ring was canted somewhat forward from the line of flight and the rear one was recessed below the top-line of the fuselage. There was transparent panelling in the rearward-sloping nose, for the bomb-aimer, and a sliding panel in

Top, Boulton & Paul Bourges with normal Scarff ring-mounting for twin Lewis guns; *lower*, gull-wing Bourges with unusual form of Scarff ring-mounting. In both views the shutter-like bomb doors are just visible between the split axles of the undercarriage.

Lion-engined Bourges, showing unusual Scarff ring-mountings for twin guns in nose and dorsal positions.

the floor behind it. Bombs were stowed internally between the lower main-plane spars.

In the summer of 1918 Boulton & Paul designed a scheme for shutter-like bomb doors, associated with laths and tensioned cords, and over a year later mentioned a stowage scheme involving three bomb-supporting beams mounted between vertical guides and supported by 'quick-pitch screws geared to a common horizontal shaft which, when free to rotate, allows the bombs to drop'. By this means each bomb in succession came to the discharge position, then left the screws and moved down laterally between oblique guides and out of the way of the next beam and its bomb.

The bomb load was of the 800/900-lb order and there appear to have been three bomb cells with transverse doors or shutters.

A special bomb-loading system was also designed for the Bourges, this taking the form of a readily attachable or detachable hoisting gear. Shafts were associated with winding drums, each shaft being carried in bearings bracketed to the upper longerons. The shafts were rotated by pawl-and-ratchet or worm gear.

The 'gulling' of the Bourges' wings has been mentioned as a factor affecting fighting efficiency, but there was another, and a greater, factor, and that was the quite extraordinary manoeuvrability of the Bourges. This was to be reproduced in later bombers of the family.

It remains to mention one other development in the story of the Bourges, appearing not only in the gull-winged variant but in the Lion-engined version, officially classified as a long-distance reconnaissance three-seater, and unofficially claimed in its day to be the fastest twin-engined aircraft in the world. On the aeroplanes mentioned, the two gun mountings were sited as previously but were of a different type. The identity and true nature

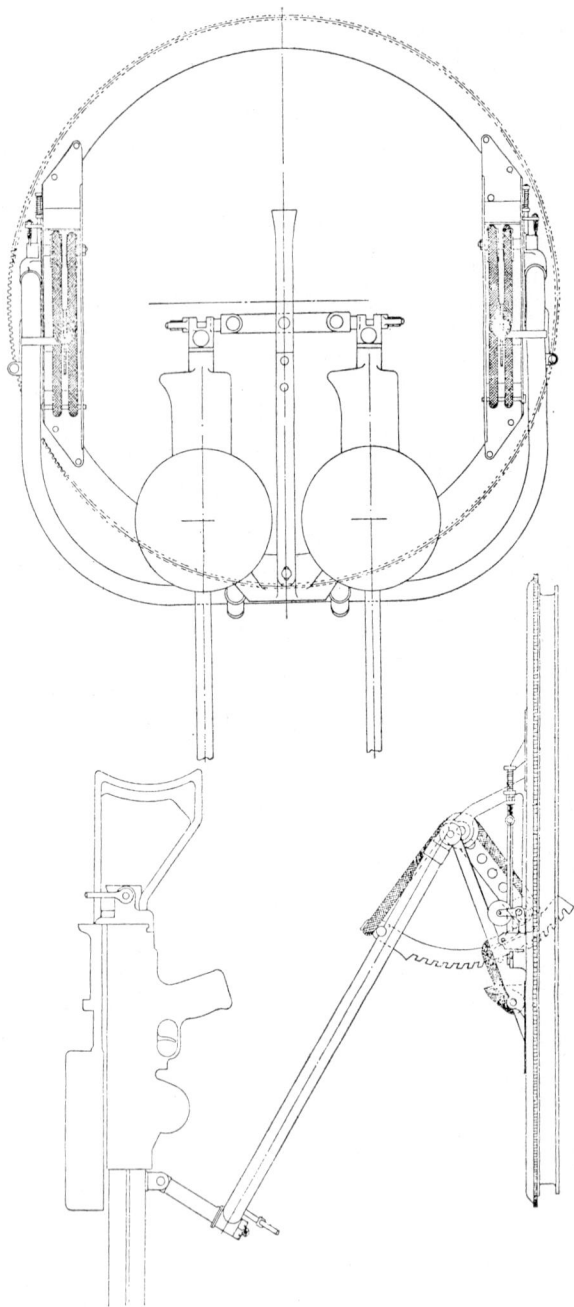

Official drawings, now first reproduced, of the unusual form of Scarff ring-mounting as installed on the gull-wing and Lion-engined Bourges. Other forms of the mounting will be illustrated and described in *British Aircraft Weapons*.

of these mountings has eluded the present writer for many years, but he is now able to attribute them to Major Scarff and to show drawings. Lightness appears to have been a primary aim in this design, which was intended for two Lewis guns but was adaptable for one. As the drawings show, the two guns were sighted with the aid of a shoulder stock and it was stated:

'The triangular frame is padded on the inner surface to prevent the operator bruising his body when pressing it against the frame to assist when turning the ring.'

Bodmin This singular aeroplane was built in 1923 and when it appeared on the Open List in December 1925 was described as '3-seat medium-range postal'. Its primary function was that of a test bed (two fuselage-mounted Lions driving four airscrews through gearing), but the structure was also very advanced. The type is included here not merely by virtue of its Service markings but because military requirements seem to have been in mind. There was a dorsal station suitable for a gun-ring, and the very long nose, with auxiliary wheels beneath it, might have lent itself as an emplacement for a heavy gun.

Bolton Produced in 1923, the Bolton had two Lion engines, and, like the Bourges with similar engines, was classed not as a bomber but as a three-seat long-reconnaissance aircraft. Standard Scarff ring-mountings for single Lewis guns were fitted in the nose and dorsal stations.
Silencers have been mentioned in connection with the Blackburn torpedo aircraft, and it is appropriate to mention here that this reconnaissance aeroplane of 1923 had special, cooled, silencers.

Bugle A three-seat medium-range bomber (official classification), the Bugle appeared in 1924. Although there appears to have been provision for internal bomb-stowage at least one of the Jupiter-engined Bugles had four bomb rails, two under the lower longerons and two a little outboard under the wings. The bombs were sighted from a prone position in the nose. Scarff ring-mountings, each for one Lewis gun, were fitted in the nose and dorsal positions, the form of the fuselage behind the latter being specially studied to allow the widest field of fire (triangular upper section). The forward ring was canted downwards towards the nose. A contemporary account declared:

'A gunner's and bomber's cockpit is in the extreme nose. This has a folding seat and gives room to lie down and observe through an opening in the bottom of the body. What amounts to a micrometer steering control, consisting of a handwheel coupled to a friction clutch and a push and pull rod, allows the bomber to control and correct the machine's course'.

Another description declared that the wheel gave 'as it were a vernier adjustment of the rudder'. As for stability, it was claimed:

The upper view of a Jupiter-engined Bugle shows to advantage the form of fuselage decking behind the dorsal gun position, designed to afford the maximum field of fire. The lower view of the Lion-engined Bugle shows how, when the petrol tanks were moved from the wings to the fuselage, the bombs were carried in a streamline structure under the fuselage.

'The machines in use in the RAF are regularly flying long distances hands-and-feet-off.'

In the Lion-engined development of the Bugle, bombs were carried under the fuselage and were faired by a light streamline structure. This installation led to the adoption of similar stowage in the Sidestrand and Overstrand, and was associated with the removal of the petrol tanks from beneath the upper wing to the inside of the fuselage.

Sidestrand Aerodynamic, structural and power plant changes differentiated between the three marks of Sidestrand, the prototype of which was flown in 1927, distilling, as it were, experience with the Bourges, Bugle and other preceding types. The Sidestrand can be regarded as a complementary type to the Fairey Fox I, representing as it did a real challenge to contemporary fighters, manifest not only in performance and manoeuvrability but in armament also. There is surviving an official account of the latter, and this remarks:

'Two Scarff ring gun mountings for Lewis guns are provided . . . in addition a special Lewis gun mounting is fitted to enable a prone gunner to fire beneath the tail of the aircraft. The rear gun ring and prone gun mounting are alternative positions; the equipment provides for two guns only, the positions which they will occupy will, of course, depend upon the position of the aeroplane in the formation in which it is flying and the objectives of that formation. Each of the three gun positions is provided with pegs for six 97-round magazine drums. Only twelve drums are normally carried, however, those for the rear gun being placed in the appropriate positions.

'The downward gun mounting consists of a semi-circular tube to whose ends are welded two straight tubes joined by a cross tube. The cross tube is mounted in bearings carried by brackets bolted to the fairing former at the mouth of the prone position fairing. The Lewis gun is pinned at the butt end to a swivel located centrally on the cross tube and also to a travelling hand grip having two roller guides engaging with the semi-circular tube. The gun can thus be moved both radially and vertically.

'A length of shock absorber cord anchored at one end of the prone position fairing is connected by a cable running over a pulley to the end of the port straight tube thus enabling the mounting to be raised or depressed without effort on the part of the prone gunner. When not in use the gun mounting is swung upward so that the gun rests in a padded channel in the rear fairing.

'The aeroplane is normally fitted with four bomb carriers, one under each centre plane, and two in the bomb cell between the rear bulkhead of the bottom monocoque and the first bay of the rear fuselage. The wing carriers are of the standard tubular pattern to take one 250 or one 230 lb bomb. The carriers are bolted to fittings on a special rib and are braced by diagonal struts to the inner end rib of the plane. The front carrier of the two in the bomb cell is of the manufacturer's own design. This carrier is slung from the sleeve fittings of the bottom cross struts of the fuselage centre portion and is bolted to brackets on the monocoque bulkhead. It is designed to carry any one of the following alternative loads: One 550 or 520 lb bomb. Two 230 or 250 lb bombs. Four 112 lb bombs. One light series bomb carrier for practice bombs. The practice bomb carrier is bolted to lugs provided on the universal rack itself. The fourth bomb carrier is also of the light series type carrying four 20 lb sighter bombs and is fitted immediately behind the universal carrier and is suspended from bolts through the bottom fairing formers in bay 1 of the rear fuselage. Practice bombs can be substituted for the 20 lb bombs on this carrier if required.'

It must be noted at this point that the special 'universal' carrier, ascribed to Boulton & Paul, is not to be confused with the Universal type developed by Blackburn and identified throughout this work by the capital U. This type of carrier was later standardised by the RAF. The official account of the Sidestrand continues:

'The bomb release control is duplicated; either pilot or bomb aimer can release the bombs. Centralised control gears of Vickers pattern and light series release controls are fitted on the cockpit flooring on the starboard side of the pilot's seat and in the front gunner's cockpit. The cables from the pilot's release controls are led through the floor and are spliced to those from the bomb aimer's controls.

'Two fusing levers are fitted in a bracket on the pilot's flooring; the levers also project below the floor and are fitted with an extension so that they can be operated by the bomb aimer. One lever fuses the bombs on the wing carriers, the other those on the universal carrier.

'A Mark IIH (high speed) course setting bomb sight is carried on a special mounting on the port side of the bomb sight aperture. When not in use the sight is swung back and the window closed.'

It must be added that the nose bombsighting station with hinged window and seat was not introduced until the Sidestrand III came into service and that the ventral gun mounting on the prototype differed noticeably at one stage from that standardised, having a prominent quadrant, forming about three-quarters of a circle, at each side. It must also be noted that, although the principal bombs in the fuselage were in a bottom fairing, they were not enclosed; this point was apparent when the first Sidestrand III was shown at Olympia in 1929 with four 112-lb (fuselage) and two 230-lb (wings).

The following points were made concerning the design of the airframe in relation to armament and special equipment:

'The front gun is carried on a Scarff ring, and owing to the narrowness of the body here this gun can be used on targets nearly vertically below.

For bombing, the occupant of this cockpit may lie down, and he has then a view from nearly dead ahead to well over vertically downwards through a window provided for this purpose. He is provided with an ingenious hand-operated fine-adjustment on the rudder control whereby he can himself correct the course steered by the pilot without in any way interfering with the pilot's freedom of control. Owing to the drop of the fuselage top forward the pilot can see ahead at an angle well below the horizontal—a point of great importance for the steering of the accurate course necessary in bombing operations.'

In the Sidestrand III the prone bomb-aimer's position was abandoned, as stated, in favour of a seat and nose window, and telephone communication between the crew was introduced. It was remarked:

'The new Irvin observer's parachute pack, which is not worn until an actual emergency occurs, is stowed in a compartment in the right side of the cockpit.'

Bittern   The Bittern was a twin-engined single-seater night fighter of 1928 and had an armament of quite exceptional interest. The first machine, it is true, hardly qualified for this distinction, having two Vickers guns fixed in the fuselage sides and firing forward in conjunction with ring-and-bead sights mounted forward of the windscreen. On the second example, however, two Lewis guns were carried in the same positions, but were movable in elevation, permitting the attack of bombers from below, though capable also of frontal fire. The guns were remotely controlled by the pilot and were interconnected with a special moving sight. This was of ring type, and was fixed to the end of an arm which, in turn, was attached and braced to an elevating hoop, somewhat resembling that of a Scarff ring-mounting, pivoted at the cockpit sides. The guns were largely contained in bulbous fairings, designed to move with them.

The Bittern, it may be noted, appeared almost simultaneously with the Westland and Vickers single-seaters with upward-firing (though fixed) C.O.W. guns. The Bittern is illustrated on page 82.

Partridge   A loser in competition with the Bristol Bulldog, the Partridge (completed 1928) had its two Vickers guns set in the bulged section of the fuselage which contained the cockpit. The top longerons formed the sole support of the guns. Although it has been stated that the lateral bulges resulted from an official demand that the guns be lowered, the makers themselves declared:

'The body is somewhat unusual in form in that there are two bulges, one on each side of the cockpit, which serve to house the two machine guns. It has been found that the superposition of these bulges on a basic form of small cross-sectional area gives a less total resistance than would a body devoid of bulges but of sufficiently increased cross-section to give equal accessibility to the guns'.

81

The Boulton Paul Bittern in the upper view has provision for two fixed Vickers guns in the fuselage sides and ring-and-bead sight forward of the windscreen. The lower view shows the version with pivoted Lewis guns and special sight.

The guns fired through sheet steel troughs between the second pair of cylinders on each side and had the usual ring-and-bead (port) and Aldis (starboard) sights. Four 20-lb bombs could be carried under the port bottom wing.

P.32 This three-engined night-bomber of 1931 was laid out like the D.H.72, the third engine being mounted on the top wing. In comment the makers declared:

'The engine arrangement, though somewhat unusual, has great practical advantages over the usual arrangement of three engines. The chief of these are that the nose of the fuselage is left clear for the use of the bomb-aimer and front gunner, giving the best conditions for bombing and gunnery, and that the fuselage is free from directly transmitted vibration.'

Nose and midships (dorsal) gun installations resembled those on the Sidestrand, but there was a third position in the extreme tail of the fuselage. This was of curious form, having a sagging lower line and a protective screen ahead of the Scarff ring-mounting. There were two Light Series carriers beneath the forward fuselage and the main stowage aft of these was semi-internal, as on the Sidestrand and Overstrand. The load might have been four or more 520/550-lb bombs or a roughly equivalent weight of 230/250-lb or 112-lb bombs. The sighting station in the nose resembled that of the modified Sidestrand.

Overstrand Any dilettante in the literature of British military aircraft will immediately and correctly identify the Overstrand (1933) as a Sidestrand development having a power-driven gun turret in the nose. It was, in fact, considerably more than this, being re-engined, strengthened, having more comfortable accommodation and better protection for all crew members, not to mention a revised bomb installation. But first the famous turret.

The Boulton Paul nose turret, as installed in the Overstrand, was a vertical cylinder with domed ends and almost entirely transparent. At the base was a bearing carried from a bracket built into the front fuselage frame and supported additionally by a roller bearing that partly surrounded the turret's upper extremity. The single Lewis gun was on a pivoted arm, and the barrel projected through a vertical slot extending the whole depth of the turret. An automatic fastening arrangement ensured that little draught entered, and in any case the turret was warmed by hot air.

The gunner's seat was supported by an hydraulic ram, connected to a pair of smaller rams coupled to the elevating gun-arm. The two sets of rams and the leverage for the second set were placed about the gun-arm, and the seat and gun-arm moved in opposite directions. Adjustment of the leverage of the rams coupled to the gun-arm permitted accurate control of the balance between gunner and gun, allowing for variations in the gunner's weight.

Power for rotation was provided by a reversible pneumatic motor, geared to the turret, thereby training the gun in response to pressure exerted by the gunner on the operating handle as he followed his target through the sights. Rapid movement of the gun vertically and horizontally thus automatically followed the small muscular efforts applied by the gunner in the normal processes of training his gun. Rotational speed was about 12 rpm. The bombsighting panel was offset to port and the sight rotated with the turret, the turret being locked during aiming. One component of the panel served as a windscreen.

There were other refinements in the Overstrand affecting armament. Thus, although the ventral gun mounting remained unchanged, the upper position was provided with a large protective screen. (It is of interest to note that the projected Superstrand development, which had a retractable undercarriage, had no mechanical turret in the nose, but a manual turret,

D   83

comprising a Scarff ring-mounting and cupola, in this and the dorsal positions).

Finally, the Overstrand carried a heavier bomb load than the Sidestrand, on carriers of the Universal pattern. Two 500-lb bombs could be stowed in the fuselage with two of 250 lb on external carriers. Two Light Series carriers could be fitted, one forward of and one behind the fuselage bombs.

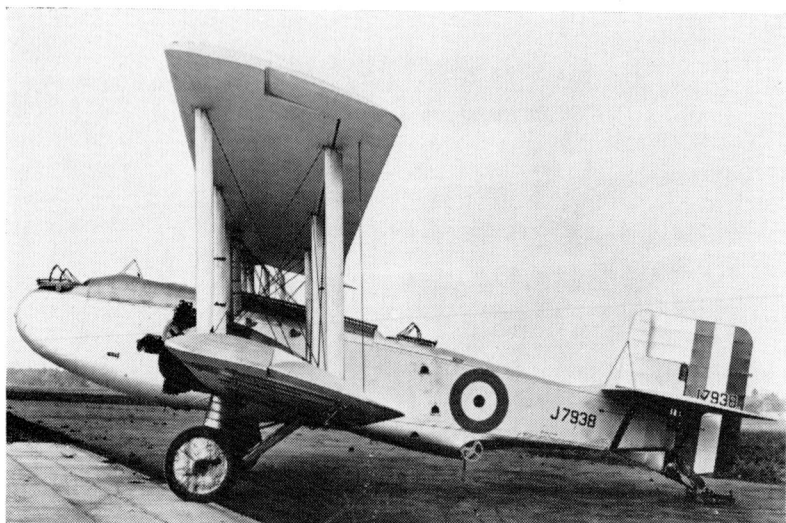

Progress in bomber defence is illustrated by these comparative views of the Boulton & Paul Sidestrand prototype (*top*) and Boulton Paul Overstrand. The ventral gun mounting of the Sidestrand was later changed to one of the type seen on the Overstrand; but note on the Overstrand the power-driven turret and screened dorsal position.

Both the Sidestrand and the Overstrand had movable nose sections, though in different senses. The upper picture shows a Sidestrand with hinged nose portion, complete with gunnery and bombing equipment, swung aside (also Jupiter engine), while the lower one shows the Overstrand turret in detail. External bombs on the Sidestrand are of 230 lb, on old-type tubular carriers. On the Overstrand they are 250-pounders of later pattern, on Universal carriers. (Lower picture, *Flight International*.)

Defiant Such was the promise extended by the power-operated gun turrets of the mid-1930s—British and French alike—that the decision was taken to supplement the fixed-gun firepower of Fighter Command with a new class of military aeroplane called 'turret fighter'. While the French had fitted turrets on an awesome scale to their *multiplace de combat* types, the British concept epitomised in the new class of day and night fighter was a wholly new departure, involving as it did the concentration of the entire armament in a power-driven four-gun turret. Heavy twin-engined aircraft to this formula were envisaged at the early stages, but the examples constructed were single-engined. These were the Defiant, Hawker Hotspur and Blackburn Roc. The Hotspur was abandoned in favour of the Defiant and the Fleet Air Arm Roc never saw action. Only the Defiant was to test the new-found formula in war.

First flown in 1937 without its turret, the Defiant was a notably clean-cut aeroplane, and, even with the turret mounted, proclaimed a remarkable compromise between aerodynamics and armament. Retractable tapered

Boulton Paul Defiant with turret at rest (*top*) and in action, with rear fairing lowered. The front fairing is not operative in this instance because the pilot's cockpit canopy is slid rearward.

fairings were installed fore and aft of the Boulton Paul Type A turret. This domed cylindrical turret was supplied with 600 rounds for each of the four Browning guns. The number of guns and other details were for some time secret, and it was not until January 1940 that one was able to caption a picture in *Flight*:

'It is only now that photographs of RAF machines with four-gun turrets have appeared in German newspapers that it is permissible to reveal some of the facts about this device. The photograph seen here was actually taken some months ago. The guns are arranged in pairs, one pair on each side of the gunner; they are all worked together with the turret and are aimed by one sight.'

There was, in fact, a single control handle, having a safety catch and firing button on top. Movement of this handle fore and aft elevated and depressed the guns while clockwise movement to the right or left controlled the rotation of the turret and the guns in a clockwise or anti-clockwise direction. The turret hydraulic system was an independent one and was not connected with any similar system outside. Weight of the turret, less guns, sights and accessories, was 361 lb. Smooth operation owed much to the Hele-Shaw-Beacham hydraulic variable-gear principle.

As already intimated, the retractable fairings were a key feature of the design, and these were thus described in a contemporary account:

'The upper fairing of the fuselage surmounting the flat decking of the fuselage frame proper is in the main a light spruce and three-ply structure. The frame of the pilot's windscreen is the main exception, being a light alloy casting. This fairing is in two main portions, corresponding to the two sections of the fuselage. The front section of this fairing carries on the cross section of the pilot's windscreen back to the gun turret cupola, but the rear portion of this windscreen tailpiece comprises a section which can collapse downwards to permit of the passage past it of the guns in the turret.

'The rear upper fairing tapers away from a section similar to that of the front fairing just aft of the turret to a slightly domed section at the tailplane. The central portion of this fairing, which is just aft of the turret, corresponds in section to the windscreen, is hinged on a transverse axis some halfway back along the rear fuselage and, like the corresponding part of the fairing ahead of the turret, may be collapsed to permit of the turret guns passing by.

'These two collapsible fairings are operated by pneumatic jacks, the control valves for which are operated automatically by cams on the turret in such a manner that the fairings collapse only when it is necessary to allow the guns to be traversed past them.'

Consideration was at one time given to the making of these fairings from inflatable air-tight fabric.

Interior of Defiant turret. The four Browning guns are not installed, but the control handle, with firing button on top, is seen in the lower foreground, slightly to right of centre.

The Defiant's operational history was brief and sharply contrasted. Of May 1940 Peter Wykeham has recorded:

'On the 13th No.264 Defiant Squadron escorted a strike of Battle bombers against targets in Breda. The Battles and their escort were intercepted near the target by a strong force of Me 109s and 110s. The Battles were badly mauled and five out of the six Defiants were destroyed. In this, as in so many of these engagements where the British formations were almost wiped out, it was impossible to discover how many of the enemy were shot down before the force met its end.'

A short time later, over Dunkirk:

'The day's operations included the last big success for the Defiants before the enemy fighters got to know their peculiar weaknesses. No.264 Squadron had already done some considerable execution. On the morning of the 20th it was ordered to patrol over Belgium, and fell in with "more enemy fighters and dive-bombers than could be counted". The Defiants at once attacked, but their lack of speed and the attentions of the escort prevented them from getting to grips with the Stukas. In a series of whirlwind battles, however, they shot down seventeen Messerschmitts without loss, and on another patrol in the afternoon they eluded an enemy escort and destroyed eleven Ju 88s and Stukas over Dunkirk.'

The Defiant served out its operational term as a night fighter. Circumstances, as much as misconceptions and deficiencies, had encompassed Britain's turret fighter, and in its intended role of bomber-destroyer it was never able to prove itself fully.

At least one Defiant was fitted with a carrier for bombs or flares under each wing, as later mentioned in connection with the Hotspur. In this context it may be remarked that the type was evaluated in the army co-operation role. Defiants used for gunnery training had only two guns.

Bristol

Bristol-Coanda Biplanes Of such exceptional interest and significance were the bomb and bombsight installations, developed for the Bristol-Coanda biplane exhibited in the Paris Salon of December 1913, that they will be described at length in Volume 2 as historic departures. Original Coanda drawings will be reproduced, together with a page of calculations which influenced the design of the sight. It must be recorded here that an aircraft of similar type, but having a simple bomb-carrier, was delivered to Rumania a few weeks before the show mentioned, and that even earlier yet another Bristol-Coanda biplane was photographed at Larkhill with a mechanic holding a bomb. One RNAS machine of the type was apparently a 'gun-carrier'.

S.S.A. Although this book is mainly concerned with armament, and not passive protection, the fitting of armour to military aeroplanes inevitably has some place, and in no more fitting instance than this single-seat 'scout', built to Coanda's designs in 1914. As in the later Sopwith Salamander, the whole of the forward fuselage, including the cockpit, was of sheet steel construction (in this case monocoque) and even the engine was protected. A few weeks before war came this aeroplane was sent to the Breguet works in France. It may be mentioned in this context that at the Olympia Aero and Marine Exhibition of 1914 The Integral Propeller Co Ltd showed 'an armoured propeller specially designed and built for warplanes'.

Scout The Scout, or Bullet, originated in 1914 as an eminently appealing creation apparently suitable for no other warlike purpose than that of carrying a man swiftly on the mission its name conveyed. Two years almost to the month from the first flight of the original machine, a Scout was at the fighting front with the first operational installation of British gun-synchronising gear. This was of the Vickers type, as was the gun itself. Many and exotic were the improvisations both before and after this historic installation. Pistols were carried not only upon the pilot's person, or in his tiny cockpit, but attached to the airframe also, the classic example being the battery of three Webley-Fosbery revolvers carried in a rack affixed to the Scout of Maj W. G. Moore. Capt Vesey Holt was credited with destroying two enemy two-seaters with a pistol. Shotguns, sometimes with choke bore, were somehow shipped aboard, firing buckshot and even chain shot, and rifles were attached, with or without their stocks, and variously stripped. A 0·45-in Martini-Henry rifle was, in one instance, lashed to a centre-section strut, firing outside the airscrew arc at an angle of 45 degrees to the line of fire. One identified load was a Short Lee-Enfield rifle without its stock, a Mauser self-loading pistol and five rifle grenades. Two rifles were fixed to the fuselage sides, firing at about 45 degrees to clear the airscrew, and a Lewis gun was mounted to fire straight ahead, and thus not to clear the airscrew, the resulting holes being filled and bound with sticky tape. (Airscrew scrapped, if holes more than three in number.) Lewis guns were also mounted for outward, upward or forward firing, in the last instance over the top wing, sometimes with a trigger extension attached to the spade grip. At least one Scout carried two Lewis guns, one on the port side and one over the top wing, pivoted at the rear and lying at its forward end in a rest carried on a pylon. In another arrangement there was one forward-firing Lewis gun on each side. Installations of the Vickers gun were not altogether crude. Attempts were made at partial fairing, and a system of channelling the empty cases and links overboard, as devised by G. H. Challenger and as will be illustrated in Volume 2, was applied. A type of cross-wire sight has been identified. In addition to the Vickers synchronising gear, there were installations of the Scarff-Dibovsky mechanism—these on RNAS Scouts. Rifle grenades were carried in external racks, and Capt G. I. Carmichael has recalled that the detonator pins 'usually had to be withdrawn by the pilot's teeth'. The rods which fitted in the rifle

Bristol Scout of the RNAS, with Lewis gun mounted on starboard side of fuselage.

Mauser self-loading ('automatic') pistol, shown with backsight raised. A pistol of this type was among several forms of small arms carried in Bristol Scouts.

barrel were sawn off and streamers were attached for stability. Ranken Darts in canisters of 24 were attached to the lower longerons, and RNAS Scouts are known to have carried two such canisters. Four bombs were carried under the nose of some RNAS Scouts.

T.T.A. This large two-seat fighter was first flown in the same month (May 1916) as the Avro Pike and there can be little doubt that it was initially intended to have been similarly armed. The 'one large gun' which was on one occasion mentioned as an alternative to the two Lewis guns with which the T.T.A. is generally associated may well have been of the Hotchkiss type, by then becoming established in French service. The pilot sat behind the wings, from which position he could see little and probably accomplish less, for he was responsible for a rearward-firing free Lewis gun. For this he had three spare 47-round drums. The gunner, remote in the nose, had five drums for his Lewis gun.

S.2A This 1916 development of the Scout, designed for the Admiralty, had side-by-side seating and was intended for fighting. The proposed armament was a Lewis gun, possibly on a pillar mounting behind the cockpit.

Fighter The Bristol Fighter of 1916/17 endures in history as a pre-eminent example of an aeroplane designed round its armament. Not only is this quite literally true of the fixed-gun installation, but in the concentration of the crew and the studied provision of an effectively emplaced free gun—this to afford not only rear protection, but to augment the pilot's fire-power for attack. Allied with excellence of all-round performance and manoeuvrability, these qualities had their summation in an aircraft of which Oliver Stewart has declared that it 'should be spoken of in terms of the heroes of classic mythology', being 'in the fullest sense a hero after their pattern—a fighter by name, inclination and aptitude'.

91

Bristol Fighter F2B, showing port for Vickers gun above radiator, sight attachments on upper centre-section, Scarff ring-mounting, and bomb rails for two 20-lb carriers beneath lower wings.

With this aeroplane the name of Frank Barnwell is identified, and it may have been Barnwell himself who declared: 'The fuselage is of rectangular section tapering to the rear to a horizontal knife-edge, thereby enabling the various tail members to be brought down low, out of the way of the gun. The top of the fuselage is kept flat for this purpose also.' It was further explained that, in order to bring the position of the pilot and the gunner as high as possible in relation to the top plane without increasing the depth of the fuselage, the latter was placed between the wings. In 1929 Barnwell remarked in a letter: 'I'm not sure that the happy guesses of ten years or so ago did not produce as efficient machines as many present-day ones. We've got performance by piling on BHP—but this is not per se advance.' Yet Barnwell's masterpiece, the Bristol Fighter, was no mere happy guess. It evolved, in fact, from 1916 designs for a two-seat reconnaissance aircraft along generally similar lines but armed with a synchronised Lewis gun to starboard and a second Lewis gun on a pillar-type mounting at the rear. This gun could be stowed in the fuselage decking as on much later multi-seaters. Field of fire was very carefully studied. Meanwhile Barnwell had been watching armament development and his fancy fell upon the Vickers gun for pilot use. Forthwith his assistant, L. G. Frise, was sent off on a

Vickers-gun course at Hythe, and, as soon as Barnwell had learned all that he needed to know concerning the gun, he decided that it should be on the centre line of his new aeroplane with the breech casing to the pilot's hand— even though this involved forming a tunnel through the petrol tank. And there it went, its presence being proclaimed only by the sights, frontal port, and low-sited ejection chute in the port side of the cowling. Proximity to the engine served to keep the lubricating oil relatively warm. The belt box was immediately behind the petrol tank and was filled through an access panel in the top fuselage decking on the starboard side, between the centre-section struts. When the Siddeley Puma engine was installed it became necessary to move the Vickers gun to starboard, and the front of the gun was then exposed near the front centre-section strut. The gunner's Lewis gun was on a Scarff ring-mounting, attached to the upper longerons immediately behind the pilot. Six or more double drums were provided, and there were firing steps and a folding seat. Production-type Fighters had both ring-and-bead and Aldis sights, the former bracketed to the top centre-section. The Aldis sight was offset to starboard and was fixed to a special fore-and-aft tubular mounting, likewise attached to the centre-section,

A Browning Model 1918, M1, Cal ·30 aircraft machine-gun (*top*) is shown installed in a Bristol Fighter of the RAF. The original photographs have been somewhat 'doctored', but there is no doubting the authenticity of the installation.

and carrying the two circular clamps. The C.C. gear was of 'B' type and the loading handle a Hyland Type B also. An official document of 1917, relating to the F.2B, gave the empty weight, including guns and mountings, as 1,700 lb and the weight of 'ammunition' as 150 lb. This figure, however, represents a total of about 2,000 rounds of 0·303-in ammunition and corresponds to the total military load for one known condition. Other figures quoted for military load are 180, 185 and 192 lb, but in this connection it must be noted that a load of up to twelve 20-lb bombs could be carried beneath the inner lower wings and centre-section. A Negative Lens bombsight could be fitted. On production aircraft the pilot's seat was not armoured as on the two prototypes.

How the earliest F.2A Fighters met disaster, until their pilots learned to use them as single-seaters with rear cover, is a thrice-told tale, but in basic armament there was little variation. On F.2Bs two Lewis guns were sometimes fitted on the ring-mounting, and on one machine at least there was a third Lewis gun, arranged to fire upwards and forwards over the top centre-section. For this gun there was a massive 'four-poster' mounting. By far the most interesting departure from standard was made on Home Defence F.2Bs for night fighting, following a similar experimental installation on an F.2A. A Neame illuminated sight was fitted on the centre-section, pointing upward at an angle of 45 degrees from the pilot's eye. The pilot took aim, and the gunner, having aligned his gun accordingly, fired on receiving a signal from the pilot. A device enabling the pilot to rotate the gun mounting himself is said to have been fitted, though the virtue of this is not apparent.

A confirmed installation of the greatest interest was the fitting of one of the earliest Browning aircraft machine-guns (Model 1918, M1, Cal ·30) on a Bristol Fighter F.2B during 1918. In general pattern this gun was similar to that which armed the Hurricane and Spitfire in the Battle of Britain, a fact which is clearly apparent in the photograph on page 93.

In post-war years the Bristol Fighter was adapted for army co-operation and general purpose duties, and during early 'A.C.' trials the guns were unshipped to make weight allowance for heavy wireless gear. In 1921 an Air Ministry order instructed that the 'C' type C.C. gear would in future be standard on all Falcon-engined Bristol Fighters, in conjunction with a new-type nose-piece for the engine in which the generator brackets were incorporated in the castings.

The last honoured years of the Bristol Fighter in RAF service have been fittingly expressed by one who shared them, thus:

'The Brisfit of North-West Frontier vintage actually carried an operational load of eight 20-lb Coopers and one 112-lb H.E. The latter was sometimes replaced by a can of 200 B.I.B. incendiaries. This was, of course, in addition to the front and rear guns, extra tropical radiator and an extra fuel tank under the rear seat. For squadron transport purposes the load was slightly different. Two bundles of bedding, complete with mosquito nets and poles (with galvanised-iron wash-bowls as nosepiece) were lashed to the wing bomb racks'.

The last variant (Mk.IV) could carry two 112-lb bombs.

M.1A,B,C   Like the Bristol Fighter, this fast monoplane single-seater was in large degree designed around the Vickers gun, though not literally so, for the gun lay exposed on top of the fuselage. The A version (1916) appears never to have been armed; the B carried a Vickers gun at the port wing root, fixed to the fuselage longeron and synchronised by Sopwith–Kauper gear or C.C. gear Type B (one example had the gun centrally mounted); and on the M.1C (the production version, and the only British monoplane in service during the 1914–18 War) the central position for the gun was standardised, the padded windscreen being divided to receive the sight. For training, the type was fitted with a camera gun. Sir Miles Thomas has related how, confronted with a stoppage caused by a thick-rimmed cartridge, and finding it impossible to get his hand high enough to give the cocking handle the required blow, he had recourse to a tin of Fray Bentos corned beef. Although this split on contact with the handle it did the trick.

M.R.1   Though a notable structural advance, the metal-built M.R.1 of 1916 carried the same armament as the Bristol Fighter and this was similarly disposed. The fuselage was built in sections, the second embodying the cockpit, Vickers gun and ammunition box and the third the observer's seat with the Scarff ring-mounting above it.

Scout F   The two Vickers guns of the Scout F (1917) were mounted externally on top of the fuselage, the land-service handle blocks flanking the windscreen. There was a ring-and-bead sight, the bead being positioned just ahead of the windscreen and the ring almost level with the front of the cooling jackets. Beneath the short ejection chutes were access panels to the belt boxes. The external fitting of the guns was regrettable, if unavoidable (because of the small fuselage dimensions), for the Scout F was of unusually clean aerodynamic design.

Badger   Like its rivals in the contemporary (1918) two-seat fighter/reconnaissance category, the Westland Weasel and Austin Greyhound, the Badger had two fixed Vickers guns, mounted much as on the Scout F, and one Lewis gun on a Scarff ring-mounting. This mounting was over a cockpit with cutaway sides to improve the gunner's view. The scheme was later reproduced in, (e.g.), the Supermarine Seamew. Brackets for the ring-and-bead and Aldis sights were attached to the upper wing.

Makers' figures for the Jupiter-engined version, which, at one stage at least, had the full complement of guns mentioned, included 170 lb for 'ammunition, bombs etc', but this figure would easily be accounted for by the three guns with a normal supply of ammunition. Mention of two guns in

Vickers gun installation on Bristol Scout F.

another makers' document suggests that one of the Vickers guns was, or would be, deleted in the event of bombs being carried.

Braemar   The Braemar four-engined triplane bomber of 1918/19 had internal cells for six 230/250-lb or twelve 112-lb + five 40-lb bombs, aimed from the nose by the front gunner, who had a Scarff ring-mounting for twin Lewis guns. For these there were six ammunition drums. Doubtless dictated by the width of the fuselage was the fitting in the dorsal position of two transversely-moving pillar mountings for one Lewis gun each. (Later large bombers, as will be seen, had laterally-sliding Scarff ring-mountings.) For this second station there were six ammunition drums. There was, additionally, a ventral position with an inverted-bow mounting for a fifth Lewis gun, and for this there were eight drums, four on each side, disposed horizontally. As the Braemar was intended for the bombing of Berlin, it is probable that the carrying of a single 3,300-lb bomb was in view, and certainly a scheme was prepared late in 1921 for fitting a torpedo-carrier under the fuselage. This installation would have placed the Braemar in the category of the Blackburn Cubaroo and Avro Ava.

A point of special note is that one contemporary document mentioned a gyro bombsight. This was said to be mounted to the rear of the pilot's seat, together with other instruments 'for bomb dropping'. In the forward compartment was a High Altitude sight.

Bullfinch During 1922/23 two Bullfinches were built as single-seat monoplane fighters and one as a two-seat fighter or fighter/reconnaissance biplane. The gun installations, like the aircraft itself, were out of the ordinary. Twin fixed Vickers guns were specified for the pilot, and, although these may never have been installed, there were flutings or troughs of very great vertical depth in the fuselage sides. With these were associated ejection chutes, above which were located sliding access doors. The gunner's cockpit of the two-seater biplane was a self-contained unit and carried a Scarff ring-mounting for a single Lewis gun.

Bloodhound An Open List of 1925 declared the Bloodhound (built 1923) to be a two-seat fighter; indeed it was otherwise known as Fighter C. The pilot had twin Vickers guns mounted in front of him, provided with 1,500 rounds of ammunition. The Scarff ring-mounting was very close behind, and there was provision for six drums of ammunition, additional to that on the gun. Wing sweep-back was intended to improve field of fire as well

Vickers gun and Scarff ring-mounting on Bristol Badger.

as field of view. 'Fittings for bombs' were mentioned in one company statement.

Berkeley   A competitor of the Hawker Horsley, Handley Page Handcross, de Havilland Derby and Westland Yeovil (the first-named proving the winner), the Berkeley was a large two-seat bomber which appeared in 1925. Though the fuselage was capacious, the bombs were carried externally, beneath the fuselage and inner wings. Possible under-wing loads were two 520/550-lb, four 230/250-lb or eight 112-lb bombs, and four 20-lb sighter bombs were carried under the fuselage. It was claimed that the bombs could be released from three positions. Respecting the operational function of the Berkeley, there is an additional point of interest in that the Frise patented balanced ailerons which were fitted were claimed to introduce no yaw which might interfere with sighting. The pilot's Vickers gun was fitted low in the cockpit on the port side, the barrel casing wholly exposed. There were fittings for ring-and-bead and Aldis sights, and notwithstanding the Berkeley's size (span 58 ft) a normal stick-type control column was fitted. The dorsal Scarff ring-mounting was behind a prominent cut-out in the wing trailing edge and carried a single Lewis gun. There was a scheme for a ventral position also (one Lewis gun).

Bristol Berkeley, showing pilot's Vickers gun above exhaust pipe, bomb-carriers beneath fuselage, window for bomb-aimer's station and Scarff ring-mounting.

Boarhound and Beaver   These were closely related types, the Boarhound appearing in 1925 and being laid out with army co-operation in mind, and the Beaver being a general purpose machine of 1927. The pilot's Vickers gun was fitted to port, well down the fuselage side, and fired through a trough. The mounting on the Beaver was stated to be of 'special adjustable type' and was probably similar to that on the Bulldog. The Scarff ring-mounting was set high, and the field of fire for the Lewis gun was enhanced by the tapering top section of the fuselage behind it. Bombs, typically four 112-lb or two 230/250-lb or sixteen 20-lb, could be carried under the lower wings and aimed from a prone position. Mention was made of two special 'multi-purpose bomb-dropping levers'. The prone position was deleted in the aircraft known as Boarhound IIs, supplied to Mexico for fighter/reconnaissance work.

Together with Bristol Fighters, Boarhound IIs were used in the Mexican Civil War (1929). It was reported:

'With one of the Boarhounds Colonel Sidar, one of the most daring officers of the Mexican Air Force, created a sensation by the capture, single-handed, of more than 2,000 rebels. Flying low, he dropped messages inviting their surrender. As a volley of rifle fire was the only response he dropped two or three bombs into their midst as a slight inducement to submit to reason, and also swept their ranks with machine-gun fire. A second application to surrender was also unavailing, so the gallant colonel again treated his adversaries to a dose of bombs. The second approach proved more effective . . .'

Bagshot As the Berkeley was a rival of the Yeovil, so did the Bristol company find themselves arrayed against their Westland neighbours in a match entailing heavy fighters, the Westland contender being the Westbury. The primary armament of two 37-mm Coventry Ordnance Works guns explains the original name Bludgeon for the Bristol machine, which materialised in 1927. A high-wing twin-engined monoplane, it had gun positions in the nose and in line with the wing trailing edge; at each of these stations was a massive trunnion mounting for one of the heavy guns. Additionally, behind the large opening for the rear cockpit, was a normal Scarff ring-

Trunnion mounting for 37-mm Coventry Ordnance Works gun forward of rear cockpit of Bristol Bagshot, with Scarff ring-mounting at rear.

A study in gun installations and fields of fire, seen in Bristol two-seaters: *reading down*, Bullfinch, Beaver, Type 101.

mounting. Not only was the airframe a failure, but the armament formula it was built to exploit against heavy bombers was abandoned. It may be added that in the early stages of the project (to a 1924 specification), the design team was denied vital information concerning armament provisions.

Type 101   Still striving to repeat the success of the incomparable Fighter, the Bristol company constructed in 1927 the Type 101 two-seater fighter biplane. The armament was two fixed Vickers guns and a free Lewis gun on a Scarff ring-mounting, which, due to its high placing in relation to the wing, and also to the special form of fuselage, had an unusually wide (theoretical) field of fire. The mounting was of the wind-balanced type but was wholly unprotected. The Vickers guns were sited lower in the fuselage sides than on previous comparable Bristol types and were provided with 1,200 rounds. There were five double drums for the Lewis gun.

Bulldog   A close-run eliminating contest between the Bristol Bulldog and the Hawker Hawfinch was the climax of a competition for a day and night fighter to replace the Armstrong Whitworth Siskin in RAF service. The victorious Bulldog was first flown in the spring of 1927, and the prototype differed principally from the production version (Mk. II) in having a shorter fuselage, but also in details of the gun installation. While the two Vickers guns were similarly located, a little below the fuselage 'shoulder' level, the characteristic bulge on the starboard side (to allow for the tilting of the gun, as later explained) was of different form. On the early production machines the cowling was carried further forward over the gun troughs, and this section incorporated vertical louvres. The scheme was later abandoned. Now follows an official account of the armament of 'The Bristol Bulldog Mark II Aeroplane':

> 'The armament consists of two Vickers ·303 in Mk.II guns, mounted one on each side of the cockpit, with link and empty case chutes emptying through the fuselage fairing on either side. Each gun is controlled, through C.C. gear, by a thumb lever in the centre of the control column spade grip, the two levers being mounted side by side. A bomb load of four 20 lb bombs, or alternatively Mk.I practice bombs, can be carried under the port bottom main plane and dropped by operation of a release on the left hand side of the pilot. A signal pistol, 1½ in, with eight cartridges is provided for the use of the pilot. The following is a list of the principal items of armament equipment.

> Gun, Vickers, ·303 in Mk.II*, R.H. feed block
> Gun, Vickers, ·303 in Mk.II*, L.H. feed block
> Cartridges, S.A., ball, ·303 in, in belt
> Gear, C.C., type C, twin
> Gear, C.C., handles, double gun control
> Sight, Aldis, 1·8 in
> Sight, ring and bead, 4½ in

Bomb, aircraft, H.E., 20 lb, Mk.I
Bomb, aircraft, practice, $8\frac{1}{2}$ lb, Mk.I
Carrier, bomb, light series, Mk.I
Carrier, bomb, light series, Mk.I attachment No.1, Mk.I
Control, bomb carrier, release, light series, Mk.I
Pistol, signal, cartridge, $1\frac{1}{2}$ in, No.2, Mk.I

'The two Vickers guns are carried outboard, one on each side of the cockpit, between the fuselage side members and the fairings. The mountings for both guns are of the same design, but that on the starboard side is arranged to tilt its gun over to the inside of the cockpit at an angle of 10 deg; this allows the pilot to insert his hand between the gun and the adjacent fairing panel to reach the loading handle, both guns being of the same hand. The gun mounting consists of two longitudinal bearer tubes, connected at the front end by a piece of channel, welded in place, each bearer being secured by a vertical bolt to a short piece of tube that projects from the side strut of frame No.2 and is attached to the front D-section fairing former. The outer of the two bearers is placed at the front to withstand the recoil shock of the gun by a stay tube which runs forward to the side diagonal strut in bay No.1. At the rear end the two bearer tubes are supported by a tubular framework from the projecting end of the pilot's seat bearer tube.

'The two fixed panels which carry the gun troughs are composed of a rear portion of aluminium, with pressed-out louvres, and a semi-circular trough. The trough, made of stainless steel to withstand the blast of the gun, is riveted to the rear portion of the panel and screwed to the fireproof bulkhead and cowling ring. At the rear end of the trough is an asbestos-lined cover with a vent hole to permit the escape of gases. This is secured at the front by a skewer and at the rear by spring catches, and lies beneath the front edge of the detachable panel fitted to the sides of the cockpit.

'The gun is fixed to the mounting by two wing bolts that screw into tapped bosses in the side plates of front and rear channel brackets. When the aeroplane leaves the manufacturer's works the centre line of the gun is set parallel to the centre line of the fuselage both in plan and elevation. To allow for small movements of the gun in setting, the front channel bracket can turn about a vertical axis, whilst the rear bracket is adjustable laterally and vertically. To obtain these movements the front bracket is fixed by a short pivot pin and nut to a platform across the two gun bearers, and the rear bracket has a tubular shank which enters an adjustment barrel carried on a horizontal bolt between lugs at the ends of the gun bearer tubes. Rotation of an adjustment screw below the barrel moves the shank of the bracket up and down within the barrel and the serrated nut on the horizontal bolt moves the complete barrel and bracket laterally. When correctly aligned the nut and locknut on the inboard end of the horizontal bolt fix the gun rigidly in position.

'The ammunition boxes, one for each gun, are made of duralumin with steel fittings and carried on a steel channel spanning the bottom longerons in the forward part of bay No.2. Each box has a capacity of 600 rounds of S.A.A. in a belt and, when in position, the two boxes meet at the centre of the fuselage with their flat upper surfaces slightly above the rudder bar heel troughs. The bottom inner corners of the box have projecting pins that engage in hooks on the bearer channel and the box is held in place by a skewer at the outer bottom corner, which retains it to lugs on the bearer channel longeron fitting. The flat top portion of the box to the inside of the fuselage is covered with wood as a protection against damage by the pilot's feet and hinges at its inboard edge to permit loading of the cartridge belt; this lid is normally secured by a skewer.

'The ammunition is conveyed on its belt from the box up to the gun through a built-up neck which is fixed to the box at the lower end and to the gun at the upper end. The neck, which is rectangular in section, is in two portions; the lower straight portion carries on its outer face a pair of toggles and wing nuts by which it is secured to a bracket on the front side diagonal member in bay No.2, whilst the upper curved portion, sweeping over to the feed block of the gun, fits over the straight portion and is attached thereto by a nut on each side screwing on a piece of threaded rod. Withdrawal of the complete ammunition box for loading is rendered easy by hinging the straight part of the neck, where it joins the box, a skewer being employed to secure it in the vertical position. Access to the curved part of the neck is given by a door on the outside of the bend . . . The means of adjustment provided for the upper neck allow the ammunition belt to be correctly aligned with the feed block of the gun. . . .

'A $4\frac{1}{2}$ in ring-and-bead sight and an Aldis sight are both fitted over the top of the fuselage, the positions of the sights being interchangeable. The normal position of the Aldis sight is a few inches to starboard of the centre line of the fuselage and that of the ring-and-bead sight very slightly to port of the centre line, the transverse distance between the two sights being $4\frac{7}{8}$ in. Both sights are supported by front and rear T-shaped brackets with slotted holes to allow lateral adjustment; vertical adjustment is given by a screwed standard secured to the front support. The sights are adjusted to be parallel to the guns, i.e., parallel to the centre line of the fuselage in both plan and elevation. The distance between the centres of the two supports for the Aldis sight and between the centre of the ring and of the bead is 18 in.

'The T-shaped supporting brackets for the sights, which project through the fixed fairing over the front of the cockpit, are mounted on a longitudinal tube, which is positioned under and parallel to the fairing. The tube is secured at the rear end to the instrument board and is supported at the front and midway along by inverted-V tube members from the top cross struts of frames Nos.1 and 2. The Aldis sight is carried in two leather-covered clamping rings, one on each end, the top of each

Development of Bulldog gun installation: *reading down*, Bulldog prototype with original bulge to clear loading handle; Bulldog II with revised bulge and louvres; Bulldog IIA in RAF service with louvres deleted and bead sight behind engine.

clamp being locked by a bolt to hold the sight in position. An alternative position for the bead sight is provided vertically over the engine plate. A piece of streamline tube bent over at right angles at the top has a slotted hole for the screwed standard of the sight and is braced by tubes to the top of the engine plate and the fireproof bulkhead . . .

'The normal bomb load consists of four 20 lb Mk.I, H.E. bombs which are loaded on a light series, Mk.I carrier fitted under the port

More Bulldog revisions: *reading down*, Danish Bulldog with lowered position for Madsen guns, associated with large bulge over breech casing; Bulldog IIIA with revised trough for Mercury engine installation; Bulldog IV with short trough.

bottom main plane; an alternative load of four Mk.I practice bombs may be carried when an attachment No.1, Mk.I, is fitted to the carrier. The release of the bombs is controlled by a light series, Mk.I, release, placed on the left hand side of the pilot's seat below and behind the port gun, and giving selective or salvo working . . .'

The type of gun heater employed was later named in the publication as 'Heater, gun, Vickers, 12 volt, 25 watt'.

The following entry appeared under 'Camera gun':

'Provision is made to fit a camera, aircraft, G3, on the top centre plane. The mounting consists of two parallel steel tubes taper-pinned at their ends to clips permanently fitted to the centre plane front and rear spars. The camera gun is fitted to the tubes by two fittings, one placed over the front spar attachment and the other approximately mid-way between the spars. The front support is pivotal, whilst the rear support can be adjusted both vertically and transversely so that means are provided for setting the camera with its centre line parallel to the datum line of the fuselage; thus adjusted, the centre line of the camera gun is parallel in elevation to that of the Vickers guns. In order to absorb shocks and vibration a pair of rubber rings is fitted between the gun and its front support. When the camera gun is to be attached to the mounting, it is placed upside down and the spade grip removed. In place of the spade grip a small bracket is fixed to the gun to form the means of attachment for the rear end.'

This armament, with its associated equipment, remained standard throughout the Bulldog's service with the RAF; likewise on the later marks, though on the Mk.IV the installation was cleaned up by shortening the exposed lengths of the gun troughs. The following extract from a Bristol brochure on the *Bulldog Mk.IV All Steel, Single Seater, General Purposes, Day and Night Fighter* is complementary to the description already given:

'Two Vickers guns are fitted to this machine, one on either side in a position that it is impossible to improve from the point of view of accessibility in the air. It is quite possible in flight to open the lid of the gun, which is held open automatically until released, and if necessary to remove and replace the lock or any part of the gun requiring attention. The loading handles are in the best position for working, and the belt box feed chutes can be opened and examined with ease. The belt boxes can be loaded, if required, in position through hinged lids although it is a simple matter to withdraw them complete through the side doors of the fuselage. The gun mountings are fitted with a patented means of adjustment, to enable the two guns to converge on a point a certain distance ahead.'

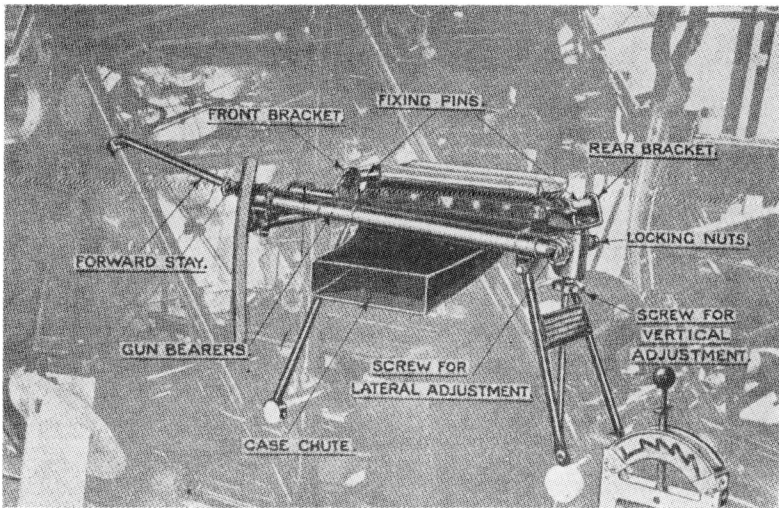

Bulldog gun installation in detail: *top*, showing mounting and case chute; *lower*, Vickers gun in place, together with trigger motor, louvres and vent pipe. The bomb-release quadrant is present in both views.

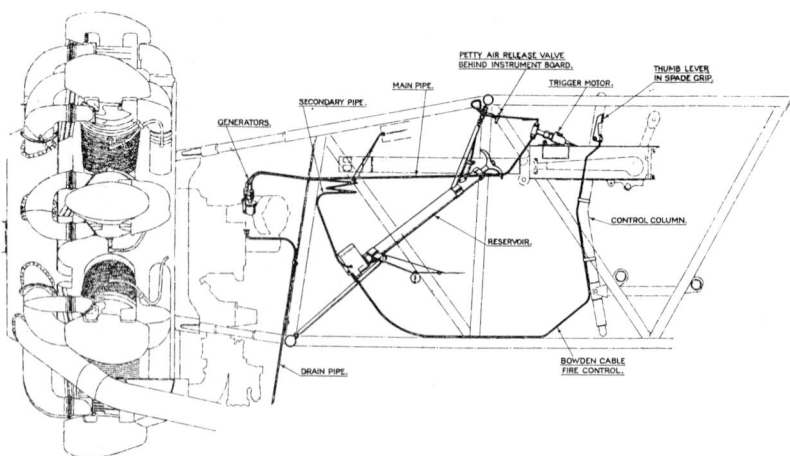

Arrangement of C.C. synchronising gear in Bulldog II. The engine shown is a
Bristol Jupiter VII.

On the Danish Bulldog II the Madsen guns were lowered to fire below, instead of above, the centre cylinder as viewed from the side, and the breech casings were covered with large fairings. No ejection chutes were in evidence on the Finnish Bulldog IV, though the ventilating port for the gun gases was present.

The Bulldog (T) dual-control trainers in RAF service had no guns but retained provision for the bomb-carrier.

Bullpup A diminutive of the Bulldog, the Bullpup (1928) was unsuccessful in the interceptor competition won by the Fury. Its armament installation was generally similar to that of the Bulldog, but no provision was made for bombs.

A point which seems hitherto to have escaped attention is that, although the Bullpup does not appear to have had supplementary armament actually installed, it was certainly offered for sale with it. During 1930 the makers declared that, in addition to the two Vickers guns, the aircraft could be armed with two or four Lewis guns, attached beneath the lower wings. This declaration preceded the appearance of the Gloster S.S.19, which, like the Bullpup, had been originally produced to meet the requirements of the 1927 interceptor specification. The Gloster fighter differed in having the additional guns installed one in each wing.

Type 118 This was an attempt on Bristol's part to produce a basically new type of general purpose aircraft, readily adaptable for its various roles and specially studied with respect to crew amenities. First flown early in 1931, it was armed generally as the Type 120, described in detail hereafter, the most noticeable difference being that the Scarff ring-mounting was unprotected, except for being sunk somewhat below the top level of the fuselage.

108

Type 120 Not only was this Type 118 development of 1932 a notable aeroplane in its own right (as was its precursor), but it marked the entry of the Bristol company into the serious business of protecting the gunner from the effect of air loads at high speed. The 'birdcage' fitted to this end achieved in its day public attention comparable with that aroused by the nose turret on the Boulton Paul Overstrand, although the Type 120 never progressed beyond the prototype stage. The essential points about the aeroplane relevant to this account were made in a makers' brochure now quoted:

'The specific duties which this aeroplane is intended to undertake are five in number, viz: Fighting, bombing, army co-operation, photography, as an ambulance. The crew normally consists of a pilot and an observer. The observer carries out the duties of rear gunner, bomb aimer and wireless operator.

'The pilot is located just behind the trailing edge of the top centre plane, and the wing section is reduced to a minimum here so that the pilot's view is practically unimpaired by the wing. The observer's cockpit is in close proximity behind that of the pilot. It is surrounded by a Scarff gun ring mounting a Lewis gun, and surmounted by a transparent turret which revolves with the gun ring. Thus comfortably installed, the observer can operate the Lewis gun at all air speeds with great precision and effect, since he is protected from the slipstream. Thus, even when the machine is flying at more than 160 m.p.h. the efficiency of the gunner is in no way impaired.

'There is considerable space between the under-side of the pilot's cockpit and the bottom of the fuselage, so that it is a perfectly simple matter for the observer to pass under the pilot and go forward to the bombing station, which is right up in the forward end of the fuselage. The bomb sight is mounted on the floor of the fuselage immediately behind the fireproof bulkhead, and a roller blind, which normally covers the sight opening, is run in to expose an aperture of sufficient length to permit sighting from 17 degrees behind the vertical to within 9 degrees of the horizontal in a forward direction. The width of the slot is sufficient to permit the maximum angle laterally for sighting for drift, and the full range of sighting angles is unobstructed because the under-carriage is divided.'

Having explained how one or two stretchers could be carried in the bombing compartment the account continued:

'The armament for which provision is made is one Vickers gun firing forward, with 600 rounds of ammunition and fired by C.C. interrupter gear, and one Lewis gun mounted on the Scarff ring to which reference has been made, with six double drums of ammunition. The Vickers gun is fitted on the port side of the pilot's cockpit on an adjustable mounting which permits vertical and lateral adjustment. After making any adjust-

The gunner who came in from the cold: eloquent comparative views of the Bristol Type 118 and Type 120, showing not only the rear gun position but the Vickers gun installation and window for the bomb-aimer's station. On the Type 120 the stem of the bead sight is seen attached to its post.

ment to the line of fire, a single bolt clamps the moving parts and thereby eliminates all backlash. The ammunition box, containing 600 rounds, can be filled without removal from the machine, but if desired its removal may be very easily effected, since it can be lowered into the open compartment under the pilot's cockpit after releasing its attachments.

'Racks on the bottom wing are provided to carry the following types of bombs: 20 lb, 112 lb, 230 or 250 lb, 500 lb. In addition, bombs may be carried in a crate beneath the fuselage. Both pilot and observer are provided with salvo-selector release gears.'

A fact which must not pass unnoticed is that the Type 120 and the somewhat later Westland Wallace provided another instance of Bristol/Westland competition—on this occasion in provision of gunner-protection while using the time-honoured Scarff ring-mounting as a basis. It may well be asked how the gunner entered the turret: this was accomplished through a triangular top-hinged door in the port side of the fuselage. A link with this turret and the powered pillar-type mounting, later to be mentioned in connection with the Bristol Type 148 army co-operation monoplane, is the mounting designed by Frank Barnwell in 1933. This carried the gun at one end of an arm, the gunner's seat being slung by hinged linkage at the other end so that the seat moved up and down in an opposite sense to the gun, the seat being automatically tilted forward as it moved up, and backward as it moved down. The weight of the gunner was balanced against that of the gun.

Type 123 A Rolls-Royce Goshawk engined Bristol four-gun fighter to the F.7/30 specification, the Type 123 was flown in 1934. The four synchronised Vickers guns were all in the fuselage and were carried on the same triangulated steel-tube framework which supported the fuel tanks. The breech casings were staggered, but were accessible to the pilot. The troughs for the upper pair were above the exhaust manifolds of the Goshawk engine and the bottom pair below.

Type 133 This four-gun monoplane fighter affords a striking comparison with the original crank-winged Supermarine Spitfire, with which it was intended to compete, being of similar layout and similarly armed, though the undercarriage, slightly outboard of which the wing guns were mounted, was retractable. All four guns were of Vickers type, though it is sometimes stated that those in the wing were Lewis guns. The two fuselage guns fired beneath the long-chord cowling of the Mercury engine, and the wing guns projected from fairings.

This notable fighter was destroyed in an accident during 1935, the year of its completion.

Bombay The prototype of the Bombay (Type 130) bomber transport was flown in 1935. There was a barrel-shaped manually operated nose turret of Bristol manufacture for one Lewis gun and provision for a gun installation in the tail. Here a Scarff ring-mounting with faired cupola was later fitted. The production version was flown in 1936 and was named in the following year. Hydraulically operated nose and tail turrets of Bristol design were installed, each having one Vickers G.O. gun, mounted on its side. The turrets were designated Bristol Types B.II and B.III respectively. Bombs were carried beneath the fuselage and were sighted from the nose. The present writer is indebted to a nameless warrior for this account of the Bombay in the offensive role:

'The armament was four Vickers "K" guns, one in the front Daimler turret, one in the rear turret, and one on each side of the fuselage, firing through a rectangular removable portion of the side wall. I believe the rear turret was found to be pretty hopeless, due to vibration. The bomb load was a load of incendiaries or eight 250-lb bombs carried on external racks, or a load of ninety 20-lb bombs carried inside the body. The 250-pounders and the sparklers (incendiaries) were released by ordinary electrical bombing gear, but the 20-lb bombs required different treatment. When near the target the wireless operator, the flight mechanic and the flight rigger would be responsible for having the bombs ready. The wireless operator would free the bomb from the floor rack to hold it steady, whilst one of the other two cut the wire holding the nose-pin propeller steady. The other member would then throw the bombs through the already opened main door. This procedure would go on until our arms and backs were aching with lifting and throwing 20-lb bombs.'

A profusion of chutes and troughs marked the installation in the Bristol Type 123 of four synchronised Vickers guns.

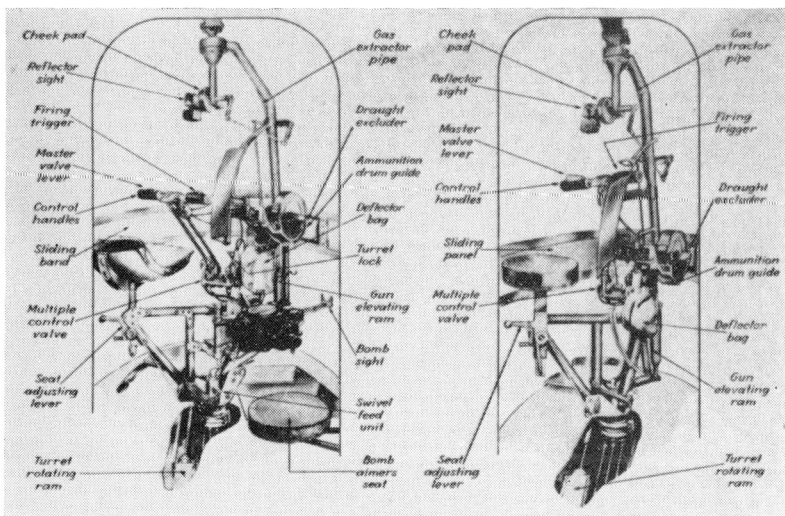

Nose and tail turrets of the Bristol Bombay. These were of Bristol design and it will be seen that the nose turret housed the bombsight as well as a gun. The gun was mounted on its side, with the ammunition drum vertical.

A less tiring method of dispensing bombs from fuselage stowage was evidently schemed, for the present writer noted, after a visit to Belfast to see early-production Bombays, that the lower half of the inner main door hinged inward to enable a bomb trolley to be run out for bombing operations. On the same occasion he observed doors in the fuselage floor for inspection of the electrical bombing gear, and a launching chute for reconnaissance flares.

A Bombay's operational crew numbered five; first pilot, second pilot, navigator/front gunner, wireless operator/port gunner and a flight mechanic and flight rigger who took the positions of rear gunner and starboard gunner. Hydraulic power for working the turrets, flaps, etc. was provided by a Bristol hydraulic pump driven by the starboard engine. The dome of the rear turret could be jettisoned by quick-release fasteners.

Type 146 This single-seat fighter materialised in 1938 as a highly individual Mercury-engined machine, initially with four wing-mounted Browning guns, later with eight. The belt boxes were integral with the wing structure, and for this aeroplane also Bristol designed a special gun-cooling system. They stated:

'Where a continuously operative cooling arrangement is provided for the breech and adjacent parts of the gun it is found that the parts are liable to be excessively cooled when the gun is out of action so that the viscosity of the lubricant increases to a point where the operation of the mechanism is adversely affected; moreover, where the firing mechanism is hydraulically operated such excess cooling causes congealing of the

113

pressure-fluid whereby the gun is rendered inoperative. On the other hand, if no cooling system is provided, a continuous burst of fire of, say, 100 rounds or more, raises the temperature of the breech and adjacent parts so high as to cause premature firing'.

The guns fired through the usual blast tubes, but the breech ends were not normally exposed to the airstream, and, when firing was initiated, air inlets were automatically opened by flaps in the lower surface of the wing.

Type 148   An aeroplane cast much in the mould of the Type 146, this was a two-seat army co-operation machine, first flown in 1937. The armament installation was quite unconventional. True, it was by this time accepted practice to provide two front guns on army co-operation machines, the pattern having been set by the Lysander, which the Type 148 was intended to succeed; but in the Bristol machine these were mounted not one in each wing, as might have been expected, but both in the starboard wing. These guns fired outside the airscrew arc. For the rear gunner a form of track-type mounting for a Lewis gun was at first provided, but a special powered mounting was developed for the aircraft. Recognising that the gunner of an army co-operation aircraft had manifold duties to perform in a confined space, the Bristol engineers devised a mounting giving minimum obstruction. This was of the powered pillar-type, in which an hydraulically operated follow-up system gave what was claimed to be 'adequate and sensitive control' over gun movement with little increase in bulk over earlier types of hand-operated pivot mountings. The single gun was of Vickers G.O. type, which was carried on an arm and was balanced by the weight of the gunner in his seat. A reflector sight was fitted.

Blenheim   The first of the legendary fast bombers in British service was the D.H.4, the second the Fairey Fox, the third the Bristol Blenheim, the fourth the D.H. Mosquito and the fifth the English Electric Canberra. The D.H.4 and the Fox will later pass under review; the Mosquito and Canberra are removed in time from these pages (though the Comet racer of 1934 will be named as the Mosquito's herald), and now for scrutiny we have the Blenheim. The operational significance of this twin-engined monoplane, first flown in 1936 and in service the following year, was precisely that of the Fox: that is, it could show contemporary fighters a clean pair of heels and further confounded its pursuers with rearward firepower. Peter Wykeham remarks in *Fighter Command,*

> 'In the manoeuvres of the 1937 exercise season, the Command had to use all its craft and skill to get within firing distance of the Blenheims at all. If the intercepting fighters could be put directly in the path of the bombers and a good deal higher, they could sometimes choose the exact moment to roll over into a vertical dive that could be pulled out just astern of the Blenheims, with enough speed built up to enable them to use their camera guns at the proper range. As this speed fell off they

had then to endure the mortification of watching the immaculate formations draw steadily away from them . . .'

The installation of weapons on the Blenheim was made with close reference to the performance of the aircraft; and this—together with the rapid introduction of Blenheims into service—must be related to the sire of the breed. The aeroplane concerned was the high-speed monoplane *Britain First* (Type 142, of 1935), which itself showed in its pedigree the Type 143, the fuselage of which was exhibited at Paris in 1934. Little known, perhaps, until recorded by C. H. Barnes, was the fact that Bristol envisaged military employment for the Type 143, a fixed 20-mm Madsen gun and a dorsal Lewis gun being a proposed armament scheme for a fighter/ bomber version. The RAF derivative of *Britain First* was ordered off the board—and promptly swept the board! A Bristol publication of the time declared:

'The Bristol Blenheim I is a high-speed day-bombing landplane. The crew of three consists of the pilot, housed in the front fuselage, a bomb-aimer/navigator, whose station is alongside the pilot on the starboard side, and a wireless-operator/gunner, in the rear fuselage. A bomb cell under the centre plane, which forms an integral part of the fuselage, provides means for carrying the various bomb loads. Light Series bomb-carriers for sighter bombs and flares are mounted on the underside of the centre plane, close to the fuselage. Two practice bomb stations are provided under the rear fuselage. The bomb fuses are set and released by electrically operated gear. A Vickers gun, operated by the pilot, is mounted in the port outer wing, and a Lewis gun is carried in the rear fuselage turret.'

Other relevant extracts are:

'The navigator's seat, which is hinged at the back, is carried on the structure support frame on the starboard side, in line with the pilot's seat. This seat is hinged back when the bomb-aimer is in action. A sliding and folding seat is provided ahead of this for use when bomb-aiming, the bomb-sight being fitted in the nose at the front on the starboard side. This sliding seat enables the bomb-aimer to adjust his position easily to suit a high or low position of the beads. A tail drift sight can be fitted in the floor, just under the bomb-sight. When not in use the bomb-aimer's seat is folded up on to the side of the fuselage.'

The specific entry under 'Armament' reads:

'The armament consists of a fixed forward gun mounted in the port wing and fired by the pilot, and a rear gun mounted in a special retractable turret. The fixed gun is mounted on a detachable cradle in the outer wing on the port side, outside the airscrew disc. The belt box is removable for reloading, access to this and the gun being by means of a detachable panel underneath the wing. The pilot's gunsight is in the nose, offset

Top, Bristol Blenheim I with the cupola of the Bristol turret extended and Lewis gun installed. *Lower*, Blenheim IV with cupola retracted. (*Flight International.*)

to the port side of the centre line. The foresight is fixed, and for the rear sight, which can be folded when not in use, vertical adjustment is provided. A camera gun can be fitted under the front fuselage.

'All bombs are carried internally on the centre of gravity in a bomb cell. Hinged doors cover the bomb cells, these doors being of double-skin construction for torsional stiffness. They are opened under the weight of the falling bombs and closed by return springs. Various types of bombs can be accommodated and for this purpose two Universal carriers are attached to the supports provided. Detachable inspection panels are provided in the sides of the fuselage. A hand winch has been devised for loading. This takes the form of a geared cable winder which operates from inside the body through the roof of the bomb compartment. The winch registers over the centre of each carrier and the cable is dropped through the floor of the body on each side of the carrier. Hooks on these cables pick up a belly-band under the bomb, when the bomb can be raised up to the hook by operating the winch. If the bomb hook does not register exactly into the release unit, the winch can be rocked sideways, causing the bomb to roll slightly until able to enter the release catch. Observation holes are provided in the roof of the bomb cells so that the operator inside can see the raising of the bombs and also communicate with the helper outside. After hooking the bomb, the stays, etc., can be adjusted through large hand-holes provided in the side and centre walls of the bomb compartments.

116

'A jettison lamp is provided in the bomb control station, which can be used to indicate that the various bomb circuits are intact. The jettison lamp is switched on before each bomb is released, and is extinguished when the bomb falls. All bombs can be released together in case of emergency'.

Under 'Pneumatic System' was this note concerning the pilot's gun:

'The firing button is fitted into the top right-hand corner of the control wheel. The air supply is tapped off the main pipe-line and carried via the control hand-wheel and leading-edge of the centre plane to the gun. When removing the gun from the aircraft the connection is broken at the junction of the flexible air pipe and the trigger motor on the gun.'

Under 'Hydraulic System' it was said of the turret:

'This turret has been specially developed by The Bristol Aeroplane Company for efficient operation in high-speed aircraft, being fitted with a retractable hood. It is a circular structure, with the necessary mechanism to train the gun over a wide field of fire, centralising near the stern. The turret has a by-pass valve worked by a spring-clip lever on the main control handle in addition to its control valves. This returns the pressure oil to the supply when the operator releases the handle, so that the turret operates automatically if the gunner is disabled.'

The turret was a notable innovation, for not only was it of remarkably small diameter (30 in) but the hood was retractable. The transparent hood was supported on pillars and moved in a guide, mounted on rollers. The pillars slid, under the tension of springs, in guides connected by a member secured to a beam of the cockpit floor and were connected through links and levers to a torque tube. One of the pillars was provided with a rack which could be engaged by a pinion to retract the hood and tension the springs. To permit the springs to raise the hood, the pinion was disengaged from the rack, against the action of a spring, on raising a handle by which the pinion could be rotated. The moving seat for the gunner was synchronised with the movement of the gun. There was also a secondary motion involving the column on which the gun was mounted. This could be operated independently to enlarge the field of fire and to cover such arcs as could not be reached by normal rotation.

Reviewing Bristol turret development during the war, L. G. Frise, then chief designer of The Bristol Aeroplane Company Ltd, said of the Blenheim type:

'The first mark of this type of turret gave partial rotation in the rear hemisphere only and carried one gun. The development of the Blenheim turret can be traced from this original model, through types with different makes, numbers and calibres of guns, different ammunition feeds, varying sights and armour protection, and with partial and complete rotation.'

The first Blenheim Is were delivered to RAF Wyton, and there the present writer was allowed to fly in the twelfth production aircraft. The following note he made on that occasion may usefully be added to the foregoing:

'The white excrescence which may sometimes be seen near the two small racks for practice bombs under the fuselage is stowage for a battery of Sashalites, which are 'fired' to simulate the dropping of bombs over the camera obscura, by means of which accuracy can be gauged.'

When war came, standard bomb loads for the Blenheim were four 250-lb or two 500-lb. Flt Lieut K. C. Doran wrote of the first bombing raid of the war:

'The war was only 24 hours old, but already the bomb load had been changed four times. Lunch-time on the 4th September found us standing by at an hour's readiness, the Blenheims bombed-up with 500-lb S.A.P. Suddenly we got more "gen". Units of the German Fleet had been sighted, but the weather in the Heligoland Bight, it appeared, was bloody, and the only attack possible would be a low-level one. We could not carry torpedoes, so off came the 500-lb S.A.P. and on went 500-lb with 11 seconds delay fuse.'

Apart from anti-personnel and incendiary loads compounded during the war there were such 'special' combinations as one carried by the Lorraine Squadron: twelve 40-lb + two 250-lb + a 1-cwt package of 40,000 leaflets.

The Blenheim Is for Sweden were modified to carry Swedish bombs, and there was one British specimen of special interest (Blenheim II) which was strengthened to operate at higher all-up weight than normal and carry two external bombs under the wing, inboard of the engine nacelles, as alternatives to extra internal tankage.

The change from the 'short' to the 'long' nose calls for mention because this was made (on the Blenheim IV, originally Bolingbroke) in the interests of navigation and bombing. The original nose was a singular structure and F. A. de V. Robertson remarked after a visit to a Blenheim squadron:

'It is not a slithy tove, certainly not a mome rath or a jub-jub bird, nor even a borrowgrove, but it is something weird. The nose, I am told by technical experts, makes up in virtue for what it lacks in beauty, and even contributes its quota to the total lift of the machine.'

The lengthened nose (some 3 ft greater) was introduced in 1938 and included a chart table and a folding seat. The section to port was fluted in the interests of pilot view.

The Blenheim Fighter is considered separately, and wartime developments special to Bomber and Coastal Commands or of a purely experimental nature can be given here only the merest mention. They included: single backward-firing Brownings in a 'blister' under the nose (later twin Brownings in Frazer-Nash F.N.54 powered mounting); backward-firing guns in the engine nacelles and rear fuselage; nose gun on gimbal mounting—and even a 37-mm C.O.W. gun carried between the spars of a Blenheim I of Coastal Command for firing vertically downwards. A similar installation will be mentioned in connection with the Short Sunderland.

Blenheim Fighter   One of the most commonly retailed items of British military-aircraft history, and one that never fails to stir the spirit and imagination alike, is the fact that the under-fuselage gun-packs for the Blenheim Fighter were produced by the Ashford workshops of the Southern Railway. The background to this undertaking is to be found in the reluctant recognition by the Air Ministry of a need for fighters having a greater range than standard types and the concomitant security of twin engines. Night operation was a subordinate consideration. Having regard to the later-demonstrated failure of the 'destroyer' formula, as typified by the Me 110 (with its heavy primary armament compromised by inferior manoeuvrability, occasioned in turn by the demands of range and a second crew-man), the irresolute official policy is hardly to be deplored. But when the call for long-range fighters came in 1939, it was the Blenheim which afforded the only immediate answer, and so it was that the 'box of Brownings' came upon the scene. The housing was an angular affair, attached beneath the bomb bay, wherein was stored 500 rounds of ammunition for each of the four guns. These were mounted side by side, with portions of the barrels and the flash-eliminators conspicuous. The dorsal turret with a Lewis or Vickers G.O. gun was retained. Both Blenheim Is and IVs were converted, receiving, in addition to the self-contained fixed-gun battery, reflector sights and armour plating. The Blenheim fighters were used in the first instance for low-level attack (25 November, 1939: minelayer base at Borkum), and three Blenheim fighters were operating at about this time with the first airborne radar equipment in Service use (A.I. Mk.III). This was a combination the full implications of which were to be abundantly realised in the Beaufighter.

As a postscript the present writer may add a personal reminiscence of participation in an attack by three Blenheim Fighters of an Auxiliary squadron on six Blenheim bombers. One can hear to this day, as over the intercomm., 'Number Three Attack, Number Three Attack—GO.' One noted in *Flight*:

'The wheel went over and the control column forward, and we were staring through our nose transparency at our swift drab targets set out in plan below. The A.S.I. needle was soon up in the 280 neighbourhood . . . Actually we reached about 300 m.p.h. before swinging out up and away, the g dragging at our temples . . .'

Colleague Maurice Smith was playing in one of the bombers a role he was all too soon acting in earnest, and described us streaking up under our quarry and raking them, thoroughly, if theoretically, with our batteries of Brownings. Maurice wrote:

'Just over Radlett three defending Blenheims in Vic formation came into view . . . In quick succession they peeled off, diving almost vertically at our tails at terrific speed. In turn they dropped down until momentarily obscured by the tailplane, only to shoot up behind us at less than fifty yards range, finally rolling practically over on their backs high above.'

For the Beaufort, the prototype of which is shown, the Bristol company developed a new type of turret, and in the interests of field of fire chose a triangular-section upper fuselage behind the turret. This view may be compared with those of the Boulton Paul Bugle on page 78. A similar scheme was observed on the Blackburn Cubaroo, a very much earlier machine intended for the same duties as the Beaufort.

Beaufort   In the lament of Flt Lieut Doran, recorded in the context of the Blenheim ('We could not carry torpedoes'), is perceived the philosophy behind the Beaufort; namely that of providing self-propelled, under-water strike capability (to ply the jargon of later days) as an alternative to the bomb in over-water missions. The prototype of this general reconnaissance torpedo-bomber flew late in 1938, and Beauforts went to the squadrons in 1940. Like the prototype, the earliest examples were identified by rounded plastic nose-windows, but thereafter the bomb-aimer was provided with flat panels of safety glass.

The 18-in torpedo (1,605 lb) was carried semi-internally slightly to port and was an alternative load to bombs or—most significantly in terms of armament—a mine; for the Beaufort was the first RAF aircraft to be developed with mine-laying seriously in prospect. The first squadron to be equipped, in fact, was quickly engaged in mining operations, and perhaps the first authentic picture of this type of work was the following, prepared by Coastal Command:

'When the aircraft approaches near to the place chosen—a shipping channel, the entrance to a port, the mouth of a fjord, or wherever it may be—it comes down low in order to pin-point its position. This is done by picking up some prominent landmark, such as a building, a headland, a lighthouse, a small island. Arrived there, the navigator sights the landmark through the bomb-sight, and, at the exact moment at which the

Beaufort passes over it, presses a stop-watch, at the same time telling the pilot to fly a course at a certain speed at a certain height for a certain time. During this, the run-up, the aircraft must be kept on an absolutely level keel. At the end of the period, calculated in seconds and fractions of seconds by means of the stop-watch, the observer releases the mine and the operation is over.'

One additional significance of the Beaufort was that the bomb load could be in the form of a single 2,000-lb bomb, and such a bomb was indeed being carried in May 1940.

Defensive armament had been carefully studied not only by the Bristol airframe designers but by their fast-growing armament team, and for the Beaufort a new pattern of dorsal turret, positioned at the rear of the deep forward fuselage, and benefiting in coverage from the reduced cross-section thereafter, was produced. The intended twin Browning guns were not forthcoming (such were the demands for fighters at the time) and Vickers G.O. guns were installed. The turret was designated B.IV Mk.I. Several turret variations followed; twin G.O. guns were mounted in the nose, together with beam guns of the same type; and backward-firing remotely-controlled Browning guns were mounted as on the Blenheim.

The background to the development of the Beaufort's armament is uncommonly interesting. The Bristol company had submitted designs to two specifications—G.24/35 (general reconnaissance) and M.15/35 (shore-based torpedo-bomber)—the requirements of which they considered could be met by one aeroplane, both types having, in any case, to carry bombs. They thereupon drew up designs for a twin-Taurus aircraft which promised to exceed official requirements in terms of speed, a promise which in the eyes of Barnwell and Frise was insufficient. A rear defensive armament of one Lewis gun had been called for, and the design as it stood did not allow for possible future developments in air-launched torpedoes. Revisions were made respecting tankage, load, stowage and armament, the bomb bay being enlarged and, most remarkable of all, a four-gun turret planned. Other notable innovations respecting armament were the incorporation of improved torpedo suspension, the semi-internal torpedo stowage and the building-in of winches for hoisting the bombs or torpedo aboard from their trolleys. All Bristol's ideas were accepted—with the exception of the four-gun turret, which was all the more remarkable for its period in having belt-fed Browning guns. The official reasoning was that in time of war insufficient guns might be available for such lavish protection in aircraft of the class. A one-gun turret was therefore designed for the aeroplane, with provision for two guns to be fitted later.

Beaufighter The bounds of historical propriety are by no means tested by remarking that the Beaufighter was to the RAF after 1939 what the Bristol Fighter had been to the RFC and RAF after 1916. Like the Fighter, the Beaufighter was a unique British conception, designed round a specific armament for a specific purpose (four 20-mm guns basic; fighting by night or at long range); and history so ordered matters that the Beaufighter was designed by the same L. G. Frise who had taken the Hythe course on the Vickers gun and had flown as test-observer in the prototype Fighter. True, there had been fixed-gun/free-gun two-seaters before the Fighter; true likewise that four-cannon twin-engined 'destroyers', or 'heavy fighters', had preceded the 'Beau'; but all of these had lacked the singleness of purpose and uncompromising preoccupation with armament which had inspired the Bristol designers and which were so strikingly apparent in the prototype which flew in 1939. Of the fully armed production type, Mr Frise was able to declare during the war:

> 'When the Beaufighter pilot presses his button the weight of lead that plasters the target is 75 times as great as that which came from the single gun I put in the old Bristol Fighter.'

The development of the Beaufighter's armament makes a story far outranging this book, and is one which is all the more intricate and romantic by reason of the diverse applications found for this initially specialised machine (yet another analogy with the Bristol Fighter). This story has been told with a singular depth of knowledge and feeling for the subject by C. H. Barnes in his book *Bristol Aircraft since 1910* (Putnam 1964). The hard core of the Beaufighter was a battery of four 20-mm British Hispano guns mounted in the bottom of the fuselage and fed by 60-round drums which were changed by a 'loader'. The guns lay in fore-and-aft housings and fired through blast troughs. A 'universal support assembly' was provided forward and there was a link assembly for fore-and-aft adjustment at the rear. Associated with the installation was a gun-control unit embodying a safety switch for each gun ('safe' up, 'fire' down) and giving the warning: 'All guns to safe before landing.' With the installation of six Browning guns in the wings a five-position Dunlop control button was provided for the pilot, giving positions for 'safe', 'light guns', 'heavy guns', 'all guns' and 'camera only'. Wartime developments included continuous feed for the cannon; dorsal turret, 40-mm guns, torpedo, bombs, reardefence guns, and rocket projectiles. Respecting versatility, in fact, the Beaufighter made even the Bristol Fighter seem unwilling.

British Aerial Transport

Bantam The Bantam single-seat light fighter of 1918/19 had an uncommonly chequered history in regard to airframe and power plant; but the armament remained as two Vickers guns. These were mounted internally at cockpit-floor level and had 500 rounds of ammunition each. They fired through ports, between the lowest pair of engine cylinders. An extraordinary feature of the Bantam was the mounting of the Aldis sight. As the pilot's head projected through a circular hole in the upper wing the sight was fixed to brackets above the wing.

Basilisk   Regarding armament, the most striking feature of this 1918 Dragonfly-engined single-seater was the deep, tapering cowl forward of the cockpit, housing the two Vickers guns and protecting the pilot. The second aircraft of the type had an even deeper cowl.

de Havilland

D.H.1   Built in 1915, the D.H.1 reconnaissance/fighter pusher—a projection of the Farnborough-designed F.E.2—had a pillar-mounted Lewis gun in the nose of the nacelle, the forward coaming of which was lowered on production aircraft to increase the gunner's freedom. Whether the mounting was of the type designed by Capt Geoffrey de Havilland and mentioned in connection with the D.H.2 is not known.

D.H.2   The 1915 prototype of this single-seat pusher fighter had a bracket-mounted Lewis gun on the port side of the nacelle, the swivelling bracket being attached to a vertical pillar which was faired throughout its length. Ahead of this mounting the port side of the nacelle was cut away to accommodate the gun. The mounting, or its successor, was designed by Capt de Havilland and was once described as having 'an upright pillar slidably adjusted, without turning, in a tubular socket fixed to the nacelle'. This pillar was said to have carried at its upper end 'a rotatably adjustable arm' which in turn carried at its outer end a mounting for the gun, adapted to permit of 'swinging movements in any direction'. A steel or rubber spring was provided to take up the weight of the pillar, arm and gun to facilitate height adjustment in the socket.

Production D.H.2s had a modified nacelle, and the gun was centrally positioned on a revised mounting. In its lowest position the gun rested in the specially cut-away nacelle nose. The windscreen moved with the gun, which had open sights and was sometimes stripped of its cooling jacket. So narrow was the nacelle that the spare ammunition drums had to be stowed in open-topped boxes flanking the cockpit. These were at first of the standard 47-round land-service type, but a form of 'double' drum is said to have been developed by Maj Lanoe Hawker and Air Mechanic W. L. French of No.24 Squadron. A drum of this type has also been ascribed to No.18 Squadron. There were several variant installations of the gun, and single and twin fixed guns were certainly fitted, for pilots had an aversion to what was described as a 'wobbly' mounting. They disliked also having to handle an aeroplane and a gun simultaneously, and the gun when elevated fouled the control column. Maj Hawker at first tried clamping

123

down the muzzle of the gun to fire straight forwards, but this scheme was officially forbidden. He then made a spring clip with a catch to hold the muzzle down but enabling it to be freed if necessary, and, though the gun was not clamped rigidly, the scheme was described as 'the best compromise possible with red tape'.

It is hoped to give considerably more information on the D.H.2 mounting in *British Aircraft Weapons*.

A point of interest concerning the D.H.2 on which no comment appears to have been made hitherto is the 'blister' under the nacelle, which on some machines was very prominent. This does not appear to have been associated with the base of the gun mounting and may have had the function of channelling or collecting the spent cartridge cases.

D.H.3   The intended operational functions of this 1916 pusher twin continue to be speculative, but fighting appears to have been as dominant a requirement as bombing. The original D.H.2 offset-gun scheme was followed, there being a pillar mounting for a Lewis gun on each side of the front and rear gunner's cockpits. Bombing provisions are unknown, although the type was clearly intended for raids on German cities. The second prototype is said to have been blazing on a factory dump in July 1917 when Gothas were bombing London.

D.H.4   The year 1916 saw the momentous advent of this progenitor of, and paragon among, fast bombers. Arguably the most significant of all British war machines, this was the true precursor of the Fairey Fox and— blood will out—the Mosquito also. It is, perhaps, not widely realised that the pilot did the bombing, while the observer, some feet astern of him, had a purely defensive function. The field of fire was a commanding one, and a speaking tube provided intercommunication, but sheer physical distance lent anything but enchantment, and crew co-ordination suffered.

The pilot's Vickers gun was carried externally to port ahead of him. Six hundred rounds of ammunition were provided and the gun was fitted, latterly at least, with a Cox Type D loading handle. Westland-built RNAS examples had two front guns, port and starboard. Constantinesco gear was standard; indeed the first Service application of this gear was on this aeroplane. The trigger motor was at first Type A, later type B. Gun installations varied in detail, but typically there was an ejection chute far down in the fuselage side. One or two Lewis guns were carried on the rear Scarff ring-mounting, which on early-production D.H.4s was attached to the upper longerons, below the top-line of the decking. It was later raised to improve the field of fire. The original machines had a single pillar mounting, and a few examples for the RNAS had two separate pillar-mounted Lewis guns. The twin-gun combination increased the drag and weight, decreasing in proportion the gunner's stamina, though, as will later be seen, it was sometimes preferred. Usually six, but occasionally as many as ten, double drums of ammunition were stowed in the gunner's cockpit, ahead of which there was a windscreen.

Top, D.H.4, showing bomb rails under wings and fuselage, at differing angular setting, owing to wing incidence, Vickers gun and ejection chute in fuselage flank, and Scarff ring-mounting, with windscreen ahead of it. *Lower*, D.H.4, showing, in particular, the Scarff ring-mounting installation.

Bombs were carried under the fuselage and wings, eight or twelve 20-lb, two or four 112-lb or two 230-lb being known combinations. It will later be shown that the 40-lb Phosphorous bomb was another type carried.

Although the D.H.4 did not achieve its full potential until the Rolls-Royce Eagle VIII engine became available, it was a remarkable aircraft from the beginning; yet, bearing the heading 'Headquarters, RFC, 20th October 1916' and signed 'H. Trenchard', a letter came for Capt de Havilland to this effect:

'. . . on the subject of the de Havilland 4. As a reconnaissance fighter I think it will be a first rate machine, but I do not think it is entirely suitable for bomb dropping. For a large machine it is extremely handy to fly. It is quick on turns with very sensitive fore and aft controls and has a very large range of speed. The criticisms I have made have been sent home to General Brancker.'

For over-water patrol the load was typically two 230-lb bombs, adapted for anti-submarine work.

A particularly ferocious anti-aircraft installation was made in two machines, which, though they flew to France, were never to see action. Firing forward and upward, with its breech extending down almost to the bottom of the rear cockpit, was a 1½-pdr Coventry Ordnance Works gun. The barrel projected through the upper centre-section, and, such was the blast, although the muzzle was well clear, that a covering of sheet metal was applied. Likewise deemed prudent was local airframe stiffening. The gun was aimed by the pilot with a bead sight mounted parallel to the gun, and the gunner fired upon the pilot's command. Some ten years were to pass before this basic concept was revived. One anti-Zeppelin aircraft had two Lewis guns on the top centre-section.

To the glory of the D.H.4 and the crews who proved worthy of it, the present writer appends this most vivid account of preparations for a daylight bombing sortie. The unknown author manned a rear seat at the turn of 1917. He recounted:

'The pilots went to their machines and got their engines running to warm up the oil, etc., while the observers went to the armoury and got out their guns and fired the usual twenty rounds into the gun-pit to see that everything was O.K. I was one of the few observers who always swore by two Lewis guns for the defence of my tail, while, of course, my pilot had his Vickers for forward work.

'Everything now being O.K., we carried our guns to our machines, where we fixed them on to the mounting and adjusted the rubber shock absorbers on the brackets. I then got out of the machine to see that the three bombs, namely a 112 lb bomb under each bottom plane and a 40 lb phosphorus bomb under the fuselage were secure. Having satisfied myself that the safety devices had been removed from the bombs, thus allowing the wind vanes to rotate immediately they were released from the rack, I got back into my cockpit.

126

'Our armourers meanwhile were assisting by carrying out drums of ammunition (usually six drums of 94 rounds each per observer), and as they were handed up to us we placed them on the racks provided . . .
'I will now describe the inside of my cockpit fixed up for this long raid. Firstly, of course, comes my "music stool", which I sit on for taking off etc., but as I cannot see below or over the sides of my machine while seated I have a special "gadget" fixed up for a seat. This is part of a safety belt fixed on each side of my cockpit and joined in the middle by a safety device so that I can undo it when scrapping. This patent seat is fixed much higher than the "music stool" so that I can rest by sitting down and yet can see everything that is going on all around and below. When scrapping I naturally have to stand up to use my guns to advantage.
'While sitting down facing over the tail I have my maps on either side, held by a piece of shock absorber; my "L-type" camera is fixed in the fuselage under the magazines with the lens just poking through the floor . . . I have four of the magazines for my Lewis guns in the racks above the camera, the other two drums on the guns . . . On the left of the Lewis magazines is my automatic pistol with spare magazines in case of emergencies. Behind this again is my Very pistol . . .'

Airborne, and heading for the target:

'I fire a few rounds from both guns into space to make certain that the oil in the recoil portions is not frozen and my pilot looks round with a yell down the telephone "Huns?". I soon put him at his ease, after which I hear "rat-tat-tat-tat". He has followed suit . . .'

Having examined specimens of the D.H.4 a German authority reported:

'The machine is provided with complete dual control. The control lever for the observer is removable. In the observer's cockpit are placed a speed indicator, a throttle and a switch for night illumination. Observer's and pilot's cockpits are placed far apart on account of the main fuel tanks being placed between them. For communication between the occupants there is a speaking tube on the right, and on the left an endless cable passing over rollers in the two cockpits. The control of the fixed machine-gun is accomplished hydraulically by a control mechanism placed immediately behind the airscrew. For loading there is either a lever on the gun or a cable running over a roller, provided with a grip. A telescopic sight is placed in front of the rectangular windscreen.
'The bomb gear, judging from the makeshift way in which the release gear is built, appears to have been added as an afterthought. Bomb racks, either arranged for four smaller or one large bomb, are placed under the lower wings and under the body. The release is accomplished from the pilot's seat by means of Bowden cable. The cables are either joined at the right of the seat or arranged separately on the outside of the body. A sighting arrangement is built in to the body immediately behind the

D.H.5, showing Vickers gun with hydraulic lead from engine-driven generator to trigger motor on top of gun. (*Flight International.*)

rudder bar. It consists of a square plane-concave glass plate, $\frac{13}{16}$ in thick at the edges and 0·2 in thick at the centre. Underneath this are three wire rods soldered at right angles to a fourth rod lying in the direction of flight. Further down about $6\frac{1}{2}$ in is another longitudinal rod, and a transverse rod working in longitudinal slots, and which can be locked in place by screws.'

[This was the Negative Lens sight, the installation of which in the pilot's cockpit of the D.H.4 will be illustrated by official drawings in Volume 2.]

Armament modifications and innovations on the American-built D.H.4s are not fittingly detailed here (eight machine-guns were fitted experimentally), but there is justification for including the following items covered at a conference on 8 April, 1918:

'Wimperis bomb sight, oil lead to synchronising generator, synchronising reservoir, cartridge chutes, magazine rack for Lewis gun, interphone box, Scarff mount, negative lens in gunner's cockpit, clothing-heating plug, gunner's seat, bomb-dropping lever, gun brackets, front and rear windshields, negative lens in pilot's cockpit, bomb-dropping rails'.

Four Marlin guns were fitted as standard to the American D.H.4s.

D.H.5 Back stagger, and excellence of pilot-view in consequence, combined with uncommon diving ability to make for the D.H.5 (1916) a more lustrous reputation for ground attack than for prowess in air combat. The type was effective, however, for low and medium-level fighting and all in all can be regarded as the Westland Whirlwind of its day. Respecting armament, the type holds a special interest, not only because, in prototype form, it exemplified one of the rare free installations of a Vickers gun, but because the installation itself was remarkable. Mounted immediately in front of the pilot, the gun, which was synchronised to fire through the

Official drawing of D.H.5, showing brackets for mounting gun and hydraulic lead running to Type A1 trigger motor.

airscrew arc, could be elevated through an arc of about 60 degrees. The synchronising gear employed was possibly of the kind devised for movable guns by G. H. Challenger, though Airco also designed a synchronising gear. Later a Vickers gun was fixed on another solitary specimen for upward-firing at an angle of some 45 degrees. The gun was offset to port and was braced to the fuselage at the muzzle end.

The standard armament of the D.H.5 was a fixed Vickers gun firing along the line of flight, offset to port ahead of the cockpit. A Cox Type D loading handle was fitted and both ring-and-bead and Aldis sights were generally fitted. When the early A1 type of trigger motor, located at the back of the gun, was fitted, the hydraulic lead from the generator on the engine was led to the rear of the gun, but when an improved pattern of trigger motor (Type B) was fitted on top of the gun the lead was carried up from the fuselage across the gun on the port side, as shown in a photograph (page 128). Ammunition supply was 750 rounds, in a Prideaux disintegrating link belt.

Further heightening the Whirlwind ground-attack analogy, the D.H.5 saw frequent action using bombs—four of 20 lb.

D.H.6   The analogy of the D.H.5 and Whirlwind is less remarkable than that adducible between the D.H.6 and Tiger Moth, the trainers of two wars which rendered arduous, if thankless, service on anti-submarine patrol. For this assignment the first-war 'Clutching Hand' carried a single 100-lb bomb or equivalent load and was generally manned by the pilot alone. The effectiveness of the type was not confined to keeping periscopes submerged, for on 30 May, 1918, an attack was made on *UC-17*, unhappily too late to prevent the torpedoing of ss *Dungeness*.

D.H.9   Scourged and derided though it was, the D.H.9 was more extensively employed than any aircraft of its class, both by the RFC and RAF. Such were the casualties inflicted by enemy fighters that formation flying was imperative. Being of an open kind this enabled the rear gun or guns to be worked effectively. The juxtaposition of the cockpits allowed not only better crew communication than in the D.H.4 but permitted internal bomb stowage also. Bombs could also be carried under each wing and under the fuselage.

The pilot's Vickers gun was located externally in a recess to port and with separate case and link chutes in the fuselage side. C.C. gear and a Hyland Type B loading handle were provided. The Scarff ring-mounting carried a Lewis gun, or occasionally two. *Royal Air Force Technical Notes* for 'de Havilland No.9' include these items under 'Order of Erection':

'Connect all Engine Controls, Revolution Indicator, and C.C. Gear; Fit Fixed Bomb Cells and Fixed Bomb Release Gear; Fit Gun Mounting and Instrument Board; Fit Ammunition Box, Shutes, and Vickers Gun; Fit Scarff Ring Mounting; Place Movable Bomb Cells in position.'

The external load of heavy bombs was typically two 230-lb or three or four 112-lb, but smaller bombs were also carried outside. With the D.H.9 the Gledhill bomb gear is mainly associated and an Air Ministry instruction dated March 1918 gave notice:

'Two sizes of this gear are being made at present. These will be issued as complete sets made up of the following units: (Λ) One fixed unit of two suspensions for 20 lb bombs. (This unit is a fixed part in the D.H.9.) (B) One movable unit of twelve suspensions for 20 lb bombs. (C) One movable unit of six suspensions for 50 lb bombs. (D) One operating mechanism and connection. Units B and C are interchangeable, and may be fitted in turn according to the type of bomb it is intended to carry. Units A, B, and C are placed in position immediately behind the engine and in front of the petrol tanks.

'In Units B and C the bomb rails carrying the slips, which are three in number, are mounted on the top of the bomb crates. The bomb crates are made of three ply wood and afford the lateral support needed by the bombs when stowed vertically. The crate in Unit B consists of 12 cells, made to fit the Cooper bomb, the crate in Unit C is similar in construction, with the exception that it is formed of six cells constructed to fit the 50 lb bombs.'

The bomb slips and release gear are described thus:

'The slip is the mechanism on which the bomb is retained, and by means of which the bomb is released. It is self-locking, and consists of a lever carrying the suspension hook and a trigger lever, both of which are pivoted. The Cooper bomb is suspended from the suspension hook by a special wire loop which replaces the nut on the tail of the bomb. The 50 lb bomb is suspended by an eye bolt which forms an integral part of the nose fuse. The suspension hook receives the suspension lug of the bomb to be stowed, and is then automatically locked by a trigger lever, which projects through a slot in a sliding bar. When this bar is pulled, as is the case when operating the release, the end of this slot depresses a lever, and so allows the suspension hook to turn on its pivot and release the bomb.

'The pilot's release lever has seven positions, as follows: (1) Locked. (2) Free. (3) Release 2 Cooper bombs from fixed unit. (4) Release 3 Cooper bombs or 1–50-lb bomb. (5) Release 3 Cooper bombs or 2–50-lb bombs. (6) Release 3 Cooper bombs or 2–50-lb bombs. (7) Release 3 Cooper bombs or 1–50-lb bomb.'

The following instructions are given for loading:

'Place the release lever in "free" position and pull down the slides at the bottom of each bomb cell which hold the safety springs aside, push the suspension lug of the bomb upwards until a click is heard. The bomb will now be automatically held in position. When all the bombs are stowed, place the release handle in the locked position. The safety springs must now be adjusted by pushing up the slides which hold them aside while stowing the bombs is in progress.'

The foregoing reference to one fixed unit of two suspensions for 20-lb bombs and one movable unit of twelve suspensions accords perfectly with one recorded test-load of fourteen 20-lb bombs.

Containers for Baby Incendiary Bombs were also carried internally, but the reported internal loads of two 230-lb or four 112-lb bombs must have been rare. Indeed, it is difficult to envisage the vertical stowage of 230-lb bombs which is stated to have been possible, for this type of bomb was $50\frac{1}{2}$ inches long, and this measurement, in addition to the length of the nose shackle and the depth of the suspension beam, would seem to be greater than the depth of the D.H.9 fuselage.

The bomb sight was of the Negative Lens type.

Eagle-engined D.H.9A prototype, showing details of gun installations, ring-and-bead sight to port and clamps for Aldis sight to starboard. Note how windscreen has been cut away to clear eyepiece of Aldis sight.

D.H.9A The fine distinction in RAF nomenclature between the terms 'day bomber', 'light bomber' and 'single-engined bomber' and the generic classification 'general purpose aircraft' is to be seen most clearly in the evolution and employment of this archetype of all 'G.P.' machines— which began its career in 1918 as a strategic bomber. Of such importance and enduring memory was the 9A in RAF service that its lineage and 'general purpose' development may now be established upon the authority of a document promulgated by the Air Ministry (Directorate of Research) in April 1922. This contained the following significant passage—possibly the original instance of the term 'general purpose' appearing in a Service publication. Thus:

> 'Though officially classed as a two-seater fighter reconnaissance type [*sic*] the functions of this aircraft cover, in practice, a wider field and it could aptly be described as a general purpose two-seater. For long-distance reconnaissance, photographic work, day or night bombing or

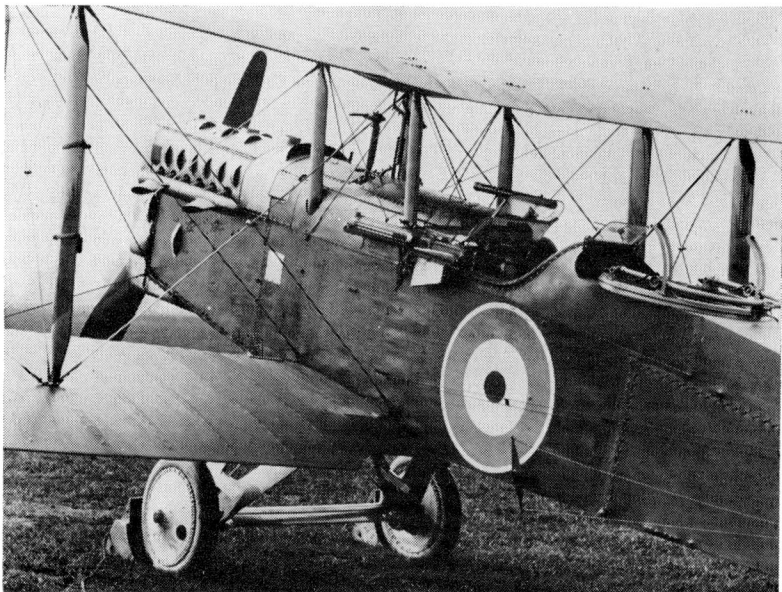

Liberty-engined D.H.9A, showing revised ejection chute on Vickers gun and Aldis sight in position. Although the pilot's windscreen has been perforated to receive the eyepiece, the hole is not here used.

> artillery observation, it is equally useful, and its high speed and strong armament render it a particularly formidable opponent.'

Armament is thereafter summarised as:

> 'Pilot, 1 Vickers gun and 750 rounds; observer, 2 Lewis guns and six drums; bombs (under fuselage), 4–20 lb, or 2–112 lb, or 1–230 lb; bombs (under each plane), 4–20 lb, or 1–112 lb.'

In a subsequent passage no mention is made of the twin Lewis installation, but there is a reference to a performance test with two 230-lb bombs.

The main account runs:

> 'The D.H.9A normally carries two guns, one fixed Vickers machine gun on the port side of the fuselage and a Mk.III Lewis gun mounted on a standard Scarff ring No.2, over the observer's cockpit. Bomb gear and a bomb sight, as well as wing-tip flare brackets, are also fitted.'

133

This information is expanded as follows:

'The Vickers gun was originally arranged parallel to the upper longerons. This position was found to be unsatisfactory, however, as, owing to the pilot's cockpit being so far back, it was impossible for the pilot to get an uninterrupted line of sight. In consequence the gun is now mounted at an angle of $3\frac{1}{2}$ degrees in relation to the top rail of the fuselage. The gun is bolted to two mild steel U brackets of 10 S.W.G., one front and one rear.

'The gun is synchronised with the propeller in the normal way by means of Constantinesco gear, and is fired by means of a Bowden lever and cable fitted on the control lever. At the rear of the engine, concentric with the crankshaft, a cam box with a splined shaft is fitted to engage with the hollow end of the crankshaft. A Type B synchronising gear with Type C trigger motor is fitted, but an adapter is supplied so that Type B lines may be used. The loading handle fitted to the gun is of the Cox D type.

'The magazine is constructed of sheet aluminium and takes a belt of 750 rounds. It is supported on sheet steel brackets, and the belt passes over a 3 in roller into the gun. The spent cartridges are ejected through a chute and fall clear of the aircraft. An Aldis sight is mounted on the starboard side of the fuselage cowling. In the corresponding position on the port side is fixed a standard ring-and-bead sight.

'The observer's cockpit is furnished with the standard Scarff gun ring, carrying a Lewis Mk.III gun fitted with a Norman vane 100 m.p.h. sight. Four pegs are provided for carrying the necessary ammunition drums and are accommodated in a special uncovered compartment immediately behind the cockpit.   Both the Vickers and Lewis guns are fitted with the standard electric gun heater.'

Of the bomb installations:

'Two similar 18 S.W.G. mild steel ribs, each of flanged U section, are bolted to four bottom fuselage struts, so that approximately one-third of each rib lies behind the rear spar. The ribs are parallel to the longitudinal axis of the aircraft and are 21-in apart. A similar pair of steel ribs, again 21-in apart, are fitted underneath each wing. Bomb gear comprises the standard bomb releasing toggles, working through stranded cable. The schedule provides for the fitting of one high-altitude drift sight and one negative lens bomb sight.'

It is pertinent to include the following note on electrical equipment:

'The D.H.9As in service at the time of writing do not carry the full standard electrical equipment. Many are either not furnished electrically or only partially equipped, while others have a war-time equipment.'

On post-war aircraft of this type, arrangements were made for eight, instead of four 20-lb bombs to be carried under each wing (two tandem carriers). The Vickers gun was often of the Mk.II pattern with small perforated barrel casing and a G.3 camera gun was sometimes mounted on the port lower wing. A prone bomb-aimer's position was incorporated, as indicated by two windows in the fuselage sides near the bottom longerons. Already the 9A was being made to carry (in the phrase which this aeroplane brought into Service currency) everything except the kitchen sink, and when geographical and climatic demands were superimposed, it became less of a war-horse and more of a beast of burden. Apart from an auxiliary radiator, oleo undercarriage (occasional), cameras, camera gun, etc, the following inventory was listed by (the writer believes) Sir Arthur Longmore: auxiliary tank, giving an endurance of seven hours; spare tyre strapped under fuselage (camel-thorn punctures); emergency rations for three days; two gallons of water; special container for beer bottles; and a gadget to work the rudder bar by hand so that the pilot could stretch.

In connection with the Handley Page O/400, mention will be made of a bomb-aiming technique involving the tying of string to the pilot's ankles, and a similar technique is known to have been employed with the D.H.9A.

Finally it may be noted that in 1921 an Air Ministry Order made allusion to modifications concerning the R.L. Launching Tube on aircraft of this type. This device had been developed by the Royal Laboratory early in the 1914–18 war with the intention of launching incendiary bombs against airships, though it was also associated with flares and markers.

D.H.9b   This designation was applied to a post-war development of the 9A, remodelled by the Aircraft Disposal Company, having an Eagle VIII engine with Lamblin radiators and augmented armament. Provision was made for three 230-lb bombs, two fixed Vickers guns, two Lewis guns on a Scarff ring-mounting and a third Lewis gun firing through the floor, for which a sliding hatch was provided.

D.H.10   Like the D.H.9, this D.H.3 bomber development of 1918 had internal as well as external stowage. The internal vertical cells could take containers for Baby Incendiary Bombs as alternatives to high-explosive types, and the heaviest load which appears on record is six 230-lb. In postwar operations eight 112-lb was one load dropped on operations. But if, in its early forms at least, the D.H.10 was undistinguished for weight-carrying, it did possess an excellent all-round performance, and one machine was actually sent to a Home Defence station for appraisal as a fighter. The installation of a Coventry Ordnance Works gun, however, in two of the early examples (following trials of the gun in a Tellier flying-boat at the Isle of Grain) sprang rather from an offensive or defensive-escort requirement. The two experimental aircraft had their noses lengthened, strengthened and fitted with wheels, and both were sent to Orfordness for trials. The Independent Force was interested to the extent of requesting examination of the possibility of fitting a similar gun in the dorsal position also.

Normal gun armament was two (or twin-yoked) Lewis guns on nose and dorsal Scarff ring-mountings.

135

D.H.11 Oxford   Though designed in wartime, this twin-engined day bomber was only about half complete at the Armistice and did not fly for many months. It was notable respecting armament because of the commanding position of the rear gunner above the wings and the interconnecting catwalk between his station and that of the nose gunner. This was made possible by the fuselage dimensions (6 ft × 4 ft). Each position had a Scarff ring-mounting. Bomb stowage was internal, and was probably of the 800–900-lb order.

D.H.14 Okapi   Dating from 1918/19 (and still extant in 1922) this high-performance single-engined bomber followed the now-established de Havilland practice of stowing the bombs internally. The bombs were suspended vertically by their noses, four of 112 lb in two double crates between the main spars and two of the same weight in single crates beneath the pilot's seat. Brown paper was used to cover the openings of the bomb cells in order to exclude draughts. The pilot had a Vickers gun, set deep in a groove in the top decking, and there were twin Lewis guns on the rear Scarff ring-mounting. For these guns six double drums of ammunition were provided. Field of fire benefited from the suppression of the tailplane top-bracing wires in favour of struts beneath.

D.H.15 Gazelle   More or less contemporary with the Okapi, the Gazelle was a direct 9A development (Galloway Atlantic engine) and armament remained unchanged.

D.H.27 Derby   Completed in 1922, this single-engined biplane was officially rated as a 'three-seat medium-range bomber', and, the undercarriage being of the divided type, could carry two 520/550-lb bombs externally under the fuselage. The navigator/bomb-aimer had a cabin and a Scarff ring-mounting with Lewis gun, the mounting being fitted well aft. Military load was given as 2,528 lb.

D.H.29 Doncaster   Although fitted in one instance with a Scarff ring-mounting aft of the wings, the Doncaster high-wing cantilever monoplane (1921) was essentially a research aircraft.

D.H.42 Dormouse   Built in 1923 to a specification issued the year before, the Dormouse was a two-seat fighter (official classification). The pilot was under the top wing, with two fixed Vickers guns mounted largely externally ahead of him and firing over the Jaguar engine. The Scarff ring-mounting for a Lewis gun was immediately aft of the trailing-edge cut-out.

D.H.42A and B Dingo   The Dingo (1924) was an army co-operation development of the D.H.42 design with one fixed Vickers gun (top port) and a Lewis gun on a Scarff ring-mounting. The ring was not countersunk, as on the Dormouse.

D.H.56 Hyena   Developed from the Dingo in 1926, the Hyena competed with the Armstrong Whitworth Atlas, Bristol Boarhound and Vickers

A de Havilland two-seat fighter of the early 1920s, the Dormouse had somewhat unusual crew arrangements. There was a hole in the centre-section above the pilot. The two Vickers guns are not installed, though the fairing for them is seen ahead of the cockpit; nor is a Lewis gun fitted on the Scarff ring-mounting. (*Flight International*.)

Vespa in the army co-operation contest won by the Atlas. Both cockpits were positioned well aft. The pilot's Vickers gun was internal (port high); there was a Lewis gun on a Scarff ring-mounting immediately behind the pilot's cockpit, and four 20-lb bombs could be carried under the port wing.

D.H.9AJ Stag This Jupiter-engined general purpose development of the D.H.9A appeared in 1926 and was beaten in competition by the Wapiti. War load was typically four 112-lb or two 230/250-lb bombs, Vickers gun (external port), and Scarff ring-mounting with Lewis gun. There was a prone bombing position, with wind deflector.

D.H.60T Moth Trainer Built in 1931, the Moth Trainer was readily fitted for fighter training (camera gun and Aldis sight) or bombing practice (four 20-lb under fuselage). Standard Gipsy II Moths were also adapted to carry four 20-lb bombs.

D.H.65 Hound A private-venture high-performance bomber, fully worthy of the D.H.4, the Hound (1926) had provision for four 112-lb or two 230/250-lb bombs under the wings, a fixed Vickers gun, and a Lewis gun on a specially designed de Havilland low-drag mounting. Redesigned with Jupiter engine and split-axle undercarriage (D.H.65J), it had a rearranged installation for the Vickers gun (starboard upper) and a prone bomb-aimer's position in the rear fuselage.

A special type of gun mounting was devised by de Havilland during the period of the Hound's existence, and this was apparently of the type fitted to the aircraft while it was being tested with the geared Napier Lion engine. In this mounting a 'gun carriage' was adjustable round a track member in the form of a ring frame extending from side to side of the cockpit, this track member being hinged to the cockpit to enable the gun to be raised or lowered. Provision was made for counterbalancing the weight of the gun in all positions by a strut, the lower end of which slid longitudinally against the action of tension or compression springs housed in the fuselage decking. The 'gun carriage' had a universal joint for the gun and an operating

137

Showing how essential features of the D.H.9A (*top*) were reproduced in the Stag (*centre*) and Hound. Note, however, that, being built to an official general purpose requirement, the Stag retains the Scarff ring-mounting and has a prone bomb-aimer's station, betokened by windows. Contributing to the clean lines of the Hound private-venture day bomber is a de Havilland low-drag mounting for the rear Lewis gun.

A requirement to use up spares for the D.H.9A (first Liberty-engined example shown at top) resulted in a strong resemblance between intended replacement types. Second is de Havilland's own submission, the Stag, third the victorious Westland Wapiti, fourth the Gloster Goral. Only the Goral has a partially faired Vickers gun; on the other types the gun is wholly external. On the Wapiti the mounting only is seen; a somewhat similar fitting on the Goral is for a wind-driven generator. The Goral also displays an unusual form of coaming round the Scarff ring-mounting. The Stag carries two 250-lb bombs.

139

handle fitted with a spring-controlled catch for engagement with holes in the track.

D.H.72 Originally this three-engined night bomber, completed by the Gloster company in 1931, was to have been a development of the Hercules airliner, which had one of its three engines mounted in the nose, but a requirement for a nose gun position caused the third engine to be moved to the upper wing. The fuselage was of small cross-section and there was no internal bomb stowage, the Universal carriers being distributed under the fuselage and inner wings. Bomb-load was probably comparable with that of the Vickers Virginia. Scarff ring-mountings for Lewis guns were fitted in the nose and tail.

Gun and gunsight installation on D.H.77 interceptor fighter. (*Flight International.*)

D.H.77 The two Vickers guns of this low-wing interceptor fighter (1929) were mounted low in the cockpit, their barrel casings exposed in the blast troughs which ran parallel with the centre line of the Halford 'H' (Rapier) engine. The Aldis and ring-and-bead sights were immediately ahead of the windscreen. The guns were removed when the aircraft became a Rapier test bed.

Tiger Moth The Tiger Moth appeared in 1931. Quickly establishing itself as a trainer, it also showed adaptability for armament practice or offensive work. Installations were made of a camera gun on the starboard lower wing and an Aldis sight bracketed to the starboard side of the fuselage, and also of a carrier for 20-lb bombs beneath the fuselage, this last in con-

Installation of Czech machine-gun and Aldis sight on de Havilland Tiger Moth
Fighter (makers' own designation).

junction with a vertical tubular sight and release quadrant. One Tiger
Moth (E.6) was built solely for offensive work as the Tiger Moth Fighter,
and the makers announced:

'We are now able to offer the Tiger Moth as a single-seater fighter
fitted with a machine gun firing forward through the propeller, and also
capable of carrying eight bombs of 20-lb each. A fairly substantial order
has been received from an important foreign Government for Tiger
single-seater fighters fitted with Gipsy Major engines, on which we have
now completed full firing tests, both on the ground and in the air. The
machine gun is air-cooled, weighs only 9·5 kilos, and is manufactured by
the Czechoslovakian Arms Factory of Prague. A Pratt and Whitney
synchronising gear is fitted, which is very light and efficient, the drive
being taken from the top half of the rear cover of the engine, where provision for hand-starting gear is normally allowed for. The gun is
mounted in the front cockpit, and shoots directly over the top engine
cowling. The ammunition box, holding 200 rounds, and the cartridge
shute, are fixed to the mounting itself, and the only connections between
the gun, gun mounting and fuselage are four holding-down bolts. The
cocking handle is connected only by a cotter pin to the lever which acts
on the gun. In order to protect the workings of the gun it has been
cowled in. An Aldis telescopic (*sic*) gun sight is provided for long-distance

141

firing. The ordinary ring-and-bead sight for "dog-fighting" can be fitted–
as an alternative, or together with the Aldis . . .'

Tests were made with a disc fitted to the propeller and it was claimed:

'The results of the official ground and air acceptance test were as
follows: (1) Pulling over the propeller by hand, the first round pene-
trated the disc 19½ deg. after top dead centre.   (2) Dispersion throughout the entire speed range occurred between the angles 45 deg. to 86 deg.;
that is to say through an arc of 41 deg. (3) Propeller speeds varied from
800 to 2,400 r.p.m. These results are absolutely satisfactory.'

Clearly D.H. were rather pleased with their little trainer as a fighting
machine, but they could hardly have foreseen that the Tiger would actually
go to war—and not in the service of a foreign nation but wearing the

Disc on Tiger Moth Fighter airscrew to test Pratt & Whitney synchronising gear,
showing dispersion of bullets.

142

roundels of the RAF. Like the D.H.5 before, it was pressed into service as an anti-submarine aircraft with four 20-lb bombs under the wings. For anti-invasion duties astonishing devices were schemed, among which a tray of Mills bombs was one of the least spectacular. These devices are beyond the scope of the present review, and Tiger Moth enthusiasts will already have been apprised of them by Messrs Bramson and Birch's *Tiger Moth Story* (Cassell, 1964). The present writer's contribution to the continuing story of the Tiger is the foregoing fragment of history.

Puss Moth As supplied to Iraq during 1932 the Puss Moth was fitted with a carrier for four 20-lb bombs beneath the fuselage.

Dragon (Military Type) The military version of the Dragon twin-engined biplane was produced in 1933 and gained export orders with somewhat varying armament. A makers' description stated:

> 'The armament consists of a fixed Lewis gun operated by the pilot, and two Lewis guns firing aft (one above and one below the fuselage) . . . These two guns are fired through holes, normally covered with detachable lids, in the roof and floor of the cabin'.

Sixteen 20-lb bombs were carried beneath the fuselage. The release gear and bombsight were located just aft of the pilot's seat, so that the pilot and bomb-aimer were closely in touch. An external feature was a guard rail to protect the tail surfaces from misdirected fire from the upper gun.

Comet Though the Mosquito is chronologically inadmissible here, and though the Comet twin-engined wooden racer of 1934 was never armed, the racer is nevertheless accorded a place by reason of the fact that the specimen called *Grosvenor House* was tested at Martlesham in Service markings and stimulated transient interest in the feasibility of unarmed bombers. This concept, brought so triumphantly to realisation in the Mosquito, was in harmony with Lord Bacon's dictum that 'the best armour is to keep out of gunshot'. The Comet racer merits mention also because of its apparent potential as a fighter, and here allusion may be made to C. G. Grey's early strictures on the pusher type of fighting aircraft, which will be recorded in Volume 2, and to the foregoing notes on the D.H.2. In 1935 'C.G.' discharged this bewildering salvo:

> 'If the Staff is really keen on having single-seat fighters so that they can carry a vast weight of ammunition for several guns instead of supplying a gunner with swivelling guns, then they can always build small high-speed twin-motor machines like the de Havilland Comet and have fixed guns sticking out of the nose, just as the single guns stuck out of an F.E.8 or a D.H.2. Any pilot who flew one of those single-seat pusher fighters will admit that as a fighting machine it was the finest thing in the war.' [The common denominator between the early pushers and the Comet was, of course, the absence of a nose engine.]

D.H.89M   This aeroplane was first produced in 1935 to compete for RAF general reconnaissance orders against the Avro Anson (or Avro 652A, as it was then known), The airframe was that of the civil Rapide, adapted to take the same war load as the Anson. On the starboard side of the pilot's cockpit was a Vickers Mk.III gun, with the breech mechanism easily accessible. The gun had a left-hand feed block, and an ammunition box for 400 rounds was beneath the pilot's seat. The pilot had a bomb release. In the front of the fuselage, where he could easily talk to the pilot, was the observer/gunner, and just to the rear of the pilot's seat was a hole with a sliding hatch for bomb sighting. Behind the Vickers gun was the electrical bomb-selector and release gear and a handle for opening the sliding hatch covering four 20-lb bombs. As the bomb-aimer lay down to sight he found in front of him an instrument board with altimeter, A.S.I. and temperature gauge. Two 100-lb bombs were slung in the middle of the fuselage and were accessible from inside through doors in a raised box on the floor. When released, the bombs fell through spring-loaded trap-doors in the belly, which then closed automatically. There was a rack for four flares. Eight 97-round drums were provided for the dorsal Lewis gun, which was on a special gun mounting of de Havilland design. The gunner sat on a swivelling seat and the gun ring was on roller races, being capable of rotation, when the gun was fitted, by the pressure of one finger. For any firing position, except air-to-ground, the gunner was seated, and the greater the angle of elevation, the higher the position of the gun. In other words, the height of the gun varied with the eye of the gunner, instead of the gunner having to adjust his height to that of the gun. When not in use, the gun and mounting could be folded away in two or three seconds and covered with a sliding hatch.

Although the D.H.89M secured no British orders, a variant type was supplied to Spain. In the nose was a Vickers Class E gun, with 200 rounds and a ring-and-bead sight. In the middle of the fuselage was a Spanish bombsight, covered with a canvas roller blind operated by cable, and to the right were releases for the twelve Spanish bombs, weighing about 27 lb each and carried under the fuselage in three rows of four. In the dorsal position was a Vickers Class F gun, with a guard and an easily detachable ring which could be folded back into the fuselage and the hatch then closed. The gunner stood on a folding platform. Firing through the floor was a second Class F gun, the hatch for which had a canvas roller-blind cover. Six 97-round drums were carried on pegs on the cabin walls.

Don   Armament training was one of the designated functions of the Don (1937), and though the type saw service only as a communications aircraft the present writer was able to fly in the turret-equipped prototype at Martlesham Heath. The turret was of Armstrong Whitworth type and carried a single Lewis gun. It was situated at the rear of a massive cabin structure which had side-by-side seating for instructor and pupil-pilot at its forward end. Built in to the bottom of the fuselage was a prone-

A de Havilland Don with practice bombs and Armstrong Whitworth manually operated turret with Lewis gun. The port for the fixed Vickers gun is seen in the wing, just inboard of the landing light. (*Flight International.*)

bombing station and under each wing was a carrier for eight practice bombs. A Vickers gun was fixed in the port wing, a little inboard of the landing light, and the prototype had two sighting beads mounted side by side on the cowling.

The Don had an additional interest in the armament context, for one machine was used by de Havilland for tests with a reversible-pitch airscrew to investigate the possibility of using this as a brake for dive-bombing aircraft.

Dyott Bomber with second form of nose, showing three Lewis guns with land-service type cooling jackets, sights and ammunition drums, but with spade grip in place of stock.

Dyott

Dyott Bomber Sometimes styled 'Dyott Twin Bomber' and sometimes 'Fighter' this adventurous aeroplane was originally intended for exploration. Undeniably advanced though it was in design, its two engines delivered no more than 240 hp, and it is difficult to imagine any useful war load additional to the astonishing array of small arms undoubtedly fitted, but possibly never lifted. The Lewis guns had land-service cooling jackets and 47-round ammunition drums. Two were on spigot mountings above the fuselage and another two were stationed at portholes in the fuselage sides. A fifth was mounted aft of the wings. These five guns alone, without ammunition or fittings, would have weighed all of 130 lb.

There were at least two versions of this aircraft. In the first a conspicuous feature was the gun-rail carried above the top decking of the fuselage and incorporating six spigot mountings, the two upper guns being interchangeable between these mountings. In the second version the decking was built up and the mounting(s)—for the gun installation may have differed from the original—were no longer visible.

Fairey

F.2 Although this twin-tractor biplane of 1916/17 has been called by the makers the Fairey Twin Bomber, it might more correctly be termed a heavy fighter, though it could doubtless carry bombs. A three-seater, it had Lewis guns in the nose and atop the fuselage aft of the wings. These were on Scarff ring-mountings, the rear one being somewhat recessed below the fuselage top-line. In the context of armament the F.2 had another association of interest, for the engines of one intended version (F.1?) were to have been products of the Brotherhood Engineering Company, which many years before had made the engines for the first Whitehead torpedoes.

Campania In common with other patrol and bombing floatplanes of its time (1916/17), the Campania carried its bombs on tubular carriers suspended a considerable distance below the fuselage and had no gun for the pilot, though there was a Lewis gun for the observer, the gun in this instance being on a Scarff ring-mounting. Military load of the developed version was about 650 lb. One identified load was two 100-lb anti-submarine bombs, carried in tandem.

Hamble Baby Although an armament of a single synchronised Lewis gun is generally ascribed to this development of the Sopwith Baby, the gun lying ahead of the cockpit, the accompanying photograph strongly suggests that there was an alternative installation of a Lewis gun, associated

Fairey Hamble Baby, showing evidence of Lewis gun associated with centre-section cut-out and attachment for bomb-carrier under fuselage.

with a centre-section cut-out. Two 65-lb anti-submarine bombs were carried under the fuselage side by side.

N.9   A Lewis gun on a Scarff ring-mounting appears to have been the sole armament of this 'catapultable' floatplane of 1917.

N.10 (Type III) and IIIA   The true begetter of the varied and versatile Fairey Series III aeroplanes, the N.10 floatplane of 1917 had a Lewis gun on a Scarff ring-mounting. The mounting was recessed considerably below the top of the fuselage, like the rear mounting on the F.2, and this type of emplacement was standardised for Fairey types to follow. No bomb load has been identified, and this also applies to the production-type Fairey IIIA, although a military load of 449 lb could be carried.

IIIB   Developed from the IIIA specifically for bombing, this seaplane had increased span and could carry a military load of up to 690 lb. The only identified bomb load is two 230-lb, the bombs being carried in tandem

The Fairey IIIB was typical of British 1914–18 floatplanes in having tubular bomb-carriers suspended well below the fuselage. In this instance they are for two 230-lb bombs. Note also recessed Scarff ring-mounting.

The original Fairey Pintail, showing Vickers gun above wing, with case chute beneath gun and link chute to port; brackets for sights to starboard; and Scarff ring-mounting with Lewis gun.

beneath the fuselage. The observer had a Lewis gun on a Scarff ring-mounting.

IIIC Superior performance distinguished this higher-powered Series III development, which appeared in 1918. In addition to the rear Lewis gun, on its recessed Scarff ring-mounting, a fixed Vickers gun for the pilot has been reported, though no such installation can be identified in photographs. Bombs were certainly carried beneath the fuselage, as on the IIIB.

Pintail A two-seat fighter seaplane or amphibian, the Pintail first appeared in 1920. It had a fixed Vickers gun for the pilot and a rear-mounted Lewis gun, and the installation of each calls for comment. The top wing being attached directly to the fuselage, and the pilot being afforded a forward view about it, the Vickers gun was fixed above the wing, standing a

Pintail IV, with repositioned Vickers gun. Note also the clear field of fire astern.

149

few inches proud on the port side of the centre-section. This resulted in the Pintail having an additional distinction, for, apart from the B.A.T. Bantam, it seems to have been the only British aeroplane to carry an Aldis sight on the top wing. The brackets were attached on the centre-section starboard side. The rear-gun installation on this first Pintail likewise had a double distinction. Not only was the gunner protected forward by the pilot's cockpit coaming, but he had an unimpeded rearward field of fire, for there were no vertical tail-surfaces above the high-set tailpane.

In later versions of the Pintail the wing was raised above the fuselage and the Vickers gun was relocated on the port side of the fuselage at the level of the pilot's cockpit coaming. The Scarff ring-mounting was now on the same level; thus the two gun installations resembled those of the Fawn.

IIID   Later to be variously engined and equipped, the IIID first appeared in 1920. The type was extensively employed for naval and land-based general purpose duties. Tubular bomb-carriers beneath the fuselage, for a typical load of two 230-lb, preserved in the floatplane version an aura of the war not long concluded, though the Scarff ring-mounting for the Lewis gun was no longer recessed below the top line of the fuselage as on the F.2 and other precursors, but was actually built up from the turtle decking. Alternatively bombs were carried under the wings, as shown. There was no fixed gun for the pilot (whose forward view, in any case, was minimal), although it was reported during 1923 that the latest IIID seaplanes in Malta were being looped, rolled and spun.

Like the floatplanes of the war not long concluded before its construction the Fairey IIID had tubular bomb-carriers beneath the fuselage. The Scarff ring-mounting for the Lewis gun was not recessed below the top line of the fuselage, as on earlier Fairey types.

On this Fairey IIID landplane carriers for two 230-lb bombs are seen beneath the wings. This particular aircraft is equipped for deck landing, as indicated by the arrester hooks attached to the axle of the undercarriage. This arrangement antedated the more familiar tail hook.

Flycatcher   To meet the same requirements as the Parnall Plover, the Flycatcher single-seat naval fighter was first flown in 1922. Its armament was two Vickers guns mounted externally on the fuselage sides—a simple enough scheme it might be supposed, although the fittings were quite complicated because provision had to be made for angular movement fore and aft and laterally for correct alignment. The guns and their belt boxes were staggered, the port installation being a little ahead of that to starboard. The mountings were supported on two transverse members, the forward one of which carried the handwheel for operating the Fairey camber-changing flaps, inherited by the Flycatcher from the Hamble Baby, from which, in truth, it was a lineal descendant. There were two patterns of mounting, the latter being identified by perforated flange plates forming both lower, as well as upper, components. In early machines the lower components were of tubular construction. After a period of service guide chutes were fitted for the empty cartridge cases. Both ring-and-bead and Aldis sights were fitted on operational Flycatchers, these being attached by brackets to the top wing. A G.3 camera gun could be fitted on the lower starboard mainplane.

In the Fleet Fighter Flights, Flycatchers replaced the few Nightjars and Plovers and became especially notorious for their converging dive-bombing attacks. For this work four 20-lb bombs were carried under the fuselage.

151

Guide chutes for the empty cartridge cases are seen in place beneath the port Vickers gun of this Fairey Flycatcher. Aldis and ring-and-bead sights are fitted.

The mounting on a Flycatcher of a 0·5-in gun has been reported. Such an installation should have been relatively easy by virtue of the external fittings mentioned, but the writer has no confirmation of such a development, although the Plover definitely carried this armament.

Fawn Designed as a day bomber and long-reconnaissance aircraft to succeed the D.H.9A, the Fawn appeared in 1923. Sir Richard Fairey himself once recalled that the specified speed was 6 mph less than that of the earlier aircraft. Comparative test-figures for the Liberty-engined D.H.9A (August 1918) and for the Fawn (March 1924) showed respective speeds at 10,000 ft of 114·5 mph and 108 mph; figures for 15,000 ft were 106 mph and 96 mph, though the latter was approximate only, for the Fawn was then above its service ceiling. The armament loads carried on these trials were: D.H.9A, two 230-lb bombs, one Vickers gun, one Lewis gun; Fawn, three 112-lb bombs, one Vickers gun, two Lewis guns. With such a performance the Fawn might well have mounted two Lewis guns, though in

Fairey Fawn prototype, with 112-lb bombs under wings and dummy Lewis gun with land-service type cooling jacket.

service these were not always fitted. They were certainly reported to have been carried in the Air Exercises of 1924, when Fawns were engaged by Snipes, Flycatchers and Nighthawks. The pilot had both ring-and-bead and Aldis sights for his Vickers gun.

Bombs were carried under the Fawn's lower wings, and possibly under the fuselage also. Though typical loadings were probably four 112-lb or two 230/250-lb, it has been said that the aircraft of No.12 Squadron at least carried the '500-lb' (presumably 520/550-lb) bomb.

Atalanta and Titania These very large four-engined flying-boats were officially classed as '6-seat open-sea reconnaissance'. The first was flown in

Fairey Titania, showing evidence of beam guns at midships hatches.

153

1923, though the design dated from 1918. It is certain that 'fighting top' gun positions were schemed for, if not actually installed on, the upper wings of Titania, and there is accompanying photographic evidence that pillars or sockets were provided at the midships hatches, possibly for the mounting of Lewis guns. A 37-mm Coventry Ordnance Works gun may well have been intended for the bow station, and bombs, if carried, would have been under the wings.

Fox I   Although the circumstances of the conception, design, development and eventual adoption of this classic light bomber are now generally known (thanks largely to the writings of Norman Macmillan, who did the test-flying) there are unfamiliar aspects of the story which may now be viewed. The original Fox (having no mark number at the time, and innocent even of markings) was completed early in 1925. Designed by Marcel Lobelle and P. A. Ralli, in accordance with ideas propounded by Richard Fairey, and made possible by his acquisition of certain American rights (notably for the Curtiss D.12 engine), it was a two-seater of uninhibited layout and exquisitely clean design. As it first appeared, with short-span wings and surface radiators alone for cooling, no rear armament was visible. This was not because the Fairey patent gun mounting (later to become familiar as the Fairey 'High-Speed' mounting) was in its stowed position, but because it had not at the time been fitted. And if the front gun for the pilot was itself in place, then its installation appeared quite different from that which was later adopted. The fabric covering of the fuselage, it must be explained, was carried forward to the metal engine-cowling, and the gun was covered by an inserted detachable panel; thus the trough through which it fired made its appearance in line with the front centre-section strut and not the rear strut as later. Nevertheless, when the Fox was sent to Martlesham Heath in this condition, it was loaded with two 230-lb bombs on standard tubular carriers close inboard under the lower wings.

An event of singular importance during 1926 was the re-equipment of No.12 Squadron RAF with the new Fairey bomber. The Foxes the squadron received (wings increased in span from the original and composite

Fairey Fox prototype with two 230-lb bombs.

154

Rolls-Royce F (Kestrel) engined Fox with 112-lb bombs.

cooling system installed) had full provision for bombs and guns. The pilot's Vickers gun was convenient to hand against the port wall of the cockpit, the reservoir for the C.C. synchronising gear close beside it. The gun was covered by a panel which could be removed in a few seconds and the mounting was adjustable transversely and vertically. The ammunition box, holding 300 rounds, was between the rudder stirrups, and fed the belt up to the gun through a swan-neck extension. The gun was fired by pressing a milled lever on top of the hollow control column, and was sighted by a ring-and-bead sight mounted on a fore-and-aft tube over the cowling ahead of the windscreen.

The Fairey 'High-Speed' gun mounting, which was almost a basic feature of the Fox, in eliminating drag when stowed, comprised, according to its designers, 'a radius member angularly movable about the centre of an arcurate member, the said members being also movable together about a trunnion axis coincident with or parallel to the chord of the arc.' Further means were provided for locking the members against movement, and the gun was connected to the free end of the radius member by a universal joint. A more detailed description appears in this book under Fairey Gordon.

For the Lewis gun on the Fairey mounting, five double ammunition drums were provided. Also in the rear cockpit (starboard side) were the release quadrants and fusing levers for the bombs—two 230-lb or four 112-lb or eight 20-lb. These were released from the prone position, being sighted through a sliding panel in the floor immediately behind the attachment of the undercarriage radius rods. A folding seat enabled the prone position to be occupied. Conveniently to hand, on vibration-absorbing mountings, were an air speed indicator, altimeter, watch and inclinometer.

During 1930, when the Fox's operational career drew to a close, it was announced that No.12 Squadron, the only one armed with this aeroplane, had achieved the best bombing average in the Camera Obscura Exercise; that the same squadron had become the first to hold the Armament

155

Officers' Bombing Trophy; and that it was the top-scoring day-bomber squadron for the third successive year.

It does not appear to be widely known that the Fox (designated in Air Ministry orders as 'Fox Cranwell') served during 1932/33 for the dual instruction of 'day bomber Cadets'. Thus did the usefulness, as well as the example, of this historic aeroplane live on.

No photographs of the Fox were allowed to be published until some months after it had flown, although it was a private venture and was, of course, frequently seen. When it put in an unofficial appearance at Andover in the summer of 1925 one experienced war-pilot said: 'That's the first real aeroplane I've seen since the Albatros. And I always used to see those from the wrong end.'

Ferret The Ferret was a precursor of the IIIF and was first flown in 1925 as a three-seat fleet reconnaissance machine, also capable of carrying bombs. The pilot had a fixed Vickers gun mounted high on the starboard

On the two-seat general purpose version of the Fairey Ferret (*lower*) a Fairey 'High-Speed' mounting for the rear Lewis gun permitted vastly cleaner lines than were possible with the Scarff ring-mounting, seen fitted on the three-seat fleet reconnaissance version (*above*). The 'G.P.' Ferret is seen with two 250-lb bombs.

156

side of the fuselage with the breech casing virtually in the cockpit beneath the windscreen and the barrel jacket exposed above the fuselage. Provision was made for ring-and-bead and Aldis sights. The three separate cockpits were very closely set, and over the third was a wind-balanced Scarff ring-mounting for a Lewis gun. As tested at Martlesham, this Ferret had under-wing tubular carriers for two 250-lb bombs, set slightly inboard of the inner interplane struts. This same aeroplane, and certainly the two other Ferrets built, appears to have had additional strong-points for bomb attachment, and the maximum intended load of the type was evidently two 230/250-lb or four 112-lb bombs and four of 20 lb, the latter outboard to port. On the first machine, at one stage, there seems to have been a fuselage carrier. The third machine was laid out for general purpose duties and had a Fairey 'High-Speed' mounting instead of the Scarff ring-mounting. This machine was tested at Martlesham Heath with two 250-lb bombs.

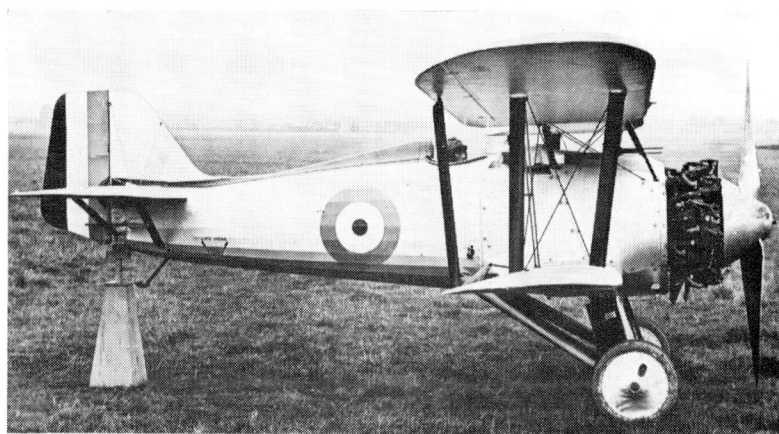

The fitting of a radial engine sometimes resulted in a far less tidy gun installation than was possible with a water-cooled unit. This is well illustrated by these comparative views of the Fairey Flycatcher II (*top*) and Firefly I. On the Flycatcher II the two Vickers guns are largely external above the cowling.

Firefly I   A companion type to the Fox, and a rival of the Hawker Horn-bill, Avro Avenger and Gloster Gorcock, this private-venture single-seat fighter of 1926 had its two Vickers guns installed in the manner of the single gun on the Fox. They were mounted with the breech casings in the cock-pit parallel with the centre line of the fuselage and fired through troughs extending almost to the nose. There were single ejection chutes, and exter-nally at least the installation was one of impeccable neatness. No sights appear to have been fitted for flight trials, but an Aldis sight was apparently intended.

Flycatcher II   In aerodynamic and structural essentials this intended metal-built replacement (1927) for the earlier wooden machine resembled the Firefly I; but it was radial-engined, and because of this, apparently, the guns were rearranged. They were transferred to the upper fuselage, a little above the pilot's shoulder level, and at first were largely external, the cooling jackets being exposed and the breech casings only partly faired. Thereafter the installation was much cleaned up, with the breech casings nicely faired and the cooling jackets lying in troughs. No sights appear to have been fitted to the aeroplane as test-flown.

Although fitted with a Scarff ring-mounting, this early Fairey IIIF presents a far neater appearance than the Gordon radial-engined development later illustrated. On the Gordon the Vickers gun was external.

IIIF   As first flown in 1926, the IIIF could fairly be described as a cleaned-up IIID, and even later developments differed relatively little except in structure. There were, however, points of interest concerning armament. The earliest production machines can be identified by the Scarff ring-mount-ing for the rear Lewis gun, but the great majority of subsequent aircraft for general purpose (two-seater) and Fleet Air Arm spotter reconnaissance (three-seater) duties had the Fairey 'High-Speed' mounting. The second prototype was apparently the first IIIF to have this fitting and calls for special comment in this regard. In order to afford the crew additional pro-tection (the Flycatcher had embodied a similar feature), but also to take the fullest advantage of the excellent streamline form made possible by the new mounting when retracted together with the gun, the sides of all three cockpits were fitted with sliding panels. These conformed to the fuselage shape, and when extended upwards did much to mitigate the 'bathtub' appearance associated with the IIIF (FAA). At least one other IIIF, the probable prototype of the IIIF (G.P.) two-seater, had a similar installation, as had the general purpose version of the Ferret.

In every IIIF constructed, the pilot's Vickers gun was identically positioned. Even the Jaguar (later Panther) engined machine which served as the Gordon prototype, as well as the experimental machine with geared Jupiter, had the gun similarly located—midway down the fuselage on the port side —though this was an external installation to clear the engine cylinders.

It may be remembered that the earlier Fairey multi-purpose aircraft, and in particular the IIID, did not have forward-firing guns; but in the IIIF the lack was made good with elegance, the installation resembling those previously made on the Fox and Firefly. The following is an Air Ministry note on the installation:

'The gun channel is formed of steel and is supported by three brackets secured to fuselage side struts Nos. 1, 2 and 3. The gun lid is held in the raised position by a spring clip fitted under the top longeron. The body of the gun is covered by a fairing panel which is humped to clear the gun projections and slotted to pass the cartridge and link chutes. A short cartridge chute is fitted to the bottom of the gun to deflect the empty cases through the fuselage fairing and clear of the aeroplane structure.'

Otherwise the standard IIIF armament installations were generally as later described for the Gordon.

Although it has been stated that IIIFs of one squadron at least were fitted to carry 500-lb bombs there appears to be no official documentary evidence that this was so, and certainly the normal load was four bombs of 112 lb or two of 230 lb or 250 lb, with four 20-pounders as sighters, as was customary at the period. The carriers for the larger bombs were of standard tubular type, the Universal pattern not having been introduced until the IIIF had been in service for some years.

Firefly II The most redoubtable opponent of the victorious Hawker Hornet (Fury) in the interceptor contest to the 1927 specification, this 1929 development of the Firefly biplane fighter series differed very considerably, though not in distribution of armament. The two Vickers guns were again mounted midway down the fuselage sides and fired through troughs, but there were two features of which the makers made a special point. One was the uncommonly good accessibility of the guns, by virtue of large side panels, allowing quick servicing and removal; the second was the fact that, by adopting a design of belt box with what Fairey called 'a twisted neck', the two guns were not staggered, as they had been, for example, in the original Flycatcher as supplied to the RAF. Aldis and ring-and-bead sights were provided as specified, the Aldis being wholly forward of the windscreen.

159

Armament and other details of the Fairey Firefly II interceptor fighter, with and without cowlings. In the upper view the Aldis sight is fitted.

Firefly III This naval counterpart of the Norn (Nimrod) appeared, like the Firefly II, in 1929, and was similarly armed, except that provision for four 20-lb bombs was made beneath the starboard lower wing.

Fox II–VII Like the Firefly II, the second mark of Fox light bomber (1929) came second best in open competition to a Hawker counterpart, in this instance the Hart. The sadness at Fairey was the greater because the requirements of the official specification were clearly based on the already established performance of the Fox I. And just as the company had ruefully compared the Fawn with the D.H.9A, so, with different intent, did they juxtapose the leading data for the wooden Fox I with Curtiss engine and the Fox Mk.II (Roll-Royce F.XIB). The dates of the respective tests were given as April 1926 and July 1930, and armament weight was quoted as 512 lb, comprising three 112-lb or two 230-lb bombs, a Vickers gun with 300 rounds and a Lewis gun with five double drums. The respective speeds at 15,000 ft were 140 mph and 145 mph and the range at a cruising speed of 125 mph almost identical (580 miles, 570 miles).

Armament provisions were essentially as for the Hart (q.v.), including the prone station for the bomb-aimer, but the Lewis gun was on a Fairey 'High-Speed' mounting. The four 112-lb bombs were carried side by side in pairs on tubular under-wing carriers. The rear-gun installation compared favourably in neatness of appearance (and doubtless in aerodynamic, if not fighting, efficiency) with the ring-encircled positions on the Hart and Antelope, the decking of the fuselage being taken very high and a windscreen provided for the gunner. The pilot had fuselage-mounted ring-and-bead sights, and for Martlesham tests the bead was immediately forward of the windscreen.

Adopted, like the Firefly II, by Belgium, the Fox II underwent extensive development. The Fox III had two front guns and Aldis sight; the Mk.VI likewise, and with the added benefit of a cockpit enclosure embodying a folding screen for the gunner; and the Mk.VII (Kangourou) single-seater had two additional guns fixed in the top wing, but no rear gun. A fuller account of Belgian developments is beyond the scope of this review.

Fleetwing The Fleetwing was first flown in 1929 and bore the same relationship to the Fox II as did the Osprey to the Hart (or, for that matter, the Firefly III to the Firefly II). It was unsuccessful in competition with the Osprey, but carried the same specified armament of one Vickers gun and one Lewis gun and four 20-lb bombs. The Vickers gun was mounted much as in the Fox II, but considerably higher, and the front lip of the rear cockpit was noticeably built up for gunner-protection. With development, this feature became even more pronounced. The mounting was of the Fairey 'High-Speed' type. The bomb-carrier was under the starboard wing. For Martlesham tests as a landplane, the Fleetwing had ring-and-bead sights only, but at Felixstowe, for trials on floats, an Aldis was also installed. Both types were intended to be standard.

161

A study in cockpit protection on Fairey two-seaters: *reading down*, original
Fleetwing; developed Fleetwing; Fox VI with canopy.

Gordon True, the Gordon, first flown in prototype form during 1930, was nothing more or less than a IIIF airframe re-engined with a Panther air-cooled radial; but it is nevertheless a type so well remembered, and so wholly representative of the RAF's general purpose class, that the production version of 1931 is accorded especially detailed treatment. An official account runs:

'The Gordon is a general purpose aeroplane fitted with a Panther Mark IIA engine. It differs from the latest type of IIIF Mark IVB all metal aeroplane only in the power plant, fuel and oil system, front fuselage, Vickers gun mounting and certain details in the layout of the electrical system . . . Armament for both offensive and defensive operations is carried. A Vickers ·303 in. air-cooled Mark II gun is fixed to the port side of the fuselage and a Mark III Lewis gun is mounted over the rear cockpit.'

Of the Vickers gun:

'The loading handle is carried on a rocking shaft mounted between bearings in the pilot's seat bearer and in a bracket on the gun. A quadrant adjustment is provided on the lever itself to suit the position of the lever to the requirements of the individual pilot. A short cartridge chute is fitted to the bottom of the gun to deflect the empty cases through the fuselage fairing and clear of the aeroplane structure. A small link chute is attached by two thumb screws to the side of the gun and the chute directs the links over the edge of the fuselage fairing.'

The foregoing official references to 'fuselage fairing' are at variance with the fact that the gun was externally mounted, and had short case and link chutes in common with other similar installations. It seems likely that the official compiler was working from a description of the Fairey IIIF. The account continues:

'The ammunition supply for the Vickers gun is carried in a metal box placed transversely across the fuselage beneath the pilot's feet. Owing to the body of the box being in this position the ammunition has to be lifted about 18 in. to reach the gun and is conveyed this distance along a built-up neck fixed to the port end of the box. The neck is rectangular in section, and, viewed from the front, is turned on a circular sweep to meet the gun feed chamber . . . The box is large enough to contain 600 rounds of ·303 in. S.A.A. in a belt, and on releasing the pins at the bottom of the neck and those on the bottom brackets, the body of the box can be withdrawn by being passed through the bottom of the fuselage; this facilitates the loading of the ammunition in the box.
'A ring-and-bead sight is used for the Vickers gun. The ring and the bead are mounted over the top of the fuselage on brackets with the bead just in front of the windscreen and the ring 18 in. further forward over the top main petrol tank. Each part of the sight has a screwed stem which

permits vertical adjustment and the stem for the bead passes through a slotted hole to give freedom for lateral setting.'

Of gun gear:

'The gear used is the Type C. single. The firing trigger is placed in the control column handle. The reservoir is placed in an inclined position on the starboard side of the pilot's seat . . . From the generator on the engine the main and secondary pipes are run together, being bound by whipcord, following the port bottom members of the fuselage structure . . . The fire control for the gear is a thumb-lever in the centre of the spade grip of the control column. This lever pulls a Bowden cable which is clipped to the control column and to a diagonal secondary strut under the seat . . .

'The Lewis gun is carried over the rear cockpit on a Fairey high speed gun mounting. This is a complete detachable component which fits over the rear part of the gunner's cockpit. The main support is given by the top longerons, each of which provides two connections. The main member of the mounting is a transverse steel tube which spans the longerons and has its ends held by clips. At each end of the tube is a quadrant and arm which lie inside and parallel to the longeron to which the arm is attached at its rear end. Between the quadrants an outer tubular member is placed over the transverse support tube on which it can rotate and can be fixed in any one of several positions by spring-loaded pins that engage holes in the quadrant framework. The ends of the outer tube are joined by a semi-circular ring which swings with the tubular member and is drilled with a series of holes. The position of the ring will therefore be determined by the pins that engage the side quadrants. At the centre of the transverse member an arm is pivoted, the arm lying against the semi-circular ring along which it is constrained to move by a sliding bearing. The position of the arm on the ring may be fixed by a spring-loaded pin that enters one of the holes of the ring. The arm is continued beyond the ring and its free end carries the Lewis gun, with the standard pin connection. Between the gun and the swinging ring a hand-grip is fitted to the arm, with a finger guard on one side and a release lever on the opposite side of the grip. The operation of the lever releases the locking pin in the ring and by means of cables inside the arm and transverse tube, it also releases the pins in the quadrants, thus freeing the mounting.

'The weight of the gun is counterbalanced by springs housed inside the mounting members. The spring for the elevating movement lies within a tube which forms the lower part of each quadrant arm, and the azimuth movement operates a spring inside the transverse tubular member. Each spring is adjustable for tension by turning a nut by a box spanner inserted in the ends of the spring housings.

'When the mountings are erected by the manufacturer, the springs are balanced and set to the correct tensions. If it becomes necessary to alter

164

Fairey Gordon with two 250-lb bombs on Universal carriers, showing also the external Vickers gun.

this setting, both springs of each pair must be altered by the same amount, which may be judged from the number of turns given to the adjusting nuts. The spring loads will tend to centralise the gun arm transversely and cause it to pass to its foremost position, i.e., the arm will swing from rear to front in elevation. When the mounting is in any other position the hand-grip release must not be operated unless there is a gun on the mounting. The ammunition is carried in six Mark II, No.2 magazines, each holding 97 rounds, five of the magazines being accommodated on pegs in the rear cockpit, with the remaining one on the gun. On the starboard side four pegs are arranged; the other peg will be found on the bulkhead separating the two cockpits.

'The total load of bombs which may be carried can be made up in several ways, the alternative loading being as follows:

Classification of loading	No of bombs	Nature of bombs
A	2	Bombs, H.E., 230 lb., or Bombs, H.E., 250 lb. and
	4	Bombs, H.E., 20 lb.
B	4	Bombs, H.E., 112 lb.
	4	Bombs, H.E., 20 lb.
C	16	Bombs, H.E., 20 lb.

The bomb carriers used for these loads are:

Nature of bomb	Type of carrier
Bomb, H.E., 230 lb.	Carrier, bomb, skeleton, tubular, 230 lb., Mark IIIF
Bomb, H.E., 112 lb.	Carrier, bomb, skeleton, tubular, 100 lb., Mark IIIF
Bomb, H.E., 20 lb.	Carrier, bomb, light series, Mark I

'The bomb loads are carried under the main planes. With loadings A and B, the large bombs are under the inner bays of the planes and the sighter bombs (H.E. 20 lb) are under the outer bay on the port side.

165

For the C type of loading the bombs are equally distributed on four carriers under the inner and outer bays on both sides.

'The bomb carriers are suspended from rails, which, in turn, are pinned to eyebolts fitted in the spars of the bottom main planes. The pins are made captive to the rails by short lengths of cable. A light series carrier requires two rails, but the skeleton tubular carrier is hung on one rail . . .

'The release of the bombs can be controlled from either of the cockpits, the observer adopting the prone position for the purpose, and the same type of control release gear is used in both cockpits. For the large bombs, which have to be fused before release, fusing levers are placed at the starboard side of the bulkhead between the cockpits, with a hole cut in the bulkhead to make the levers accessible to both pilot and observer. The pilot's control release is placed on the starboard seat with an upward pull and the observer's control is fitted on the starboard side of the bombing aperture in the floor with a horizontal pull, and is protected by a light detachable cover. The bomb control release combines the functions of selective, salvo, and light series releases.

'The observer is provided with a course setting bomb sight Mark VI, which is fitted with a duralumin flanged plate. The mounting, which is an aluminium alloy casting with two standard wedge strips screwed to its upper surface, is bolted to the port side of the bombing aperture in the floor. An air speed indicator and an altimeter are also fitted in the lower part of the cockpit, where they can be read from the prone position.

'A metal holster is provided on the starboard side of the pilot's cockpit to carry a pistol, signal, cartridge, $1\frac{1}{2}$ in., No.2, Mark I.'

It must be added that, although this official description indicates that the main bomb-carriers were of the old tubular skeleton type, the Universal pattern was later fitted.

And finally a short burst from C. G. Grey on seeing the Vickers-gun mounting:

'. . . they stick a gun out on the one side just at the most critical place in the evolution of the air-flow along the fuselage. The gun stands out on a platform big enough to hold a baby's bassinet . . .'

Seal The Seal was the three-seat fleet spotter reconnaissance Fleet Air Arm counterpart of the Gordon two-seat general purpose aeroplane, and as in the case of the Gordon, the prototype (1931) was a converted Panther-engined IIIF. The first production Seal was flown in 1932, and was a considerably different aircraft, not only from the prototype, but from the production Gordon. As in the IIIF (FAA) the crew comprised pilot, air gunner/telegraphist, and observer/bomb-aimer. An official document gives these details: pilot's gun, Vickers Mk.II with 600 rounds and ring-and-bead sight; rear gun, Lewis Mk.III on Fairey 'High-Speed' mounting;

bomb load (under wings) two 250-lb or four 100, 112 or 120-lb. Light Series carrier for four 20-lb or four 8½-lb practice bombs. Provision for G.3 camera gun on bottom starboard wing.

Points of interest here are the listing of the 100-lb bomb, revived at about this time for anti-submarine work, the new 120-lb bomb and the 8½-lb practice bomb.

Passing recognition must be accorded the fitting of a long-chord cowling over the Panther VI engine (non-standard in British Seals) and the resulting 'dimpling' necessitated by the front gun's line of fire. To record that this was a masterly piece of tin-bashing is enough.

Hendon I and II The Hendon twin-engined cantilever monoplane night bomber was taken into RAF service late in life. The prototype, with Jupiter engines, was first air-tested towards the end of 1930, and the same machine, re-engined with Kestrels, during the following year. The developed production version (Hendon II) entered service, on a restricted scale, in 1936. Thus the type was more or less contemporary with the Handley Page Heyford, and it may have been in a sense of emulation that Fairey claimed for it that it had no blind spot 'outside twenty feet from the aircraft', that no lowering of turrets was necessary, and that all gunners were visible to the pilot. Another undisputed virtue of the Hendon was that there was a catwalk from nose to tail, thus linking the gun positions in the nose, mid-upper position and extreme tail (behind the twin fins and rudders). To what extent this virtue stemmed from the Hendon's ability to carry 15–20 fully armed troops may be conjectured.

The Hendon is worth study for the deployment, protection and effectiveness of its crew and armament. As originally tested, the Hendon I had an enclosure for the pilot, though the gun positions were open and screened with folding panels. In the second version (Kestrels) the enclosure was deleted. Because of its troop-carrying propensity the Hendon's fuse-

'A masterly piece of tin-bashing': the Fairey Seal with Panther VI engine, having a dimpled long-chord cowling to clear the line of fire of the Vickers gun. Marine markers are attached to the under-wing bomb-carrier and the Lewis gun is raised from its well.

167

A further study in Fairey cockpit protection: the Hendon prototype with open crew-stations (*top*) contrasted with a production aircraft having enclosed nose turret, stepped-up enclosures for pilot and navigator, and rear gun positions with folding screens. (Lower picture, *Flight International*.)

lage was relatively broad-beamed at the top (it was of inverted-triangle section towards the rear) and problems in gunnery were evidently posed. These can be related to a special type of Fairey gun mounting 'for use in cases where it is necessary that a gun shall be capable of being sighted at will upon a target in substantially any position relative to the gun itself'. After a description had been given by the company of 'the common type of ring mounting' it was stated that the prime object of the new mounting was so to mount a gun as to enable it to be fired over the sides of a wide fuselage. It was explained:

'A gun is carried by a gun-mounting of circular-track design, i.e., two rings, of which the upper turns co-axially upon the lower, and this gun-ring, in addition to permitting rotary movement about its centre is mounted for bodily movement about a pivot pin arranged at the after part of the ring and at the central longitudinal vertical plane of the aircraft. At its forward part the gun-ring is provided with slides or rollers which support [it] on or in an arcurate track or guideway, curved about the pivot pin as a centre, so that said ring may be moved laterally of the aircraft to enable the gun to be fired vertically downwards over the side of the fuselage.'

On the Hendon the rings carried one Lewis gun each. The makers said of the gun installation:

'The gun mountings are of Fairey design and provision is made with each mounting for internal stowage of the gun while remaining on the mounting ready for action.'

They stated further:

'The form of construction employed allows access to the fuselage without the use of ladders; mechanics are thus able to install equipment, wireless and gun armament etc. in the minimum of time. The operation of the bomb hoist, the installation of the bomb fuses and setting of releases is carried out with ample room and is independent of other gear. Standard Universal bomb racks are used and are mounted inside the wing, the bombs dropping through hinged doors. These doors are kept closed by interchangeable lengths of shock-absorber cord. Access for loading is obtained by means of hinged flaps on the upper surface of the wing, and a loading winch is provided which enables the bombs to be hoisted into position in a reasonable time with a minimum of effort.'

In RAF service the Hendon carried a crew of five. There were tandem stepped-up cockpits for pilot and navigator and a transparent cupola in the nose position, incorporating a revised bomb-aimer's station with projecting circular panel. The bombs were sighted from the sitting position. Dorsal and tail-gun positions had sliding covers, and the gunners were protected from the air-stream by massive folding screens. The bomb load was given by the makers as 1,600 lb (possibly six 250-lb or twelve 112-lb). In service, Light Series carriers, for four sighter or practice bombs each, were attached externally behind the wheel fairings.

G.4/31 There was something reminiscent of the old Avro Aldershot bomber about this Fairey general purpose/torpedo-carrier, first flown in 1934, for it was a large single-engined biplane (though by no means as massive as the Aldershot), having internal, as well as external, crew accommodation, and seating the pilot behind the wings. For dive-bombing and torpedo-dropping the pilot was afforded a reasonable view by virtue of his high position and the pronounced fall-away of the nose ahead of him. Beneath the wings were six Universal carriers, the two inner ones taking 500-lb bombs and the outers 250-lb. Outboard of these (starboard) was a Light Series carrier. The torpedo, of course, would have been carried beneath the fuselage, though no cradle seems to have been actually in-

Like the Hendon, the Fairey G.4/31 in its first form had hinged-screen protection for the gunner, but in this instance the screen was transparent.

stalled. The pilot's fixed Vickers gun is not discernible in photographs, though the specification called for such a gun. The free Lewis gun was carried on a new type of Fairey retractable mounting, of the general type described under 'Battle'. There were two forms of the cockpit wherein this was emplaced. The first had deeply cutaway sides and a massive hinged transparent screen at the forward end to protect the gunner when operating the gun on the erected mounting; the second had a continuous top line.

S.9/30 Remarkable in allying the 'high-speed' upper-wing coolant condensers of the early Fox with the ample two-bay wing cellule of the T.S.R. machines, this fleet spotter reconnaissance biplane, first flown in 1935, was undistinguished in armament. The possible exception might be made that the pilot's Vickers gun was mounted not to starboard, as on the T.S.Rs, but to port, firing along a trough in the top cowling. The observer's Lewis gun was on a Fairey 'High-Speed' mounting, and under-wing strong-points were incorporated for bombs or marine pyrotechnics.

Fantôme (Féroce) The zenith of British fighter-biplane design was attained by the private-venture Fantôme of 1935. (The name Féroce was conferred later.) An entrant for the Belgian fighter competition promoted to find a successor to the Firefly II, it had provision for a French Hispano-Suiza 12Ycrs *moteur canon* with an Oerlikon 20-mm gun firing through the airscrew hub and four rifle-bore Browning guns, as made in Belgium by the Fabrique Nationale. The installation of these Brownings (only two of which were intended to be fitted in addition to the cannon), was of uncommon interest and neatness. Two were mounted in the upper fuselage forward of the cockpit and the other pair one in each lower mainplane,

170

The Fairey Féroce supplied to the RAF, showing Browning gun in lower wing, ejection chute for fuselage gun behind exhaust stubs, and port for gun above front stub.

the principal point of interest being that the fuselage guns, as well as those in the wings, were remotely controlled. The position of the fuselage guns is indicated in the photograph of the single RAF Féroce by the location of the ejection chutes a little aft of the forward centre-section bracing struts. The only additional evidence of the fuselage installation was twin ports in the upper cowling, extending rearwards only to the first pair of engine exhaust ports. The machine-guns were loaded and cocked pneumatically, compressed air also being used for the trigger motors of the wing guns and for the firing control of the fuselage guns. Gun-selector switches were fitted at the pilot's right hand, ring-and-bead sights were mounted on the fuselage centre line, and design provision was made for four 10-kg bombs.

In connection with the Fantôme, the Fairey company, already eminent in the field of aircraft armament, developed a pneumatic piston-and-cylinder device for actuating the loading handles of the Browning guns, this being so arranged that the handle was retained at the end of the outstroke of the piston by a detent, which was automatically released just before the piston reached the end of the return stroke.

Swordfish   Torpedo, mine, bomb, rocket projectile, gun: all these were the weapons of the Swordfish at one time or another, and with the exception of the R.P., which is beyond the chronological scope of this review, provisions for all will be described. But first a note on how the airframe design was influenced by operational considerations, especially the torpedo requirement. The makers declared:

'The pilot's view has been very carefully studied, and the centre-section struts have been brought to an inverted V in front of the windscreen.'

171

Respecting the torpedo, no caption is required for this picture of a pre-production Fairey Swordfish, the inscription on the nose being sufficient. Also seen are the Vickers gun and Aldis sight, and torpedo sighting-bar beneath the leading edge of the top wing.

Having laid claim to advantages for 'landing on' they continued:

'This arrangement is also particularly effective for the torpedo-dropping case. The centre-section has been designed and positioned to give the minimum interference during the dive down to the dropping height, when the strut arrangement gives a sighting view of the target which is completely free from obstruction.'

The prototypes of the Swordfish were the T.S.R. 1 and 2, of 1933 and '34

Swordfish floatplane with six 250-lb bombs and eight practice bombs on outboard carriers.

172

respectively. Beyond remarking that 'T.S.R.' signified the introduction of a new official category for Fleet Air Arm aircraft—torpedo-spotter-reconnaissance—it is unnecessary to give these machines any further attention, for their armament provisions were essentially the same as those which appeared on the production Swordfish (1936). The following makers' description was drawn up during, or shortly following, that year:

'Alternative bomb services are provided for six $\times$ 250 lb and four $\times$ 20 lb; two $\times$ 500 lb and four $\times$ 20 lb: or three $\times$ 500 lb. Bombs and torpedo are all released by electrically operated cartridge releases controlled by switches in the bomb-aimer's station and duplicated in the pilot's cockpit. Selector switches are provided for each bomb and a firing switch completes the circuits of all those pre-selected. At each station there is also provided a jettison switch which will release the whole load of bombs irrespective of the selector switches. Current for the bomb circuits is provided by an accumulator located on the floor of the observer's cockpit. Alternatively, the current can be obtained from

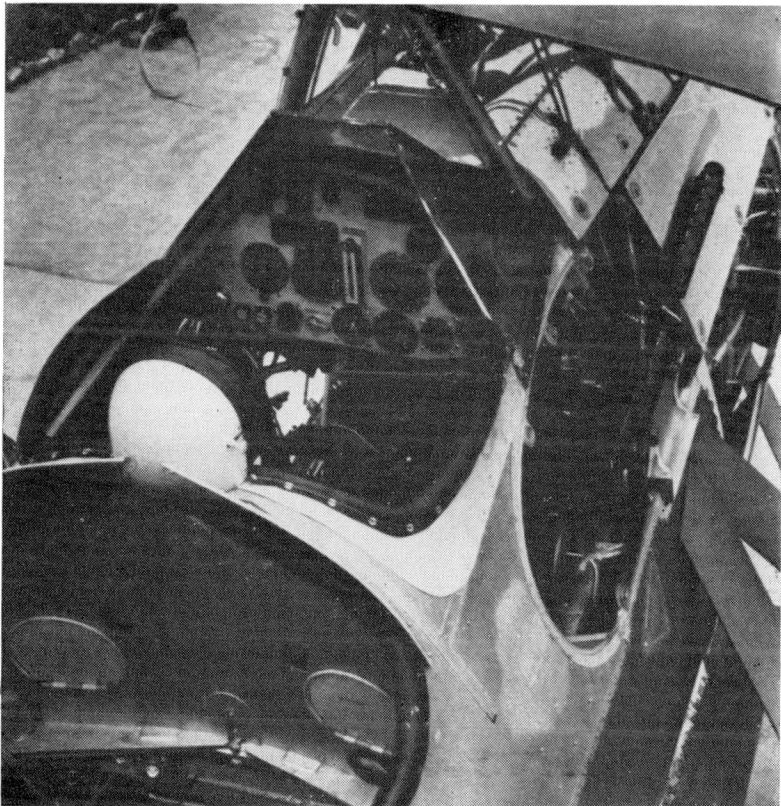

Pilot's cockpit of Fairey Swordfish, with Vickers gun to starboard. The access panel over the gun has been removed.

173

Rear cockpit of Swordfish with Fairey 'High-Speed' gun mounting and stowage-
well for gun.

the main electric services, a plug point for this being provided. Fusing
of bombs is also done electrically.

'The torpedo is carried below the centre of the fuselage and is held up
against two crutches by twin support wires or slings. The sling wires are
anchored at one end to the fuselage structure—one on each side, the
other ends being held by release units. Both units are operated simultaneously, releasing the slings and the torpedo. The release switches for
the torpedo are located with the bomb switches. A manual release is also
provided for the torpedo. It consists of a hand lever located at the left
of the pilot. Provision is made for heating the torpedo, the current for
this being provided by a separate generator which is attached to an
undercarriage strut and driven by a windmill.

'The Vickers front gun is placed at the pilot's right hand in an accessible position, and is fed from an ammunition magazine which is stowed
in the centre of the cockpit between his knees. A map case is attached to
the rear face of the magazine. Also to the pilot's right is the C.C.
reservoir handle.

'The Lewis type rear gun is carried on a Fairey High-Speed Mounting
which allows the gun to be stowed away in the top rear fairing. A slid-

ing shutter is fitted below the gun mounting. This can be rolled up and over the mounting to cover it when not in use.'

Not mentioned on this occasion was the fact that the spare ammunition drums were stowed on the gun-mounting decking, one on each side of the gun, and others near at hand. The torpedo sight-bars extended laterally to the plane of the inner wing-bracing struts. They were attached to two forward-sloping struts, set at the same angle as the two front struts of the aircraft's characteristic pyramidal centre-section cabane which carried the leads for illuminating the sight-bar at night. The ring sight was fixed to the top wing, and the bead was on a horizontal post fixed to the port front centre-section strut. An Aldis sight was sometimes fitted to starboard, slightly ahead of the windscreen.

The Swordfish was one of two types of aircraft available at the coming of war to carry mines, these being dimensioned for the standard torpedo crutches. The other type was the Bristol Beaufort. Under-wing rails for eight 25-lb A.P. or 60-lb H.E. rocket projectiles were a later fitment. In addition to the bombs mentioned earlier the Swordfish carried 40-lb bombs during the war.

Finally it must be noted that there is a recorded instance of a revolver having been used from the rear cockpit of a Swordfish against an Italian fighter.

Battle Welcomed though it was under the Expansion Scheme, the Battle single-engined medium bomber (for such was its original classification) proved deficient in performance and armament for the tasks it was called on to perform in war. This, however, cast no blame on the makers. Like the B.E.2c a quarter-century before, its operations were often conducted beyond the call of duties imposed but not foreseen. As with the B.E., armament was improvised in war. As originally built for the RAF, the Battle (first flown 1936) answered to the following contemporary account by the makers:

'The cabin houses the bomb-aimer for whom full equipment is installed, including a chest pad for use in the prone position. In the centre of the floor, forward, is the bomb-aimer's aperture which is normally closed by a sliding shutter. Provision is made for the bomb-aimer's equipment to be available for use in the prone bombing position.' (This apparently signified that his instrument panel was in front of him.) 'Equipment is provided for a third man to act as navigator when required. Aft of the cabin and yet an integral part of it is the rear cockpit which is used by air gunner or wireless operator. The transparent hooding over this end is hinged at each side so that it can be rotated up and forward to form an effective wind shield. A swivelling seat is placed in the rear cockpit and this can be elevated or depressed on releasing its locking catch by a hand lever attached to the assembly.

'Front gun: The gun body and ammunition box are located between the spars with the barrel of the gun projecting in a blast tube through the spar and leading edge. A container for empty cartridge cases and links is fitted in line with the gun and beneath it, while abreast of it and on its port side is the ammunition box with a capacity of 400 rounds. The box is held in position by release pins and shipped through an aperture in the underside of the wing normally closed by a hinged cover. Through this opening also the gun itself is mounted and maintained. Firing of the gun is effected by means of a pneumatically operated trigger motor, fed by pipe line from the air reservoir and controlled by a press button on the pilot's control column hand grip.

'A Lewis gun is carried in the rear of the fuselage on a mounting which allows the whole installation to be stowed away in the top fuselage fairing behind the rear cockpit. Pegs for ammunition drums are placed on the sides of the gunner's cockpit while a swivelling seat is provided for the gunner.

'Bombs are carried on racks or carriers which are located within the thickness of the main planes, in cells formed by spaces between the spars and ribs . . . there is a small cell for the light series carriers. The cells are covered by double doors to each cell, hinged downwards from the ribs. In the case of the main cells the bomb carriers on each plane are supported by a central hydraulic jack which lowers the racks for loading and then retracts them complete with bombs into the cells. Link gear attached to the carriers operates the doors so that these are opened as the carriers are lowered. Electric switches in the release circuits of the bombs and operated by the action of the carriers prevent the releasing of a bomb before the doors are opened or the racks are lowered. The light series bomb racks are rigidly attached to the plane but the doors in their case are opened by a separate small hydraulic jack coupled directly to the doors. The light series racks are normally used for flares, two being fitted in each cell port and starboard. Ground equipment is provided for loading bombs, while their release is effected electro-magnetically. An additional external rack on each plane can be carried when required, lugs being provided for these.'

Briefly stated, the bomb load was 1,000 lb (1,500 lb overload). The makers explained:

'Bomb loading schemes: 4 reconnaissance flares Mk.I, 4-250 lb bombs, internally stowed; 2-250 lb bombs on external carriers and 2-500 lb bombs mounted externally on internal carriers; six bombs—any arrangement from types 100 lb, 112 lb, 120 lb or 250 lb.

'Provision is made for carrying an external universal bomb carrier, No.1, port and starboard. Bombs are fused and released electro magnetically.

'The mounting for the camera gun is in the starboard main plane below the Vickers gun. The shutter of the gun is operated pneumatically.'

The special Fairey gun mounting fitted to the Battle was described as a stowable mounting in which the gun-support post was turned down about a transverse axle to collapse the mounting within the fairing, the post also carrying a toothed sector over which the post was movable to one side or the other of its mid position. In order to compensate for the weight of the gun during its movement over the sector, levers were engaged by the post to stress a spring from either end according to which side the gun was moved. The teeth of the sector permitted locking the gun in its adjusted position by a bolt operated by a Bowden cable. During this adjustment the training pivot of the gun was kept vertical by its connection with a link forming part of a parallelogram linkage. To stow the gun, toggle-links supporting the post were broken by operating a hand lever; this moved a cam lever with which was associated a hook for locking the gun in its stowed position. The mounting was turned down through a slot into a barrel-shaped container, the radial arms of which were supported on brackets so that the barrel could be rotated through 90 degrees to invert the mounting and close the opening in the fairing.

To the original Fairey description of the Battle's armament quoted earlier the following notes may be added:

The hydraulic jacks mentioned in connection with the internally stowed bombs could be used not only for the loading of the bombs but for their transference into free air for dive-bombing attacks. In place of the external Universal carriers mentioned, two Light Series carriers for practice bombs were generally fitted. The pilot had a bomb-release switch. For the pilot's Vickers gun there were ring-and-bead sights. The Lewis gun was latterly superseded by the Vickers G.O. In stress of war an additional gun of this type was mounted well below the belly of the aircraft in line with the wing trailing edge. This had a small angular movement and was remotely oper-ated. Sighting was done by means of a mirror, in conjunction with a ring-and-bead. The Germans were impressed by the extent of armour-plating (about 4 mm thickness), arranged to give protection from the front, rear and below (for low attack).

Later in the war the Battle was adapted as a 'turret trainer', with a Bristol Type I Mk.III turret modified to incorporate a 'break-out' panel.

Seafox The *Graf Spee* action, wherein a Seafox catapulted from the cruiser HMS *Ajax* made a telling contribution to the destruction of the German battleship, is the event by which this twin-float seaplane, first flown in 1936, will be remembered. Otherwise it was undistinguished in achievement, though distinctive in character. Being intended as a 'light reconnaissance' aircraft solely for cruiser operation, it carried no front gun, though the observer/gunner had a Lewis gun on a special Fairey rocking-pillar mounting. His station was provided with a hinged canopy. Pegs were fitted for six double drums of ammunition. Under each wing could be attached a Universal No.1 carrier for a 100-lb anti-submarine bomb. Other possibilities were eight 20-lb bombs or eight smoke floats. Bomb-release and fusing was electro-magnetic.

The observer/gunner of the Fairey Seafox was well protected. The objects beneath the wings are not in this instance bombs but marine markers.

P.4/34 A latter-day Fox in all respects, this most elegant of British bombers up to its time (1936) was in competition with the Hawker Henley; but although the Henley was ordered in quantity, it never served in the role for which these two fine aeroplanes were intended—namely high-speed day bombing (including dive-bombing) with a bomb load up to 1,000 lb. The Fairey machine was of particular interest because, although the rival Henley had internal stowage for its main bomb load in its deep

Extreme neatness characterised the gunner's enclosure on the Fairey Battle (*top*) and P.4/34. The Battle prototype is shown; production machines differed in detail. Two 250-lb bombs are seen under the starboard wing of the P.4/34.

fuselage, the Fairey designers elected to preserve the lines of an extremely slender body by carrying the bombs externally under the wings. This practice, it might be supposed, was no advance on the Fox of 1925, and yet it was, for, although the bombs themselves were exposed to the airstream, the carriers were snug inside the wing. A photograph reproduced is evidence that only the crutches were external. This system was not only intrinsically neat, but it allowed dive-bombing without the complication of ejector gear. The pilot sat just behind the leading edge and had a Vickers or Browning gun set in the starboard wing and provided with pneumatic control and ring-and-bead sights. The bead was attached to the engine-cowling structure and the ring to the pilot's windscreen. Over the trailing edge was the station for the gunner/W.T. operator/prone bomb-aimer. His cockpit enclosure was flush with the fuselage top line and had a rotating hood, the hinge pins being in a horizontal plane. A Lewis gun was the rear armament, and this, according to one pronouncement based on official information, had a 'deflector sight'. (It will be grasped that 'reflector' was intended; and yet the evident misprint has a coincident authenticity in the context of gun-laying deflection.) The mounting for the rear gun was of the type installed on the Battle, and when not in use formed part of the fuselage fairing.

Albacore Emphasis was placed in the design requirements for this intended successor to the Swordfish on dive-bombing capability. This was not only achieved but was duly exploited in war, wherein the Albacore

Fairey Albacore, with the characteristic curved torpedo sighting bar forward of the windscreen and pillar-mounted bead sight.

became recognised not as a Swordfish successor but rather as a companion type. The first Albacore was flown in 1938. Pilot-view, so vital in torpedo-dropping and dive-bombing, was exceptional. The pilot sat in line with the wing leading edge and immediately in front of his windscreen was the torpedo-sight bar, curved in plan, with the bead sight mounted sturdily before it on a faired pillar. The pilot's fixed Browning gun was in the upper starboard wing. The gunner was over the trailing edge at the rear of a lengthy enclosure, the final segment of which hinged upwards for gunnery as on the Battle. The Battle-type pillar mounting carried a Lewis or Vickers G.O. gun (occasionally twin G.O. guns). The torpedo-carrier was similar to that of the Swordfish, and, as alternatives to the torpedo, six 250-lb or four 500-lb bombs could be carried under the lower wings. Light Series carriers were fitted outboard.

Fulmar   As soon as the P.4/34 appeared (and doubtless before) the remark was frequently passed in comprehending circles that it should make an excellent fighter. Its high all-round performance was obviously much in its favour and the slender lines of the fuselage, as already remarked, were uninhibited by internal bomb-stowage. It came to pass in 1939 that this aeroplane was, in fact, developed as a naval carrier-borne fighter, a counterpart of the RAF's Hurricane and Spitfire in its intended employment, but hampered in agility by a necessary navigator, and, by reason of its greater size and weight, slower than the shore-based single-seaters. As Terence Horsley, who knew the type well enough, remarked in his book *Find, Fix and Strike*, 'It merely lacked the fighter's first essential—speed. Unless the pilot's first burst made a kill, he rarely got a second chance.'

The eight Browning guns were installed in two compact batteries of four, well outboard, and staggered as in the Hurricane. The pilot had a reflector sight. A Light Series bomb-carrier was sometimes fitted beneath the starboard wing, and as a wartime emergency measure a Vickers G.O. gun was mounted in the rear cockpit.

Felixstowe

Porte Baby   The design of this three-engined flying-boat dated back to 1916, and during its existence the craft was used for some notable armament experiments. Thus, a 6-pdr Davis recoilless gun was fitted in the bows, and on another occasion two 14-in torpedoes were slung one beneath each lower wing. The effectiveness of machine-gun armament was restricted by hull-form and construction, but hatchway or window guns may well have been intended or installed behind the cockpit.

The carrying of a fighter aeroplane (Bristol Scout) on the top wing, and a successful launching in flight, is a further distinction to the credit of this early flying-boat, and one which may fairly be included under the heading of 'armament'.

F.2A Extraordinary technical and military qualities were possessed by this most famous of the 'Felixstowe boats' and only in comparatively recent years have these qualities received full recognition. Dating from 1917, the F.2A had an armament of Lewis guns concentrated in the forward part of the hull and at the waist. Typically, there was a Scarff ring-mounting in the bow for one or twin-yoked guns. This was sometimes, perhaps generally, of the familiar No.2 pattern, though there is some evidence to suggest that in a few instances a type of Scarff ring-mounting wherein the quadrant moved with the gun-carrying 'bow', and was invisible when the bow was at its lowest position, may have been fitted. This type of mounting, which will be mentioned again in connection with the Handley Page O/400 and which will be shown in official drawings in Volume 2, was one of several mountings designed by F. W. Scarff. Sometimes the F.2A had a pillar-mounted Lewis gun on top of the pilot's cock-

In this view of F.2A number 8677 a man is obstructing the waist hatch. Clearly, however, the mounting above the hatch is not of the Scarff No.2 type, and there is doubt, moreover, if the mounting in the bow is of this pattern. Even the Lewis guns appear non-standard. Beneath the wing is a flat-nosed 230-lb anti-submarine bomb. (*Imperial War Museum.*)

pit canopy; there was a single Lewis gun at each waist hatch behind the wings; and atop the hull in this same area was another gun, or sometimes twin-yoked guns. In some instances at least the waist guns appear to have had the Scarff compensating sight. The pillar carrying each gun was mounted at the outer ends of two superimposed struts, braced to an inboard member and allowing the assembly to be swung outboard. There was under-wing provision for two 230-lb bombs just outboard of the attachments of the wing/hull bracing struts, the carrier being stayed to the wing inboard. One experimental F.2A had two 'howdah' or 'fighting-top' gun-nacelles, each with twin-yoked Lewis guns on a Scarff ring-mounting at its forward end, built on to the upper wing. These guns further broadened an already commanding field of fire; for, compared with the H.12 type of boat, the F.2 was well endowed in this regard, having a 'cocked-up' rear hull which permitted the midships beam guns to be swung outboard on their pillars so that their lines of fire could meet little more than twenty feet astern.

For comparison with the Sunderland, and with flying-boats between, this contemporary description of accommodation and battle stations is offered:

'A gunner is located immediately below the fore gun-ring, and a table for his use extends from his seat to the nose of the hull. Underneath the table is an ammunition box and trays . . . Abaft is the station for the pilot and assistant pilot . . . Their seats are well upholstered with kapok cushions, which act as lifebuoys if required. The assistant-pilot's seat is made to hinge, so that a clear passage may be obtained for walking fore and aft. A few feet behind the pilot is the wireless cabinet, with operator's seat, while at the port side of this a ration box is fitted. The engineer's accommodation is situated aft, with a ladder giving access to the top deck. Further aft is the second gun ring, with an adjustable platform to allow a gunner to have a good range of heights . . .'

In a photograph showing an F.2A built by the Aircraft Manufacturing Co, the sights on the beam gun are mounted on an arm on the gun's left side, with an eye-piece for the rear component. The forward gun, on its Scarff No.2 ring-mounting, does not have Norman vane-type sights, but apparently a form of ring-and-bead sight mounted laterally on the gun's axis.

F.2C One experimental installation on this F.2A development was a compressed-air bomb-release system, eliminating the usual Bowden cable, but introducing its own problems of complexity and reliability. Only one F.2C was built. Flown by Wg Cdr J. C. Porte, to whom the greatest honour is due for developing the F-boats, this shared with two other machines of the same formation in the destruction of a submarine.

Although in this picture of an F.5 the guns and mountings are not installed it affords an excellent idea of the fields of fire possible with the beam guns, mounted at the sliding hatches amidships.

F.3 and F.5   Emphasis was placed, in the arming of these two flying-boats (1917 and 1918 respectively), upon anti-submarine operations, and the bomb load was accordingly increased to four 230-lb bombs. Machine-gun deployment was much as on the F.2 boats, the standard arrangement, as shown in an official publication on the F.5, being single Lewis guns at bow, dorsal and beam positions. No installation of a Davis gun or other heavy ordnance is known to have been made on a British F.3 or F.5, although interest in such armament was very much alive at this period and the American-built F.5 had an installation of the Davis gun. One Lion-engined F.5 for Japan is said to have had a revised bow cockpit for a '1-pounder shell-firing gun'.

Fury   The armament potential of this very large flying-boat triplane (1918) does not appear to have been fully realised; nor is it likely that this was of primary concern during development flying. Provision was made for at least four Lewis guns.

Gloster

Nightjar   A Bentley-engined Nieuport Nighthawk development for carrier operation, the Nightjar (1922) had its two Vickers guns mounted externally on brackets projecting from the fuselage sides, outboard of the centre-section struts and at the level of the cockpit coaming. Aldis and ring-and-bead sights were bracketed to the wing centre-section.

On the Gloster Sparrowhawk the two Vickers guns were of wartime pattern (Class C) and were largely faired.

Sparrowhawk   Contemporary counterpart of the Nightjar for Japan, this fighter had its Vickers guns moved inboard of the centre-section struts. The guns were largely faired by a 'hump' at the rear, the ejection chutes lying flush with the fairing.

Jupiter-Nighthawk and Jaguar-Nighthawk   These more powerful Night-hawk developments of 1922/24 were not always armed, some being engine-development aircraft, but Jaguar-engined machines for Greece and the RAF had their two Vickers guns positioned as on the Sparrowhawk, though without fairings.

Grebe   The Grebe appeared in 1923 as a new Jaguar-engined single-seat fighter for the RAF. On the two prototypes the two Vickers guns were carried on brackets, or 'cradles', close in to the windscreen. For trials at Martlesham Heath, dummy guns were fitted and partial fairings were tried. On these prototypes the Aldis (port) and ring-and-bead (starboard) sights were attached to the top wings (there was no centre-section on the Grebe). The case chutes, in the fuselage sides, were considerably lower than the link chutes. Ammunition supply was 1,200 rounds. A weight breakdown

184

listed the gun mountings at 10 lb, and guns, ammunition, sights and C.C. gear at 170 lb.

On production Grebes the guns were almost wholly exposed, and external link chutes were a prominent feature. The sights were now attached to the fuselage. Notwithstanding the exposed nature of the installation, it was claimed:

> 'The machine guns are housed inside the fuselage fairings, so that the pilot can change his ammunition drums (*sic*) and generally attend to his guns without having to put his hands over the side, which, at the high speeds and great altitudes attained, would quickly become numbed with cold.'

This was doubtless a sniping shot at the fuselage-side arrangement on the Fairey Flycatcher and Hawker Woodcock. In service, carriers for four 20-lb or practice bombs were fitted under each wing; this was an alternative arrangement to a single carrier under the fuselage. The Grebes for New Zealand had built-up fairings round the guns and rails for a bomb-carrier under the fuselage.

On the Gloster Grebe the guns were of Class E type, with small-diameter jackets, and were largely exposed.

185

In this vivid study of Gloster Grebes the carriers for four 20-lb bombs are seen under each wing. Guns, sights and chutes are also in evidence. (*Flight International.*)

Gamecock The Gamecock appeared in 1925 as a development of the Grebe, having the Bristol Jupiter instead of the Armstrong Siddeley Jaguar engine. The Jupiter was of considerably larger diameter than the Jaguar, and the roomier fuselage associated with it allowed a complete redesign of the gun installation. When the Gamecock appeared in the New Types Park at Hendon it was remarked:

'The machine-gun mounting appears to be in the nature of a victory for the aircraft designer over the Air Ministry equipment expert. In a large number of recent British war machines the synchronised guns have been carried beside the pilot, and outside the fuselage, in the interests of accessibility. It has been held necessary that the pilot should have both the room and the light to change a complete lock in the air, if necessary, and a position for the breech of the gun just alongside the seat is apparently considered to be the best for this particular purpose. As there is usually not a great deal of room inside the fuselage the gun has been fitted outside in a good many cases. In the Gamecock the guns are mounted inside a fairly large-diameter body in the required position, and their muzzles brought out into grooves recessed in the sides of the body with their lines of fire close in to the crankcase and between the pairs of cylinders of the Jupiter engine. Indeed, there seems no reason why the resistance should not further be reduced by sticking a piece of fabric over the gun-tunnels, and allowing the gun to shoot its own bullet exit through the fabric.'

This last remark appears to be a valid one, for the drag created by the deep troughs, or tunnels as the commentator chose to call them, must have been considerable. There was at least one instance of the troughs being faired over for racing.

The comments made when the Gamecock made its first appearance at Hendon—a rare instance of a lively journalistic interest in armament—

186

might have been even more *à propos* had they pointed out that it was impossible to fire between the cylinders of a fourteen-cylinder radial engine, as fitted to the Grebe.

An official Air Publication, issued after the Gamecock had entered service in 1926, referred to 'two fixed ·303-in Vickers guns, synchronised by C.C. gear', and described their installation in some detail. Each gun mounting, it was said, was braced at its front end by a recoil tube, carried across to the bottom of a bulkhead. The mounting was built up of steel plates in the form of a trough, in which the gun fitted, and this was attached to two bulkheads. The gun was held in position by two pins, one at the front end of the mounting and the other towards the rear end. The rear end of the mounting was supported by a saddle plate on the projecting portion of a bulkhead, and between the mounting and the saddle plate

The Gloster Gamecock, the prototype of which is shown, was a Jupiter-engined Grebe development with a completely revised gun installation, as seen.

aluminium shims were used to give the correct vertical alignment of the gun. The lateral alignment was effected by an adjusting screw which engaged a nut brazed on to the inner flange of the mounting. The lid of each gun, when lifted, could be held in the raised position by engagement with a spring clip attached to the top longeron. The clip was so shaped that the lid snapped into position. Further extracts are now quoted verbatim:

'The two guns are fed with ·303-in Mark VII ammunition, which is stored in two ammunition boxes, one for each gun, and each box contains 600 rounds. Each box is a separate unit, but the two are bolted together, and in this form they span the width of the fuselage. The top of each box has a lid which is in two portions separately hinged, so that either one or both portions of the lid may be lifted. The smaller lid covers the exit of the ammunition belt, and the larger one gives access to the body of the box. Both the hinges are secured by draw pins, the end of each pin being bent back to lie over the lid, to which it is held by

187

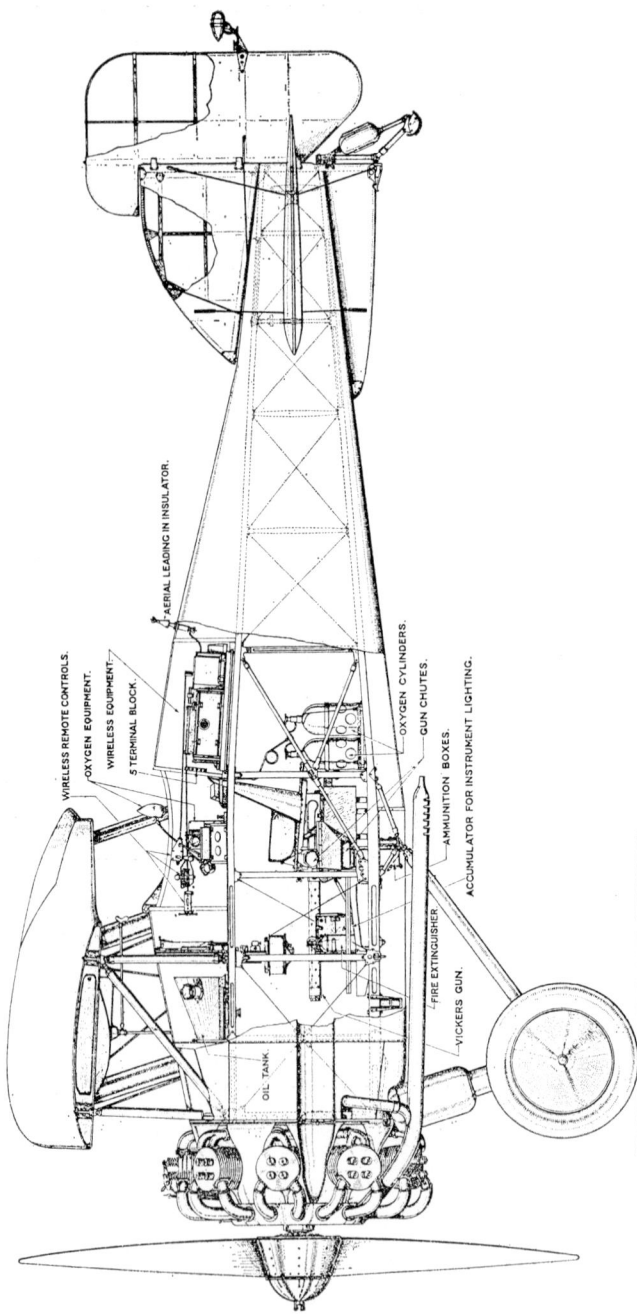

WIRELESS REMOTE CONTROLS.

OXYGEN EQUIPMENT.

WIRELESS EQUIPMENT.

5 TERMINAL BLOCK.

AERIAL LEADING IN INSULATOR.

OXYGEN CYLINDERS.

GUN CHUTES.

AMMUNITION BOXES.

ACCUMULATOR FOR INSTRUMENT LIGHTING.

FIRE EXTINGUISHER

VICKERS GUN.

OIL TANK.

Distribution of Service equipment, including Vickers guns, on Gloster Gamecock.

188

a spring clip. The ammunition belt is fed from the box through a rectangular aperture in the top outer corner. This portion of the box is shaped to a radius of 1·5 in. and the bearing face for the belt is covered with a steel liner. The front and rear faces of the belt exit are fitted with a lip which engages the feed block.

'The empty cartridge cases from each gun are conveyed to the outside of the aeroplane by means of a cartridge chute. This is connected over the ejector chamber at the bottom of the gun, and is slightly curved to provide a smooth path for the fall of the cartridge cases. The top edge of the chute is padded with felt which forms a bearing against the inside faces of the gun-mounting flanges. The link chute which is attached to each gun carries the disintegrated links from the gun to the outside of the fuselage. The link chute is connected to the gun by means of a flange plate, the bolts used for this purpose being locked by wire, after they have been tightened.

Gamecock in RAF service with Vickers guns and ring sight fitted. Compared with the prototype the link chutes (uppermost of the two apparent) are of modified form, and there are other differences in detail.

189

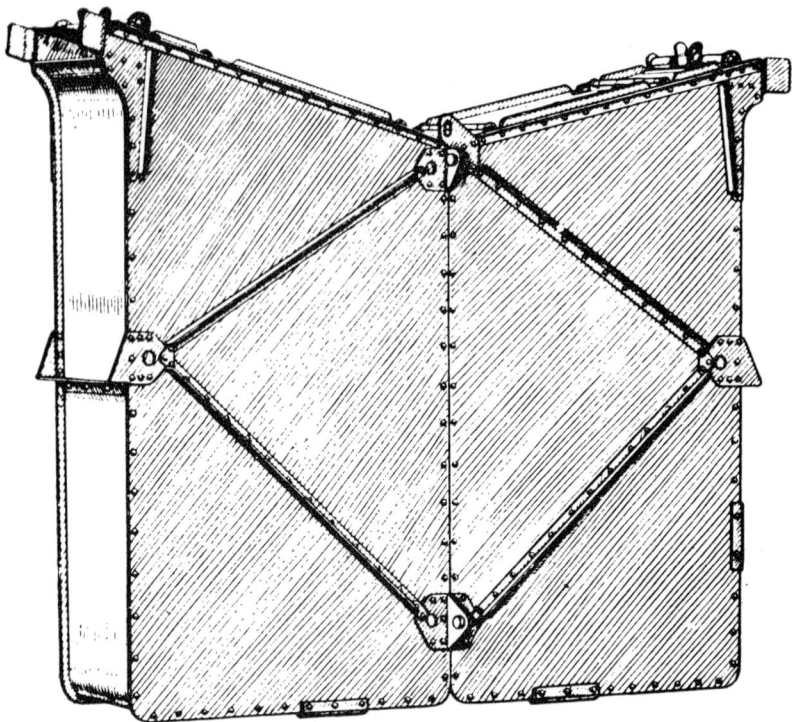

Belt boxes for Vickers guns of Gloster Gamecock.

'Two sights are provided for use with the guns, the Aldis sight, and the ring and bead sight. The positions of the sights are interchangeable, but the normal position of the Aldis sight is over the centre line of the fuselage, and that of the ring and bead sight on the starboard side of the fuselage. The Aldis sight is carried in two clips, one at each end, each lined with a leather strip. Each clip is in two portions held together by bolts. When the sight is fixed, its centre line must be parallel to the centre line of the aeroplane both in side view and in plan view. To allow the sight to be correctly set, adjustment in side view is provided by a screw thread on the studs that support the clips, while the correct setting in plan is obtained by moving the stud of the front clip in a transverse slot in the front bracket.

'The two portions of the ring and bead sight are mounted on screwed studs, similar to those used by the Aldis sight, and the supporting brackets are fixed to similar parts of the fuselage.

'The Aldis sight, in its normal position, necessitates the use of a special windscreen in which is cut a hole to pass the body of the sight and make the rear end accessible to the pilot.

190

'Provision is made to carry four bombs under the fuselage. The bombs are slung from a light series bomb carrier which in turn is suspended from special fittings on the fuselage members. Channel shaped members are carried between the fittings; the bomb carrier is connected to the channel members. The release mechanism for the bomb gear is actuated through a cable by a bomb release control, situated on the port side of the cockpit. Two types of release control are provided for; one— which is usually adopted—consisting of a lever moving in a quadrant with a stranded cable connection to the carrier. The other release is of the 'toggle' type and operates the release gear on the carrier through a length of Bowden cable . . .'

Concerning heating and lighting it was stated:

'The Mark VII switchbox in the cockpit contains six switch units which control the following services: gun heater, wing tip flares, navigation lights, body, hands, feet. The gun heater switch is No. 1 on the switch box, and another gun switch unit is fixed lower down the side of the cockpit'.

The control column was described as a brass tube, fitted at the top with a circular handgrip, bound with cord, and embodying two short levers for the operation of the guns.

On the first Gamecock the gun troughs (or, in this instance, perhaps, 'channels', their mountings themselves having been likened to troughs in the official notes) were carefully faired in at the rear, and similar, though not identical, treatment was applied on the later Mk.III variant. The 'channels' on RAF Gamecocks were of such depth that squadron markings were painted clean across them.

A G.3 camera gun was fitted on the lower starboard wing of RAF machines.

It may finally be remarked of the Gamecock that it represented a notable advance in gun accessibility; there were large detachable panels covering the whole of the gun-mounting area and incorporating slots for the ejection chutes.

Gorcock and Guan The Lion-engined Gorcock fighters and the turbo-supercharged Guan dated from 1925, and though their guns were disposed as in the Gamecock, local differences in fuselage and cowling shape caused variations. Points of interest were the prominent 'blister' or 'teardrop' fairing on the starboard side of Gorcocks, giving the pilot better access to the loading handle of the gun, and the fitting on the 'high-altitude' Guan of the standard bomb-carrier under the fuselage. Ammunition capacity (1,200 rounds) remained undiminished on these machines.

Gambet The Gambet was a naval development of the Gamecock, built in 1926. Standard Gamecock armament was retained.

Showing how features of the installation of the starboard Vickers gun on the Gloster Gorcock (*top*), were reproduced in the Gauntlet. As explained in the text, the bulge in the cowling was for a different purpose in each case. (Lower picture, *Flight International*.)

Goring This two-seat day bomber was completed in 1928 and was flown both as a landplane and as a seaplane. The pilot, who sat well forward, below the trailing edge, had a Vickers gun let in to the fuselage on the port side, and for this there were ring-and-bead sights. Over the gunner's cockpit, somewhat removed to the rear, was a wind-balanced Scarff ring-mounting with one Lewis gun. This commanded an excellent field of fire by virtue of the small cross-section of the fuselage—small enough, indeed, to necessitate a slight 'lip', on which the ring was partly mounted. One Gloster document mentioned a gun firing through the floor, but in any case there was a prone bombing position, lit by a window on the port side. From here auxiliary rudder control was possible. Tubular bomb carriers were fitted under the wings. Bomb loads were given as four 112-lb, two 230/250-lb or sixteen 20-lb. The observer's seat was fitted with rollers at each end, running in channels fixed to the sides of the fuselage. This seat was held in the lowered position by a bolt, which, when released, allowed the seat to be 'shot into a concealed position out of the way of the observer, thus giving him full freedom for fighting'. It was further stated:

'Ailerons and elevators are operated by a very short control column, which is pivoted to the elevator cross-shaft by a compact universal joint designed so as not to obstruct the bomber when in the prone position below the pilot. Instead of the normal type rudder bar two stirrups are provided, each mounted on a pair of fore-and-aft steel-tube slides. The arrangement provides the pilot with a clear view of the bomber.'

The Gloster Goring as a floatplane, showing under-wing installation of two 250-lb bombs on tubular carriers. (*Flight International*.)

Goral The Gloster entry in the competition for a new RAF general purpose aircraft won by the Westland Wapiti, the Goral was built in 1928. Though generally resembling the Wapiti (especially in wing cellule) it had a fuselage of somewhat finer lines, and though the pilot's Vickers gun was exposed it lay in a trough at the upper port side of the cockpit, the case chute being a short distance down the fuselage side. The wind-balanced Scarff ring-mounting for the Lewis gun was close behind the pilot, at the forward end of an angular structure built up from the main portion of the fuselage. Specified main bomb loads were four 112-lb or two 230/250-lb.

Goldfinch This metal-constructed Gamecock development was flown in 1928. Armament remained essentially unchanged, but the rear ends of the gun troughs were faired. A Light Series bomb carrier (four 20-lb) was fitted under the fuselage.

Gnatsnapper The Gnatsnapper single-seat fleet fighter (1929) underwent much re-engining and modification. As originally built (Mercury or Jupiter engine) it was armed almost exactly as the Gamecock, though at the rear ends of the gun troughs there were louvred fairings. These covered more than half the length of the gun cooling jackets. The point made earlier (Grebe/Gamecock) concerning the impossibility of firing between the cylinders of a 14-cylinder radial engine was most effectively illustrated when the Gnatsnapper was re-engined with a Jaguar. With the reversion

Vickers gun installation in the Gloster Gnatsnapper, with Armstrong Siddeley Jaguar engine on hinged mounting forward of troughs in the top decking. One of the two guns is seen at upper right, with its fore-and-aft belt box below it in the fuselage side.

to this type of engine, a reversion of gun position was also entailed—to the top of the fuselage, as on the Grebe. The installation was, of course, very much cleaner, the presence of the guns being betrayed only by ports in the top cowling over the hinged engine-mounting. Even the familiar case and link chutes were invisible. The guns were, in fact fed from belt boxes which were themselves in the fuselage sides, the belts being fed upwards to the guns through twisted necks. Had the evaporatively cooled Rolls-Royce engine installation been developed to become standard, as intended, no further modifications to the gun installation would have been necessary.

As the Gnatsnapper was originally designed to be a Flycatcher replacement, design provision would have been made for four 20-lb bombs.

S.S.18   This two-bay biplane was built in 1929 for the single-seat interceptor fighter competition then in prospect. The two Vickers guns (1,200 rounds) were disposed in the manner originated in the Gamecock, but the troughs were shallower and there were louvred fairings at the rear, as on the original Gnatsnapper. An Aldis sight was mounted on the centre line, forward of the windscreen, and there were posts for a ring-and-bead sight a little to starboard. Being a pure interceptor, this aeroplane had no provision for bombs.

S.S.19 ('Multi-Gun')   The original S.S.18 airframe (Service number J9125) appeared during 1932 in modified form, still in the basic 'interceptor' configuration, i.e., carrying no night-flying equipment but having

194

wireless equipment and armed with four Lewis guns in addition to the twin-Vickers installation, which remained unaltered. The aircraft now became known as the Gloster Multi-Gun Fighter. The Lewis guns were described by the makers as 'an optional additional armament', and were installed one in each wing, in fairings slightly inboard of the inner pairs of interplane struts. Ammunition supply was 1,200 rounds for the Vickers guns and four 97-round drums for the Lewis guns. The installation was intended to give a 'cone of fire', the streams of bullets converging 100–300 yards ahead of the machine.

C.16/28 During 1932 Gloster completed a very large four-engined aircraft to the foregoing specification. It was designed to carry up to thirty fully equipped soldiers in its primary role or bombs in a secondary role. Troop and alternative bomb loads were given as thirty or 6,600 lb, twenty-five or 5,500 lb, twenty or 4,400 lb, fifteen or 3,300 lb, or ten or 2,200 lb. These figures were quoted for fuel-and-oil weights ranging from 2,000 lb to 6,600 lb. A typical bomb load, as on the Vickers machine to the same specification, would probably be twelve 250-lb + four 20-lb. There were strong-points for bomb-carriers under the fuselage and a bomb-aimer's position in the nose. Mountings for Lewis guns were provided for in the extreme nose and tail and at two staggered hatches in the fuselage sides, between the wings and tail.

Gauntlet During 1932/33 the Gloster fighter J9125 was developed to meet Air Ministry requirements for a day and night fighter to replace the Bristol Bulldog and carrying a similar Service load. The Vickers gun installation was retained and the Lewis guns deleted. Provision was made under the port wing for a Light Series bomb-carrier. As development proceeded alterations were made to the gunsights: the bead was set up on a pedestal immediately behind the engine, and the Aldis sight was rearranged so that its rear end projected behind the windscreen through a hole. When an experimental cowling of lengthened chord was fitted to the Bristol Mercury engine, by this time installed, the trailing edge was slotted to receive the bead-sight pedestal. Bearing the name Gauntlet, production aircraft appeared in 1934. These at first had no need of the slotted cowling mentioned in connection with the J9125 prototype, but this was later required as the cowling chord was extended. To increase their resistance to blast, the gun troughs were made of mild steel instead of light alloy, and the ejection chutes were slightly reshaped to protect the tail bracing wires against the empty cases and links. Eventually large 'tear-drop' fairings were fitted to retain the 'empties' aboard. A G.22 camera gun could be mounted on the starboard lower wing. Three-lobed gun cams for the C.C. gear became necessary when three-bladed Fairey metal airscrews were fitted to a proportion of aircraft.

A trial installation of Browning guns is reported to have been made on one Gauntlet (K4095).

Permutations of armament on Gloster fighters: *top*, S.S.19, with two Vickers guns and four Lewis guns; *lower*, Gauntlet with two Vickers guns.

F.7/30   As a private venture to the specification named (which called for four guns) the Gloster company built in 1934 their S.S.37 fighter, which later flew with the Service number K5200. The fuselage gun installation was identical with that of the Gauntlet, but two Lewis guns were carried beneath the single-bay wings. The fairings somewhat resembled those on the 'Multi-Gun' machine, but were much bulkier because they housed not only the greater part of each gun but the ammunition drum also. Outboard of the port fairing were attachment points for a Light Series bomb-carrier. At a later stage of development two Vickers guns displaced the Lewis guns, and the fairings for these were quite remarkably compact, for the belt-fed guns were so mounted that their barrels were close against the under-surface of the wing, with their breech casings lying under metal access covers let in to the top surface. Running inboard at right angles to these panels were two other panels over the belt boxes in the wing. Ring-and-bead sights were initially fitted and latterly a sight of the reflector type.

In September 1934 this aeroplane was sent to Martlesham Heath for competitive trials; a production order was announced in July of the following year. Shortly afterwards the name 'Gladiator' was announced for the production type.

The F.7/30 had attachment points for a four 20-lb bomb-carrier just outboard of the Lewis gun on the port side.

S.15/33 Otherwise known as the T.S.R.38, this torpedo-spotter-reconnaissance aircraft of 1934 had an uncommonly interesting installation of the pilot's Vickers gun; this was installed low in the port side, and the trough through which it fired was shared by the exhaust tail-pipe of the Goshawk engine. An external collector box was at first fitted, this resembling the type fitted to the Fury and other Hawker machines; but when the aircraft was undergoing trials at Martlesham Heath, this was not in place. The ring-and-bead sight was fitted on a fore-and-aft tubular

More permutations: *top*, F.7/30, with two Vickers guns and two Lewis guns; *lower*, Gladiator with four Vickers guns. (Lower picture, *Flight International*.)

member. The Lewis gun in the rear cockpit was on a Fairey 'High-Speed' mounting, and lay flush when stowed. Attachment points were provided in the lower wings for six Universal bomb-carriers, representative loads being six 250-lb or two 500-lb plus four 250-lb. Outboard of the main carriers, Light Series carriers could be fitted. There was a prone bomb-aiming position beneath the pilot. The massively braced steel torpedo-carrier was detachable (the 18-in Mk.VIII torpedo being an alternative load to the bombs) and was set so that the torpedo was parallel to the ground line. A G.22 camera gun could be fitted on the lower starboard wing.

Gladiator   The production-type Gladiator appeared in 1937, having been greatly developed in all-round effectiveness from the private-venture prototype of 1934. The first machines had four Vickers guns. Armament features, dating back to the prototype Gamecock of 1925, were now incorporated in a machine which was itself to fight like a gamecock in the coming war. The makers were able to proclaim:

'The aeroplane provides a very steady gun platform and adjustment of the guns is simple and easy to actuate. Particular attention has been given to ease of maintenance on the ground. The guns, ammunition boxes and cartridge chutes are readily accessible and removable'.

Gone were the long-familiar case and link chutes in the cowling panels behind the gun troughs; gone, too, the 'teardrop' fairings of the later Gauntlets. The cowling was so designed that only the daintiest little hummock was in evidence, with a vent for the gun-gases ahead of it. A subtle touch was evident in the engine cowling, the nose collector-ring of which was lipped over to give a better entry, necessitating two exquisitely fashioned scallops, or dimples, in way of the gun troughs. The wing-gun fairings were much as on the prototype, with case chutes in the bottom and link chutes on the outboard side. The guns in the fuselage had 600 rounds each; the wing guns, 400 rounds each. As Browning guns became available, they were installed in all four positions, only the more slender, slotted, barrel casings betokening the change. Absent ahead of the windscreen was the staunch companion of the fighter pilot, the Aldis sight; absent, too, the carrier for 'four 20-lb Coopers' of the 1914–18 war. Only the C.C. gear remained from Camel days. Spent ammunition was collected in boxes shaped to fit in the bottom of the fuselage. The changing of the times was thus expressed by A/Cdre Allen Wheeler:

'If the Gladiator could be criticised at all, I might say that, flying it, one was perhaps conscious of beginning to lose that sense of being actually part of the machine. Fighters had by then started to get big.'

The Sea Gladiator was similarly armed, and only minor alterations were needed to meet the demands of foreign customers.

F.5/34 This single-seater, which flew in 1937, was the first eight-gun fighter to be ordered. The guns were grouped as on the Hurricane, and there were large access panels in the top surface of the wing between the ailerons and undercarriage. A reflector sight was fitted in the Gladiator-type cockpit enclosure.

F.9/37 The first (Taurus-engined) example of this twin-engined single-seat fighter was initially flown in 1939 without armament, but with blanking plates over two obvious gun ports low in the nose. The second example, with Peregrine engines, flew in 1940 and had armament installed. The two guns, mounted low in the forward fuselage, with their barrels projecting a few inches, and with ejection ports in the bottom of the fuselage near the junction with the wing, were of 20-mm Hispano-type. Photographic evidence is presented suggesting four additional guns of the same type (not 0·303-in Brownings, as generally stated hitherto) installed in a wholly unorthodox manner. These appear to have been grouped in two pairs in the top of the fuselage, each gun having a portion of its barrel exposed through ports a little aft of the transparent panelling behind the cockpit. The centre guns were somewhat forward of those outboard. Thus the

A photograph which appears to disprove long-expressed belief concerning the armament of the Gloster F.9/37. The original indicates that the guns behind the cockpit are of the same type as those in the nose, namely 20-mm Hispano.

Another aspect of the Gloster F.9/37, with the two nose guns clearly in evidence and the muzzle of one of the guns behind the cockpit just discernible above the spinner of the starboard engine.

guns fired over the pilot's head. The guns were probably staggered to accommodate the 60-round ammunition drums, of the type then standard for the Hispano gun, and it appears that there were large hinged access panels for servicing and rearming.

Should confirmation be forthcoming that the rear 20-mm guns were four in number, as appears probable, then the Gloster F.9/37 may be accorded the distinction of having been the most heavily armed single-seat fighter in the world during the fateful year 1940. Indeed, as Bristol Beaufighters were initially delivered without their wing-mounted machine-guns, it may well have been the most heavily armed fighter of all.

Grahame-White

1913 War Plane (Type 6)   A Browning machine-gun on a British fighting aeroplane of 1913: this was but one blood-quickening feature of this pusher biplane, exhibited at Olympia early in the year mentioned. A second feature was the arrangement of the power plant to allow the free mounting of a gun. Thus *The Aero*:

> 'The engine is coupled up to a long shaft mounted on ball bearings which extends back to behind the pilot's seat, where it carries a chain sprocket driving the propeller through a twin roller chain. The propeller is mounted so that the upper longitudinal member of the triangular-section fuselage is taken through its hub, the principal reason for this being that with this design the arrangement of the fuselage is simplified, and the engine can be carried in front without introducing the necessity for the pilot and passengers to sit immediately in the slip stream of the screw.'

Almost as an afterthought there was appended to a lengthier description the simple observation:

> 'The machine is shown equipped with a quick-firing gun'.

Let it now be placed on record, after well over half a century, that this layout was schemed by Horatio Barber; that the detail design was the work of John D. North, who was to adapt a Box Kite for a Lewis gun demonstration at Bisley in November of the same year (the War Plane never flew) and who in later years became a pre-eminent figure in aircraft-armament development; and that the gun at Olympia, though correctly described by the commercial name Colt, was of the type called Browning Model of 1895 (or 'potato digger'). Like the later Lewis, this gun was air-cooled. The gun-pillar was associated with a quadrant fixed in a vertical plane under the gun. Elevation was said to be possible over an arc of 50 deg and traverse over 180 deg. The allusion to 'passengers', it may be noted, signified that an observer was carried in this aeroplane as well as a gunner.

Scout Type Pusher (Type II)   To J. D. North's design in 1914 Grahame-White produced this two-seater, which has a minor place here because it was seriously intended as a 'gun machine', although armament never materialised. It was announced that for tests the pilot would be in front, the positions being reversed for the gun.

Type 18   For the RNAS this very large single-engined four-bay folding biplane was produced as a bomber in 1916. The observer had a ring-mounted Lewis gun and the intended bomb load probably corresponded to that of the comparable Short and Wight single-engined bombers.

Ganymede   Designed before the Armistice for long-range day bombing, and completed during 1918/19, this three-engined biplane was laid out to provide effective defensive firepower, which its intended mission would obviously demand. In the nose of the central nacelle was the bomb-aimer's station, with windows, and a gunner at a Scarff ring-mounting, and there were similar gun mountings dorsally placed on each of the two fuselages. In the bottom of each fuselage was a hatch, affording downward and rearward protection, but further details of defensive armament and bomb load are unknown.

Handley Page

Anzani Biplane   Although never intended for warlike purposes this biplane of 1913 (sometimes called Type G) serves to introduce the Handley Page military aeroplanes by reason of an anecdote beloved of 'H.P.' himself. This was simply recounted:

> 'When war began in 1914, this aircraft was bought by the Royal Naval Air Service and stationed for training and defence at Hendon. Its offensive and defensive potentialities were limited to one Webley revolver, worn by the pilot. During a patrol, the biplane was mistaken by London's defenders for a Taube and riddled with bullets, but without serious effect.'

O/100 and O/400   The legend of the 'bloody paralyser', requested of Mr Handley Page by Cdre Murray Sueter, is abiding testimony to the foreseen destructive powers of the RNAS 'patrol bomber' styled O/100. The original specification was dated 28/9/14 and called for pilot, 'passenger', six 100-lb bombs, bombsight, rifle, ammunition, armour and wireless. The armour was to be provided by the contractor and was described as Firth's manganese steel, of the best resistance compatible with two prescribed gauges—10 S.W.G. underneath and 14 S.W.G. sides and engines. The radiators were to be safe from bullets nearer the vertical than 45 degrees and the petrol tanks were to be protected all over (could, in fact, be made entirely of armour plate). The bombsight was to be supplied and fitted by the Admiralty and was to weigh not more than 100 lb (*sic*). For the Service rifle 100 rounds of ammunition were demanded. As it materialised, the O/100 was officially described as having a machine-gun over the pilot's head, firing forward, and a cylindrical, rotating bomb gear which proved to require excessive manual effort. The crew and engine nacelles originally had armour protection, but this was later removed. In the developed aircraft up to sixteen 112-lb bombs could be carried internally. These were suspended by their noses in cells which had spring-loaded doors opened by the falling bombs. On 23 April, 1917, three O/100s, each carrying fourteen 65-lb bombs, bombed German destroyers off Ostend. The load is an interesting one because the standard 65-lb bomb was suitable for horizontal stowage only. Production aircraft (late 1916) had a Scarff ring-mounting in the nose, and in some instances at least this was of the 'disappearing-quadrant' type, apparently known as No. 3. Dorsal and ventral armament appears to have been as described in the succeeding paragraph.

September 1917 saw the emergence of the essentially similar O/400 with revised nacelles and tankage arrangements. This was officially stated to carry four Lewis guns and 17 double drums of ammunition. There was a Scarff ring-mounting in the nose; the two dorsal guns were carried on brackets, one on each side of the fuselage (alternatively, a single gun on a rocking pillar); and the ventral gun was officially described as being on a swivelling bar for firing under the tail. For the dorsal guns two separate firing platforms were provided. One official document gave the weight of the four Lewis guns as 66 lb, ammunition as 108 lb and mountings as 61 lb. Trial installations were made of a 6-pdr and a 2-pdr Davis recoilless gun. These guns were regarded as offensive weapons, but bombs were judged superior. The gun mounting in the nose sometimes had two Lewis guns, and in the nose position also, mounted on the cockpit rim, was a Bomb Sight, High Altitude, Mk.IA. There was at least one instance of the sight being transferred to the trapdoor position in the floor of the forward fuselage, where it was shielded from the main force of the air stream. Provision was made for the following alternative loads: sixteen 112-lb or eight 250-lb (internal), or three 520/550-lb or one 1,650-lb (external). On earlier aircraft more varied loads were carried; in one raid on Ostend in 1917 four Handley Pages dropped sixteen 112-lb, eight 100-lb and sixteen 65-lb bombs between them. There follows a contemporary account of crew and armament provisions on the O/400:

'Accommodations are made for one pilot and two or three gunners, and an observer who operates the bomb-dropping devices. Their placing is as follows: At the forward end of the fuselage is the gunner who operates a pair of Lewis guns. Bowden cables at one side of the cockpit permit the release of bombs. Behind the gunner is the pilot's cockpit from which the gunner's cockpit is reached through an opening in the bulkhead segregating the two compartments. The pilot is seated at the right side of the cockpit. Beside him is the observer's seat, hinged so it may be raised to permit access. Bomb-releasing controls are placed on the left side of the observer, extending to the forward gunner's compartment and running back to the bomb racks, located in the fuselage between the wings. The forward compartments are reached via a triangular door in the under-side of the fuselage.

'Aft of the bomb-rack compartment the rear gunners are placed. Two guns are located at the top of the fuselage and a third is arranged to fire through an opening in the underside of the fuselage. One gunner may have charge of all the rear guns, although usually two gunners man them. A platform is set half-way between the upper and lower longerons, upon which the gunner stands when operating the upper guns.'

The same account gives the dimensions of the 'bomb section' as: 3 ft $5\frac{3}{4}$ in $\times$ 5 ft $2\frac{15}{16}$ in $\times$ 4 ft 5 in.

In May 1918 the newly established Air Ministry issued an impressive document entitled *Bombing Gear in Handley Page Machine*. The massive, bewildering equipment installed in this true 'giant battle plane' is thus described:

'The Bomb Crates are built into the fuselage and are not detachable, the framework on which the bomb slips are supported being built into the framework of the centre section. The framework of the Bomb Crate consists at its top of two longitudinal members of 3 in $\times$ 4 in spruce 5 ft 2 in long, one on either side of the machine. On these two longitudinal members are carried four transverse members, also of spruce, termed *Bomb Beams* . . .

'From each of the bomb beams are suspended four metal supports or brackets; these brackets are called *Adapters*. The adapters extend downwards nine inches and at their ends are carried the bomb slips, on which the bombs are hung.

'From each of these adapters is also supported a bomb cell skeleton framework constructed of four $\frac{5}{8}$ in steel tubes. The upper ends of these tubes are shaped to the approximate outline of the nose of the bomb. These tubes are termed the *Bomb Guides*, and are fitted with narrow strips of ash bolted to them, the latter being named guide plates. The function of the bomb guides and guide plates is to steady the bomb when it is released, preventing it falling sideways as it slips through the bomb crate. The lower ends of the bomb guides forming each bomb cell skeleton framework are in each case secured to the centres of their corresponding squares in a series of shallow cells arranged on the floor level between the longerons immediately below the bomb beams. These enclosed cells are called the *Honeycomb*, their purpose being to give lateral support to the bombs as they fall through the crate when released, and also to check any tendency on the part of the bomb to rotate.

'The walls of the honeycomb cells are aluminium, reinforced with wood, and fill in the space between the bottom longerons.

'Each bomb slip is actuated by an individual control cable consisting of Bowden Standard No.51 wire of 270-lbs strength. The bombs are released in salvos of four, or separately as desired. Dropping bombs singly is not easy, and cannot be relied on, but they may be released positively in pairs, if the release handle is pulled over only one point on the ratchet on top of the control box in place of pulling it over two points, as in the release of a salvo. In either case the order of release is the same, *i.e.*, the aft port side bomb is the first to fall, and is followed in order by the next three bombs to starboard of it; this completes the first salvo. In the second salvo the port side bombs of the second transverse row of bomb cells working forward is the first to be released, followed by the remaining three bombs of the second salvo. The third and fourth salvos are released in the same order, always from port to starboard, and always opening with the port side bomb.'

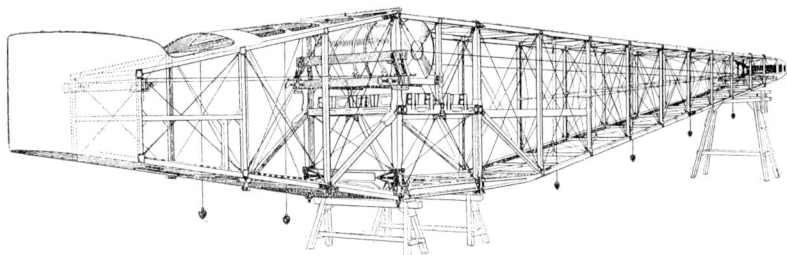

Although the wartime Handley Page bombers had internal bomb stowage, the post-war Hyderabad and Hinaidi carried their bombs externally. The four transverse bomb beams in the O/400 are seen in the drawing, and in the photograph below it the extent of the bomb compartment is shown by an external member. Gun positions are also seen on the O/400; likewise on the third view, of an Hinaidi carrying a 250-lb bomb under each wing.

'The control cables are sixteen in number', it is explained, 'and run from port to starboard in four distinct groups of four cables each.'

There ensues a lengthy dissertation on the disposition of these, involving a set of four pulleys 'termed the *Pulley Nest Block*', from which the control cables ran through fairlead blocks to the salvo release gear. Devices termed *Safety Springs* and *Tension Springs* were involved.

Next followed an account of 'Salvo Release Gear, Mark IV', which the reader may be spared for the present, though a description and picture will appear in Volume 2. There could be no more dramatic illustration than this of advances in bomb-dropping technique during the First World War.

Instructions are given for 'Alterations for Stowing 250 lb Bombs' on a remaining set of eight bomb slips; and there is a concluding item headed 'Handley Page Bomb Slip' which has a particular fascination. This declares in essence:

'The bomb slip is the mechanism on which the bomb is retained, and by means of which the bomb is released. The slip has five parts: Framework; suspension hook; retaining trigger; retaining trigger spring; electro-explosive release. The electrical release is never used and need not be considered. It will not be present in the latest designs.'

Fascinating, as remarked, when Handley Page's post-war successes with electrical bomb- and torpedo-release gear is recalled; and this was not taken into RAF service until 1930. It may be added that during 1921 the Handley Page company was awarded royalties on a war-time invention which permitted 'locking of the release gear so that the bombs were held steady until the moment the release was complete'.

Official loading instructions may now be quoted for bombs, H.E.R.L., 112-lb, Mks.III, V, VI and VII (all heavy-case). The last two marks of bombs, it may be mentioned, differed considerably from the others and could be identified by their angular fins. The instructions ran:

'The total number of bombs to be carried, having been carefully fused, should be laid gently on the ground with safety pins in position at a convenient distance from the aeroplane. The release slips on the carrying gear should now be tested before stowing the bombs. If the slips are found to be working satisfactorily the suspension hooks of all slips should now be placed open in readiness for stowing bombs. The bombs may then be stowed in order of the salvos, from port to starboard. The safety pin in the nose fuse of each bomb should not be removed until it is actually being handled for stowing, when, with the nose fuse safety pin removed, the bomb is pushed up into its cell from beneath the centre section by two or more men, as required. The suspension lug on the nose fuse now engages with the suspension hook of the release slip, which it automatically closes and locks, so retaining the bomb. Before allowing the weight of the bomb to fall on the release slip, the greatest care must be taken by the Officer or NCO superintending the stowing to ascertain that the arm of the suspension hook is securely locked by the locking arm of the release slip. The tail fuse arming vanes are now prevented from rotating by a locking arm, the fingers of which go over one of the arming vanes. The nose fuse arming vane is automatically held from rotating by the fact of its suspension lug being engaged in the release slip.'

As for the heavy externally carried bombs, it is known that a load of three 550-pounders was aimed at the lock gates at Zeebrugge, and Aircraftman Welland, who served with a Handley Page squadron in 1918, has recalled:

'About September a bomb was delivered to the squadron which weighed about 1,750-lb and was about twenty feet long. When it was first seen, the astonishment was great, and many doubts were expressed about a Handley ever getting off the ground with it. The armourers fitted a couple of chains under a plane and the idea was to sling it, as no proper bomb rack had been supplied . . .'

This reminiscence need only be qualified by noting that the weight of the bomb (nominally 1,650 lb) was almost exact, although the length was much overstated; and although it was stated that 'no proper bomb rack had been supplied' it is known that 'Carrier, Bomb, S.N., Mk.1' was in existence or in prospect during October 1918.

For the O/400 in post-war years an electrical bombing aid was developed. The bomb-aimer was in a prone position some six feet behind the pilot, who was kept on the desired course by coloured lights on his instrument panel. How this system failed on one important occasion, and how a string was attached to the pilot's ankles with remarkable effect, will be related in Volume 2.

One of the last O/400s in RAF service was used at the Isle of Grain for gas and smoke experiments and a vastly spectacular feat of pyrotechnics was performed by such an aircraft at the RAF Pageant of 1921. It was thus described:

'The stolid Handley Page was forging slowly ahead, when, from about 100 ft below it, there was a shattering explosion, and, gradually swelling upward from the centre of the burst, a beautiful cumulus cloud appeared. From it a million rain-streams of pale fire descended in an umbrella shape. Behind the cloud the great form of the R.33 disappeared quickly from view, and was soon completely obliterated by the smoke.'

R/200   Reconnaissance was the mission of this compact single-engined biplane, built for the RNAS in 1917. A Lewis gun on a dorsal Scarff ring-mounting apparently comprised the sole armament.

V/1500   At the end of 1917 it was considered to be worth attempting to bomb Berlin from a base in England. For those days this was indeed a long-range project, entailing, it was reckoned, a point-to-point sortie of some 450 miles and a minimum endurance equivalent to 1,100 miles. Operation in daylight, as well as by night, was therefore necessary, and a heavy defensive armament was a corollary. This demanded a crew of seven. Their stations were once enumerated by Mr Frederick Handley Page, who prefaced his remarks with this most typical reflection: 'If this aeroplane did not bomb Berlin we may find consolation in the fact that perhaps the Germans knew it was coming and saw it was time to give up.' He explained:

'As in the O/400, the bomber sits in the front, and also has a gun; behind him is the pilot and the captain of the vessel, and behind them again is the mechanic, who looks after all the engine equipment. On another platform at the back there are two gunners, one who fires upwards against hostile attack and another who fires downwards. Right at the tail of the machine there is another gun position, in which a man sits and fires back to beat off attacks from the rear.'

Thus 'H.P.', speaking in 1919, the year after his V/1500 four-engined bomber had been built and flown; and Gen Trenchard, describing Independent Force operations at about the same time:

'The 27th Group was established in England under the command of Col. R. H. Mulock, D S O, for the purpose of bombing Berlin and other centres. This group only received the machines capable of carrying out this work at the end of October, and though all ranks worked day and night in order to get the machines ready for the attack on Berlin, they were only completed three days before the signing of the Armistice.'

Respecting armament, the two most remarkable features of the 'Super Handley' were the tail gun position, with a catwalk giving access, and the very heavy bomb load. Neither the tail gun nor the fuselage access were the first of their kind, for in 1916 Igor Sikorsky had applied such armament to giant aircraft of the *Mouromets* class. He has said:

'Finally the officers of the Squadron worked out a scheme for mounting a machine gun at the rear of the fuselage and I was given the problem of designing it. I increased the stabiliser so as to take care of the weight of a man with a machine gun and ammunition. At the end of the fuselage a cockpit was arranged for the gunner, with a sort of windshield as protection from the stream of air. It was difficult to provide means of reaching the rear gunner's nest in flight, because inside the fuselage were wire crosses . . . A device was invented which the flying crews called the 'trolley car'. It consisted of a pair of light rails running along the whole fuselage and of a low couch mounted on rollers. When necessary a man could lie down on the couch and move easily below the wire crosses . . .'

The present writer makes a particular point of the V/1500's tail gun position, of which Handley Page were justifiably proud, because he will later be recording their arguments for not adopting such a position for the Hampden. The V/1500 tail position, it may be mentioned, proved the means of saving the life of the British flying pioneer Alec Ogilvie. He was occupying this station when one of the great bombers crashed near Golders Green and caught fire. The rest of the crew were killed.

The tail gunner in the V/1500 had a Scarff ring-mounting for a Lewis gun. There was a similar installation in the nose and on top of the fuselage aft of the wings. Alternatively, this last position had a central socket-and-pillar mounting or two such mountings, one on each side. The whole of the centre portion of the fuselage formed the bomb bay. Twenty-four 230-lb bombs was a load quoted by Handley Page, but up to thirty 250-lb bombs could be taken for short ranges.

The new 3,300-lb bomb, designed especially for the V/1500, was about 15 ft long, and one or two of these were to be carried beneath the fuselage. The bombsight was of Wimperis course-setting type.

Hanley   Like its Blackburn counterpart the Swift, the Hanley was a single-seater deck-landing torpedo-carrier and had no gun for the pilot. Built in 1922, it was required to carry a Mk.VIII or Mk.IX torpedo with heating arrangements (the exhaust tail-pipes were led past the torpedo) and to carry as an alternative load two 520-lb bombs under the wings. A pistol stop, to engage with the nose vane-wheel of the Mk.IX torpedo, was fitted beneath the engine cowling. Ring-type torpedo-sights flanked the windscreen.

Hyderabad   The Hyderabad was the first Handley Page twin-engined bomber to follow the O/400. Built to a 1922 specification, it was initially flown in 1923; but times were leisurely, and the official publication later quoted was dated 1928. Tail design and other features altered, but armament remained essentially unchanged. It will be noted that the Handley Page electrical bomb-release system had not yet been taken up for Service use. The official publication observed:

'The Hyderabad is a large aeroplane, constructed principally of wood, and is designed for the duty of medium range night bombing. It normally carries a crew of four, consisting of a first pilot in the forward part of the fuselage, a second pilot, who also acts as navigating and bombing officer, a forward gunner, who also does wireless duties, and a rear gunner, who controls two guns, one at the top and the other at the bottom of the fuselage, the latter gun being manipulated at the prone position.

'Scarff rings for mounting Lewis guns are fitted over the nose and rear cockpits, also a special mounting is arranged beneath the rear cockpit for downward firing. Bombs are carried under the fuselage centre portion, and under the bottom main planes, the bomb sight aperture being made in the flooring at the prone bombing position, situated at the front portion of the fuselage. Bomb releases are fitted at the prone position and an emergency release is provided in the second pilot's cockpit.

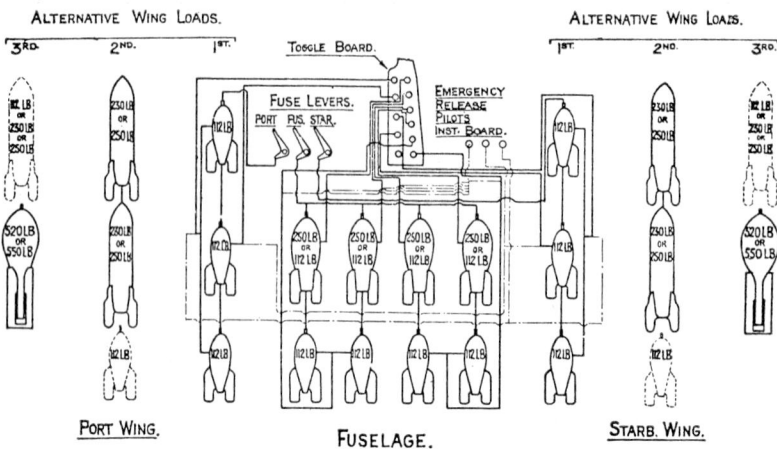

Bomb-loading diagram for Handley Page Hyderabad and Hinaidi. This should be studied jointly with the descriptive matter for the Hyderabad.

'*Bomb installation and controls.* The bomb load may be distributed under the fuselage and under the lower planes. There are several alternative loadings at either of these stations. That section under the fuselage, between the front and rear spars, provides for two alternatives, i.e., eight 112 lb bombs, or four 112 lb bombs with four 250 lb bombs. If the bomb load is carried under the lower planes then three alternatives are provided for, i.e., two 520–550 lb bombs or four 230–250 lb bombs, or six 112 lb bombs. In addition, a light series rack for sighter bombs is fitted under the starboard side of the fuselage forward of the rear spar. For practice purposes a temporary rack for light series bombs is fitted under the fuselage, immediately to the rear of the front spar . . . Some modifications may be found in the bomb system of later aircraft.

'The bombs are released by toggle pulls arranged on a board fitted at the prone bombing position, the fuse levers being mounted on a lay shaft supported in brackets at the forward ledge of the raised platform of the centre-section. The light series bomb releases are controlled separately by levers in standard quadrants fitted to the flooring immediately to the right of the heavy bomb release toggles. Emergency bomb release toggles, for use by the pilot, are fitted at the left-hand bottom corner of the rear instrument board, one toggle being fitted for salvo release (fuselage) and one toggle each for 500 lb and 250 lb bombs (planes).

'*Bomb-sight mounting.* The mounting for the course-setting bomb-sight, Mark IIa, Ref. No. 11/276, comprises an outer and an inner tube of duralumin, the lower end of the latter being fitted with a base plate having three bolt attachments for the bomb-sight, the upper end of the inner tube being made to slide in brass bearings fitted in the main outer tube. The base plate fitting bridges a guide tube, which also slides in an

210

outer tube, the guide being fitted to the side of the main mounting tube. Adjustment of the sliding tube is effected by means of a small hand wheel mounted on a screwed stud fitted in a top bridge or cross head which is split and is made to nip the sliding tube at any desired position by means of the stud and wheel. The inner, or sliding, tube is pulled out from the main mounting tube against the tension of a rubber elastic cord fitted centrally in the tubes and is anchored at its top end to the bolt securing the complete mounting to a lug fitting on the pilot's seat bearer unit. The lower end of the bomb-sight mounting tube is secured to the fuselage flooring by means of plate attachments fixed by wood screws to a wooden support, the bolts securing the top bridge in position also passing through the attachment plates and support.

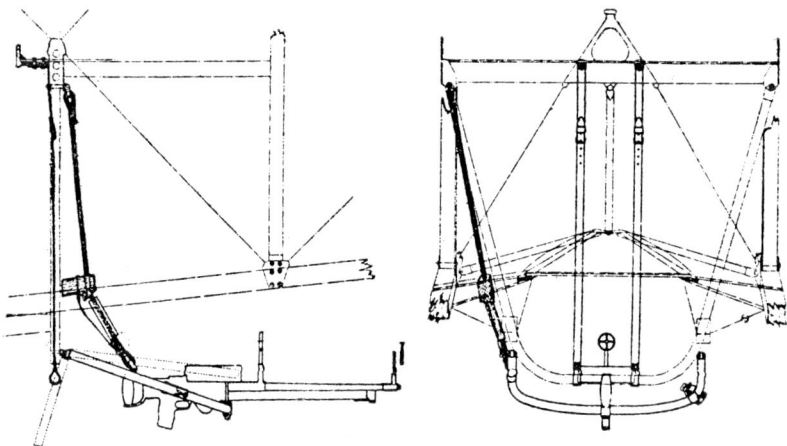

Makers' drawings of the ventral gun installation for the Hyderabad and Hinaidi, described under 'Hyderabad'.

'*Guns.* The aircraft is equipped with three Lewis guns, two of which are mounted on Scarff rings and one specially mounted for firing downwards from the rear prone position in the fuselage. The woodwork over the nose and rear cockpits provides for either the No.2 or No.7 Scarff rings. The special mounting is pivoted to two eyebolts secured to the fuselage side struts at the rear gunner's position, and is suspended below the fuselage flooring by a length of braided elastic cord. The cord is shackled to the elevator arm, or mounting, and has its upper end anchored to an eyebolt secured to a fitting on the gun platform supporting structure. A stop limiting the upward movement of the mounting is fitted to the elastic cord, and is in contact with a fairlead through which the cord passes inside the fuselage, a short length of 5 cwt. cable, for retaining the mounting in the normal position, being fitted from an eyebolt secured to the fairlead fixing block with a spring hook connection to the mounting. A hinged door locked by spring bolts is arranged in the flooring over the gun, and a large portion of the flooring structure of the fuselage at the forward end of the gun mounting is fitted over with a hammock of two thicknesses of Willesden canvas, reinforced by a cradle of 10 cwt. cable. The gunner, resting in the hammock, is provided with safety straps secured to the fuselage and to the open rear end of the hammock. A padded wooden swinging seat is fitted on the top gun platform.

'Ammunition for the guns is carried in drums, each of 97 rounds, six drums being stowed on pegs at each gun position, i.e., the nose cockpit, the top rear gun cockpit and at the prone gun position under the top rear gun platform.

'The camera, type P.7, is mounted within a table structure with drawer, the legs of the mounting being let in flush and screwed to plate socket fittings secured to the flooring at the rear of the wireless platform.'

Under the heading 'Instruments' the following appears:

'An altimeter (Mk.Va, Ref. No. 6 A/7) and an airspeed indicator (Mk.IVa, Ref. No.6A/107) are mounted on the small board arranged at the prone bombing position. A special air temperature thermometer is fitted under the nose cockpit, with dial indicator reading from -30 deg.C to $+55$ deg. C, the dial indicator being mounted by means of brackets on the upper end of the bomb-sight mounting.

'An observation mirror, reflecting from the prone bomber's position, is provided for the use of the pilot. This is a 4 in. diam. convex mirror secured inside the cockpit by a light steel plate bracket screwed to the starboard side of the fuselage.

'The pilot's safety belts are each secured by eyebolts fitted to the seat back rest. The front and rear gunners' harness connections are made to eyeplates bolted to each gun platform.'

A point of interest and importance not made in this official description is that the dorsal gun-ring was on transverse rails along which it was slid to give a steep angle of fire over the fuselage sides. The gunner stood on a platform, which had a firing step at each side. In squadron service some Hyderabads carried on the dorsal ring-mounting a Lewis gun having a large land-service type of cooling jacket.

H.P.21   Being intended for the U.S. Navy, this single-seat fighter (1923) had two Marlin machine-guns, totally enclosed beneath the top cowling and firing out through short troughs or ports. The ejection chutes were half-way down the fuselage sides. The weight of the armament installation was given as 150 lb.

Hendon   Built in 1924 as a two-seater development of the Hanley, having a Scarff ring-mounting for a single Lewis gun immediately behind the pilot, but still no pilot's gun, the Hendon was supplied to the RAF to the extent of six examples. A Hendon was tested at Martlesham Heath with a dummy Mk.VIII torpedo (very snug against the fuselage in crutches, as on the

Hanley), and with Lewis gun and under-wing bomb carriers (two 520-lb) in place. Torpedo sighting bars were attached transversely and fore-and-aft to the centre-section struts.

Handcross Produced in 1924 for competition with the Westland Yeovil, Bristol Berkeley and victorious Hawker Horsley, the Handcross had bomb-carriers under the lower wings, outboard of the undercarriage attachments, though other carriers are said to have been provided within the light fairing under the fuselage. However, this fairing also seems to have housed the prone bombing position, and there may have been some intention of installing a ventral Lewis gun at the rear. Bomb load was probably as given for the Bristol Berkeley. The pilot was seated beneath the top wing and had a Vickers gun in the upper port cowling. A Scarff ring-mounting for a single Lewis gun was mounted dorsally a little behind the trailing edge.

Harrow The Harrow of 1926 was a two-seat torpedo-bomber shipplane (to use the idiom of its day). A counterpart of the Blackburn Ripon, it carried a similar load, the Mk.VIII torpedo being slung parallel with the fuselage datum line and having the customary two steel crutches. There was, however, one point of interest concerning the torpedo installation, or specifically the torpedo sight. The commonly used form of centre-section bracing being absent, the transverse bar carrying the sighting beads was attached to the inboard pair of interplane struts and was thus of unusual length. A similar installation has already been noted for the Blackburn Swift and Dart. The pilot had a fixed Vickers gun which was neatly installed in the starboard side of the fuselage, firing through a short trough in the sloping turtle deck. The Harrow I had a built-up rear fuselage for the Scarff ring-mounting (one Lewis gun), but on the Mk.II aircraft (1928) the fuselage was cut away and the ring thus afforded a degree of shelter. Bombs (two 520-lb was a possible loading) were carried under the wings at

Handley Page Harrow floatplane, showing torpedo installation and relatively protected emplacement for Scarff ring-mounting.

points where they cleared the floats of the seaplane version. This version, it may be mentioned, was tested at Felixstowe with a torpedo.

Hinaidi Dating from 1927, when the first (wooden) version was flown, the Jupiter-engined Hinaidi was supplied in its metal form to the RAF. Except for structural material and power plant it was identical with the Hyderabad, and was similarly armed. In a contemporary description Handley Page described the ventral 'hammock' installation as a 'movable chair for firing below the fuselage'.

Handley Page Hare with two standard loads for RAF day bombers: *top*, Jupiter-engined machine with two 230-lb bombs; *lower*, Panther-engined machine with two 250-lb bombs. (Top picture, *Flight International*.)

214

As seen in the uppermost picture the Handley Page Hare is in developed form, with Armstrong Siddeley Panther engine and split undercarriage. It carries four 112-lb bombs, and a dummy Lewis gun is seen on the Scarff ring-mounting. In the lower view it appears in its original form, with Bristol Jupiter engine and cross-axle undercarriage. The gunner's folding seat and a spare ammunition drum for the Lewis gun are visible; likewise the rear of the pilot's Vickers gun.

Hare The Hare two-seat day bomber/torpedo-carrier was built in 1928 for competition with the Hawker Harrier and Blackburn Beagle. It was much developed and variously engined. As originally built it had a cross-axle undercarriage, but the fitting of a split undercarriage allowed a torpedo to be carried under the fuselage, and a torpedo-carrier, with two steel crutches, braced fore-and-aft and laterally, was fitted at the development stage when the Hare was flying with Panther engine and Townend ring. Tubular under-wing carriers were fitted slightly outboard of the wheels, and the aircraft was flown at various times with two 230-lb or 250-lb bombs and also with four 112-lb bombs, these last in tandem pairs. The bombs were aimed from a prone sighting station lit by a window in the starboard side. For the pilot there was a Vickers gun, fixed in the port upper fuselage side and having ring-and-bead sights close in front of the cockpit. Behind the pilot's cockpit the fuselage was cut away to receive a wind-balanced Scarff ring-mounting with a single Lewis gun, the mounting being recessed. The makers claimed:

'A draughtless gunner's cockpit has been obtained by careful arrangement of the fuselage contour and of the top plane relative to the fuselage.'

Clive Contemporarily described as a 'troop carrier' and as a 'medium-range troop carrier and day bomber', the Clive (1928) had five main loading possibilities: 17 fully armed troops; three Jupiter, or similar, engines;

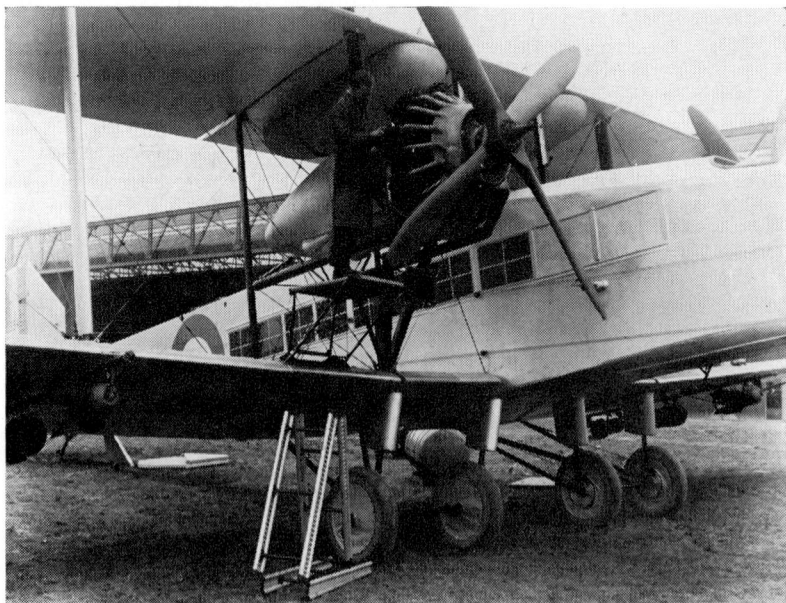

Handley Page Clive carrying four 112-lb bombs on front and rear carriers and two 250-lb bombs at the centre of the groups. (*Flight International*.)

400 gal of petrol in special tanks; about 1,300 lb of bombs with fuel for 765 miles; or two stretcher cases and eight sitting cases. Although the aircraft was first flown without provisions for armament, the nose was later extended to take a Scarff ring-mounting for a Lewis gun, and a similar installation was made at the rear of the cabin above the fuselage. This mounting slid on transverse tracks, as in the Hyderabad and Hinaidi. Bombs were carried beneath the wings, an indentified load being two 250-lb and four 112-lb. The three bombs under each wing were carried in tandem, with the large one between the two smaller ones. There was a prone position for sighting on the starboard side of the fuselage, slightly behind the pilot, with a bracket for a course-setting sight.

Heyford The prototype of the Heyford twin-engined night bomber (then known by its specification number B.19/27) first flew in the summer of 1930 and marked a departure in defensive and offensive armament. There were three gun positions; nose, dorsal and ventral. Because the fuselage was attached directly to the top wing, the front gunner (who also acted as bomb-aimer and navigator) had a field of fire not only in the frontal hemisphere, but also aft above the pilot's head. The field of fire of the dorsal gun likewise benefited from the placing of the fuselage, as well as from the narrowness of the fuselage and the twin fins and rudders. The ventral gun was carried in a retractable, rotatable, manually operated turret, or 'dustbin' as it was quickly named. As initially flown, the Heyford had no gun mountings, but in due time rings of Hawker type were applied to the nose and dorsal positions, each carrying a Lewis gun. A folding protective screen was fitted forward of the dorsal mounting. A single Lewis gun was likewise the armament of the retractable turret. It was the makers' claim that all blind spots were eliminated, as the concerted fire from at least two gun positions could be brought to bear on any practical point of attack round the aircraft. The loss of speed due to the drag of the extended turret was said to be 'negligible', but the greatest care was taken to eliminate any possible extra drag due to the bombs by air-sealing (by means of spring doors) the separate main bomb cells, which virtually filled the centre-section of the lower wing. The bombs were all disposed laterally. Centrally there was provision for four 500-pounders and, on each side of this clutch, for three 250-pounders. This was the heaviest possible internal load, for the 500-lb bomb was at the time the largest available to the RAF. Outboard of the undercarriage on each side were carriers for three bombs of 120 lb, and outboard of these for four 20-lb bombs or reconnaissance flares. The maximum bomb load was stated to be normally 2,660 lb, although 3,300 lb could be lifted for short range. The following combinations were possible: ten 250-lb; four 500-lb; sixteen 112-lb; or six 250-lb—additional in each case to eight 20-lb. Load for full range was 1,600 lb. It was one of the makers' favourite claims for the Heyford that the bombs could be loaded while the engines were running, by virtue of the placing of the engines on the top wing. Though the value of this possibility in actual warfare may seem obscure, it should be related to a more significant facility. This was the provision made for reducing rearming time by adjusting the bombs on the carriers and setting the fuses before hoisting the assemblies by a special winch. On reaching its locating point each carrier was instantly locked in place and it was only necessary to plug in the electrical leads for fusing and release. For the Handley Page electrical bomb-release system, the switch panel and release were to the right of the bomb-aimer's instrument panel.

A single aircraft, nominally known to the manufacturers as Heyford II, though not corresponding to the standard RAF variant so designated, had, among other improvements, developed armament installations. An improvement in fighting qualities was claimed by reason of an enclosed pilot's cockpit, with screening so arranged that the pilot could put his head outside the windows and look vertically down or horizontally forward without hindrance from the air stream, and by the sheltering of the dorsal gunner by a faired superstructure carried aft from the upper wing. This second modification eliminated the need for an adjustable screen, reduced drag, and, it was claimed, screened the gunner at all speeds.

In December 1933 Handley Page gave comparative data for the Heyford and a typical single-engined bomber, which may be assumed to approximate to the Hawker Hart. Figures for the SEB are given in brackets, thus: bomb load, 2,800 lb (500 lb); endurance $4\frac{1}{2}$ hr ($3\frac{1}{2}$ hr); cost £15,000 (£6,000); operational height 13,000 ft (15,000 ft); crew 4 (2).

So well remembered is the Heyford today for its eye-catching and breath-catching 'dustbin' that the present writer ruefully admits that this was one of the few types of pre-1939 RAF turret that he never occupied.

Handley Page Hyderabad, showing gun positions and under-wing bomb-carriers.
(*Flight International.*)

Handley Page Heyford, showing gun positions, with turret lowered, and bomb doors open. (*Flight International.*)

F. D. Bradbrooke did, however, do so in the Air Exercises of 1936, and he left a sparkling account:

'This is a strange battle station,' he wrote. 'It has some comfort, not because there is an inch clearance for back, knees or feet, but because it is tailored accurately to fit. If a can-opener had been handy I might, in fact, have eased mine slightly at the arm-pits. The rim of the little balcony reaches barely to the knees as one sits, and a re-entrant bulge between them adds to the field of fire that little extra something which we hope others haven't got. When the opening faces dead aft there is an eddy which calls for goggles, but when turned abeam there is no draught. The sensation when winding this pill-box round is at least novel. The solemn rotation above empty space brings to mind the observation cars which the Zeppelins used to trail far below them on a single cable— surely one of the most fearsome habitacles ever devised. By contrast the dust-bin at once felt cosy and solid to a degree.'

The same writer, looking dead astern, saw fit to remark that a fighter might 'stymie' him with his own tail-wheel; and, having ascended to the upper gun-ring, was able to record:

'I looked out in time to see a red glow reflected from the tail-plane. Hostilities must be starting, and the weather had cleared annoyingly south of Hatfield so that the fighters might come at us from any angle. Further reports drew attention to a trail of archie-bursts behind us. In accordance with the sporting custom of Set Pieces we, the target, were providing these by means of Very pistols for gunners down below. The

219

smell of powder drifting back through the fuselage somehow added a touch of reminiscent realism to the characteristic atmosphere of a military aeroplane.—The narrow fuselage with its steel tubes and wondrous variety of war baggage, cables flapping, fabric shivering and a seemingly all-pervading film of oil. Above all the beat of twin motors . . .

'From the upper gun ring I saw that a squadron of Bulldogs was wheeling to get on our tails. Still out of range, the flights formed line astern and began a dive. They were obviously intending to zoom at us from below; so I clambered down, and reached the dust-bin just in time to see a file of them boring up from the depths . . . Before my imaginary gun could be brought to bear they had zoomed up past the tail and made off.

'I sat down to evolve a better scheme at leisure. I was undoubtedly dead and had lots of time.'

H.P.43   This three-engined bomber transport biplane appeared in 1932. It was of interest in marking a revival of the tail gun position, pioneered (though not initiated) in the V/1500. In this position, as in the nose, was a Scarff ring-mounting for a Lewis gun. The nose also carried a bomb-aiming station for an external (fuselage) load.

H.P.46   Otherwise known by its specification number M.1/30, this torpedo-bomber has always been something of a mystery aeroplane by reason of the fact that no photograph survives. Perhaps the present writer is one of the few living persons who actually saw this rarity and admired its appearance. (The admiration was scarcely shared by the makers, one of whose executives annotated an official listing of the type 'N.B.G.'.) The intended war load would obviously have corresponded to that of the Blackburn and Vickers machines built to the same specification, i.e., an 18-in Mk.VIII torpedo or bombs (e.g. four 500-lb or eight 250-lb) in addition to the usual Vickers gun for the pilot and Lewis gun for the observer. The Vickers gun was in the fuselage port side and the Lewis gun commanded an excellent field of fire by virtue of its high placing and the narrow fuselage.

H.P.47   It will already have been gathered that Handley Page were much concerned in designing their aeroplanes to provide the most effective field of fire, and their concern was especially apparent in this general purpose machine of 1935. Behind the main section of the fuselage (roomy enough to carry four soldiers in emergency) the tail was carried on a circular boom of small cross section. The dorsal ring-mounting was on a section of the fuselage deeper than the boom itself, to broaden the field of fire, but well below the top line of the fuselage proper, to afford protection for the gunner. The ring, which carried a single Lewis gun, was of a special type, the gun being carried on an offset arm. The pilot's Vickers gun was tidily housed in the fuselage port side and fired through a trough. There were ring-and-bead sights. The 18-in torpedo was carried at a distinctly nose-down angle under the fuselage, this being made possible by a type of split undercarriage introduced for a similar purpose on the Hare. Bombs (e.g. two 250-lb or 500-lb) were hung externally on Universal carriers beneath the inner wings. The bombs were sighted through a panel in the bottom of the forward fuselage, provided with a wind-deflector at its forward end.

H.P.51   Up to 4,000 lb of bombs could be lifted by this monoplane conversion (1935) of the H.P.43. The bombs were carried beneath the fuselage and were associated with the usual Handley Page electrical fusing and release system. The defensive provisions of the H.P.43 were retained.

A study in fields of fire, especially for rear defence: *reading down*, Handley Page Hinaidi, with Scarff ring-mounting slid to port; Heyford; Harrow; and Hampden. (First three pictures, *Flight International*.)

Harrow The Harrow of 1936 was a hasty, but by no means ineffectual, conversion of the H.P.51 for duty as a heavy bomber under the newly introduced RAF Expansion Scheme. In terms of armament, it marked the arrival of power-operated turrets for British bombers, but these were not at first installed, their places being taken by fixed glazing. The turrets were two in number, though a third (dorsal) powered installation has been mistakenly recorded. Designed by Handley Page themselves, the turrets (nose and tail), had Nash and Thompson driving mechanism, and housed in each were the guns—two Lewis (rear) and one Lewis (front), aimed by means of reflector sights. Vickers G.O. guns were later fitted. Into the nose turret was built a projecting section incorporating an optically flat panel for the bomb-aimer. Early Harrows had temporary turret installations, and although the distinction between the Mk.I and Mk.II aircraft was officially the fitting in the latter of Pegasus XX engines in place of Pegasus Xs a colleague wrote after visiting a Harrow squadron:

> 'Externally, the difference seems to be that the goldfish bowls in the nose and tail have no fish in them in the Mk.I, while in the Mk.II the bowls are fully stocked. A light-hearted young pilot explained that the authorities evidently expected some of the first Harrows to get a bit bent and did not want expensive articles of machinery to get smashed up as well.'

The Harrow's nose and tail turrets were distinctive in design, and were not strictly 'rotatable' as sometimes asserted. The turret proper was in fact fixed, and the rotatable portion was in the form of a belt set low in a shallow embrasure and carrying the gun(s), which were elevated about a trunnion axis and had a wide field of fire in elevation and azimuth. This installation was associated with the reflector sight, the gunner's seat and a support for his feet. One advantage claimed was easy aerodynamic sealing. The sight was connected with the gun(s) by a parallel-link motion.

The Harrow's dorsal gun position was more or less in line with the trailing edge of the high-set wing and originally had a dummy fairing. The operational installation was a single Lewis gun in a manually operated cupola resembling that of the Armstrong Whitworth turret. The makers remarked that as the tail turret did not project above the top line of the fuselage, the dorsal gunner could fire past the twin fins and rudders and reduce the blind area to the rear almost to nothing. A bomb load of some 3,000 lb could be carried internally, and the Handley Page system of fusing and release control was naturally provided. The bomb bay extended beneath the floor of the fuselage centre-section, and above this ran a walkway connecting all crew stations.

An historic pair of pictures, (*top*) showing King George V in the cockpit of a Handley ▶
Page O/100; (*lower*) showing King George VI inspecting a Harrow. The gun-mounting on the O/100 is of the Scarff 'disappearing-quadrant' type. The Harrow turret, designed by Handley Page, but having Nash and Thompson driving mechanism, houses a single Lewis gun—precisely as on the O/100 of over twenty years earlier. The bomb doors are open.

222

Harrows served during the war as transports (their antecedents serving them well in this regard), and the type was also used for the sowing of aerial mines under the code-name Mutton.

Hampden   In prototype form (B.9/32), the Hampden was flown some four months before the first Harrow and represented a philosophy very far removed from turret armament. In a paper expostulating against these devices and entitled *The Future Defence of Bombers* the makers declared:

> 'These turrets do provide suitable positions for gunners, and a high degree of accuracy can be obtained in air firing from them. But they have to be paid for, and the price is exceedingly heavy . . . To take a hypothetical case, a tail-gunner's turret, by demanding modifications in the rest of the machine to balance the additional weight at the extreme tail, by such things as the moving forward of the engine mountings, may exact a price of 700–1,000 lb in load. Similarly, the front turret exacts its price, and the outcome of these two turrets is a considerable reduction in bomb load and in performance.'

In laying emphasis on performance rather than defensive firepower the company went further, even to the point of terming the Hampden a 'fighting bomber' and a 'fighter bomber'. They went so far, in fact, as to give the pilot a fixed gun, a feature which had last appeared on a large RAF bomber in the early 1920s. This earlier installation was on the single-engined Avro Aldershot: weight, about 11,000 lb, span, 68 ft. The corresponding figures for the twin-engined Hampden were about 19,000 lb and span about a foot greater. Further comment on armament may well be prefaced by reference to a Handley Page publication issued shortly after the Hampden had come into production. This claimed:

> 'Defence is provided by two gun stations forward and two aft covering wide angles of attack and completely shielded from the air stream'; and further: 'The aeroplane is designed to give the greatest economy in structure weight and the highest degree of manoeuvrability. It is well defended by two forward and two rearward guns and has enclosed accommodation for a crew of four, consisting of pilot, who also operates front fixed gun; navigator bomber, who operates front lower gun; wireless operator and top rear gunner; lower rear gunner. The central cabin forms an enclosed flying gun platform with the crew enclosed in special cockpits . . . The fixed gun is easily operated by the pilot and is clear of the flying controls . . .', etc.

That in stress of war the Hampden's armament proved grievously inadequate has long been history; nor did the design of the aircraft permit truly effective augmentation. That losses must in any case have been high is of course allowable; but less justified are the early claims by the makers for their 'fighter bomber'. The movable front gun was in an elementary hand-held installation, with the barrel protruding through a small hinged window in the glazed nose-section, immediately below and behind the large oval optically flat Triplex bomb-aiming panel. This gun could be detached from its mounting and stowed in the fuselage. That the fixed gun was 'easily operated by the pilot' is difficult to substantiate, for this was mounted wholly forward of the cockpit—'clear of the flying controls', as Handley Page put it, because there was no room for it as well as the controls. If for 'operated' the word 'fired' be read the claim then may be admitted, but though the present writer experienced some lively flights in Hampdens, he could never reconcile that fixed front gun with the Hampden's intended role. The two rear guns were neatly emplaced, though Sir Arthur Harris described the lower position as 'hopelessly cramped'.

The pilot's gun was a belt-fed Vickers or Browning, mounted forward of the cockpit a little to port, with the muzzle and flash eliminator exposed. There was a ring-and-bead sight. The pillar-mounted dorsal Lewis or Vickers G.O. gun was stowed when out of use in the fuselage decking and the gunner's position was protected by a deep folding spring-loaded transparent dome faired into the forward fuselage. The ventral position was similarly armed, and the upper segment of the rear transparency hinged upward for action. Behind the upper gun-position was provision for flare/chutes or a camera.

One historical note on defensive armament: the prototype carried no guns, and the gun positions were at first tentative and inoperative. Thus one wrote after the 1937 S.B.A.C. Display: 'The lower rear gun position on the Hampden has been revised. Even now it seems to be only temporary.' Nevertheless, provision was made for a Lewis gun in this position, and one such gun was certainly installed dorsally. After war came twin Vickers G.O. guns were fitted at the dorsal and ventral stations, the former in conjunction with bow-shaped steel guards to protect the structure. Beam guns were added near the wireless-operator's position.

As for offensive load, the Hampden carried 4,000 lb of bombs in a bay extending from a point below the pilot's cockpit almost to the lower gun position, and at the coming of war there was provision for two 2,000-lb or four 500-lb bombs. There were strong-points for 'overload' bombs outboard of the engine nacelles below the wings. The bomb doors were opened by a massive lever in the pilot's cockpit. Handley Page's electrical fusing and release system was fitted, with selector switches at the bomb-aimer's station, which had a folding seat, and to the pilot's right.

The Hampden was quickly adapted for mine-laying, and the disclosure was made in due time:

'The mines carried by the Hampdens are dropped from varying heights. A canvas parachute opens automatically after release to break the mine's fall so that it does not explode or receive damage on impact with the sea. The mine fields are worked out to a perfect plan and the Hampdens take care that they are exactly over the selected spot. If they encounter difficulties that make the dropping of the mine at the pre-

225

arranged place impossible, it can be jettisoned, but the exact position must be carefully noted so that all Allied shipping can be warned, if necessary, of its location.'

The 2,000-lb H.C. bomb was also carried by Hampdens, and the type was further used as a torpedo-bomber, with one 18-in torpedo and provision for two 500-lb bombs under the wings outboard of the nacelles. Extensive armour-plating was installed.

Hereford The armament provisions on this Dagger-engined Hampden conversion (first built 1939) conformed with those of standard production Hampdens.

Halifax The Halifax four-engined heavy bomber is accorded a place here more for convenience of reference than as a matter of strict historical obligation, for, although the first example flew in 1939, it carried no armament. For the record, the Halifax I had Boulton Paul turrets at nose and tail (two and four guns respectively) and two hand-held beam guns. The main bomb bay was 22-ft long and there were additional cells in the wing. The Halifax II had no beam guns, but, in their place, a two-gun Boulton Paul dorsal turret. Developments and variations in armament were numerous.

Hawker

Duiker A parasol monoplane corps reconnaissance two-seater of 1923, this counterpart of the Armstrong Whitworth Wolf and Short Springbok had centre-section cut-outs for the closely emplaced pilot and gunner, field of view being a primary consideration. The pilot had a fixed Vickers gun mounted on the port top shoulder of the fuselage and there was a Scarff ring-mounting, probably for twin Lewis guns. There is no evidence of bombs.

Woodcock The Jaguar-engined Woodcock I night fighter first appeared, in 1923, with its two Vickers guns set high on the fuselage flanks, their breech casings being a little above the cockpit coaming. On the Jupiter-engined version, they were lowered somewhat, doubtless to clear the engine cylinders. The mountings were of bracket type, on four supporting tubular members. On the single-bay Jupiter-engined prototype Woodcock II, the guns were in approximately the same position, though the mountings were of new design with, at one stage at least, prominent fairings below the guns. The guns themselves remained fully exposed. In production aircraft the mountings were altered yet again and the fairings were removed; and then there followed a new type of mounting and the addition of the large squarish collector boxes which became such a prominent feature of the

226

Armament development on the Hawker Woodcock II: *reading down*, prototype with early gun mountings; production type with redesigned gun mountings; aircraft in squadron service with collector boxes.

Woodcock in RAF service. The new mounting was of the type described by the Hawker company in 1926 as incorporating means for effecting fine adjustments about horizontal and vertical axes for alignment purposes. The gun was connected by bolts by fixed U-shaped brackets, a turning movement of the bolt effecting one adjustment and axial displacement of the bolt, or of bushes associated with it, effecting the other.

It was claimed that the position of the guns on the Woodcock prevented muzzle flash from interfering with the pilot's vision at night.

There were variations in the mounting of the sights, which were originally bracketed to the upper wing. The standard Service Woodcock had both Aldis and ring-and-bead sights, these being supported on a tubular fore-and-aft mounting. For each gun, 750 rounds were provided, and there were rails for a four 20-lb bomb-carrier beneath the lower port wing.

Although, as already intimated, the Woodcock was a night fighter, being the first specialised type in that category to be supplied to the RAF, it was required to carry its bomb load for emergency use by reason of the stringent economy then being imposed. For the same reason much armament equipment, including bombs and carriers and the Scarff ring-mounting for the Lewis gun, were retained in service during the 1920s and early 1930s either in original state or slightly modified. The Woodcock's guns, however, were of the newly introduced Mk. II pattern (Class E).

Hedgehog The Hedgehog was a three-seater fleet reconnaissance biplane built in 1924. During 1925 it was reported that the observer was in the front cockpit, the pilot second and the gunner third, but in photographs the pilot's Vickers gun and sights are seen forward of the first cockpit. The ring-and-bead sight was central and there was an Aldis sight to starboard, with the gun lying nearby. Six hundred rounds were provided. A Lewis gun was carried on a Scarff ring-mounting beneath the large centre-section cut-out. This gun had five double drums. There was under-wing provision for bombs, probably two 230-lb.

Danecock Like the Woodcock from which it was developed in 1925, the Jaguar-engined Danecock had externally mounted guns. These were 7·7-mm Madsens, with 720 rounds apiece. The sights were carried on a fore-and-aft tube. There were two rails under the port wing for the attachment of a carrier for four light bombs.

Heron The gun installation of the Heron single-seat fighter of 1925 appears in some early photographs to be the only untidy feature, in that the two Vickers guns are seen exposed. They were located as on the contemporary Gloster Grebe, at the shoulders of the fuselage ahead of the cockpit, the coaming of which was specially formed to receive the breech casings. The cooling jackets lay in dimples. In the completed installation the breeches were faired over and the fairing of the rear centre-section struts cut away to clear the ejection chutes. There were brackets for (apparently) Aldis and ring-and-bead sights. Provision was made for 600 rounds per gun.

The Heron was the last Hawker fighter to carry its guns more or less externally, at the shoulders of the fuselage.

Horsley The Horsley appeared in its original day bomber form during 1925 and proved victorious over the Bristol Berkeley, Handley Page Handcross, de Havilland Derby and Westland Yeovil. In 1927 it was adapted as a torpedo-bomber. The original prototype differed considerably from its successors in having a ventral position for a Lewis gun. In the first state of the machine, with lateral radiators, this was faired off at the rear, but, when the aircraft was remodelled with 'chin' radiator, the mounting was conspicuous beneath the gunner's cockpit. The gun was carried on a quadrant-mounted arm and the gunner lay in the compartment over the wing which had side windows for bomb-aiming. There was a prominent fairing below the fuselage aft of the trailing edge. In this first Horsley the installation of the pilot's fixed Vickers gun differed from that on later examples, the gun being offset to starboard, instead of to port, of the centre line. In the production-type installation, the gun fired through a trough

Hawker Horsley prototype, with ventral gun position below cockpits.

229

running forward, just inboard of the port centre-section struts, almost to the engine nose-cowling. This gun had 600 rounds, and there was provision for ring-and-bead and Aldis sights. Immediately behind the pilot there was a Scarff ring-mounting for a Lewis gun, for which six 97-round ammunition drums were provided. Tubular bomb-carriers were fitted outboard of the undercarriage under the wings for two 230/250-lb or four 112-lb bombs, these last in tandem. Alternative provision was made under the starboard wing for four 20-lb bombs. Beneath each lower longeron was provision for a 520/550-lb carrier. A single carrier to port appears to have been standard practice, but the Leopard-engined specimen, if not others, had a carrier to starboard. On the production-type bombers, the windows lighting the bomb-aimer's prone position, the hatch for which was close behind the radiator, were lower than on the prototype. The bombsight was of the Mk.IIB pattern, and the bomb-aimer had an indicator for correcting the pilot during the bombing run. In 1926 Hawker developed a special mounting for the bombsight, comprising a pair of telescopic members, one of which carried the sight. The sight was mounted at the lower end of a tube, arranged to slide without rotation within another tube attached to the cockpit. The first tube was moved axially by a screwed spindle operated by a handle at the top and was clamped in position by a split ring.

The torpedo-bomber Horsley had two heavily braced tubular steel crutches under the fuselage for a torpedo of Mk.VIII or Type K pattern

Hawker Horsley torpedo-bomber with 520-lb bomb on port Universal carrier under fuselage and 250-lb bomb on Universal carrier under port wing. The pistol stop for the torpedo is seen beneath the radiator, the sighting bar runs across the top of the picture and the ejection chutes for the Vickers gun are visible just forward of the pilot's cockpit.

Features associated with the Horsley's torpedo installation apparent here are the ring sights flanking the pilot's windscreen, sighting bar, pistol stop and crutch. A tubular bomb-carrier is seen beneath the wing. (*Flight International.*)

or one of 2,150 lb. Consideration was apparently given to carrying a 21-in torpedo of some 2,800 lb. The torpedo sighting bar was attached beneath the upper wing on two brackets very near the attachment points for the forward inner wing-bracing struts. Two sighting rings were mounted just forward of the pilot's windscreen, one on each side, and a pistol stop was attached beneath the radiator. Both the pilot and the gunner had a torpedo release. On production torpedo-bombers, the Scarff ring-mounting was of wind-balanced type. The torpedo-bomber Horsley with the geared Leopard engine had its pistol stop attached beneath the reduction-gear housing. An installation was made of Universal bomb-carriers, as shown in a photograph herewith. The two carriers under the fuselage were of the No.2 pattern (50/550-lb); No.1 carriers (50/250-lb) were fitted beneath the wings. On the aircraft depicted, an installation was also made well aft under the fuselage for a carrier for four 20-lb bombs, also suitable for marine markers.

Hornbill The Hornbill single-seat fighter of 1926 sacrificed armament to performance: there was only one gun, and so narrow was the fuselage that jam-clearance was more difficult than usual, if not impossible. The single Vickers gun was mounted low in the port side of the cockpit and fired through a long blast channel. Provision was apparently made for some-

The Hawker Hornbill had a single Vickers gun, mounted low in the fuselage.

thing like twice the normal quantity of ammunition (1,000 rounds) and the ejection chutes were faired. A tubular gunsight mounting was fitted at a development stage when the aircraft had a direct-drive Condor engine.

Hawfinch Redoubtable opponent of the Bristol Bulldog in the competition for an RAF day and night fighter to replace the Siskin IIIA, the Hawfinch appeared in 1927. The two Vickers guns were installed high in the top of the fuselage and fired through troughs which ended in line with the forward centre-section struts. A similar disposition of the guns was to continue throughout the line of Hawker biplane single-seaters. Behind each trough was a fairing, apparently over the trigger motor. The two guns and equipment were listed as weighing 88 lb, and 1,200 rounds of ammunition accounted for another 100 lb. There was a fore-and-aft tube ahead of the windscreen upon which an Aldis or a ring-and-bead sight could be mounted. Beneath the port wing were rails for a four 20-lb bomb-carrier.

Harrier The Harrier was a two-seat day bomber/torpedo-carrier, competitive with the Handley Page Hare and Blackburn Beagle. The pilot's Vickers gun was installed much as on the Horsley. There was a ring-and-bead sight on a tube mounting. The Scarff ring-mounting for a Lewis gun was immediately behind the pilot and was of wind-balanced pattern. The gunner's seat was retractable to allow him to adopt a prone position for bomb-aiming. Tests were conducted at Martlesham with two 230-lb bombs on tubular carriers beneath the wings, but four 112-lb bombs could be carried in their place, and the maximum designed bomb load appears to have been the same as for the Beagle, namely eight 112-lb or four 230-lb bombs.

When the bomb-carriers were removed and torpedo crutches were fitted under the fuselage, a torpedo of some 2,150 lb was intended to be carried as an alternative to the lighter Mk.VIII.

Air Ministry Specification 23/25, to which the Harrier was ordered in February 1927, was perhaps the most exacting to be issued during the 1920s requiring as it did the reconcilement of high performance at altitude while carrying a bomb load with the low-level qualities of a

232

A Hawker Hart of the original development batch, showing how the 112-lb bombs were carried in tandem. On later Harts they were side by side.

Hart and Hart (Special) The Hart light bomber, or single-engined day bomber, as it came to be classed (SEDB), dated from 1928 and was competitive with the Avro Antelope and Fairey Fox II. The influence of the original Fox on the specification is self-evident, but the Hart proved uncommonly adaptable and was the sire of numerous variants which are individually treated. The following official account covers armament features common to most, and even takes account of the 'development Harts', which had a bomb installation differing from standard. The two guns were a Vickers Mk.II and a Lewis Mk.III. Official notes follow:

'The Vickers gun is carried on the port side of the fuselage 1-in above the airscrew thrust line. The gun mounting brackets are riveted to a support tube bolted to the fuselage side struts. The rear bracket is provided with vertical and lateral adjustment. A short cartridge chute is fitted below the gun to deflect the empty cases through the fuselage fairing and clear of the aeroplane structure. A small link chute is attached by two thumb screws to the side of the gun and the chute directs the links over the edge of the fuselage fairing. The chute has a steel frame round it and this frame fits another frame which is screwed to the body of the gun. The ammunition supply is carried in a metal box placed transversely across the fuselage beneath the pilot's feet. The box is located in guides by two trigger catches, and when these are released the box can be drawn downwards through the bomb sight bay leaving the upper conduit in position. The top of the box body, which is large enough to contain 500 rounds of ·303 in S.A.A. in clips [*sic*] is fitted with a door to permit loading of the ammunition.

'Ring and bead sights are used for the Vickers gun. The sights are carried on a tube mounted on brackets on the fireproof bulkhead and the decking in front of the windscreen. The tube is provided with three transverse slotted holes. Normally the ring sight is fitted in the middle slot, which is approximately the regulation 36-in in front of the pilot's

235

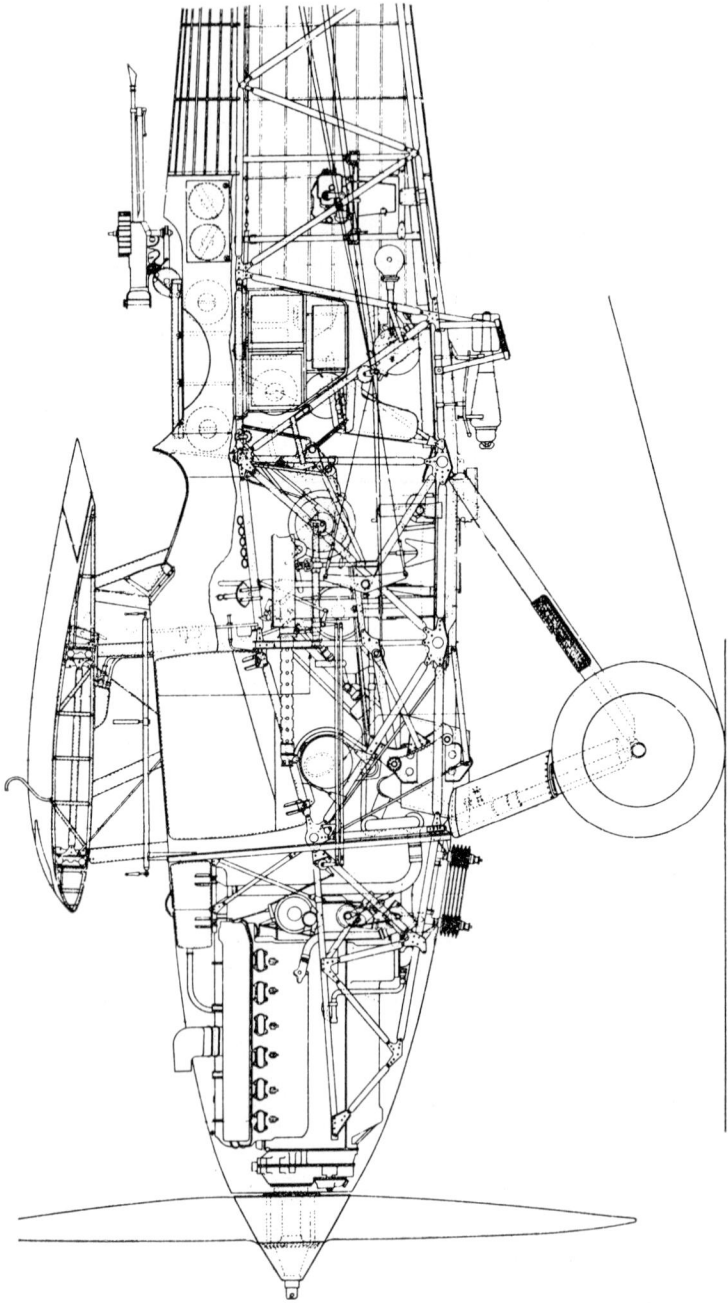

Makers' drawing showing installation of military equipment in the Hawker Hart, including a Light Series bomb-carrier under the fuselage.

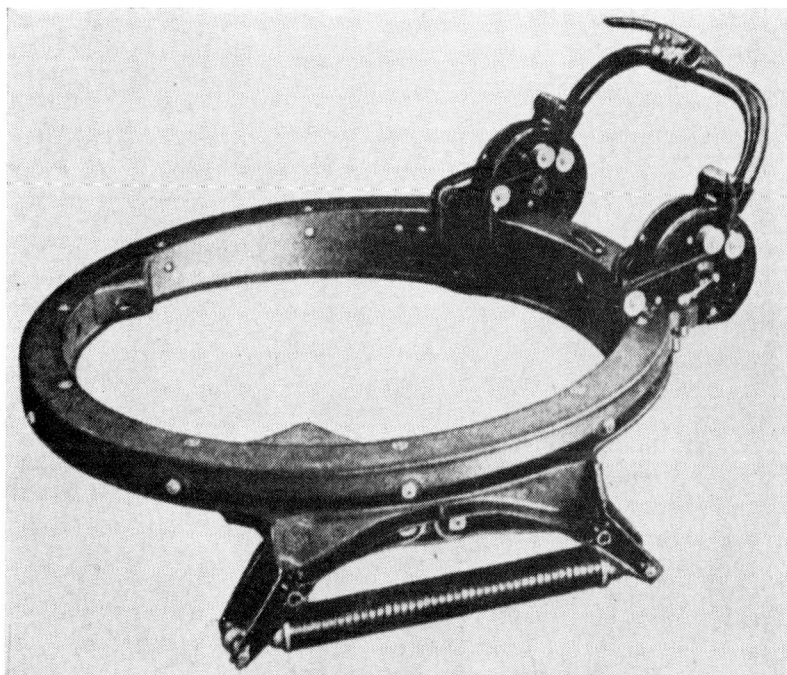

Hawker ring-mounting, as fitted to Hart and variants.

eye, and the bead in the slot immediately in front of the windscreen. When attacking ground targets, however, these positions may be reversed. If preferred by the pilot, the bead may be fitted in the front slot or in both front and rear slots, but for air targets the ring should of course always be fitted in the middle slot.

'The gear used is the Type C single. The firing trigger is placed in the control column handle. The reservoir is placed in an inclined position on the starboard side of the pilot's seat.

'The Lewis gun Mk.III is carried over the rear cockpit on a special gun ring of the manufacturer's own design. This consists of a rotating ring carrying ten vertical and ten horizontal rollers which run on a second ring fixed to the cockpit decking. Both rings are aluminium-silicon castings. The rotating ring is formed with a varying depth of section so that its bottom surface provides a cam contour on which run two spring-loaded rollers. The rollers are deflected to their lowest positions and the spring consequently fully compressed when the gun is in its aftermost position, and the cam contour is so formed that as the gun ring is rotated either way from due aft the rollers exert on it a progressively greater deflecting force which serves to balance the air forces on the gun due to the slipstream. The adjustment of the spring tension should not be interfered with as a very small reduction in its effective

237

length would cause blocking of the spring and consequent failure of the tension rod.

'The gun elevating gear consists of a tubular steel arch hinged to the rotating ring and located in the desired position by stop pins engaging with quadrants. The stop pins are actuated by the normal type of lever on the arch through Bowden wires to a cam and tappet mechanism, which also operates the locking pins for the rotating ring. The weight of

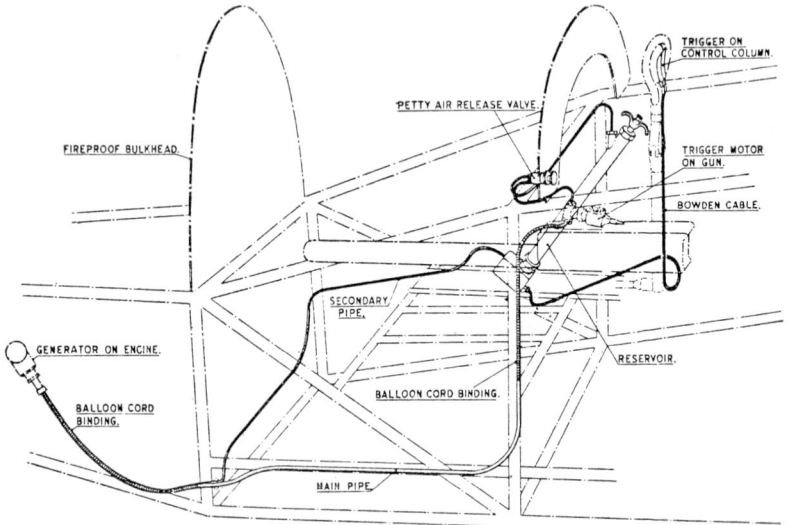

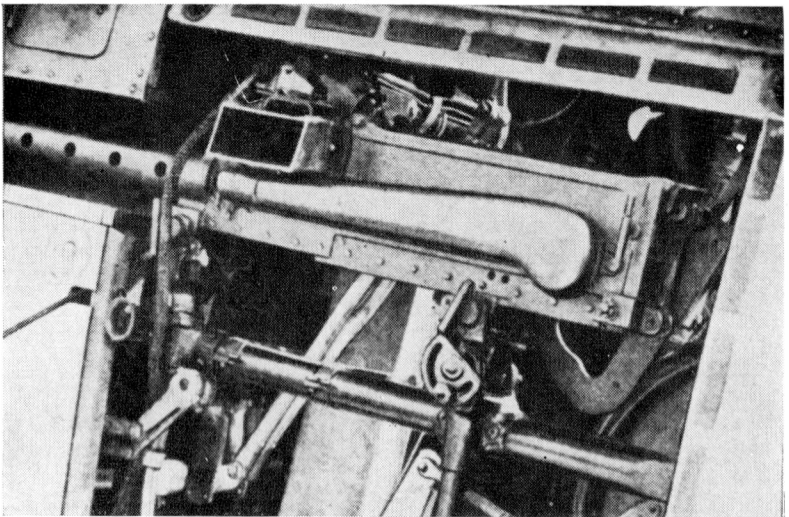

Cause and effect (1): installation of Vickers gun in Hawker Hart, the drawing showing details of the C.C. synchronising gear, and the photograph, the gun with link chute fitted.

Cause and effect (2): testing the Vickers gun of a Hart at the stop butts. An ejected link is clearly visible below its chute. (*Flight International.*)

the gun is balanced by elastic cord loops. The ammunition is carried in eight Mk.II No.2 magazines (97 rounds), seven of the magazines being accommodated on pegs in the rear cockpit and the remaining one on the gun.' [On the Hart prototype the gun mounting was in an early stage of development.]

Twin Vickers guns in the Hawker Hornet, showing fireproof bulkhead cut away to accept troughs.

Persian Fury with Bristol Mercury engine, showing special form of ring cowling to clear the lines of fire of the guns. (*Flight International.*)

The official account continued:

'Bombs are carried under the main planes only. The total load of bombs which may be carried can be made up in several ways, the alternative loadings being as follows:

Port plane	Starboard plane
Universal carrier	Universal carrier—Light series carriers
2—112 lb	2—112 lb⎫
or 1—230 lb	or 1—230 lb⎪
or 1—250 lb	or 1—250 lb⎬ and 4—20 lb
*or 4— 20 lb	⎪
† ———	or 4— 20 lb⎭

* Electro-mechanical release⎱ Port and starboard Universal
† Mechanical release ⎰ carriers removed

'The fifteen development Hart aeroplanes, service numbers J9933 to J9947, are fitted to carry the 112 lb bomb racks in tandem. Subsequent Hart aeroplanes are fitted with an intermediate bomb girder in place of the outboard lugs fitted to the development aeroplanes, and the 112-lb bombs are carried side by side. A light series carrier outboard of the universal carrier attachments is provided on the starboard plane.

'The release of the bombs can be controlled from either of the cockpits, the air gunner adopting the prone position for the purpose, and both stations are equipped with salvo and light series releases. For the large bombs which are fitted with fusing gear a fusing lever is clipped to the

240

starboard fuselage side strut ED where it is accessible to both pilot and air gunner. The air gunner's salvo and light series releases are bolted to the wood framing on the starboard side of the cockpit. The fusing lever controls both port and starboard plane bomb loads and gives the usual three positions: "Safety", "Tail fuse", "Both fuses".

'Electro-magnetic bomb release is fitted only to special instructions. When electro-magnetic bomb release is fitted, fusing is effected either electrically or mechanically.

'The air gunner is provided with a course setting bomb sight Mk.VI. A small instrument board immediately in front of the bombing aperture carries an air speed indicator, an altimeter and a cross level where they can be conveniently read from the prone position.

'Provision is made to fit a camera gun (Camera, aircraft, G.3) on the top of the port bottom main plane.

'De Havilland type speaking tubes are fitted for intercommunication between pilot and air gunner, connections being available for the latter in both seated and prone positions.

Hart (Special) Aeroplane

'The Hart (Special) Aeroplane is an Audax aeroplane modified to carry out, as far as possible, the duties of a Hart day bomber.

Hart with Armstrong Siddeley Panther engine, showing special trough in ring cowling, front and rear gun installations and 250-lb bombs.

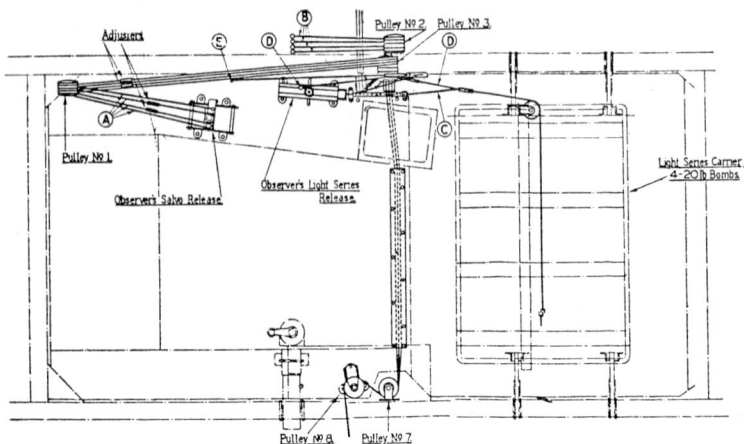

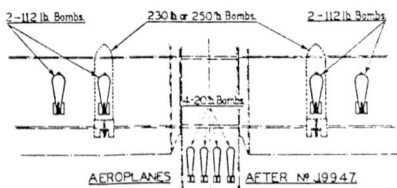

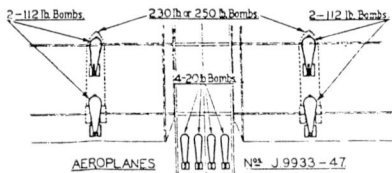

Makers' drawings of bomb installation in Hawker Hart.
On the Hart (Special) there were differences in detail.

A. Observers Salvo
B. Pilots Salvo.
C. Observer's Light Series.
D. Pilot's Light Series.
E. Fusing Control.

Pulley Nº 2. Joint E.

Pilots Salvo Release.

Pilots Light Series Release.

Fusing Lever.

Pulley Nº 3.

Junction of fusing wires for
Port and Starboard Bombs.

Junction of Pilots and Observers
Salvo for Port Bombs.

Junction of Pilots and Observers
Salvo for Starboard Bombs.

Junction of Pilots and Observers
Light Series Cables.

Pulley Nº 1.

Observer's Salvo Release.
Observer's Light Series Release.
Pulley Nº 4.
Pulley Nº 5.
Pulley Nº 6.

Joint F.
Joint H.

Pulley Nº 2.

Pulley Nº 3.

Pulley Nº 5.
Pulley Nº 4.
Pulley Nº 8.

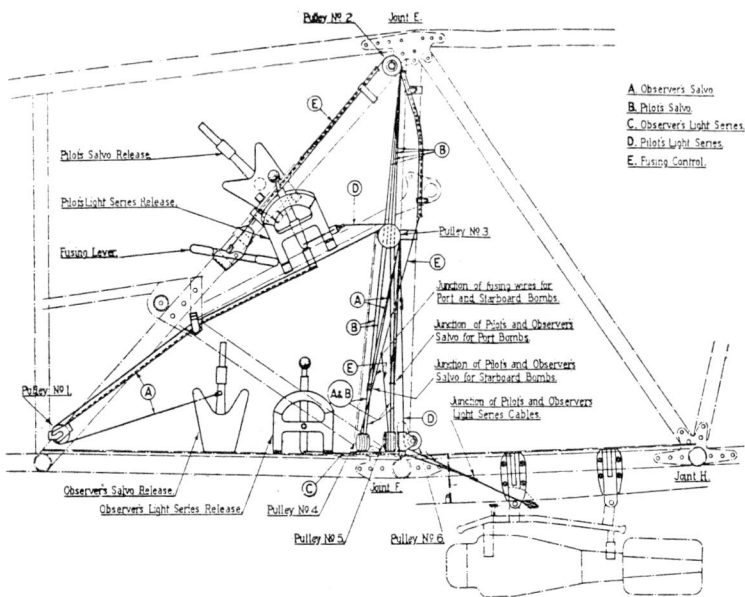

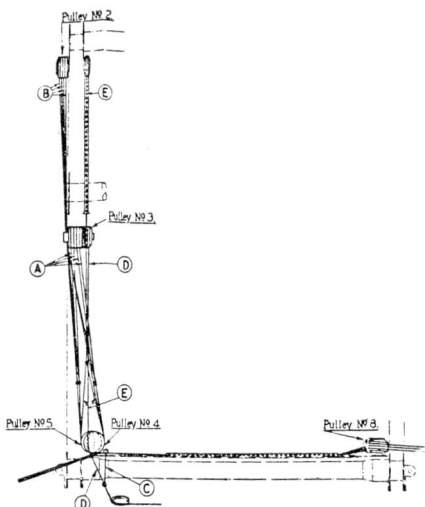

Makers' drawings showing details of the Light Series bomb-carrier installation
(four 20-lb) under the fuselage of the Hawker Hart.

I   243

Hart (Special) day bomber of No.600 (City of London) Squadron prior to re-equipment of the squadron with Demons. Note squadron markings and installation of G.3 camera gun on lower wing. (*Flight International.*)

'The bomb release gear is electro-mechanically operated. The Mk.II gun synchronising gear is fitted. The ammunition is carried in seven Mk.II No.2 magazines (97 rounds) . . . The release of all bombs is electro-magnetically operated. Selector, release and jettison switches are mounted in the pilot's cockpit and in the air gunner's prone position, thus giving independent bomb release control.'

In service the Light Series carrier was fitted under the fuselage, together with a second carrier of the same type for practice bombs. Although the development Harts had tubular carriers for the main bomb load under the wings, the true production-type Hart had Universal carriers. A large window was let in to the starboard side of the fuselage to light the bomb-aimer's position, to which warm air could be ducted. As production progressed the gun trough was deepened at the forward end and sometimes a collector box was fitted over and below the case and link chutes. A restraining clip for the Lewis gun was fitted on the fuselage decking behind the gun ring. When the 120-lb bomb came into service, this was an alternative to the 112-lb.

Detail variations in aircraft of basic Hart type equipped to foreign order are too numerous to list, but mention must be made of the following: Esthonian Hart with two front guns; Panther-Hart (tested at Martlesham Heath with two 250-lb bombs), with short gun-trough and dimpled ring

244

cowling in continuation of line of fire; Jupiter-Hart and Pegasus-Hart with gun lowered to clear cylinders; Dagger-Hart (also tested with two 250-lb bombs) with special gun-trough to suit engine cowling; Swedish Pegasus-Hart with front gun on starboard side instead of port.

For use with the camera gun, the Hart Trainer (which was unarmed) could have an Aldis sight on the tube forward of the front windscreen and a similar sight on the starboard side of the rear windscreen.

Osprey Although the production-type Osprey carrier-borne two-seat fleet fighter reconnaissance aircraft did not appear until 1932, the true prototype appeared in 1929 as the 'Naval Hart', this being an adaptation of the prototype day bomber airframe. The 'fighter' element in the make-up of the 'navalised' aircraft was betokened by an Aldis sight in addition to ring-and-bead sight, fixed to a fore-and-aft tube. Otherwise gun armament followed Hart practice. On the production Osprey, the tube carrying the sights was much longer, as on the production Hart, and provision was made for a Light Series (four 20-lb) bomb-carrier under the port wing— unlike the Nimrod, which had its carrier to starboard. In service a collector box was sometimes fitted for the Vickers gun.

Hornet This interceptor of 1929 had virtually the same armament installation as the F.20/27, though the cooling jackets of the guns were more prominent in the troughs. As the aircraft was tested at Martlesham Heath, an Aldis sight was installed on the centre line forward of the windscreen, and at one stage at least, a ring-and-bead sight was also fitted. The pillars for the sights were not faired as on the F.20/27. There was a transverse access panel above each ejection chute and a second panel fore-and-aft over each breech casing.

Nimrod Closely related both to the Hornet and the Hoopoe, the Nimrod (at first, 1930, called Norn) had the same armament provisions. In production aircraft, the Aldis and ring-and-bead sights were interchangeable (centre line or starboard) and from the beginning there was provision for a Light Series (four 20-lb) bomb-carrier under the starboard wing. A camera gun could be fitted above the lower starboard wing.

Like its predecessor in service, the Fairey Flycatcher, the Nimrod carried its bombs primarily for diving and low-flying attacks against suitable targets, whether by sea or land. In the former instance the anti-aircraft armament of warships was considered a primary objective, but it is of interest to note that the British Fleet fighters (for so the class was officially designated) were never called upon to carry relatively heavy bombs as were their U.S. Navy counterparts. The Curtiss Goshawk, for example, had provision for either four 116-lb bombs under the wings or a single bomb of 474 lb under the fuselage. Similarly, the Curtiss Helldiver, the nearest American counterpart of the Nimrod's two-seater companion type the Osprey, made its name as a dive-bomber, although having a fighter designation. This type also carried double the Osprey's complement of machine-guns, two being fixed and two free.

Three Hawker single-seat fighters, illustrating stages in the development of machine-gun armament: (*top*) Nimrod; (*centre*), Fury with collector boxes; (*third*), Yugoslav Fury with two additional guns in fairings far outboard under wings to clear propeller arc.

246

Fury All British variants of the Fury interceptor (1931), including the 'Super' and 'High-Speed' versions, had the same armament installation, with the positions of the ring-and-bead and Aldis sights interchangeable between the centre line or to starboard, 600 rounds per gun (Vickers Mk.II, III and V progressively fitted) and provision for camera gun above the starboard lower wing. The following is a weight breakdown for the military load of the Fury and other British interceptors of its period:

Quantity	Item	Weight in lb
2	Vickers 0·303-in guns	60
1 set	Synchronising gear (double)	18
2	Belts S.A.A. (1,200 rounds)	87
2	Gun sights	4
1	Safety belt	3
1	Irvin parachute	20
1	Very pistol and 8 cartridges	7
1 set	Oxygen apparatus	20
1 set	Electrical heating	24
		243

Collector boxes for the empty cases and links were fitted on some squadron aircraft recalling the Woodcock of former years.

The export models included a version of the Yugoslav Fury with two additional guns enclosed in fairings under the lower wings. By reason of the large-diameter airscrew, these were almost as far outboard as the interplane-strut attachments. The Iranian Fury was fitted with a Light Series bomb-carrier beneath the fuselage and was further distinguished by having two inverted channels formed in the top segment of the Townend ring cowling over the Mercury engine to clear the lines of fire of the guns.

It is not inappropriate to append the following description of air-firing practice as demonstrated at a Hendon display by three Furies, the target being a drogue towed by a Fairey Gordon:

'Breaking from flight formation above and astern of the target the Furies attacked. Their leader dived, fired a burst and pulled up in a rocket loop, getting into position for a second dive. The remaining two Furies attacked from the quarter, one passing above and the other diving below the sleeve. As the Gordon repeated its run over the aerodrome the fighters approached in echelon starboard. They dived in as a flight and made a beam attack in succession. Then, before taking up formation, the leader attacked from below and the others from both sides.'

Hart Fighter and Demon In March 1931 the Air Ministry announced that, during the three months ending June that year, one flight of No.23 (Fighter) Squadron would be equipped with Hawker Hart two-seat fighters. This Hart variant, the Hart Fighter, was the forerunner of the Demon, and marked the re-entry of this class of aircraft into RAF service. In addition

Doyen among British armament-development aircraft, J9933 is seen in two forms: *top*, Hart Fighter prototype, with dummy Lewis gun; *lower*, Hart Fighter development aircraft with screens for gunner.

to a fully supercharged engine and night-flying equipment the type had ring-and-bead and Aldis sights, as on the Osprey, and retained the single Vickers gun on the port side. There was, however, a more noticeable difference, namely the canting forward of the Hawker ring-mounting so that its forward rim rested on the top longeron, and not on the built-up decking as formerly. Less noticeable, but serving the same purpose of improving the gunner's field of fire, was the lowering of the top line of the fuselage behind the gun mounting. The more slender fuselage which resulted was one of several features which distinguished the Demon from other Hart variants.

The armament-development aircraft on which this rearrangement was initially made was the first production-type Hart, J9933, and this machine, before it became the prototype of the Turret Demon, was fitted with protective screens at the forward edge of the gunner's cockpit and on another occasion with a massive angular canopy. In this latter state the aircraft had an experimental collector arrangement for the Vickers gun ejection chutes. The collector extended downwards almost to the lower wing.

The standard production Demon had two Vickers guns with 600 rounds each and provision for two Light Series bomb-carriers, one under each wing.

The present writer flew in Demons at every opportunity, and after a trip in a squadron aircraft wrote:

'The parachute (observer's type) is carried either stowed in a recess behind the pilot's seat, where it is easily accessible and yet does not interfere with gunnery, or is attached to two hooks on the harness over the lower part of the chest. There is a small folding seat in the forward portion of the cockpit, which, when extended, allows the occupant to sit in a normal fashion if he faces astern, or to straddle it and face forward, when he can rest his elbows on, or grip, the gun ring. No form of Sutton harness is provided for the man in the back seat. He is anchored to the floor by a "safety wire" embodying a quick-release, and connects an eye on the harness at his nethermost portion to a fixture on the floor.

Two more forms of J9933: *top*, Hart Fighter development aircraft with cockpit protection and collector box; *lower*, Turret Demon prototype, with Nash and Thompson power-operated turret, manned in this instance by the author. (Lower picture, *Flight International*.)

249

In addition there is a metal hoop on which the air gunner, should he wish to use his gun at a steep angle over the side of the machine, can stand, or against which he can brace himself during rapid manoeuvres.'

In 1936 the Air Ministry announced that certain Demon aircraft were being fitted with 'F.N. turrets with cupola heads'. They were to be converted by the contractors. The development of the Nash and Thompson turret concerned will be described in Volume 2; meanwhile some impres-

Details of J9933 in the last two forms shown on the previous pages.

Two forms of the Hawker Demon: *top*, Australian Demon, showing Universal bomb-
carriers and collector boxes; *lower*, standard RAF Demon. The form of the rear gun
positions may be compared, that of the Australian machine being of Hind type.
(Lower picture, *Flight International*.)

sions of the turret, formed by the present writer when he was permitted to
try it in the air, may be given. One recorded in *Flight*:

'Those with a memory for such things will recall that at the time of
the formation of Parnall Aircraft in 1935 it was announced that a Nash
and Thompson turret had been fitted experimentally to the Demon
J9933. Since that time this amazing piece of mechanism has been ex-
haustively tested at Martlesham and one counted oneself fortunate in
being permitted to fly in the machine and to manipulate the turret, details of which must perforce be withheld. It is the most human gadget
imaginable; one has only to think of the direction in which one wishes
to aim the gun and the indescribable mechanism seems to do the rest.'

On that same day the writer flew in a standard Demon of No.64 Squadron
and was left with no doubt of the turret's significance. The slipstream was
a cold, hard fact.

The Demon's turret was mounted on the fuselage top longerons and the upper decking was cut away accordingly, as seen in the photographs. In his book *Hawker Aircraft since 1920* (Putnam, 1961), Francis K. Mason has recorded that the weight of the turret moved the c.g. of the Demon to its aft safe limit, but that Service clearance was achieved after spinning trials at Brooklands and Martlesham. Some Turret Demons were built as new by Boulton Paul, others were retrospectively modified standard Demons.

Parnall Aircraft Ltd said of the turret:

'In the Nash and Thompson "Demon" turret the application of hydraulic power has given to the aerial gunner personal protection against hostile fire and increased effectiveness of his own fire at high speeds. Because of the smoothness of operation of this turret the gunner's fire has become of much superior accuracy. The design provides for the seat to be linked to the gun, thus giving him comparative comfort in all firing positions. This factor, coupled with ease of manipulation, makes firing as successful as possible at high speeds and gives improved marksmanship. To cater for the varying size of gunners, adjustments are possible both for height and for chin-to-eye level measurements. To eliminate possible danger of shooting away parts of the aircraft structure a rotational trip mechanism has been evolved. The gunner is thus able to concentrate fully on his target without the necessity of giving thought to his own machine. Addition of a folding cupola to the turret has overcome the effects of increased wind pressure on the gunner. It follows all gun movements and thus gives the gunner perfect protection. With the cupola closed and the gun in the stowed position little drag is added to the machine, while its shielding effect on the rudder is negligible. The turret is equipped with special heating for the body, hands and feet, intercommunication phones, gun heating, oxygen supply, lighting for reflector sight, and parachute stowage.'

The Australian Demon was a considerably different aircraft and was essentially a Hind with two front guns. Certainly the rear-gun position was that of the Hind and not of the Demon. Provision was made for two 250-lb +sixteen 20-lb or four 112-lb + eight 20-lb bombs. There was a prone bomb-aimer's station with Mk.VII sight and electrical release controls. The Vickers guns were of the Mk.V pattern, made in Australia.

Audax The Audax went into production during 1931 as an army co-operation Hart derivative. Reference to armament has already been made in connection with the Hart Special. Normal bomb load for army co-operation work was eight 20-lb bombs, but two 112-lb bombs was a possible load and two 250-lb bombs were carried during the Habbaniyah operations in 1941. A more usual load on the two Universal carriers was two cylindrical supply-dropping containers, sometimes confused with bombs. These, in turn, should not be confused with the box-like containers

Hawker Audax as used for armament training, releasing three practice bombs. One bomb remains on the carrier. The pilot has an Aldis as well as a ring-and-bead sight.

for desert equipment, holding tool kit, covers for engine and airscrew, rations boxes, or 4-gallon fuel cans.

A ring-and-bead sight was normal on the Audax, but aircraft of the type used for armament training had an Aldis sight.

Attaching a supply-dropping container to a Universal bomb-carrier on an Audax.

253

Egyptian Audax with fairing for Vickers gun and 'dimpled' long-chord cowling over Panther engine.

On the versions of the Audax with Pratt & Whitney Hornet or Bristol Pegasus engine, the front gun was lowered in the fuselage to clear the cylinders. An especially interesting installation of the front gun was to be seen on the Audax with Panther engine, the body of the gun being virtually outside the fuselage proper but housed within a massive 'blister' fairing with case and link chutes let in. The long-chord engine cowling had a corresponding 'dimple' as on the similarly engined Fairey Seal.

During 1933 an Audax was used for trials with the Vickers Mk.V gun.

The three-seat Hawker Dantorp differed considerably from the Horsley, from which it was developed. The torpedo pistol stop is seen in place.

Hawker Hardy prototype, with containers for desert equipment outboard of Universal bomb-carriers. A G.3 camera gun is installed on the port lower wing.

Dantorp The Dantorp was developed in 1932 from the Leopard-engined Horsley, from which it differed considerably. It was arranged as a three-seater, the third cockpit being between the pilot and the ring-mounting. This mounting had to be moved aft in consequence; it was of the Scarff type, but of Danish pattern, differing in detail from the British. The 1,500-lb torpedo was likewise of Danish pattern. There was no fixed gun for the pilot, as on the Horsley. Eight 50-kg bombs formed an alternative loading to the torpedo.

Hardy The Hardy was developed during 1934 as a general purpose aircraft and greatly resembled the Audax. There were four under-wing Universal carriers for four 112-lb or two 250-lb bombs, and outboard of these on each side was a Light Series carrier.

P.V.3 (F.7/30) This last type of Hawker biplane fighter (1934) had two Vickers guns mounted as on the Fury and associated types—in the cockpit

Case and link chutes low in the fuselage and a deep trough ahead mark the positioning of the lower pair of Vickers guns in the Hawker P.V.3. Similarly located were the fuselage guns of the Fury Monoplane, which eventually became the Hurricane.

at shoulder-level—and a second pair low in the sides. A similar position was retained for the Fury Monoplane. Ammunition supply totalled 1,800 rounds. The guns were installed with extreme neatness, the upper pair firing for a short distance through blast tubes and thence through short troughs. The external troughs for the lower guns commenced in the same region as the upper ones—in way of the forward undercarriage and centre-section struts. Case and link chutes for the lower guns were separate. Provision appears to have been made for a reflector sight, although a bead sight was mounted on the cowling. As on the Nimrod II, to which the P.V.3 was closely related, there was provision for four 20-lb bombs under the starboard wing.

Hind In essence the Hind day bomber of 1934 was a Hart with a fully supercharged engine (as distinct from normally aspirated, high compression); but in detail it was considerably more. Among visual distinctions from the Hart bomber was the forward-canted ring-mounting, following Demon practice, though the installation differed quite considerably from that on the Demon, for the rear fuselage was of full depth and the mounting was higher on the decking, necessitating a small projecting lip on each side. This 'female of the species' differed further from the Hart bomber in having the metal cowling panels extended rearwards. Thus, on the starboard side, the bomb-aimer's side window, introduced on the Hart, had a metal surround, and to port there was a corresponding window, let in to the same panel as the case and link chutes for the pilot's Vickers gun.

Bomb load was the same as the Hart's, except that Light Series carriers

The Hawker Hind (*left*) has four Universal bomb-carriers, and a Light Series carrier outboard on the port side. Note also installation of Vickers and Lewis guns and bomb-aimer's window let in to metal cowling. The above view of a Hind shows a 230-lb bomb on a Universal carrier.

do not appear to have been fitted under the fuselage, although they were sometimes fitted under the starboard, as well as the port, wing. An Aldis sight was occasionally fitted in addition to the ring-and-bead type.

The gun trough on the Yugoslav Hind was noticeably deeper at the rear, and the link and case chutes were in tandem. On a Swiss Hind a collector box for links (but not, apparently, for cases) has been identified, and on the Latvian and Iranian Hinds the gun was low-set as on the radial-engined Harts. These last-named Hinds had a Mercury engine and the leading-edge exhaust-collector ring was grooved to clear the line of fire, as on the Gloster Gladiator.

P.V.4 This two-seat biplane of 1935 can justly be regarded as Britain's first specialised dive-bomber. It was designed as a private venture to the G.4/31 specification but without provision for the torpedo at first demanded. The pilot's Vickers gun was installed much in the manner of the lower guns on the P.V.3 fighter; that is, the gun fired through a blast tube which terminated in line with the front centre-section struts. Forward of this was a short trough. There were 600 rounds for this gun and a ring-and-bead sight was fitted on the usual Hawker fore-and-aft tube. The case

257

The Hawker P.V.4 was capable of delivering four 250-lb bombs in a diving attack. That 'precision' bombing was also possible is indicated by the sliding panel in the bottom of the fuselage. (*Flight International.*)

chute was flush and the link chute was faired. The installation of the Lewis gun, for which there were six double drums, was of exceptional interest. The base-ring of the mounting was canted as on the Demon, but the coaming around it was very carefully modelled and faired. The mounting itself was not of the usual Hawker type, but was described as a 'Somers' mounting.

The normal load was four 112-lb or two 250-lb plus four 20-lb bombs, but diving was possible with two 500-lb bombs. It may be mentioned that, notwithstanding the high factors involved, the aircraft was claimed to carry 93 per cent of its own weight as disposable load. The Pegasus X engine installed at one phase of testing was the original engine which performed the type-tests for the series and repeatedly attained 3,050 rpm in diving tests although the normal figure was 2,250. Level 'precision' bombing was possible by virtue of a prone bomb-aiming station similar to that on the Hart.

Hartbees   Like the Australian Demon, the South African Hartbees (1935) had two fixed Vickers guns in addition to the Lewis gun on a Hawker ring-mounting. There were under-wing bomb-carriers, and two machines were armoured to allow them to 'get close to disturbances'. Plating was attached round the engine, side panels and under the fuselage.

Hector The Hector (1936) was an army co-operation development of the Dagger-Hart and Audax, and differed considerably from other Hart variants—more, indeed, than its massive new engine and straight top wing suggested, and more, it appears, than historians have hitherto recorded. It had, in fact, an entirely new type of gun mounting, as the present writer recollected over the years when he came to compile these notes. His recollection is confirmed by this report of a practice dive-bombing sortie. This he offers not only as an historical reminiscence but as a memorial to the dive-bombing of German troops by six Hectors near Calais on 26 May, 1940:

'We note the marked offsetting of the Hector's fin (to counteract torque), the radio aerial overhead, and read "Barr and Stroud" on the wind-balanced gun ring. We are surrounded by switches, R/T gear and pegs for the ammunition drums. The chest-pack parachute, detached from

Hawker Hector, showing Barr & Stroud ring-mounting for Lewis gun, pilot's Vickers gun and sights, trough in cowling of Napier Dagger engine and Light Series bomb-carriers inboard of containers for desert equipment.

259

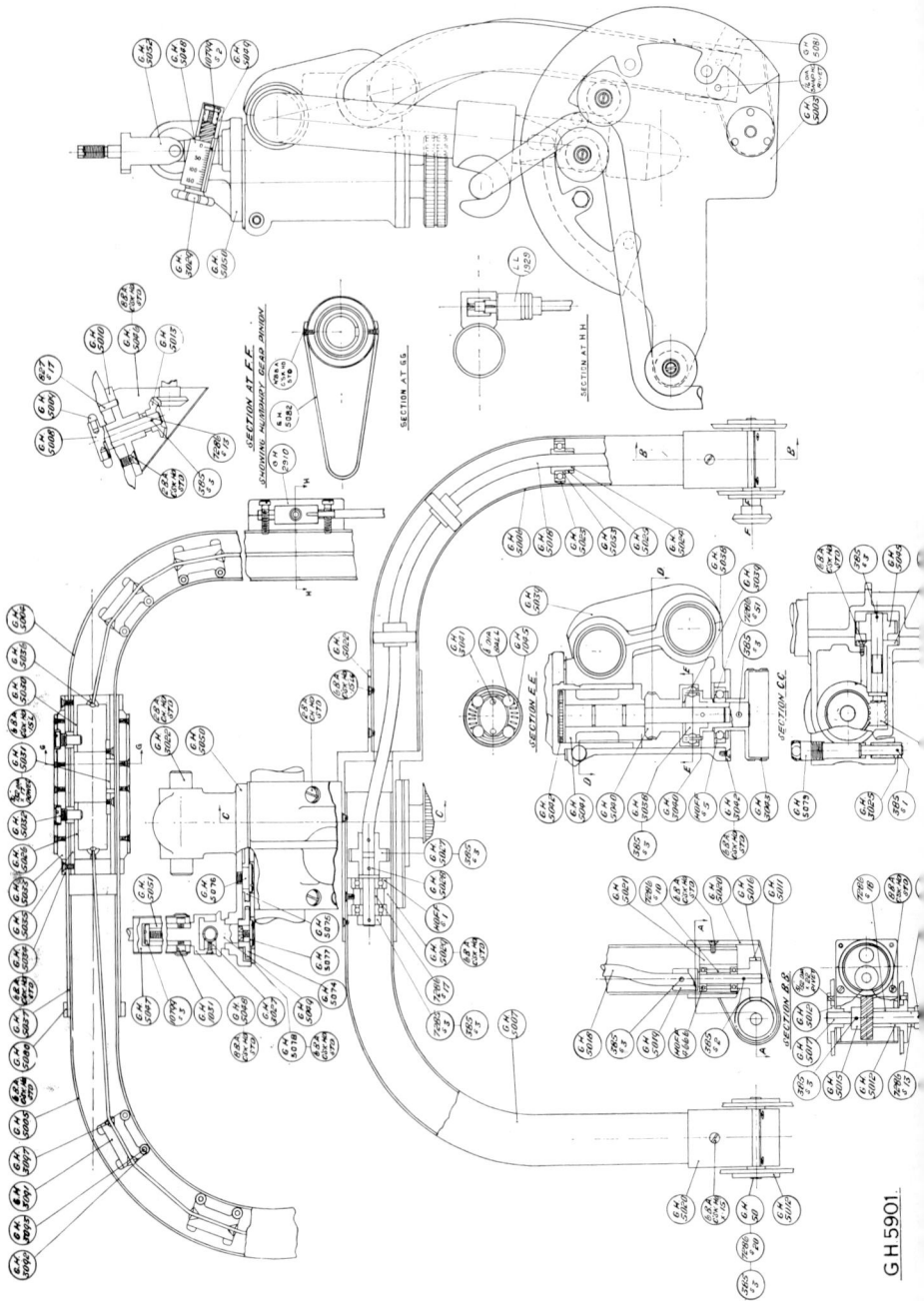

Makers' drawing of Barr & Stroud gun mounting for Hawker Hector.

the big stainless-steel hooks on our harness to give freedom of movement, is stowed in its rack on the forward wall of the cockpit. The black butt of a Very pistol protrudes conveniently from its canvas holster. As the Hectors change to a wide echelon formation we reaffirm that the "dog chain", or safety wire which connects with our parachute and anchors us to the floor, is securely attached. Our height is 3,000 feet . . .
'Then the horizon tilts crazily. The other Hectors seem to be drawn up and away by some ethereal vacuum cleaner . . . we are approaching the target in a 65 degree dive. The target passes beneath the nose cowl of the Dagger and the pilot shifts his bomb-release lever on its quadrant . . . The aerodrome drops away under our tail and we glimpse the drifting white smoke from our bombs, augmented as the other Hectors start unloading . . .'

Normal provision was made for eight 20-lb or two 112-lb or 120-lb bombs. When the writer flew in an early specimen at Martlesham Heath, it was fitted with an Aldis, as well as a ring-and-bead sight, but this was not normal. Compared with the Demon and Hind (which latter type it most resembled in rear-gun installation) it displayed a much larger flat surface of fuselage behind the gun ring mounting.

In 1968 the writer approached Barr & Stroud Ltd and a director of this renowned Scottish company confirmed that a mounting of the company's design was indeed supplied for the Hector. Though regretting that no description or photograph could be supplied, he nevertheless produced from the company archives the drawing which accompanies these notes.

Hurricane   Having prepared the Goshawk-engined P.V.3 biplane design to the F.7/30 specification, Hawker designer Sydney Camm was led to consider a monoplane, and the 'Fury Monoplane' was projected at Kingston. From this similarly-powered Goshawk-engined project grew the 'Interceptor Monoplane', to take the Rolls-Royce P.V.12 (later Merlin) engine and foreseen as having two Vickers guns in the fuselage and two Browning or Vickers guns outboard in the thick cantilever wing. As will be described in Volume 2, it was Sir Ralph Sorley (then Sqn Ldr Sorley) of the Air Ministry Operational Requirements branch whose ideas were so largely the basis of Specification F.5/34, calling for six or eight Browning guns. The eight-gun formula for which he was personally pressing stemmed from an Air Ministry conference on 19 July, 1934, on which occasion Capt F. W. Hill, senior ballistics officer at the A. and A.E.E., Martlesham Heath, showed that at least that number of guns, firing at 1,000 rounds a minute, would be required to destroy a bomber in two seconds. Meanwhile Sydney Camm did much practical work on the four-gun monoplane, leading to the F.36/34 specification, requiring four guns with twenty seconds firing time. At this point R. J. Mitchell's Supermarine Spitfire must be introduced, for upon Mitchell's proposals, emphasising climb and manoeuvrability, the specification calling for eight guns was formally written.

With increased ammunition capacity, Hawker's own 'F.36/34 Single-seat Fighter High-speed Monoplane' went ahead, but by January 1935 the company had proposals whereby the eight-gun armament requirement could be met. Even at this stage it was not known whether a licence could be negotiated for the Colt/Browning gun adapted for British 0·303-in ammunition. In February 1935 the Air Ministry contracted for one aircraft having no guns installed but ballasted for two Vickers Mk.V guns in the fuselage and a Browning or Vickers gun in each wing. But even when a licence was ratified in July 1935, and provision was made for eight outboard Browning guns, a similar Vickers gun installation was schemed as an alternative.

First production Hawker Hurricane I, with the positions of the eight Browning guns indicated by ports and ejection chutes.

Two points concerning the Hurricane may be instanced to illustrate how armament could influence structural design. The first concerns the two Vickers guns originally fitted in the fuselage, and which were responsible for the fuselage of the production-type aircraft being a trifle wider than was strictly necessary, the second—the introduction by Hawker of all-metal stressed-skin wings in place of their original, and ingenious, fabric-covered type—stemmed from the eight-gun decision. Ballasted for its eight guns, ammunition and radio, the Hurricane prototype first flew on 6 November, 1935.

Armament was first installed on the Hurricane in August 1936. On the first production Hurricane I (1937) the eight guns were harmonised for their lines of fire to converge at 650 yards, a distance thereafter progressively reduced. The Hurricane I which served specifically for armament development was L1695. Armour-plate and bullet-proof windscreen were added to production aircraft and two 20-mm guns were installed under the wings of a Hurricane in the spring of 1939, purely for test purposes. There was little immediate thought of their specific application to the Hawker fighter, but rather to the Westland Whirlwind. The Belgian Hurricanes had four 0·5-in Browning guns.

Although proposals for a cannon-armed Hurricane had been made as long before as late 1935, a trial installation of two guns was not made until May 1939, and the prototype Hurricane IIC (the first production variant

Just inboard of the landing lights of the Hawker Hotspur turret fighter were attachments for carriers for bombs or flares.

with cannon armament) was not in the air until February 1941. The development of the Hurricane's cannon armament has no genealogical claim on the present volume, nor has the twelve-Browning scheme.

The standard armament of the Hurricane I was:

8 Browning guns and accessories	212 lb
Case and link chutes	9 lb
Ammunition and boxes (2,660 rounds)	202 lb

Henley Built in 1937 to compete against the Fairey P.4/34 for RAF light-bomber orders, which never, in fact, materialised, the Henley differed very noticeably from its rival in having internal (fuselage) bomb stowage. Two 250-lb bombs were a typical internal load and two additional bombs of the same type were disposed under the wings on faired carriers. These carriers, together with bombs, were actually fitted during the summer of 1937 and were alternatives to Light Series carriers. A Vickers gun for the pilot was mounted in the wing, and a Lewis gun at the rear had a form of pillar mounting.

Hotspur The Hotspur turret fighter was built in 1938 and was a counterpart of the Boulton Paul Defiant. Although it is generally known that the turret fitted was a dummy, it appears to have escaped notice that there were attachments under the wings for two carriers for flares or bombs. There were no retractable fairings for the turret, as on the Defiant.

On the Hawker Hotspur the turret was a dummy, and there were no retractable fairings as on the Boulton Paul Defiant.

Tornado and Typhoon The design of both these single-seat fighters can be traced back to a Hawker proposal of April 1937, wherein an armament of twelve Browning guns was envisaged. The Tornado was flown, without armament, in 1939, and the first Typhoon early in 1940, so no detailed review of armament development is warranted here. Four 20-mm guns formed the alternative armament.

Kennedy

Giant No armament was ever fitted to this great biplane (142 ft span) of 1916, but mention is warranted because of the designer's earlier association with Igor Sikorsky (see under Handley Page V/1500) and the clear intention to install a tail turret, as betokened by the depth of rear fuselage. The following item in *The Aeroplane* of 28 February, 1923, is relevant:

'On Feb. 21 the trustee in bankruptcy of Mr Chessborough J. Mac-Kenzie Kennedy, the author of the famous super-Sikorsky which has so long decorated or disfigured (according to taste) the landscape at Northolt, sued the Air Council in respect of the rights to use the idea of a gun-pit in the tail of an aeroplane. The Plaintiff alleged that the War Office agreed with one Hamilton Edwards to take an aeroplane designed by Mr. Kennedy, having a gun-pit in the tail and engines mounted on the wings . . . It was further alleged that in the autumn of 1917 the Air Board lent their designing and technical staff to Handley Page Ltd., who disclosed to that firm Kennedy's confidential reports and that the Handley Page V/1500, which had a gun-pit in the tail, was the result. Mr. Frederick Handley Page applied for a patent for the tail gun-pit on March 15, 1918, and Mr. Kennedy applied for a patent on March 16.'

The action was dismissed.

The ultimate layout as planned by Kennedy was remarkably advanced. In the nose of the fuselage was a gun position, and there was an enclosed flight deck immediately behind. A second gun position was on top of the fuselage aft of the wings, and behind the tail (which had twin fins and rudders) was the controversial 'gun-pit'. The designer schemed for this position a kind of cushion, which could be arranged to act as a knee-pad or seat, according to the direction in which the gunner was firing. Two guns were planned for this station, but Kennedy was mindful of the weight problems involved and spoke of extending the nose accordingly.

Careful attention was likewise paid to the bomb installation. Each bomb was to be carried vertically, nose-down, by a pair of arms, pivoted laterally at one end and formed with interlocking cups at the other end to hold the nose of the bomb. The arms were to be controlled through selector gear, associated with an indicator, in the form of a figured drum, which showed the number of bombs dropped or still held.

Mann, Egerton

Type B   This was a seaplane of 1916, using Short 184 components and armed with one free Lewis gun (dorsal) and bombs under the fuselage.

Type H   Answering to the same requirements as the Beardmore W.B.IV, this 'ship's fighter', or 'seaborne scout' as the makers called it, was built in 1917. It had a fixed Vickers gun mounted on the fuselage to port (250 rounds), and a Lewis gun above the centre-section (three 97-round drums).

Mann & Grimmer

M.1   The two men responsible for this imaginative single-engined twin-airscrew biplane of 1914/15 will be named in the second volume of this work because of Mr Grimmer's particular interest in military aeronautics as expressed in *Flight*. It was intended to arm the M.1 with a Lewis gun, installed in the cockpit behind the nose-mounted engine, under the wing leading edge.

Martin-Baker

M.B.2   Of the many ingenious features which distinguished this private-venture eight-gun fighter of 1938, not the least was the installation of the Browning guns. It is gratifying that a first-hand account, by an ex-RAF armourer, can be quoted. This gentleman wrote:

'We of the ground crew could scarcely believe our good fortune in working on such a delightful machine. From my armament point of view everything had been made absurdly easy. There were four fixed machine-guns in each wing. I had no access-doors to baffle me with their exasperating locking buttons which wouldn't. One turn of a small handle and the whole upper surface of the wing stood up obligingly on end, allowing free access to the guns and ammunition. A trapezium-section rubber-covered seat, which fitted along the rear of the gun bay, brought luxury to the job. It also eliminated, by its shape, the curve of the wing surface, and so provided a flat top for tools and so on. The guns and ammunition tanks were locked in position with pins, conveniently looped, so that removal of four guns and tanks took five minutes instead of at least fifty on any conventional fighter.'

In *The British Fighter since 1912* (Putnam, 1965) Peter Lewis states that the M.B.2 was not a good gun platform. But it was undoubtedly an excellent armourer's platform.

The Martin-Baker M.B.2, a fighter of singular appearance, displayed great ingenuity of design, notably in regard to armament. Ports for eight Browning guns are seen.

With the name of Martin-Baker, and in particular with the name of James (later Sir James) Martin himself, the ingenious ideas incorporated in the design of the M.B.2 are especially associated. In the field of aircraft safety the same names have an even more enduring association, and in the joint contexts of safety and armament it may be noted with special interest that Sir James observed in 1937:

'It has been found in practice that where machine guns are mounted in the wings of aeroplanes there is a very great liability for the mechanism of the guns to become frozen or jammed on account of cold affecting the mechanism. This applies particularly to the lock, which is liable to become completely frozen up or to be so sluggish in operation that it jams and the gun does not fire freely. When this occurs there is a liability that the guns may go off automatically at some later time, for example when the machine is landing, Under these circumstances when the machine descends from a high altitude the mechanism of the guns may become freed and the jolt of landing may cause them to fire, thus endangering the lives of the ground staff of an aerodrome or other persons in the vicinity.'

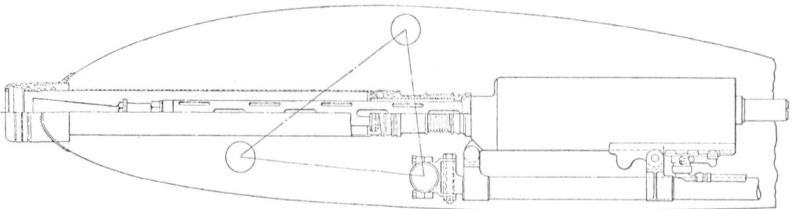

Installation of Browning gun in wing of Martin-Baker M.B.2, showing mounting, blast tube and triangulated wing spar.

These remarks were made by Sir James in connection with a system of hot-air circulation he designed for the M.B.2. He was also much concerned with the screening and shielding of the wing interior from the effects of air rushing in at the gun ports and down the blast tubes, and of the fumes, flash and blast of the guns. As already noted, accessibility was another preoccupying factor in the design of the M.B.2. This was a forerunner of the M.B.5, undoubtedly the most perfect fighting aeroplane of its kind and of its time.

Martinsyde

S.1 'In my eyes,' recorded Capt L. A. Strange of this single-seat scout (built 1914), 'all defects were outweighed by the fact that it had a Lewis gun mounted on its top plane, which could be fired forward and upward.' The installation mentioned was made in the spring of 1915, and it was during May of that year that Capt Strange had the historic experience of saving his life in an inverted spin by hanging on to an ammunition drum which had jammed on the gun. Concerning other forms of armament, specific details are lacking, but rifles were carried, and for Home Defence the following loads have been mentioned in connection with a 'Martinsyde Scout' : '6 Carcass bombs (3·45-in R.L. tube for discharge); 12 Hale Naval grenades; 150 incendiary darts; carriers for five powder bombs.' Small bombs were apparently carried for attacking ground targets, and an S.1 of No.5 Squadron (Capt G. I. Carmichael) was adapted to take a 100-lb bomb, sighted through a hole cut in the floor. Previously provision had been made for 20-lb bombs under the wings.

G.100 and G.102 Dating from 1915, these large, robust single-seaters were well suited to carry armament, and the RFC name 'Elephant' seems to have been inevitable. On early production aircraft a Lewis gun fired over the centre-section; and for rearward fire a second Lewis gun was later clamped to a cranked pillar mounting just aft of the coaming on the port side. The over-wing gun was carried above the rear spar on a massive pyramid structure, itself braced to the front spar by a fore-and-aft tube. J. M. Bruce has recorded two forms of this mounting, designated Mk.I and Mk.II, the latter having the two elements which comprised the rear attachment pivoted on the underside of the spar. The gun was fired by Bowden cable and carried a long vertical handle attached to the spade grip. By means of this handle the gun could be swung down for reloading.   An experimental installation was made of a triple-gun mounting of the Eeman (or, according to one official publication, Eaman) type, which was also tested by the Army. In this instance the fuselage-mounted guns fired upwards at 45 degrees through slots in the centre-section. There was an Aldis sight at the same angle. At least one aircraft had a non-standard mounting for a single Lewis gun offset to starboard.

As bombers, these Martinsydes were popular and successful, and in particular the more powerful G.102. Bombs were carried beneath the fuselage and wings, and among recorded loads were four 65-lb, one or two 112-lb, two 100-lb, one 230-lb, one 100-lb + four 20-lb, and twelve 20-lb. The constructors declared that the type was 'one of the few machines that could carry large 3 cwt bombs'. The bomb concerned was carried singly under the fuselage and was of the 336-lb type, designed at the Royal Aircraft Factory, Farnborough. At that establishment and also at Orfordness during the summer of 1916, tests were made with an 'Elephant' fitted with an experimental periscopic sight. The 'Bomb, H.E., 336 lbs., Heavy Case, Mk.I' was nearly five feet long in its original form, in which it is known to have been carried by the 'Elephant'. It was later shortened to allow it to be carried on a 230-lb carrier. Mr Bruce reports that the periscopic bombsight was not developed sufficiently to see operational use in 'Elephants', but, though this may well have been so, a sight of the type was certainly made in quantity.

R.G. Designed late in 1916, the R.G. was initially armed with a fixed Vickers gun to port and a Lewis gun, having a restricted field of fire, from the starboard side of the cockpit. Later two fixed Vickers guns were substituted, the guns lying exposed forward of the windscreen. These guns do not appear to have had Constantinesco gear; they retained the land-service grips and firing levers at the rear and may have had a mechanical gear to allow them to fire through the airscrew arc or to have been intended for the Martinsyde electrical synchronising gear. This, however, dated from early 1916, and may have been entirely abandoned by the time the R.G. underwent official tests at Farnborough in 1917. Certainly the R.G. must have rivalled the Sopwith Camel very closely indeed for the distinction of being the first British fighter to have twin Vickers guns.

F.1 The mystery that surrounds this two-seat fighter of 1917 may be dispelled in some degree by evidence later adduced in connection with the Vickers F.B.24E, an aircraft of similar layout. The author inclines to the view that both aircraft were designed for the Vickers mounting described and illustrated in the context of the Vickers type named.

F.2 An all-round improvement on the F.1, the F.2 was more or less contemporary and had a normal armament. A fixed Vickers gun lay externally to port, and the gunner had a Lewis gun on a Scarff ring-mounting.

F.3 'A great advance on all existing fighting scouts' was one official pronouncement on this experimental single-seater of 1917 ('Mother' in the Martinsyde family). In addition to two fixed Vickers guns, there was provision, in deference to an Air Board specification then current, for a Lewis gun on the top centre-section. This gun was apparently never fitted. Compared with the R.G., the F.3 had a deeper fuselage forward of the cockpit, and this allowed the guns to be completely cowled in and to fire through

The armament installation on the Martinsyde F.4 Buzzard was perhaps the most advanced of any 1914–18 fighter. This view shows brackets for an Aldis sight and should be studied jointly with others under the heading 'Aircraft Disposal Company'. A panel covers the ejection chute.

ports in the top decking. A single aperture for the ejection of cases and links was located just forward of the rear centre-section strut on each side.

F.4 The F.4, or Buzzard, was built in 1918 and had a generally similar Vickers gun installation to that of the F.3. An important feature, however, was the excellent system devised for accessibility, described and illustrated in connection with the Aircraft Disposal Company's A.D.C.1. Brackets for

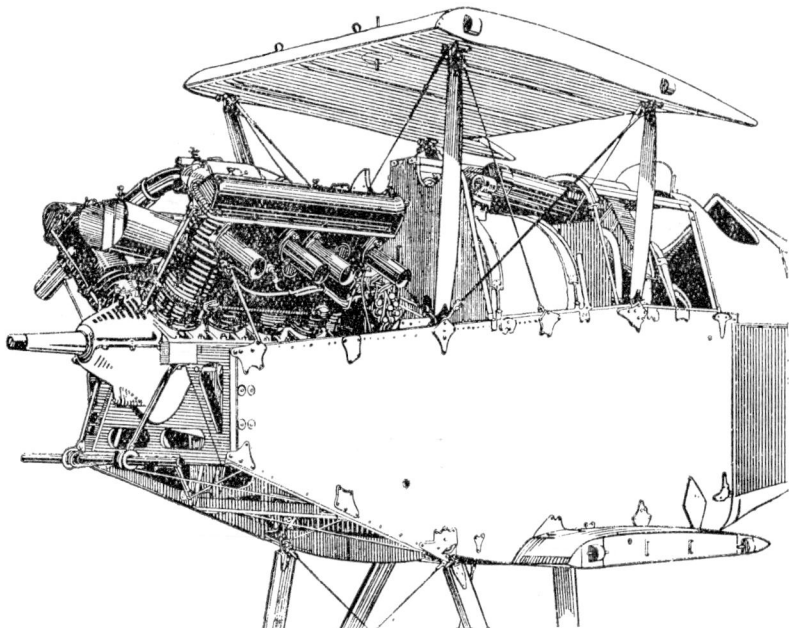

Official drawing showing Hispano-Suiza engine and gun installation of Martinsyde F.4 Buzzard.

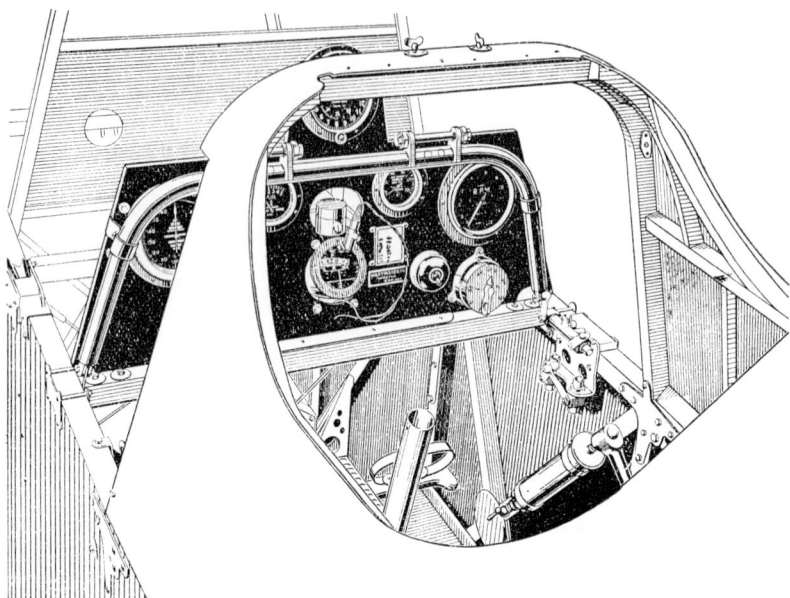

Forward of the instrument board of the Martinsyde F.4 Buzzard is a tubular frame with fittings for attachment to the rear trunnions of the two Vickers guns. The reservoir for the C.C. synchronising gear is seen at the right, but the top of the control column, with firing levers, is absent.

an Aldis sight were fitted forward of the cockpit and provision was made for a bomb-carrier (four 20-lb) under the fuselage.

A point of some interest is that on the prototype and on the production aircraft illustrated, the ejection aperture was panelled over, but whether with the object of retaining the spent cartridge cases and belt links aboard cannot be determined.

F.4a This designation was applied to a post-war (1921) two-seater development of the F.4 having a Scarff ring-mounting for a Lewis gun.

Miles

Master I The Master I advanced trainer of 1939 had a single Vickers or Browning gun in the starboard wing, aimed with a reflector sight associated with an optically flat windscreen panel. Provision was made for a Light Series bomb-carrier under the inner portion of the wing on each side. Particularly commended was the grouping in a single unit in each cockpit of an adjustable rudder bar and control column and the gun firing gear.

Nieuport

B.N.1 A counterpart of the Sopwith Snipe, and resembling that type and other contemporary single-seaters in having provision for an over-wing Lewis gun as well as two Vickers guns with C.C. gear, the B.N.1 was designed in March 1918. The Lewis gun was actually fitted on this machine, being positioned somewhat to starboard, and the Vickers guns were semi-internally mounted, beneath a humped cowling. The makers advanced the claim that although the 'anti-airship' Lewis gun installation on the top wings of other fighters was disliked by many pilots, being too high above their heads 'to permit it to be directly sighted on a target in the best fighting attitudes', the gun on the B.N.1 was 'practically in line with the pilot's eyes'.

Nighthawk Being designed specifically for the A.B.C. Dragonfly radial engine, and having the petrol tanks flanking the pilot's cockpit and shap-

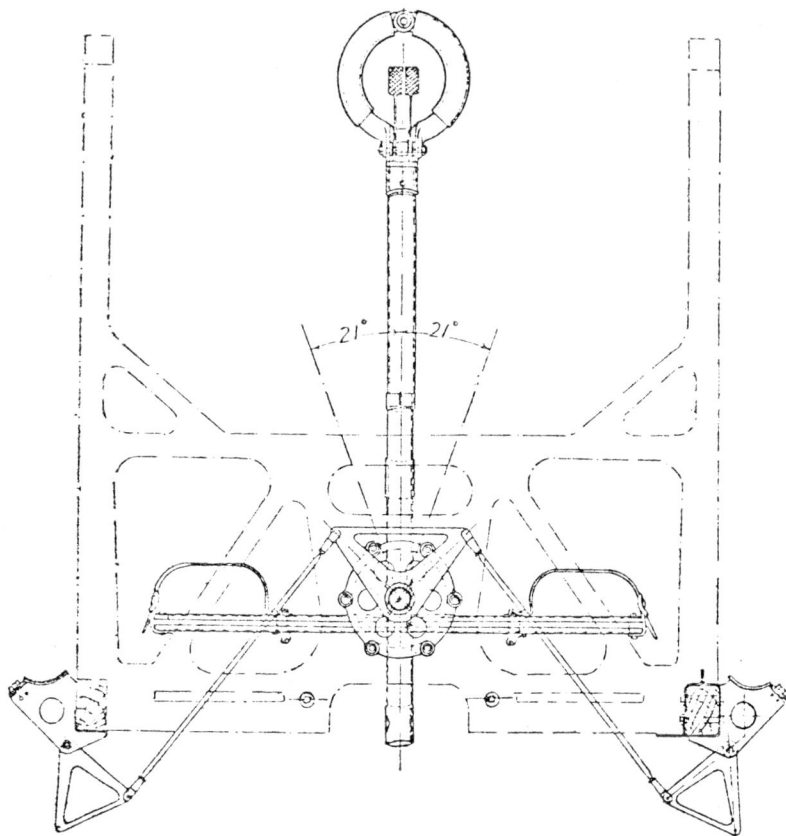

Standard RAF control column with gun-firing levers, in the Nieuport Nighthawk.

ing the fuselage contours, the Nighthawk had a commodious fore-part. This enabled the two Vickers guns to be enclosed beneath the top decking, firing through ports located one on each side of the topmost cylinder of the Dragonfly engine. Aldis and ring-and-bead sights were bracketed to the upper centre-section. As on the contemporary Siddeley Siskin there was provision for 2,000 rounds of ammunition. It was stated that the head of the control column was of 'standard RAF type', the ring being covered in rubber, having a magneto switch at the top and the two gun triggers at the centre. Design provision was made for four 20-lb bombs.

Double-yoked Lewis guns on a Scarff ring-mounting in the nose of the Nieuport London bomber.

London This Nieuport triplane night bomber (designed 1918, flown 1920) was quite literally a flying bomb-box, for the fuselage had quarter-inch matchboard covering and the bombs were stowed internally. The maximum load was carried only over short ranges (up to about 400 miles) and was made up of nine 250-pounders. These were carried nose-up, were taken aboard in threes, and could be released singly or in salvo. The bombs were aimed from the nose position, where twin-yoked Lewis guns were installed on a Scarff ring-mounting. There were no rear guns, and it may be supposed that the guns in the nose were intended as much for shooting out searchlights as for shooting down fighters.

Parnall

Zeppelin Scout Built in 1916 for 'Zeppelin strafing at night', this large single-seater had a gun mounted in the starboard side of the cockpit and firing forward and upward at 45 degrees. This gun appears to have been, or to have been intended to be, a Crayford rocket gun, as installed in the Vickers F.B.25 and the N.E.1 built by the Royal Aircraft Factory. The makers stated in June 1916 that, in order to provide maximum field of vision, the upper wing was placed substantially in the line of forward horizontal vision of the pilot, and the lower wing was arranged substantially symmetrically below his seat. Mention was made of a cut-out in the upper trailing edge to allow downward vision, and the seat could be adjusted up and down.

Panther Built in 1917 as a 'ship's aeroplane' for reconnaissance, the Panther was armed (according to a Ministry of Munitions publication) with a Lewis gun on a 'special pillar mounting' and supplied with 'three double trays'. This armament was supplemented on one example at least by a Vickers gun on the port side of the cockpit, with the breech casing faired in.

Puffin A counterpart of the Fairey Pintail, this two-seater amphibian fighter of 1921 had a Scarff ring-mounting, somewhat built up from the fuselage coaming, carrying a Lewis gun. The field of fire (as on the rival Fairey Pintail) was unimpeded by vertical tail surfaces above the fuselage. There was a fixed Vickers gun for the pilot.

Possum Like the Boulton & Paul Bodmin, which it resembled in being an experimental aircraft with fuselage-mounted power plant driving outboard airscrews, this similarly styled 'three-seat medium-range postal' machine of 1923 was fitted with two Scarff ring-mountings. One was set some distance back from the sloping nose, ahead of the pilot, and the second was in line with the trailing edge of the centre wing (the machine was a triplane). It was once said to be equipped for 'reconnaissance and bombing'.

Plover This counterpart of the Fairey Flycatcher (1923) had a more refined armament installation, the two Vickers guns being mounted with their breech casings in the cockpit and firing through ports in the sloping cowling. The case and link chutes were in the fuselage flanks and the Aldis sight was bracketed to the upper centre-section. An installation of the Vickers 0·5-in gun will be illustrated in *British Aircraft Weapons*.

An unusual emplacement for the Scarff ring-mounting was a feature of the Parnall Pike.

Pike Built in 1925 as a three-seat Naval reconnaissance aircraft, the Pike had a comprehensive armament installation. The pilot's fixed Vickers gun was mounted in the port side of the cockpit, the barrel protruding into a short trough above and behind the port cylinder bank. There were separate case and link chutes and a bracket for an Aldis sight ahead of the windscreen. The top wing was attached directly to the fuselage, and a Scarff ring-mounting for a Lewis gun was set largely ahead of the trailing edge. Tubular carriers were fitted beneath the lower wings for (e.g.) four 112-lb bombs.

Pipit Accessibility of armament and other Service equipment was a notable characteristic of this single-seat fleet fighter (1929). The two Vickers guns were mounted with their breech casings mid-way down the cockpit sides and fired through troughs of distinctive form, deepening very noticeably as the cowling curved under the nose. Aft of the starboard trough was a bulge to afford access to the gun loading handle. Aldis and ring-and-bead sights were fixed to the top cowling ahead of the windscreen and there were rails beneath the lower port wing for a bomb-carrier (four 20-lb).

G.4/31 Built in 1935, this general purpose biplane was doubtless intended to carry the same projectile loads as the Fairey machine to the same specification. The heavy bombs were carried under the wings and there was a Light Series carrier under the fuselage. The Vickers gun was mounted high to port and had a collector box. The ring-and-bead sight was on a fore-and-aft tube, braced to the sharply sloping cowling by inverted-V

A fine study of the installation of the Rolls-Royce F (Kestrel) engine and of the port Vickers gun on the Parnall Pipit. The case and link chutes are seen.

The Parnall G.4/31, showing screened rear gun position, Light Series bomb-carrier under fuselage, window for bomb-aimer and mounting for ring-and-bead sight.

Parnall Heck used for armament development, with wing-mounted Browning guns and reflector sight.

struts. There was a Scarff ring-mounting for a Lewis gun well behind the wings, set a little below the fuselage top line in the shelter of a large windshield.

Heck In 1937 a Heck light touring aircraft was made available for trial installations of Browning guns and reflector sights. Pairs of guns were installed with short lengths of barrel projecting from the leading edge outboard of the fixed undercarriage. There were associated under-wing fairings.

Pemberton-Billing

P.B.23E and P.B.25 The P.B.23E pusher 'scout' of 1915 carried a fixed Lewis gun in the nose of the nacelle and was almost certainly the first British aircraft to be armed with a fixed gun. The gun on the P.B.23E was set low in the nacelle; in the succeeding P.B.25 it was raised to the top.

P.B.29 Designed and built in 1915 to 'stand still in the air in a 28mph breeze and lie in wait for Zeppelins' this 'patrol fighter' quadruplane appears to have been intended to carry a Lewis gun in a cockpit structure between the topmost wings.

Phoenix (English Electric)

Cork Designed to Air Board requirements for anti-submarine patrol, the Cork twin-engined flying-boat (1918) had a Scarff ring-mounting in the bows and two waist hatches aft of the wing trailing edge. The mountings appear to have carried single Lewis guns, though five guns were mentioned in a company document issued some time after the boat was built. The second machine of the type had two 'fighting top' positions at the trailing edge of the top wing in line with the second set of interplane struts from the tip. These carried Scarff ring-mountings, possibly with double-yoked guns, for the company mentioned seven Lewis guns as the armament. The gunners in the 'fighting tops' ascended to their positions by way of steps on the interplane struts. They are said to have suffered not only from a sense of isolation but from a form of airsickness also, brought on by 'unusual movements' of their emplacements. Four 250-lb or two 520/550-lb bombs could be carried under the inner wings.

Kingston This Cork development of 1924 had no gun positions on the top wing, but on the Mk.II version there was a gunner with a Scarff ring-mounting in a massive faired nacelle position behind each of the two engines. Like the 'fighting tops' of the Cork, these emplacements appear to have achieved no great popularity with the gunners, in this instance by reason of engine fumes and heat, and they were deleted in the Kingston

English Electric Kingston with gun positions behind engines. A 520-lb bomb is seen below the port inner wing.

III. The nose mounting on this version could be slid rearwards for mooring. Bomb load of the Kingston was identical with that of the Cork.

Ayr The Ayr single-engined reconnaissance flying-boat of 1923 had a Scarff ring-mounting for a Lewis gun in the bow and a similar installation on the hull abaft the wing. The massive sponsons (or sponson/wings), sharply swept up from the hull, are said to have carried bombs, but these would have been well below the water line when the machine was afloat.

Port Victoria

P.V.1 This was an experimental seaplane of 1916, having a Sopwith Baby fuselage and high-lift wings with a view to improving take-off with two 65-lb bombs.

P.V.2 and P.V.2bis In 1916 the Davis recoilless gun was still viewed hopefully as an anti-Zeppelin weapon, and the P.V.2 single-seat seaplane was designed to carry a 2-pounder gun of the type. It was to be fitted over the top wing and be accessible for loading (ten rounds provided). Before the airframe was completed, the Davis gun was abandoned, and with two Lewis guns above the raised top wing the aircraft was designated P.V.2bis.

P.V.4 Another 1916 Port Victoria design, the P.V.4 pusher two-seater, did not fly until the following year. There was a Scarff ring-mounting for a Lewis gun in the nose, commanding a field of fire even over the top wing.

P.V.5 and P.V.5a   The P.V.5 of 1917 was a fighter/bomber, carrying two 65-lb bombs internally. The pilot had a Vickers gun mounted on top of the fuselage.

P.V.7 (Grain Kitten)   Designed specially for anti-Zeppelin operations from small naval craft, this tiny single-seat biplane of 1917 had a single Lewis gun above the centre-section, the trailing edge of which was cut away for elevation. Three drums of ammunition were specified.

P.V.8 (Eastchurch Kitten)   Built to meet the same requirements as the P.V.7, the P.V.8 had its Lewis gun offset to starboard. This type likewise had a cut-away trailing edge to allow elevation, though it was officially reported that the gun would be awkward to fire because of the pilot's cramped position.

P.V.9   Intended for the escort of flying-boats, this advanced single-seat seaplane of 1917 had a synchronised Vickers gun on top of the fuselage and a Lewis gun over the top centre-section, firing upwards and forwards over the airscrew.

Grain Griffin   This 1918 conversion of a Sopwith Bomber as a two-seater fleet reconnaissance aircraft had a Lewis gun on a pillar-mounted swivelling bracket behind the rear cockpit.

Robey

Robey-Peters Gun Carrier   In June 1916 J. A. Peters, who designed this large three-seat three-bay tractor biplane as a Zeppelin fighter, drew up a scheme for mounting gun (or engine) nacelles under the top wing of an aeroplane. It was stated that the gun mountings were placed above the nacelles 'on the top plane, which is cut away to facilitate operation of the guns'. On the aircraft as built, the nacelles were carried close inboard on two pairs of upright V struts. There were, in fact, two cut-outs in the upper surface of the wing above each nacelle, the rear ones, apparently, for the gunners, and the forward pair for the mountings to take two Davis recoilless guns. The pilot sat far aft in the mid-mounted fuselage.

Two solutions to the problem of attaining a wide field of fire: *top*, Robey-Peters Gun Carrier with emplacements on top wings; *lower*, Sage Type 2, in which the gunner stood to wield his gun through a hole.

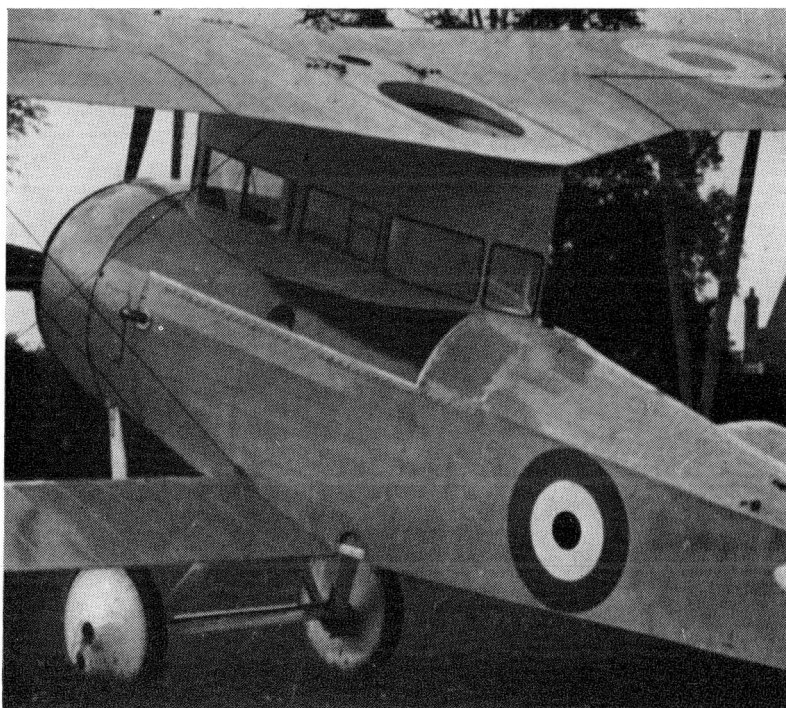

Royal Aircraft Factory

A.E.3 (Ram)   Among the unusual features of this two-seat armoured ground-attack aircraft of 1918 was the use (or evident intended use) of a tubular optical sight in conjunction with the primary armament of two Lewis guns. This installation was probably devised at Farnborough, although, as will be noted in Volume 2, A. C. W. Aldis designed a gun mounting with which an Aldis sight was used. The guns were yoked together in the extreme nose of the nacelle and the sight was mounted between and above them. Vertical downward fire was possible, though field of fire was limited, and the provision of thirty-two double drums of ammunition was specified. These would be shared by a third Lewis gun on a pillar mounting, for rearward fire above the top wing. The pillar was apparently capable of transverse movement, as on the first Sopwith Buffalo.

The armoured nacelle of the A.E.3 was of structural type, as were the forward fuselage sections of the Sopwith Salamander and Buffalo. The floor and front were of double thickness (10-gauge outer, 5-gauge inner).

B.E.2, 2a and 2b   The most famous armed exploit by an early aircraft of the B.E. series, which originated in 1912, was the dropping of a 100-lb bomb by 2nd-Lieut W. B. Rhodes-Moorhouse from a B.E.2a on Courtrai railway station on 26 April, 1915. Smaller bombs were carried, including two 20-lb, and one B.E.2a , flying without observer, was armed with one petrol bomb and 'as many grenades as the pilot could manage'. Late in 1914 the Royal Aircraft Factory produced a bomb-carrier for the B.E.2a. This held three bombs and was suspended well below the fuselage forward of the undercarriage axle. Other types of carrier were attached between the rear struts of the undercarriage. Pistols, rifles and carbines were carried, and No.50 is known to have had a rifle clamped to the side of the fuselage. One B.E.2a was used to test the Fiery Grapnel weapon, developed at the Royal Aircraft Factory for entanglement with, and explosion upon, airships. Grenades were carried on anti-airship patrols.

J. M. Bruce has recorded that at about mid-1912 it was reported that experiments were being conducted at Farnborough with a type of Vickers gun on a B.E. aircraft piloted by Geoffrey de Havilland. The gun was rumoured to weigh only 15 lb complete and to fire at the rate of 400 rounds per minute. *Flight* reported early in November 1912 that a biplane of B.E. type was being used at Aldershot for experiments with a Maxim gun, but whether this was a confusion with the F.E.2 (which, as a photograph shows, was definitely fitted with a Maxim gun) cannot be determined. The most diligent research gives no hint of a Vickers gun weighing 15 lb, and even the 'stripped' Lewis gun weighed 17 lb. The only aircraft machine-gun known to the author which approached the reported weight was the French Darne, an experimental model of which was chambered for the British 0·303-in cartridge and which weighed $15\frac{1}{2}$ lb, but this gun did not exist in 1912.

B.E.2c, d and e The B.E.2c was never intended to carry armament, but to provide a stable platform for reconnaissance. This very stability was to prove a severe handicap in combat, and even though armament schemes were quickly improvised the firing of a gun from the front (observer's) seat was a matter of great difficulty because of the adjacent wings and bracing members. Rifles, carbines and pistols were carried, and an accompanying photograph is possibly unique in showing a carbine in simulated use. This is of Lee-Metford type. Lewis guns were variously installed. In some instances four sockets were disposed round the observer's cockpit, the gun or guns being interchanged between these sockets as necessary. Sockets were also provided at the sides of the rear cockpit, or behind it, for rearward fire. Capt L. A. Strange of No.12 Squadron mounted a Lewis gun on the side of the fuselage at such an angle that the line of fire cleared the airscrew, but whether this was the first arrangement of its kind (requiring the pilot to fly crab-fashion) cannot be determined. The common type of mounting which became known as the 'Strange mounting' was of cranked pillar type, having a toothed quadrant and illustrated in connection with the B.E.2e and B.E.12. In March 1917 the Strange mounting for the Lewis gun was improved by Sgt Hutton of No.39 Squadron by fitting a release stud which made the gun or mounting easier to manoeuvre. Other

Demonstrating the use of a Lee-Metford carbine from an early B.E.2c.

281

patterns of cranked pillar mounting were improvised and to these the description 'candlestick' mounting was applied. In apparent refutation of the B.E's inferior manoeuvring qualities it has been recorded: 'The Huns were a poor lot and had one violent manoeuvre not dislodged the Lewis guns from their silly candlestick mountings the B.E. might have driven them off.' Some B.E.2cs of the RNAS carried a single Lewis gun on a tall bracket mounting ahead of the cockpit, allowing the gun to be fired under the centre-section but above the airscrew arc. There was at least one instance of a hole being made in the centre-section through which the observer put his head and shoulders to use an unspecified weapon, and there was also an installation of a Lewis gun above the top wing. As many as four guns were carried at a time. One B.E.2c carried two Lewis guns and a Mauser pistol. Oliver Stewart has recalled:

'Sometimes the observer knelt or stood on his seat to use Lewis guns mounted on brackets linked by a bar between the rear pair of centre-section struts. Sometimes a Lewis gun which could be fired downwards was fitted on the left side of the fuselage alongside the pilot's seat. Another mounting, which was found in numerous forms in the B.E., had one or two Lewis guns on splayed brackets which kept the bullets clear of the disc swept by the airscrew.'

For Home Defence one or two Lewis guns were installed on Strange mountings to fire behind the centre-section, the ammunition drums being loaded with a mixture of ordinary and 'special' ammunition. Home Defence B.E.2cs and 2es also carried four, six or eight Le Prieur rockets, attached to the outer interplane struts, the launching tubes being set at an upward angle. Armament for Home Defence also included canisters of Ranken Darts, two 20-lb high-explosive bombs and two 16-lb incendiary bombs. 'Bomb boxes' were mentioned, and the R.L. Tube was used to launch incendiary bombs. The Fiery Grapnel, already mentioned in connection with the B.E.2a, was also tested on a B.E.2c. Two of these weapons were carried side by side under the fuselage. In No.6 Squadron a winch was fitted on a B.E.2c to lower a lead weight on a steel cable, the object being to foul the airscrew of an enemy aircraft.

Bombs were carried either loose in the fuselage or beneath the inner lower wings and fuselage. Some B.E.2cs of the RNAS carried three small bombs under the engine. With the heavier bomb loads the aircraft were flown as single-seaters. Identified loads are four to ten 20-lb, or one 112-lb + four 20-lb, or two 112-lb bombs, and as early as 10 March, 1915, Capt Strange dropped three French bombs weighing 25 lb on Courtrai station. B.E.2cs are known to have been used on anti-submarine operations, and in this connection it may be noted that the standard bombs used for this work were of 65-lb, 100-lb and 230-lb weight. Loads for the B.E.2e included two 100-lb or one 100-lb + eight 20-lb.

In August 1916 a B.E.2c was used to test the first installation of the Constantinesco synchronising gear for the Vickers gun, but the only aircraft of

Lewis gun on Strange mounting between cockpits of B.E.2e.

Lewis gun on 'candlestick' mounting on B.E.2e.

the type to have such an installation as standard were those modified by the Belgians. The gun in this instance was mounted above the engine, and a ring-mounting of Nieuport type was fitted over the rear cockpit.

Armoured seats were developed at the Royal Aircraft Factory and during 1916 an armoured version of the B.E.2c was produced at the same establishment. The armour weighed 445 lb, and armoured B.E.2cs were operated successfully against entrenched German troops. Other applications were low-level photography and the attack of kite balloons. One single-seat B.E.2c had a repositioned and specially armoured cockpit, the armour being built up round the pilot's head and shoulders in a manner reminiscent of Ned Kelly himself. It remains to mention the now-famous installation of five Lewis guns made on a B.E.2c by Lieut C. J. Chabot. The guns were within the undercarriage structure and fired downward at a shallow angle. The installation was never used operationally.

No aircraft of 1914–18 was fitted with a greater variety of armament than the B.E.2c, and, notwithstanding its handicaps in combat with other aeroplanes, it endures as the greatest airship-destroyer of all time. On 31 March, 1916, 2nd-Lieut A. de B. Brandon dropped Ranken Darts and an incendiary bomb on the crippled L.15, which then came down on the sea. Some months later, on 3 September, 1916, Lieut W. Leefe Robinson shot down S.L.11 in flames, using a Lewis gun installed on a Strange mounting, of the type illustrated herewith on a B.E.2e. The Lewis gun, firing special ammunition, was also the chosen instrument in the destruction of L.32 (2nd-Lieut F. Sowrey, 24 September, 1916), L.31 (2nd-Lieut W. J. Tempest, 31 October, 1916), L.34 (2nd-Lieut I. V. Pyott, 27 November, 1916) and L.21 (Flt Lieut E. Cadbury, Flt Sub-Lieut G. W. R. Fane and Flt Sub-Lieut E. L. Pulling, 28 November, 1916).

The stability which cost the B.E.2c so dearly in daylight operations in face of opposing aircraft rendered this same aeroplane a steady platform for what was to become perhaps the most famous aircraft machine-gun of all.

B.E.8 and 8a　A single 100-lb bomb could be carried by aircraft of this type and it is likely that the usual small arms, though not machine-guns, were also taken into the air.

B.E.9　This much-modified development of the B.E.2c was one of the more radical attempts to overcome the absence, in 1915, of a gear allowing a gun to be fired through the disc of a revolving airscrew. A gunner's compartment, generally resembling that of contemporary pushers, was built out in front of the airscrew, and this was officially declared to have as its object provision of a 'wide angle of fire'. Although 'The Pulpit' (as it could hardly fail to be called) went to France there is no record that a gun was actually installed.

B.E.12　The earliest recorded armament tests with a B.E.12 involved the dropping of bombs and darts (Farnborough, September 1915). By March

Vickers gun, with Vickers synchronising gear, on B.E.12. A Strange mounting for a Lewis gun is also seen. Note the chute for leading the webbing belt of the Vickers gun back into the fuselage.

1916 an experimental gun-mounting of indeterminate type had been installed, and in June of the same year one machine was tested with a Lewis gun and deflector plates on the airscrew. A fixed Lewis gun on the starboard side, firing through the disc swept by an airscrew having deflector plates, was to be numbered among standard installations, and Oliver Stewart records 'one or two Lewis guns mounted to clear the disc swept by the airscrew'. He comments: 'There were brackets alongside the pilot, and the guns fixed to these brackets were splayed outwards. Control of the guns was either directly by hand or by means of Bowden cables.' Not surprisingly, the complicated problems of deflection involved in the 'crab' method of attack necessitated gave poor results. In May 1916 the Central Flying School tested a B.E.12 having a fixed Vickers gun with Vickers synchronising gear, and this was to become another standard installation, together with a Lewis gun on a Strange mounting, as illustrated. Sometimes there were two Lewis guns on Strange mountings. A Lewis gun actuated by the Vickers gear is also on record. For Home Defence work the Vickers gun was fed with ordinary ball ammunition, with one round of Sparklet in five, whereas the Lewis gun fired explosive/incendiary ammunition. Some Home Defence B.E.12s had as many as four Lewis guns, and Le Prieur rockets were also fitted. Probably the most spectacular installation was that involving a six-pdr Davis recoilless gun. This gun fired upwards at 45 degrees; the muzzle was at the level of the upper wing, which was cut

285

away accordingly as far as the front spar. For reloading the gun was lowered to the horizontal.

Bomb loads were one or two 112-lb or up to sixteen 20-lb.

B.E.12a   When used as a bomber (typically with one 112-lb bomb under the fuselage) this aircraft sometimes had a Lewis gun on a Strange mounting ahead of the cockpit. There was also an installation of a fixed Vickers gun.

B.E.12b   Although it could carry two 112-lb bombs under the lower inner wings, this single-seater was introduced in 1917 primarily for Home Defence. The armament for this duty was one or two Lewis guns, mounted over the centre-section and firing special ammunition above the airscrew arc. The Neame illuminated sight was fitted (on the starboard gun when a pair was mounted). Additionally there was a ring-and-bead sight, the two elements of which were attached to the starboard centre-section struts. The mounting for the gun(s) was one of the most elaborate of the war. Running between the rear centre-section struts was a cross-bar, and pivoted to this was a steel-tube assembly which constituted the mounting proper. A cable running over a pulley at the top of the front forward centre-section strut connected the mounting to a large lever attached outside the cockpit on the starboard side, somewhat reminiscent of the multi-purpose lever in the Blackburn Blackburd. With the lever pulled to the rear the gun(s) were in a position to fire forwards above the airscrew; when the lever was moved forward the gun(s) were moved into a vertical position for reloading or upward firing.

C.E.1   Two 230-lb anti-submarine bombs could be carried by this single-engined pusher flying-boat. There were three pillar-type mountings for Lewis guns, one in the front cockpit and two between the cockpits, one on each side of the hull.

F.E.2   The genesis of the F.E.2 is of exceptional interest, especially in respect of armament. It first appeared, with 50-hp Gnome engine, in September 1911, having been rebuilt from the crashed F.E.1, which was Geoffrey de Havilland's second aeroplane (Farman Experimental No.1). By the time of the British Military trials, on Salisbury Plain in August 1912, this aircraft had been fitted with a Maxim machine-gun, as a photograph shows. The gun, which appears to have been of 0·303-in calibre, was mounted on trunnions in a fork-shaped member some distance aft from the nose of the nacelle, allowing the muzzle end of the barrel casing to rest on the tip of the nacelle. The gun was lashed in this position by two lengths of rope. As rebuilt early in 1913 with a 70-hp Renault engine the F.E.2 had a nacelle of revised form, associated with a very large gun-carrying member as seen in another photograph. That in this form the aircraft was intended to carry a heavy gun is suggested by a statement by F. W. Lanchester that the F.E.2 was designed to carry a 'gun weight' of 300 lb. This figure probably included mounting and ammunition, and

An historic picture showing the F.E.2 with Gnome engine and Maxim gun.

Rebuilt F.E.2 with Renault engine and mounting for large gun.

the weapon concerned may well have been the Coventry Ordnance Works 1-pounder as tested in the F.E.3 during 1913.

F.E.2a A single Lewis gun was the armament of this fighter/reconnaissance two-seater, first constructed in 1915. The gun was mounted on a tubular arm, pivoted to the floor of the front cockpit. The underside of the nacelle was armoured and an angular tubular framework built over the nose may have afforded protection for the aircraft structure against misdirected fire from the gun.

F.E.2b To the single pillar-mounted Lewis gun of the F.E.2a, which had an arc of fire of about 180 degrees, there was added, as a more or less standard fitment on the F.E.2b, a second Lewis gun on a telescopic pillar mounting between the cockpits. In order to man this gun, the gunner stood on the cupboard which contained spare parts and miscellanea and fired rearwards above the pilot's head. The pilot could fly with one hand and operate the rear gun with the other. Sometimes two pillar-mounted guns were installed between the cockpits. When the pillar or pillars were fully extended, the gunner's insteps were on the upper rim of the plywood-covered nacelle. An F.E. gunner was almost as much acrobat as marksman. Arch Whitehouse recalls of one energetic occasion:

'By the time we were back opposite Arras, the empty gun drums were rattling around the bottom of my nacelle and the canvas bag bolted to the side of my gun to catch the empty cartridges was jammed to its capacity.'

In the spring of 1916 an experimental installation was made of a Vickers 1-pounder 'Pom-pom', of the type which had been used in the Boer War, and two aircraft having this armament were delivered about a year later to No.100 Squadron for ground-attack work. No.102 Squadron used the same armament. Among difficulties encountered were malfunctioning of the gun, the fierce recoil—which on one occasion at least snapped the engine holding-down bolts—and the shell cases which were blown back into the airscrew. The Pom-pom gunner sat to the pilot's right and could elevate or depress the gun in a slot formed in the nacelle. A special form of sight appears to have been fitted on a fore-and-aft tube on top of the nacelle. A few F.E.2bs used for Home Defence had a Pom-pom gun; two had a 0·45-in Maxim gun, and some had a Lewis gun on an Anderson mounting. This type of mounting comprised a tubular inverted-U member braced to the nacelle and having a central pivoted pillar to which the gun was attached. At Farnborough early in 1917 an installation was made of two Lewis guns, one fixed to each side of a Harle searchlight for simultaneous training. There was also an installation of twin-yoked Lewis guns without the light. Some Home Defence F.E.2bs were single-seaters, either with the front cockpit faired over or with a special top decking. One or two fixed Lewis guns sometimes formed the armament and there were instances of a

Lewis gun on a normal telescopic mounting. In training units a Scarff ring-mounting was fitted.

Good load-carrying ability, tractability and field of view made the F.E.2b an attractive proposition as a bomber. A single 230-lb bomb could be carried, but two of 112 lb was a commoner load. Three 112-lb bombs could be lifted. Other types of bomb carried were of 100 lb (anti-submarine F.E.2bs carried two), 40-lb Phosphorus and 20 lb, the last-named up to fourteen in number. One identified load was one 112-lb + eight 20-lb. Bomb rails were fitted under the lower inner wings and fuselage, and a C.F.S. bombsight was mounted at the starboard side of the pilot's cockpit. The F.E.2bs of No.149 Squadron were adaptable for bombing or reconnaissance, having special carriers designed by one of the squadron mechanics to take bombs or Michelin flares without modification.

F.E.2c In this relatively little known F.E. variant the crew positions were transposed and the shape of the nacelle was much modified. The pilot sat considerably aft of the nose, and a Lewis gun was mounted low in the nacelle ahead of him. This gun could be trained by the pilot over a limited arc in conjunction with a sighting bar forward of the windscreen. A second Lewis gun, worked by the observer, was fitted on an Anderson mounting behind the pilot's seat. Some parts of the nacelle were armoured.

One F.E.2c was fitted with an experimental gun mounting of unknown type and another was used for gyroscope tests, though whether these were in connection with bombsight development is not known.

The designation F.E.2c was also applied to a version of the F.E.2b bomber with transposed crew stations.

F.E.2d The F.E.2d and its armament are epitomised in the following excerpts from two memorable articles by W. C. Cambray, MC, (No.20 Squadron) which appeared in *Flight International* during December 1968 under the title 'We Stood to Fight':

'On joining the unit I became friendly with a Canadian observer, and we found ourselves greatly impressed by the F.E.2d biplane and its armament—250 h.p. Rolls-Royce engine, 47 ft wing span, three Lewis guns, a camera, eight Cooper 20-lb bombs and 1,000 rounds of ammunition (one in every three of them tracer). We realised immediately that to stay alive we must become 100 per cent familiar with the machine. We spent much time in jumping from the front gun to the rear gun, standing up in the cockpit to fire over the back and then jumping down again. We practised, also, lying on the range with loaded Lewis guns by our sides, and at a shout of "Now!" seeing who could fire at the target first. This, I think, was one good reason why we both managed to survive the experiences that were to follow.

'As No.20 was mainly a fighter squadron an observer quite often went west during his first encounter. If he was lucky enough to return he was good for one more; and if he returned after *three* fights he was so experienced that, with luck, he would last six months and return to England for Home Establishment. But the proportion who thus returned was indeed small.

'The usual perch for the observer was on the side of the cockpit, always on the watch above and to the rear. As leader of a patrol my pilot would instruct other pilots in the formation of three, five or eight to keep close—"but not too damned close, for fear of collision". I well remember a dog-fight in which another machine passed over us so close that I could have reached up and touched it; a nasty thought, for we had no parachutes.

'The enemy usually collected a formation of six, then perhaps an additional eight, and when there were about 20 of theirs to five of ours they would come close in to attack. I would thereupon fire a red Very light, which told our formation we were going to fight.

'We would then go round and round in a big circle, each pilot following the tail of the man in front, and always making the whole circle approach gradually closer to our own lines. Should a Hun dive to attack,

F.E.2d with two free Lewis guns and one fixed. Note also rails for bomb-carriers under wings.

the observer of one machine in the circle would fire his top gun and the observer of the next machine would use his front gun, so that at any given time the attacker would have two guns firing at him.

'A close understanding between pilot and observer was essential. On one occasion I was with a new—but good—pilot who had not previously been in a fight. We were flying in a formation of only three aircraft when we became engaged in a brief but rather exciting encounter. A Hun dived from our rear and I could see his tracer bullets going under us as I stood up firing over the tail. I signalled to the pilot to throw the machine about to get rid of him; but, to my surprise, he did only a simple aerodrome-style turn. The Hun climbed again and made another attack, and this time I was fortunate enough to hit him and see him going down out of control while we did a second aerodrome turn. On returning to the squadron I asked my pilot in no uncertain terms why he had not thrown the machine all over the place. "I was afraid I'd chuck you out," he answered. I replied that it was my job to stay in. A very minor incident, perhaps, but one illustrating the necessity of close co-operation.

'Our ceiling was 17,500 ft and we did our best to get there, because the anti-aircraft fire was pretty accurate; but a little drift to the left, a little to the right and an occasional about-turn kept us reasonably safe. On the odd occasion the machine would give an appreciable lift as air was displaced by a passing shell that eventually burst well above us. At this height, with no oxygen, of course, the moving from one gun to the other was quite an exertion and made one pant a good deal.

'A useful manoeuvre in dog-fights was the Immelmann turn, but it could be disconcerting when the machine hung momentarily on one wing-tip and everything, including the observer, started to fall out of it. However, the F.E.2d usually scooped everything up in the nick of time and all was in order again. Which reminds me that another pilot and I decided to try to loop one of these machines. We had arranged for it to be rigged tail-light to help it to get over, and we intended to strap ourselves well and truly in. However, the pilot was killed before we could try; and nobody else was game—which, on mature consideration, was probably just as well.

'Bombing was something of an experience, as it was necessary to fly over the target once to set the bomb sight and a second time to release the bombs. We loaded our 20-lb Cooper bombs four under each wing. They were released by pulling a Bowden cable in the pilot's cockpit; as they fell away their wind vanes would rotate, making them live before reaching the ground.

'There was the odd occasion when the bomb fell forward but was caught by its tail in the rack. The vane began to rotate, and soon the bomb was live. The observer would signal the pilot to throw the machine about, and it was then a relief to see the bomb fall clear.

'At one time we were told we would have Bristol Fighters to replace

Early F.E.2d with two partially faired pillar mountings for a Lewis gun.

the F.E.2ds. We were not at all pleased, as the pusher's rear-mounted engine gave the Hun something to fire into and was a protection for the pilot and observer. The Bristol, being a tractor machine, made the observer feel he was rather easy meat.'

It remains to add to the foregoing stirring account that of the three Lewis guns mentioned one was fixed for the pilot's use, as shown in a photograph. Sometimes two fixed guns were fitted, and there was also an installation of twin pillar mountings in the nose of the nacelle, also illustrated. The '1,000 rounds' of ammunition mentioned would comprise ten 97-round drums.

F.E.3 The F.E.3 was a remarkable aeroplane, especially so as it was built as early as 1913. The tail was carried on a single boom, which passed through the hollow airscrew shaft, and the armament was a 1-pounder Coventry Ordnance Works gun. This gun was apparently never fired from the aircraft in flight but was tested in the summer of 1913 with the F.E.3 suspended by ropes from a gantry. It was established that flight stability would not be unduly affected.

F.E.4 The gun which was to form the primary armament of this very large three-seat fighter was a Coventry Ordnance Works product, but was of the newly introduced 1½-pounder type, which continued in very restricted service with the RAF until the Second World War. This gun will be described in Volume 2. There is no indication that the gun was ever fitted, although two F.E.4s were built in 1916. The pilot sat at the front of a 'bathtub' cockpit in the fuselage nose, and, if the gun was to have been in a free installation, it is difficult to see how the gunner could have wielded it effectively. Aft of the wings was a second gun position, in this instance for a Lewis gun. On the second F.E.4 this position was deleted, but there was a gunner's station above the upper wing. This second aircraft had two Lewis guns on cranked pillar mountings at the sides of the forward gunner's cockpit. These mountings allowed the guns to be swung outboard for frontal fire.

F.E.6 This two-seat pusher fighter was built in 1914 as a development of the F.E.3 theme and was similarly armed with a Coventry Ordnance Works 1-pounder gun. This was (or was to be) installed on a pillar mounting in the nose.

F.E.8 It is sometimes contended that the F.E.8, which was first constructed in 1915 and remained operational until July 1917, was the last pusher fighter in British service, though that distinction appears more rightly to belong to the F.E.2d, which was serving with No.20 Squadron until the autumn of 1917. As with other pusher types, the object of the design was to obviate the use of deflector plates or synchronising gear. A single Lewis gun was initially installed low in the nose of the metal nacelle, with the barrel projecting through a circular hole. This arrangement permitted the gun to be trained over small arcs in conjunction with a sighting bar ahead of the windscreen, control being by means of a pistol grip. This position of the gun rendered difficult the clearing of stoppages and the changing of magazines, and on production aircraft the gun was raised to the level of the pilot's eyes. The form of pillar mounting has been described by Oliver Stewart as 'slightly different' from that of the D.H.2. As on the similar de Havilland fighter, the spare ammunition magazines were carried in 'panniers' at the sides of the cockpit. The magazines were four in number.

F.E.9 Provision of a wide field of fire was evidently the governing consideration in the designing of the F.E.9 in the summer of 1916, for not only was this two-seater of pusher layout, but the nacelle was positioned only slightly below the top wing. Following earlier F.E. practice, Lewis guns were provided for frontal and rearward fire. The guns, one in the nose of the nacelle and one behind the gunner's cockpit, were on pillar mountings.

N.E.1 The N.E.1 was first constructed late in 1917 as a specialised night fighter. It had a counterpart in the Vickers F.B.25 and was developed from a design bearing the designation F.E.12. In this design the pilot was in the front cockpit and was provided with a Lewis gun. The primary armament, however, was a Vickers rocket gun, manned by a gunner at the rear. For this gun two mountings were provided, one for frontal fire and one for firing rearwards above the top wing. Provision was made for two searchlights, one in the nose of the nacelle and one on the forward mounting for the rocket gun.

As first flown in 1917 the N.E.1 had no searchlight on the forward rocket-gun mounting, and later the light in the nose was discarded. This enabled the gunner to be brought forward to the front cockpit, where he was afforded a wider field of fire. The rocket gun was on a bipod mounting at the front lip of the cockpit, and on the starboard side of the fuselage was a fixed Lewis gun. Provision may also have been made, or intended, for a pillar-mounted Lewis gun for rearward fire.

Early in 1918 one N.E.1 was used for bombing experiments.

R.E.5 Some of the earliest bombing raids of the 1914–18 War were made by aircraft of this type. On 30 September, 1914, an R.E.5 flown by Sqn Cdr A. M. Longmore bombed Courtrai railway station. Two or three improvised French bombs were thrown overboard by the observer, Flt Lieut Osmond. Later a load of three 20-lb Hales bombs was carried, and one R.E.5 was used to test the carrier and release gear for the 336-lb bomb developed at the Royal Aircraft Factory and associated particularly with the R.E.7 and Martinsyde 'Elephant'.

Pistols and rifles were carried as defensive armament.

R.E.7 Official figures for 'military load plus crew' for three versions of this early 'heavy' bomber give an indication of its load-carrying ability. With the 160-hp Beardmore engine the figure was 520 lb, with the RAF 4a, 730 lb, and with the 250-hp Rolls-Royce, 802 lb. The bomb most generally associated with the type is the RAF 336-pounder, previously mentioned. This was carried with the nose distance-piece in a bracket fixed to the rear V-strut assembly of the undercarriage and with the rear of the characteristic central tube secured by an inverted pylon beneath the fuselage aft of the wings. Nevertheless, the 336-pounder does not appear to have been the heaviest bomb carried by the R.E.7, for a bomb of 500 lb has also been associated with the type, together with the periscopic bombsight developed at the Royal Aircraft Factory. Bombs of 112 lb and 20 lb are also known to have been carried.

As on the B.E.2c, the observer occupied the front cockpit, and the employment of pistol, rifle or Lewis gun must have been similarly inhibited; but there were remarkable developments in defensive armament. One of these was the addition of a third cockpit behind the pilot, this being provided with a Lewis gun on a Nieuport-type mounting. Another development was the forming of a gunner's station in the top wing above the front cockpit. Oliver Stewart, who personally flew the aircraft concerned for inspection by Gen Trenchard, mentions 'the front gunner standing up in the middle of the centre section with head and shoulders through a large hole'; and with a position of this kind a Scarff ring-mounting has been associated. This is said to have come adrift on one occasion and to have finished up in the pilot's cockpit. An installation of a Lewis gun on the fuselage ahead of the pilot has been positively identified, and mention has also been made of a synchronised Vickers gun.

The R.E.7 has yet a further interest in the context of armament, for aircraft of the type were among the earliest to tow aerial targets.

R.E.8 The development of the pilot's fixed-gun installation on the R.E.8 two-seat reconnaissance aircraft, first flown in the summer of 1916, involved at the beginning a crude installation of deflector plates and towards the end the latest type of Constantinesco synchronising gear. As originally schemed early in 1916 there was provision for a Lewis gun inside the cockpit on the starboard side. This gun was sited low and considerably ahead of the pilot and was fired remotely by a lever on the top longeron. Five 47-round drums were specified. A Lewis gun for the pilot appears to have been actually installed on the first two R.E.s, though there is no evidence of deflector plates; but by October 1916 the first installation had been made of a Vickers gun with Vickers synchronising gear. This gun was at first internal, on the port side of the cockpit, firing through a triangular port, below which was a long casing for the actuating shaft from the engine. What it possessed in neatness, however, this installation lacked in accessibility, and the gun was quickly transferred to the outside of the fuselage. In the standard installation, the gun was carried on two triangular brackets. Constantinesco gear eventually succeeded the Vickers gear, the trigger motor being of the Type B. The loading handle was the Hyland Type C, and both a ring-and-bead and an Aldis sight were fitted, the latter being to starboard of the pilot's windscreen. By 1917 these sights had become standard in the British flying services, though late in 1916 a Le Prieur frame-type sight had been installed experimentally. This type of sight, of which more will be said in Volume 2, was considered complicated, clumsy and a source of danger to the pilot in the event of a crash, and was accordingly abandoned.

The installation of the rear Lewis gun likewise underwent considerable development. In the original design already mentioned, this was shown as being of extensible 'lazy tongs' form, allowing the gun to be fired forward over the top wing, and this is how it materialised on the first prototype. The basis of the mounting was a ring, and a ring-mounting of different form, incorporating a simple pillar, was fitted on early production R.Es. The Scarff ring-mounting was eventually standardised, and sometimes this carried twin Lewis guns. In one such installation the drums were of 'single' (47-round) type. A point to the credit of the R.E.8's designer(s), which may not previously have been made, is that, in order to secure the widest possible field of fire from the mounting, the fuselage in the immediate vicinity was contoured with extreme care and the rearmost portion was made very small in cross-section.

The bomb-carriers were attached to rails under the lower inner wings. Identified loads were two 112-lb, four 65-lb or eight 20-lb. The bombsight was of C.F.S.4B pattern. One bomb installation made by a squadron in the field has been described in these terms by one acquainted with it: 'For the R.E.8 we improvised a most effective device for bombing the enemy transport on roads. It consisted of a 48-compartment box with a chain and sprocket-operated sliding base, cut off at an angle. Each division of the box was loaded with a Hale's rifle grenade and, as the aircraft flew up the line of enemy traffic, the observer turned a bicycle crank to withdraw the base and release the grenades one by one.'

Better known than this installation was the fitting of a Davis recoilless gun on an R.E.8 of 'A' Flight, No.30 Squadron. The gun was fixed to the starboard side of the fuselage, firing forward and downward at 45 degrees, and was reloaded by the observer/gunner, whose Scarff ring-mounting retained its Lewis gun. The forward muzzle of the Davis gun was roughly on the level of the undercarriage axle; the rear muzzle was above and behind the rear cockpit. The installation was considered successful, although the gun could not be sighted accurately.

R.E.9 This R.E.8 development was apparently intended to be armed as the standard version of the earlier aircraft.

S.E.2 Two rifles, one on each side of the fuselage, pointing outwards to clear the airscrew, appear to have formed the earliest armament of this single-seater. These were later discarded, and only a pistol was then carried.

S.E.4a On at least one single-seater of this type (built 1915) there were brackets for a gun, probably of Lewis type, well above the top wing on the centre line. The gun fired above the airscrew.

S.E.5 The weight of armament (100–107 lb) carried by the standard S.E.5 and 5a single-seaters, which fought with such telling effect in harness with the Camel, approximated closely to that carried by the Sopwith fighter, but in type of armament, as in other basic respects, the Royal Aircraft Factory product differed widely.

From the beginning the S.E.5 design was associated with the Lewis gun. As will be explained in Volume 2, the idea of a fixed gun firing through the hollow airscrew shaft of an engine was an early British idea, though not, it appears, as early as Louis Blériot's scheme for such an installation in 1911. This same arrangement was adopted in the summer of 1916 for a proposed tractor single-seat fighter designated S.E.5, an alternative design to another, designated F.E.10, which perpetuated the B.E.9 theme, but which was mercifully abandoned in favour of the S.E.5. The Lewis gun in the early S.E.5 design was to fire between the cylinder banks of the Hispano-Suiza engine and through the hollow airscrew shaft. The 47-round magazine was envisaged. This scheme was abandoned, and by December 1916 the second S.E.5 was fitted with a basic armament which set the standard pattern, namely a Lewis gun on a Foster mounting above the centre-section and a synchronised Vickers gun semi-internally to port. There is good reason for supposing that the large 'greenhouse' windshield associated with the earliest S.E.5s was adopted to facilitate the changing of ammunition drums, for the lower end of the quadrant which constituted the rear member of the Foster mounting, and down which the gun was swung for reloading or upward firing, was anchored to the top of the canopy; thus, with the gun at its lowest position, the drum was largely shielded from the slipstream. Certainly the changing of 97-round drums in later S.Es, which had ordinary windscreens, could be a difficult business, almost, on occasions, breaking a pilot's wrist. The large windshield was perforated to starboard to receive the eyepiece of the Aldis sight, the rear clamp for which was attached to the windshield framework, and the front one to a substantial pylon on the fuselage decking. The Vickers gun, which had a Type A trigger motor for the Constantinesco gear, was recessed into the main petrol tank. There was an ejection chute in the port upper cowling. When a plain windscreen was fitted it became necessary to modify the fuselage decking to enclose the breech casing of the gun.

Capt Albert Ball, whose ideas may well have influenced the adoption of the Lewis gun and Foster mounting for the S.E.5, quickly discarded the Vickers gun on his aircraft, but mounted instead a second Lewis gun, firing downwards through the bottom of the fuselage. Later this gun was discarded in turn, and the Vickers gun was reinstated, though it was now wholly external, presumably because the earlier gun-trough had been replaced by increased petrol capacity. On Ball's aircraft the lower end of the Foster mounting was braced by two wires, but a tubular structure was standardised. So that the lines of fire of the two guns could converge at a range of 50 yards, the Foster mounting was slightly raised at its rear end.

S.E.5a and b   The S.E.5a had the 200-hp Hispano-Suiza engine, and the larger airscrew needed to absorb this greater power caused the Foster mounting to be raised very noticeably above the wing on two supports, over the front and rear spars. For the Lewis gun on this mounting, one ammunition drum was carried on the gun and three in the cockpit. For the Vickers gun, which, on late aircraft at least, had the Type B trigger

The nearest line of S.E.5as in production display a cut-out in the forward bulkhead for the Vickers gun. In the second line the Vickers gun is already installed, at least in the aircraft the Service number of which is largely visible. In the third line the Foster mounting is in place. Note access panel for Vickers gun, with built-in ejection chute, on two aircraft at top right.

motor on top of the gun and the Hyland Type E loading handle, there were 400 rounds. Both guns were aligned 5 degrees up from the line of flight. Fitzgerald jam-clearers have been mentioned in connection with the S.E.5a. Both Aldis and ring-and-bead sights were fitted, and provision was made under the fuselage for a four 20-lb bomb-carrier. Two 20-lb bombs are known to have been carried loose in the cockpit. Early troubles were experienced with the Constantinesco gear, but the S.E.5a proved an exemplary gun platform. Fire could thus be opened at relatively long range, and there is a reference to the guns being set for their lines of fire to converge at 200 yards. A distinctive feature of the S.E.5a was the gear wheel and the associated 'box' type generator for the Constantinesco gear, visible beneath and behind the airscrew hub.

No.41 Squadron is said to have attempted to install twin Vickers guns, and one machine had twin Lewis guns. There was, too, an experimental installation of the Eeman triple-gun mounting, wherein the three Lewis guns fired forwards and upwards through apertures in the centre-section. A report that an installation of a rearward-firing Vickers gun was made in 1917 cannot be corroborated. At least one night-flying example had a greatly lengthened pistol grip on the Lewis gun.

The S.E.5b appears to have been armed as the standard S.E.5a.

Sage

Type 2   The uncompleted Sage Type 1 of 1916 was a twin-engined bomber with nose, upper and floor guns; the Type 2 of the same year was a two-seat single-engined fighter, the design of which represented one of many attempts to surmount the difficulties which persisted until gun synchronising gears became available. They were, in fact, already becoming available as the aircraft was constructed. The layout adopted resembled one that had been schemed by the Short company, the gunner standing largely in a faired superstructure between the fuselage and top wing, the upper surface of which was cut away to permit the use of a Lewis gun. The pilot, who was unarmed, sat, wholly enclosed, at the forward end of the superstructure. The Type 2 is illustrated on page 279.

Type 3   A carrier for four 20-lb bombs appears to have been fitted beneath the fuselage of this 1917 trainer, though the makers quoted the military load as 64 lb. It may be conjectured that anti-submarine operation with a 65-lb bomb was envisaged.

Type 4   There were three versions of this successor to the Type 3, the first of which was a patrol seaplane. No armament appears to have been installed.

Saunders

T.1 No photograph exists of this two-seater of 1917, but a makers' sketch suggests a fixed Lewis gun for the pilot, mounted above the decking, and a rear Lewis gun on a pillar mounting.

Saunders-Roe
(formerly S. E. Saunders)

Valkyrie Generally comparable with the Blackburn Iris, the Valkyrie three-engined flying-boat was built in 1927. In the bow was a Scarff ring-mounting for a Lewis gun, and behind it two pilots in tandem. Below and behind the rear pilot were the navigator's and wireless operator's compartments, and aft of the wings were two staggered Scarff ring-mountings, each for a single Lewis gun. The under-surface of the lower wing centre-section was plywood, and to this, on each side, were attached the bomb-carriers. The load could be two 520/550-lb or four 230/250-lb.

Early in the year of the Valkyrie's production H. Knowler of S. E. Saunders developed arrangements for displacing a gun mounting from the cockpit opening 'to permit the use of the cockpit for other purposes'. In one form the mounting was turned down about a pivot on the hull, but it was stated that the mounting could alternatively be 'displaced on rails attached to the deck'. The principal among the 'other purposes' mentioned was mooring, and sliding rings for this purpose were thereafter to become familiar fittings on British flying-boats.

Severn The Severn three-engined flying-boat of 1930 was a totally different aircraft from the Valkyrie, and the armament provisions differed considerably. The Scarff ring-mounting in the bow was arranged to slide rearwards, and the midships dorsal ring could be covered by a watertight hatch. There was a third Scarff ring-mounting in the extreme stern of the hull.

The difficulty of conducting mooring operations from a flying-boat having a Scarff ring-mounting in the bow were noted in connection with the Blackburn Sydney. In the Saunders-Roe Severn these were overcome by arranging for the mounting to be slid rearwards, as seen here.

The mountings carried one Lewis gun each. Normal bomb load was the same as the Valkyrie's, but an overload of the same weight was apparently possible. Cut-outs in the trailing edges of the lower wings, close inboard, may have been associated with the intended carrying of two torpedoes.

A.10 To Specification F.11/27 Saunders-Roe built, and flew in 1929, a single-seat fighter of exceptional interest in having four Vickers guns instead of the customary two. The two most readily apparent were mounted low in the cockpit sides, firing through troughs and having their breech casings covered by bulged fairings containing the case and link chutes. An access door was let in to the upper side. The other two guns were staggered in side elevation, being considerably further forward and much higher, so that they fired along troughs in the uppermost part of the engine

A four-gun fighter of 1929 was the Saunders-Roe A.10. The location of the lower pair of Vickers guns is clearly shown in this view, and the more forward position of the pair in the top of the fuselage is indicated by the case and link chutes between the centre-section struts. Brackets for an Aldis sight are fitted, and the 'lorgnette' form of the front bracket is unusual.

Saunders-Roe London with two 500-lb bombs and eight marine markers inboard.

cowling. The ejection chutes were on a lower level. An Aldis sight was mounted on brackets forward of the windscreen.

London On 19 December, 1939, the type of ring-mounting developed for the Lewis gun by F. W. Scarff in 1916 (though now wind-balanced) was in action in a London flying-boat against German aircraft.

The London dated from 1934, and its armament and equipment were so representative of its period as to warrant quotation from makers' descriptive notes, contained in a brochure bearing the title *The Saro London Mark A27 twin-engined flying boat for open sea reconnaissance, coastal defence and patrol, convoy and general purpose duties.* This reads (verbatim):

'The bow Scarff gun ring is fitted on sliding rails: below this is the bomb aimer's station. The latter operates his bomb sight and releases whilst sitting in a sheltered position in line with the gunner's floor, a hinged and wind-balanced shield or door in the extreme nose of the machine opening outwards through which sighting and aiming can be carried out. A bulkhead with a sliding door separates this compartment from the pilot's cabin . . . The mid gun ring is behind the crew's compartment,

301

Bow compartment of London, showing bomb-aimer's position, with bombsight in place; forward-opening wind-balanced panel ahead of sight; electrical bomb-release gears (right); bombing instruments (above sight); base of Scarff ring-mounting; spare ammunition drums for Lewis gun; and anchor.

Midships gun position of London, with protective cover lowered on the left; spare ammunition drums for Lewis gun; stowage for marine distress signals; stowage for cooking stove and refrigerator; bilge pumps for hull and wing-tip floats; engineer's bench, with vice; drinking-water tanks; suitcase stowage; and dinghy stowage (beneath step).

302

with raised flooring and stowages for ammunition drums. From this gun ring is an external access to the drogue box, which is fitted with outside door and drainage so that wet ropes and cordage are not brought into the hull. In the extreme tail a Scarff ring covers the whole of the after field of fire. This cockpit is fitted with a seat and pegs for ammunition drums, and in common with all other openings can be closed with a sliding watertight hatch.'

The gunner's emplacement in the extreme stern of the London, showing gunner's platform with firing steps at side, for firing downwards at a sharp angle; spare ammunition drums for Lewis gun; and parachute stowage (left).

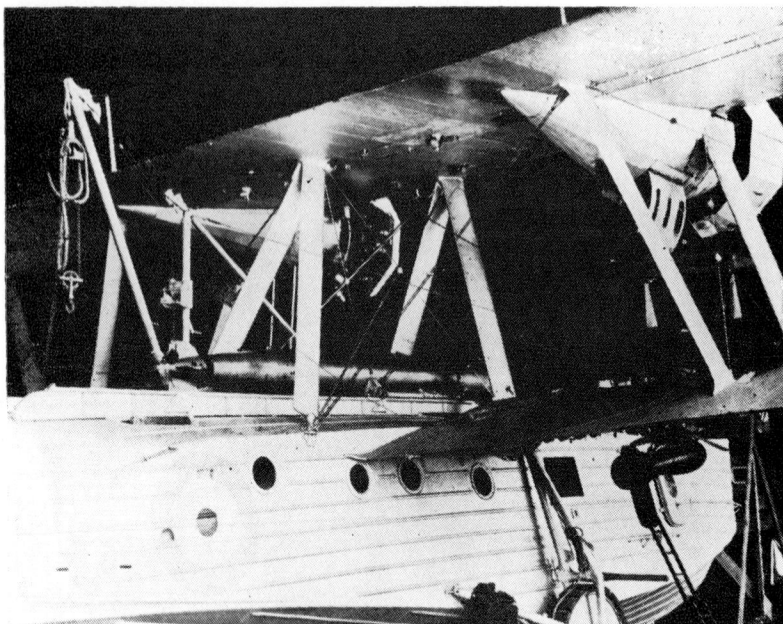

Transporting a torpedo on the hull of a flying-boat was quite a common practice between the wars, and an 18-in specimen is seen on a Saunders-Roe London. The under-wing loading is that shown in an earlier picture; but the bombs and torpedo would not normally be carried together. The torpedo could not be launched.

Later the following notes appear:

> 'The three guns are on wind balanced Scarff gun rings Mark X: five drums are allowed for each gun. The hoods in the amidships and tail gun stations give very adequate protection from the airstream, no fatigue being experienced by the gunners in operating the guns.
>
> 'The bomb controls are electrically operated through twelve release selector switches and one bomb aimer's firing switch; there is also a pilot's jettison release switch conveniently and safely placed, and protected by a small hinged metal guard. All the release selector switches and other controls are adequately protected by a hinged metal cover from dust, water and corrosion. Accessibility, control and attachment of nose and tail fusing wires is carefully arranged, functions being mechanical.'

Bombs are quoted as eight 20-lb; eight $8\frac{1}{2}$-lb practice; or four flares 4-in Mk.I; or four smoke floats, Aircraft Navigation, Mk.I (all the foregoing on Light Series carriers), and four 250-lb, or two 500-lb, 520-lb or 550-lb bombs, the first combination on two No.1 (50/250-lb) and two No.2 (50/550-lb) Universal carriers, and the last three on two No.2 Universal carriers. Of bomb loading it is remarked:

304

'The Saunder-Roe patent bomb-lifting gear consists of a direct-lifting winch placed immediately over the bomb positions. The average time taken to prepare and load one 500 lb bomb is 2 min 25 sec on the slipway. The aircraft whilst at moorings can also be loaded from a general-purpose dinghy under good weather conditions . . . The time taken from the dinghy coming alongside until four 250 lb bombs are secured is under 15 min.'

Special strong anchorages were provided on the London's hull for transporting a torpedo, flying qualities, it was claimed, remaining unchanged in this condition.

Cutty Sark For export the Cutty Sark light flying-boat/amphibian (1930) was stated to be equipped with a Vickers 7-mm gun in the bow and carriers for eight 20-lb bombs.

Cloud This larger contemporary of the Cutty Sark was adopted by the Air Ministry primarily for 'flying, navigation and bomb training'. It was stated that there were two Light Series Mk.I carriers under the starboard wing for smoke floats. The type was offered with a ring-mounting for a gun in the bows and under-wing provision for four 50-lb bombs.

A.33 As built in 1938, this four-engined flying-boat had the following tentative armament provisions: Armstrong Whitworth manually operated turret in bow, with bomb-aiming window immediately below; two beam gun positions with sliding hatches in the long dorsal fairing behind the parasol wing, and a position in the extreme stern of the hull with 'lobster tail' cover. Development was terminated by an accident.

Lerwick As originally flown in 1938, the Lerwick twin-engined flying-boat had mocked-up armament installations. The second and subsequent machines had three Frazer-Nash turrets. The bow and stern turrets were as on the Sunderland (one gun and four guns respectively) and in the mid-upper turret were two guns. The bow gun was a Vickers G.O.; the others Brownings. The main bomb load was four 500-lb or eight 250-lb.

The second Saunders-Roe Lerwick, with full complement of turrets and guns.

305

Short

S.38   A pioneer installation of a Maxim gun, probably of 0·45-in calibre, was made in 1913 on a Short pusher biplane of this type (No.66). This was dubbed 'Eastchurch Gun Machine' and was used for armament trials. The gun was mounted on a pillar in the nose of the nacelle. In wartime, rifles were carried aboard aircraft of the same type. No.34 was associated with early armament trials.

S.81 Gun-carrier   A pusher seaplane of this description (No.126) was built in 1914 with a specially stressed nacelle for the mounting and firing of a 1½-pounder Vickers gun. This development was preceded by the mounting of the gun on the Sopwith pusher seaplane No.127. It was reported in 1914 that 'excellent practice has been done in firing at targets both in the air and on the sea'. During March 1915, a 6-pounder Davis recoilless gun was tested in the same machine.

The original caption affixed to this news-agency photograph reads: 'WAR SCENES. ENGLAND MAKES READY HER AERIAL FLEET. Seaplane No.126 all ready in Ramsgate Harbour to go off at a moment's notice, she has one of the latest machine guns fitted and only awaits the order to go.' Clearly, however, the weapon is the 1½-pounder Vickers gun, inherited by No.126 from Sopwith No.127.

Short Tractor Seaplanes 'A certain 160 hp Short seaplane', identified by C. H. Barnes in *Shorts Aircraft since 1900* (Putnam, 1967) as No.121, was a third type of Short aircraft to play a pioneering part in the development of aircraft armament, for it was this machine that was earmarked by Sir Arthur Longmore for the earliest British torpedo-dropping trials. These were made at Calshot in July 1914 with a 14-in torpedo. Although crutches are said to have been attached to each of two specially arched cross-bars, hastily designed by Horace Short, early drawings, which it is intended to reproduce in Volume 2, show a seaplane of Short type having cross-bracing of X form, the torpedo being carried at the apex of the lower inverted V. The release mechanism was designed by Lieut D. Hyde-Thomson, who also adapted the torpedo.

Four other Short seaplanes of the type used in the Calshot experiments are said to have been arranged for torpedo-dropping at a later date, and aircraft having the Service numbers 178 and 186 have been associated with torpedo installations, the latter being listed as 'Type B'. This designation is of particular interest having regard to the Sopwith torpedo seaplane known as the 'Type C'.

On the Short tractor seaplanes, bombs were carried loose or on carriers. One identified load was one 100-lb bomb and four of 20 lb.

A fact of the greatest interest in the present context, and one which seems to have eluded historians hitherto, is that the famous S.41 was fitted with a machine-gun and was the first British naval aircraft to be so armed. Thus, Shorts may claim yet a fourth type of pioneering armament-development aircraft. In 1930 Cdr Sampson declared:

'It was in 1912 that we made our first seaplane, known first as Hydro-aeroplane H 1 and later as Short No.10. . . . She was an historic machine. I used her from March 1912 till the war came and never broke a piece of wood in her. I flew her in the Army manoeuvres of 1912, took her to Scotland by train for submarine experiments at Scapa Flow, used her for similar work at Harwich, and made the seaplane duration flight with her from Sheerness to Portsmouth. She was the first machine to which folding wings were fitted and the first from which a machine gun was fired.'

Samson added that the gun was a 0·45-in Maxim.

The seaplanes Types 166, 827 and 830 and that which had had the 140-hp Salmson engine all carried bombs under the fuselage. The first West-land-built 166s had arched cross-bracing struts between the floats to enable them to carry a 14-in torpedo, but all later examples had a stand-ardised installation of three 112-lb bombs. These same aircraft could have a Lewis gun in the rear cockpit, provided with six 47-round drums. A Lewis gun on a centre-section mounting was carried by at least one Type 830, and a similar installation appears to have been made on the 140-hp Salmson type.

The Short 184 Type D carried nine 65-lb bombs internally, the location of the bomb beams being indicated in the original of this photograph by three dark fittings on the side of the fuselage forward of the cockpit.

Type 184 This type—the 'Short 225', by reason of its original horse-power—was designed in 1914 specifically for operation with a 14-in torpedo, with which it achieved an early, spectacular and variously chronicled success in the Dardanelles campaign of 1915 (Flt Cdr C. H. K. Edmonds and Flt Lieut G. B. Dacre). Aircraft of the type were also employed in pioneering experiments with heavy bombs and operated with various forms of bomb installations and gun mountings.

The first examples had arched cross-bracing tubes to accommodate a torpedo, as on the early Type 166s. The release-strop was at the centre of the rear tube. One experimental Type 184 had the rear cockpit faired over, and standard RAF torpedo aircraft were to be single-seaters until the adoption of the Blackburn Ripon and Hawker Horsley.

In the early phases of the war at least, bombs were sometimes carried loose, for example, one of 16 lb plus six petrol bombs plus one incendiary bomb in addition to two bombs of 65 lb on carriers. A number of 16-lb bombs were in one instance carried loose in addition to three of 65 lb on carriers. Experiments were made with an installation of four 65-lb bombs under the wings, in line with the inner pair of interplane struts, but the carriers were normally installed in tandem on a long bomb-beam slung well below the fuselage. Identified loads include the following: four 65-lb, 100-lb or 112-lb; three 100-lb + one 112-lb; two 230-lb + one 100-lb; one 500-lb or 520-lb; and—aimed at the German cruiser *Goeben* when a Type

184 had failed to leave the water with a complete torpedo—an 18-in torpedo warhead. In May 1916 a 500-lb bomb was dropped experimentally at Kingsnorth, being aimed with a C.F.S. sight, and there appears to have been some intention of carrying such a bomb internally. In the Type D single-seat bomber variant, nine 65-lb bombs were slung nose-up internally, forward of the cockpit.

Mountings for a Lewis gun were improvised, but a Scarff ring-mounting was eventually standardised. A number of aircraft had a Whitehouse mounting. As in the usual installation of the Scarff mounting this was set considerably below the top line of the fuselage. It appears that the gun-arm was associated with a semi-circular bow, and, although the precise characteristics of the mounting are not known, they were apparently such that a recommendation was made that aircraft having this type of mounting should have a sliding panel in the floor to permit downward fire under the tail float. From one machine, in April 1916, tests were made with a 2-pdr Davis gun fitted with a Hamilton sight.

Bomber Whereas it was usual for the Short seaplanes of 1915 onwards to carry their bombs on a succession of tubular carriers under the fuselage, a feature which heightened their already distinctive appearance, the type of landplane bomber developed from them in 1916 had instead under-wing carriers. In order to save weight, Short Bros developed carriers of their own design, the bombs being suspended horizontally by their nose rings, but the official Government pattern appears to have been standardised eventually. The carrier attachments were braced by cables to upper-wing

Short Bomber with four 112-lb bombs on carriers devised by the makers themselves. The ring-mounting for the Lewis gun is not of Scarff type, though a Scarff compensating sight may be fitted.

strut attachments. Eight bombs of 65 lb or 112 lb, in tandem pairs under each wing were typical loads, and sometimes small bombs, e.g. five incendiaries, were carried internally; but four 230-lb bombs could be taken, and in preparation for the great raid on Zeebrugge, which materialised on St George's Day 1917, 520-lb bombs were delivered by aircraft of this type. On the first aircraft, a Lewis gun on the top wing could be manned by the observer standing exposed to the slipstream on the decking of the fuselage between the cockpits. Later machines had a Scarff ring-mounting or, it appears, a mounting of a type incorporating wheels running on rollers and associated with the name of W. K. Boyne. The Phoenix-built aircraft were stated by the makers to have had 'bullet-proof tanks', but armour-protection for the tanks was probably specified, as for the original Handley Page O/100.

Short Type 320, showing installation of Scarff ring-mounting behind cut-out in top wing.

Type 320 On this seaplane of 1916 the placing of the massive radiator immediately ahead of the pilot's windscreen, coupled with the presence of a float-bracing cross-tie directly beneath the torpedo-carrier, might have appeared to render the aircraft wholly useless for its intended purpose of dropping an 18-in Mk.IX torpedo. But although the radiator was immovable, and the pilot was committed to making the most of his field of view on either side, the cross-tie between the floats was removable. Before an intended raid by Short 320s on Durazzo harbour, the aircraft were towed out into the Adriatic by Naval launches, and volunteers from the launches swam out to the seaplanes and unbolted the ties. On occasions when the tie was to be removed, the floats were fitted with extra struts, which braced their inner faces.

Although as torpedo-carriers these aircraft achieved no operational success, as had the Type 184, they were used for valuable trials at Calshot early in 1918.

Mostly the Short 320s were used for patrol and bombing, without provision for the torpedo but carrying bombs and a Lewis gun. The bombs

310

were carried in the customary Short fashion under the fuselage, typical loads being two 230-lb or four 112-lb. A standard installation of a Lewis gun was made. This took the form of a Scarff ring-mounting located behind a cut-out in the top wing, the base of the ring being braced to the fuselage by two struts. The observer/gunner was in the front seat, and to use the Lewis gun he stood up in his cockpit, being thus exposed to the slipstream.

310-hp Seaplane, Type B This was the designation applied to the 'North Sea Scout' type of Short seaplane, produced in 1916 as a 'Zeppelin fighter' to carry a 6-pdr Davis recoilless gun, in addition to a Lewis gun for its own defence. The big gun was shackled to a member across the rear cockpit, and fired upward and forward. Accordingly, the centre-section of the top wing was left open, and the radiator was made in two blocks instead of one. The Lewis gun mounting was apparently developed at Grain, where the aircraft was tested.

N.2B A two-seater patrol seaplane of 1917, this type carried two 230-lb bombs (or equivalent) side by side under the fuselage. The pilot had no gun, but there was a Lewis gun on a Scarff ring for the observer. An earlier experimental machine of this general type carried two 65-lb bombs.

Shirl Like its counterpart the Blackburn Blackburd, the Shirl (1918) was a single-seat torpedo-carrier, designed specifically to operate with the 18-in Mk.VIII torpedo. Each of the two crutches was stayed by two inverted V-struts.

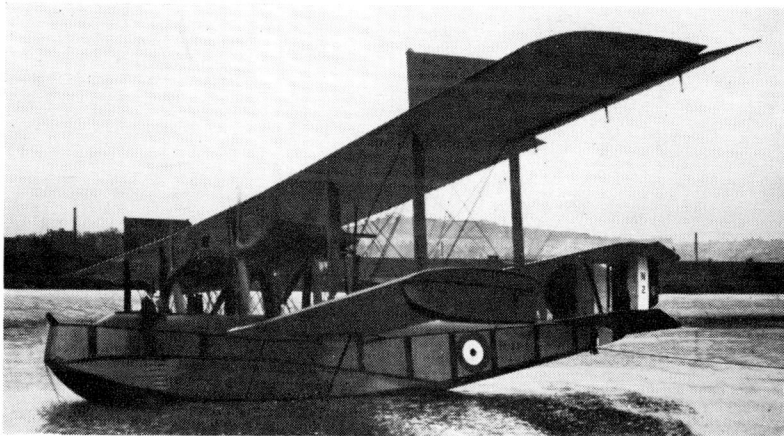

Short Cromarty, with mounting for 37-mm Coventry Ordnance Works gun in bow.

Cromarty This large twin-engined flying-boat, for 'fleet co-operation', had a counterpart in the Vickers Valentia, and was similarly armed with a 37-mm Coventry Ordnance Works gun in the bow. The gunner's cockpit was oval in planform. 'Fighting top' positions, otherwise known as 'crow's nests', for Lewis guns were planned for, but not installed on, the top wing,

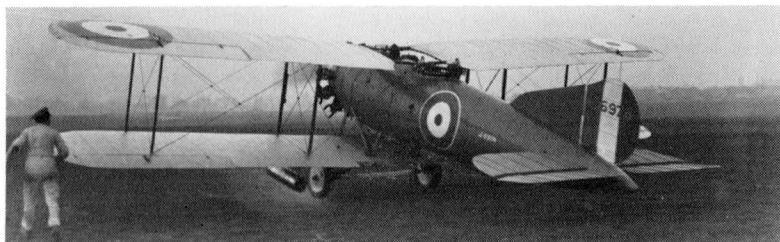

Short Springbok, showing emplacement for Scarff ring-mounting and supply container on bomb-carrier. (*Flight International.*)

outboard of the engines. Instead, a dorsal position for a Lewis gun was incorporated. This was later given a raised coaming, to afford the gunner better protection. The bomb load was two 520/550-lb or four 230/250-lb.

Springbok The Springbok was a corps reconnaissance (army co-opera-tion) two-seater built in 1923. The pilot had a fixed Vickers gun, low-set to port and firing through a trough between the cylinders of the Jupiter engine. This gun was not at first installed. For the observer, there was a Scarff ring-mounting carrying one Lewis gun. Four bomb rails were fitted inboard under the lower wings, and on these the Springbok could carry supply containers. During November 1923, in fact, an aircraft of this type gave a demonstration of dropping ammunition and supplies by parachute. The Springbok II had an open rib-bay at the root of the port lower wing to facilitate (it was said) the use of a bombsight or camera, and certainly to allow the pilot a view vertically downwards. The gunner was afforded a degree of protection by the raising of the forward coaming.

F.5 (Metal Hull) Late in 1924 the upperworks of a Felixstowe F.5 flying-boat were fitted to an experimental metal hull of Short construction. Notwithstanding its experimental nature, this hull had two Scarff ring-mountings for Lewis guns. One was in the bow and the second in line with the trailing edges of the wings.

Singapore This first aircraft in the Singapore flying-boat series (built 1926) was twin-engined and had three Scarff ring-mountings for Lewis guns, one in the bow and two offset to port and starboard on top of the hull just aft of the wings. Of these two mountings, that to port was con-siderably forward of the other. The makers quoted the weight of guns and ammunition as 280 lb and 'bombs and gear' as 1,180 lb. The bomb load, carried under the lower wings just outboard of the centre-section bracing struts, was, in fact, four 230/250-lb or two 520/550-lb.

Chamois The Chamois was a rebuilt Springbok (1927) and was similarly armed.

Sturgeon Like the earlier Hawker Hedgehog, the Sturgeon (1927) was a three-seat fleet reconnaissance aircraft. The pilot's Vickers gun was mounted to port in a massive and unbecoming bulge, with separate case

312

Top, F.5 (Metal Hull) with Scarff ring-mountings in bow and amidships. The lower view of the Singapore I shows two mountings of the same type amidships.

and link chutes, and behind the second cockpit, under a large cut-out in the trailing edge of the top wing, was a Scarff ring-mounting for a Lewis gun. Strong-points were provided in the bottom wings for bomb-carriers. These were well outboard so that the bombs would clear the float under-carriage. Probable loads were four 112-lb or two 230/250-lb + four 20-lb. There was a prone aiming position, with sliding hatch.

Gurnard A two-seat fleet fighter reconnaissance aircraft of 1929, the Gurnard was fitted with a new type of mounting designed by Short Brothers. This combined features of the pillar type and ring type. Like the Hawker and Avro mountings it was basically of the wind-balanced ring type, but the gun was carried on a curved vertical pillar instead of on a 'bow'. The ring was countersunk well below the top line of the fuselage, and the gunner was afforded some protection by a considerable depth of fuselage behind the pilot's cockpit. A single Lewis gun was fitted. The pilot's Vickers gun was mounted high in the cockpit to port and fired through a trough. There was an ejection chute a short distance down the fuselage side. Aldis and ring-and-bead sights were fitted. Curiously, the

The Short company developed its own type of ring-mounting for the Gurnard, seen here installed on the amphibian version of the aircraft.

Gurnard had provision for Light Series bomb-carriers under both lower wings, whereas its competitors, the Hawker Osprey and Blackburn Nautilus, allowed for only one. There were brackets for a camera gun on the starboard lower wing.

Rangoon On the Rangoon three-engined flying-boat of 1930 the Scarff ring-mounting in the bow was mounted on rails and could be moved aft for mooring. This mounting carried one Lewis gun, as did the two additional ones on top of the hull behind the wings. These were staggered (port ring foremost) and were installed on structures built out from the main body of the hull. Universal carriers were fitted under the wings, just outboard of the wing/hull bracing struts, for four 250-lb or two 500/520/550-lb bombs, and there was a Light Series carrier outboard to port.

Short Rangoon, showing the distinctive form of emplacement for a Scarff ring-mounting in the midships position. The bow mounting is slid aft. The dark object on the hull may be a drogue.

K.F.1 Built for Japan in 1930, this three-engined flying-boat had Scarff ring-mountings for Lewis guns in the bow (sliding for mooring), on the hull aft of the wings (two staggered rings), and in the extreme stern. This last position was accessible from the interior and was perched atop a swan-neck rear hull section of commanding elegance. There was under-wing provision for bombs.

Singapore II An experimental four-engined Singapore development of 1930, this flying-boat had a revised armament scheme, with four Scarff ring-mountings for Lewis guns: one (rearward-sliding for mooring) in the bow; two staggered on the hull aft of the wings, as on the original Singapore; and one in the extreme stern. The emplacement for the stern gun resembled that on the Blackburn Iris and Sydney.

Sarafand This very large six-engined flying-boat of 1932 had provision in the nose for a 37-mm Coventry Ordnance Works gun as an alternative to the Lewis gun on a rearward-sliding Scarff ring-mounting actually installed. In this same nose position was a hatch for a bombsight, together with fusing and release gear. Amidships were two staggered Scarff ring-

Comparative views of Short Singapore III (*top*) and Sarafand. In each instance the Scarff ring-mounting in the bow is slid to the rear. One of the recessed midships mountings on the Sarafand is seen. (Top picture, *Flight International*.)

315

mountings, deeply recessed into the canted decking, and in the extreme stern was a fourth mounting of the type, with a folding screen ahead of it. Under-wing provision was made for bombs up to an unstated weight ('military load' was quoted as 5,970 lb). It was stated:

'Provision is made for loading the bombs by the supply of a suitable winch and pulleys, which can be transferred to any of the bomb positions, the winch being operated from the top of the lower plane, with the hoisting cables passing through the plane.'

R.24/31 The armament of the twin-engined flying-boat built to the foregoing specification, and known as the Knuckleduster, was described by the makers as follows:

'Three Lewis guns are fitted at the bow, mid and tail cockpits. The mid gun ring is mounted on transverse rails to enable the gun to be operated from either side as required. Windshields are provided for both mid and tail cockpits. The bomb load consists of two 500-lb or four 250-lb bombs, which are carried together with four light series bombs and four reconnaissance flares. The main bombs are hoisted by a transportable winch which can be positioned at each bomb position, thus obviating the fitting of heavy bomb ribs. Mechanical fusing and electrical cartridge firing is used. Provision is made for transporting one 18-in torpedo under the starboard wing root against the hull side.'

Short R.24/31. A 500-lb bomb is seen on a Universal carrier, with marine markers outboard. The three Lewis guns are in position.

During one flight the fairing over the tail-gunner's position collapsed, and how this was later changed for a quarter-spherical tilting cupola is told in the book by C. H. Barnes already named.

Singapore III In 1934 appeared this definitive Singapore, as ordered for the RAF. Three Lewis guns were disposed on Scarff ring-mountings, one in the bow (rearward-sliding), one mid-way between wings and tail (sliding athwartships) and one in the stern behind the centre fin and rudder. The second of these mountings was in a recess well below the top line of the hull and had a folding screen forward. The tail mounting was similarly

Winching 250-lb bombs, with Universal carriers, aboard a Singapore III.

screened. Bombing facilities and loads were the same as those for the R.24/31.

John Yoxall, who was at home in practically every type of British multi-seater Service aircraft between the wars, in the dual capacities of photographer and journalist, gave these impressions of a Singapore III after the Coast Defence Exercises of 1937. They may be compared with similar notes included for the F boats and the Sunderland. Mr Yoxall said:

'Right at the rear of the hull is the gunner's cockpit, with a hemispherical field of fire to discourage any fighter who thinks flying boats are easy meat. Then, in the portion of the hull aft of the step, there is provision for carrying all sorts of stores, including two spare props. Moving forward, one next comes to the centre gunner's cockpit, with a sea drogue tucked in at each side. In action one would hope to have a cool-headed gunner at this particular point, as the field is rather limited and enthusiasm might be the cause of several punctures in the wing-tip floats and tail.'

Sunderland Although Mr Barnes's researches have brought to light a projected installation of a 37-mm Coventry Ordnance Works gun in the bow of the Sunderland, there was a far more ambitious scheme. In this installation two C.O.W. guns were arranged to fire vertically downwards through apertures in the planing bottom, which were to be made watertight to enable the guns to be stowed horizontally within the hull. For firing vertically downwards, the recoil would be directed towards the centre of gravity of the aircraft. Gimbal mountings would permit limited traverse.

317

Short Sunderland prototype, showing bomb-hatch in the side of the hull under the wing and distribution of gun positions.

The Sunderland prototype appeared in 1937 with temporary turrets, but the development and production machines had, in respect of guns, a primary armament corresponding to the Whitley's: that is, a Nash and Thompson F.N.13 four-gun turret (Brownings) in the stern of the hull and a turret of the same manufacture (F.N.11 with one Vickers G.O. gun) in the bow. Selection of the heavy tail armament afforded another instance of how armament could influence airframe design, for not only was the aircraft centre of gravity moved aft, calling for sweepback on the wings, but it was necessary to move the rear planing-bottom step further aft than on the Empire boat, to which the Sunderland was closely related. In the prototype, hatches were provided in the hull decking aft of the wing, and these were developed to accommodate one Vickers G.O. gun each, on manually operated pillar mountings, for which there were metal windshields. There was a hinged bomb-aimer's panel in the bow, and the bomb load was carried internally within the hull. Before release, the bombs were run outboard on rails through two large hatches in the sides of the hull below the wing. The carriers were guided on rollers running in two box-beams and were moved by hand-operated winches working a worm-and-rack mechanism. Bomb loads were eight 100-lb or 250-lb or four 500-lb.

The Sunderland must be selected for a more detailed description of internal accommodation and armament distribution for comparison with the F boat, Singapore III, London and Whitley. It may be judged from the following contemporary account that the interior of a Sunderland in action had something in common with a first-rate of Nelson's time. Thus:

'The hull is extraordinarily deep and is divided into an upper and a lower deck. In the bow is a power-operated gun turret, beneath which is the bomb-aimer's position and stowage for mooring equipment. The turret is arranged to slide aft to permit mooring operations. On the upper deck aft of the bow compartment is the pilots' cabin, which has dual controls and is accessible by a communicating ladder from the lower deck. Aft of the pilots' cabin, on the port side, is the wireless-operator's station, and on the starboard side the navigator's seat and table and a position for the engineer. The galley, which also serves as a drogue-operating station, is partitioned from the wardroom. There is a ladder from the galley to the engineer's compartment. Aft of the galley are two compartments for the crew, that forward housing the main bomb load. Farther aft, approximately on a level with the upper deck, is the platform for the midship gun stations. In the extreme tail is another power-operated turret, accessible by a catwalk in continuation of the main flooring.'

Of the nose position, wherein the turret slid on rails:

'The floor of the front gun position is hinged; when this is folded down the position may be used for mooring, and when up the floor acts as a foot-rest for the gunner. There is a small flap which forms the bomb-aimer's seat.'

Subsequent modifications and additions to the Sunderland's armament, including substitution of an F.N.7 two-gun turret for the two hand-held midships guns and replacement of the F.N.13 (tail) with 500 rpg by the F.N.4a (1,000 rpg) are outside the compass of this survey. Eventually the Sunderland had eighteen guns—including the same fixed armament as the Gloster Gladiator.

Stirling Although the first Stirling four-engined bomber flew during 1939, it carried no armament, and the first production aircraft were not completed until well into 1940.

Siddeley

R.T.1 This two-seat reconnaissance machine of 1917 had one Lewis gun on a Scarff ring-mounting, the level of which was raised during development by building up the coaming of the fuselage. There was a second Lewis gun for the pilot, over the centre-section to starboard, firing above the airscrew at a slight upward angle.

(*For other Siddeley types see under Armstrong Whitworth*)

Sopwith

Bat Boat   The first flying-boat of this type was bought by the Admiralty in 1913 and was used for armament experiments with which the names of Lieut A. W. Bigsworth and Sub-Lieut J. L. Travers are particularly associated. The dropping of darts and practice bombs was preceded by the discharge of potatoes. Naval ratings observed the fall of shot. Data on bomb aiming were thus accumulated.

Pusher Seaplane Gun-carrier No.127   The identity and significance of this historic aircraft is apparently now established for the first time, the significance being that it was armed with the $1\frac{1}{2}$-pdr Vickers gun before that weapon was transferred to Short S.81 No.126. First, there is the testimony of Sir Arthur Longmore that 'one of our Sopwith pusher seaplanes' (at Calshot before the 1914 war) carried a $1\frac{1}{2}$-pdr gun weighing 265 lb, with which Lieut R. H. Clark-Hall conducted many successful tests. Second, it was stated on the occasion of the Naval Review in July 1914 that a 'Sopwith Gun Carrier' with 200-hp Salmson (Canton-Unné) engine was unable to fly because of tail alterations. On this same occasion the Short S.81 No.126 was present carrying a $1\frac{1}{2}$-pdr gun and it was remarked:

'The gun on the Short is the biggest weapon yet used in aircraft. It was first used on the Sopwith, and later was used to test the Short's ability to stand the recoil.'

Aircraft No.127 is on record as being a Sopwith with 200-hp Canton-Unné engine, and it may be supposed that this and the Short machine were ordered as a pair for trials with heavy guns. That No.127 was of the well-known Greek Gun Bus type (see below) is certainly open to question, having regard to the fact that this was a much smaller machine than the Short No.126, the respective wing spans being 50 ft and 67 ft; and there can be little doubt that No.127 was the Hydro Biplane Type S of 80 ft span, already associated by J. M. Bruce with a quick-firing gun. Thus No.127 must take its place in history, not only on account of its big gun, but as the largest British aeroplane of its time.

One Sopwith seaplane with 120-hp Austro-Daimler engine has also been recorded as having a gun. This was probably No.93.

Tractor Biplanes   A Sopwith tractor biplane with 80-hp Gnome engine and having a machine-gun appears to have been at Eastchurch in 1914, and there is some indication that one such machine with Anzani engine may have had a pillar mounting for a gun at an early stage of the war. The pillar appears to have been fitted between the two tandem cockpits, beneath the cut-out in the trailing edge of the top wing.

Tabloid   On 28 December, 1914, the following letter was received by the Sopwith Company from the Director of the Admiralty Air Department:

'Gentlemen, With reference to the recent attack on the German air-[ship] sheds at Cologne and Dusseldorf, carried out by Sqn Cdr Spenser D. A. Grey and Fl Licut R. L. G. Marix, you may be interested to learn that the machines used were your Sopwith Tabloid aeroplanes.'

The bombs employed in this famous raid, in which Marix destroyed Z.IX and Spenser Grey had to transfer his attack to Cologne station, were of the 20-lb Hales pattern.

The Tabloid first appeared in 1913. As early as February 1915, Tabloids of Cdr Sampson's squadron were fitted with a mounting for a Lewis gun above the top wing. This mounting was devised by Lieut T. Warner and Warrant Officer J. G. Brownridge. Other installations were made on the side of the fuselage. More primitive weapons, apart from pistols and perhaps rifles, included steel darts (as carried by Lieut N. C. Spratt when he forced an enemy aircraft to land after manoeuvring in 'an aggressive manner'), a grapnel and hand grenades. On one occasion an attempt was made by Lieut Spratt to tie a grenade to a length of control cable with the intention of fouling the enemy's airscrew. This device was never used.

Gordon Bennett Racer   Almost identical with the Tabloid, one of two machines of this type was fitted in 1915 with a fixed, stripped Lewis gun on the starboard side of the fuselage. The airscrew was provided with plates to deflect the bullets. A minute written by Winston Churchill in April 1915, calling for a single-seat Naval aircraft 'with a Lewis gun firing through the deflector propeller', may be mentioned in this context.

Type C   The first British-built aeroplane designed specifically for torpedo-dropping, the Type C tractor seaplane, was built in 1914. It arrived at Calshot shortly after Sir Arthur Longmore (then Squadron Commander) had made his first torpedo-drop from a Short, and he and his pilots made drops from the new Sopwith product. It was a four-bay biplane of very large span, with overhang, and it may be wondered if the wing cellule was similar to that of No.127. As on the A.D. 1000 the two floats were quite independent, in order to allow the torpedo to be dropped. Each float was strut-braced to the lower longerons and to the attachment points of the inner interplane struts. This arrangement probably represented the first major influence of armament on aircraft design.

Gun Bus   A photograph overleaf shows the installation of a Lewis gun on one of three pusher landplanes, of a type first constructed in 1913, in RNAS service. It will be seen that the nose of the nacelle is of such a form as to allow the gunner a certain angle of downward fire. The gun, of land-service pattern, is secured to a cranked pillar by a V-shaped attachment on the cooling jacket, and a collector box is fitted to catch the spent cartridge

The Sopwith Gun Bus as a 'gun-carrier' and 'bomb-carrier' (to use the terminology of 1914/15): *top*, with Lewis gun on cranked pillar mounting; *lower*, with bomb-carriers outboard of revised undercarriage.

cases. With narrow-track two-wheel undercarriage, machines of this same type were fitted to carry four bombs under the lower wings, two on each side just outboard of the second pair of interplane struts.

Type 807 Early in 1915 two tractor seaplanes of this type were sent to German East Africa for operations against the German cruiser *Königsberg*. One was loaded with two 50-lb and four 16-lb bombs, but was unable to lift them.

Type 860 Like its contemporary, the Short Type 184, this tractor seaplane of 1915 was designed to carry a 14-in torpedo. The crutches were attached to the two cross-ties joining the floats. There was a cut-out in the top centre-section, but whether this was associated with a gun mounting has not been established.

Two-seater Scout This derivative of the 'Daily Mail', or 'Circuit of Britain' type tractor two-seater (1914), was in one instance equipped for anti-Zeppelin work with a Lee-Enfield rifle firing Hales grenades and in another with a Mauser rifle firing German incendiary ammunition. A shotgun firing chain shot and a Very pistol have also been associated with the type. On specimens with lengthened undercarriage a bomb-carrier was attached beneath the fuselage immediately behind the undercarriage.

Schneider and Baby The original Sopwith Schneider racing seaplane was built in 1913, and developed versions for the RNAS were in service during 1915. At least two different installations of a Lewis gun were made. The first entailed the fitting of deflector plates on the airscrew, and the second the attachment of the gun on the centre-section at an angle sufficient for the bullets to clear the airscrew disc. The rear end projected through an aperture. This second installation was for anti-airship work, and for the same purpose H.E. and incendiary bombs could be carried. One identified load was four 20-lb H.E. bombs and an incendiary bomb. The armament later standardised for the Baby was a Lewis gun, with mechanical synchronising gear on the fuselage centre line and projecting backwards through the windscreen, or alternatively offset to starboard. For anti-submarine work there was provision for two 65-lb bombs (the Schneider carried one) in tandem under the fuselage. The gun and ammunition weighed 55 lb and only one bomb could be carried in addition. There were instances of a Lewis gun mounted on the starboard side of the fuselage and of the gun attached to the port centre-section struts, turned on its side, and firing upwards at about 45 degrees to the line of flight. In at least one instance Le Prieur rockets were attached to the interplane struts, and one batch of Blackburn-built Babies initially carried Ranken Darts to the exclusion of other armament. A photograph overleaf shows one of these aircraft later armed with a Lewis gun and having also a carrier for, apparently, four 20-lb bombs.

Top, Sopwith Baby with Lewis gun through centre-section; *lower*, Sopwith Baby with synchronised Lewis gun and bomb-carriers.

1½ Strutter Although justly remembered as the archetype of the classic two-seat fighter (pilot with fixed gun, gunner with free gun), this biplane of 1915/16 was also constructed as a specialised bomber and as a 'ship's aeroplane'. In all three forms the armament differed. While the fighter and bomber had a fixed Vickers gun, the third variant did not. The prototype and some production aircraft were flown without armament, the reason in part being a shortage of Vickers guns. While at least one early specimen had the gun mounted on the port upper longeron, with the breech casing lying under the built-up coaming of the cockpit, on all standard production fighters and bombers thereafter the gun was mounted on the centre line of the fuselage immediately ahead of the pilot, with the firing lever projecting from the gun above the control column. The Sopwith patented padded windscreen was fitted, and plain open or ring-and-bead sights were mounted on the gun. The ammunition was fed from the right, and a metal plate on the left, forward of the feed block, served to prevent the canvas belt from twisting in the slipstream before entering the protection of the fuselage. On some early examples the rear of the gun was partly faired. The first machines for the RFC (A and B Flights of No.70 Squadron) had gun-synchronising gear of the Vickers type, but C Flight of the same unit had aircraft intended for the RNAS and fitted with the Scarff–Dibovsky gear developed for, and standardised by, that Service. Gears of the Ross and Sopwith–Kauper types were also fitted. The advantages of the Vickers gun, with its continuous belt feed, over the drum-fed Lewis, which demanded the breaking-off of an engagement for the changing of drums, was quickly apparent.

That the Scarff No.2 ring-mounting for the Lewis gun was developed with the assistance of the Sopwith company is not generally known, and it is with this most famous of all aircraft gun mountings that the 1½ Strutter is most intimately associated. Early examples, however, had either a Strange cranked pillar mounting or a ring-mounting of the French Nieuport type. The Scarff No.2 mounting was first introduced in the ex-RNAS aircraft of C Flight, No.70 Squadron, already mentioned in connection with the Scarff–Dibovsky gear. It was mounted directly on the top longerons, and thus below the fuselage top line, and its diameter was slightly greater than the fuselage width. Standard ammunition provision on the 1½ Strutter two-seater was 300 rounds in a fabric belt for the Vickers gun and five double drums for the Lewis gun. On one aircraft of B Flight, No.70 Squadron, an auxiliary armament of an automatic pistol with oversize magazine was attached to the starboard undercarriage struts to fire outside the airscrew arc. On certain Home Defence aircraft, the Vickers gun was dismounted, the front cockpit was faired over, the pilot was moved to the rear and a Lewis gun was mounted over the top wing to fire above the airscrew and obviate the risk of using 'special' ammunition in the synchronised gun. One aircraft had two upward-firing Lewis guns mounted forward of the cockpit in a special installation, and another carried the same armament on a twin mounting of Foster type.

Apart from its Scarff ring-mounting and Sopwith padded screen, the 1½ Strutter was notable also for its tailplane incidence-adjusting gear, a primary purpose of which was to compensate for gunners of different weights. For this aeroplane, also, Sopwith developed a special gunner's seat, capable of all-round movement about an eccentric pivot on a fixed stand. Means were provided for automatically locking the seat to the stand when the seat was occupied and for unlocking the seat when it was relieved of the gunner's weight. A wooden frame carried a vertical pivot having a

'No fighting aeroplane ever introduced as many novel armament features as this Sopwith two-seater': the 1½ Strutter, showing synchronised Vickers gun with Sopwith padded screen and Scarff No.2 ring-mounting.

toothed ring which was pressed, by the weight of the gunner acting against a spring, into engagement with a toothed ring carried by a fixed socket supported by legs. The engagement between the teeth served to fix the seat in the desired position, but disengagement automatically took place under the action of the spring when the gunner raised himself, and the seat could then be freely rotated in the socket.

No fighting aeroplane ever introduced as many novel armament features as this Sopwith two-seater.

Bomb rails were sometimes fitted beneath the lower wings and/or fuse-lage of 1½ Strutter two-seaters, and possible loads were four or eight 20-lb or two 65-lb. The potential of these aircraft as long-range bombers was quickly recognised by the RNAS; indeed the 1½ Strutter had been origin-ally designed for bombing and has a place in history as one of the first truly 'strategic' bombers. A specialised single-seat bomber type was developed, and this carried its bombs internally in a compartment which took the place of the gunner's cockpit. Official rigging notes indicate that the rear flying wires on bombers were shorter than on fighters. The standard load was four 50-lb or 65-lb bombs, horizontally stowed. The four trapdoors beneath the bomb compartment were opened by the weight of the falling bombs and were closed again by shock-absorber cord. Two small inspec-tion and access panels were let in to each side of the bomb compartment. On the single-seat bomber, 500 rounds were provided for the Vickers gun.

Occasionally a Lewis gun was fixed to fire over the top wing of bombers as auxiliary armament, but the drum for this could not be changed in flight. The 'Sopwith Bomber (Clerget)' was declared obsolete in an Air Ministry Order of 1921.

Pup 'Tiny little things just big enough for one man and a machine gun' was the first impression made by Pups as recorded in *War Birds*. In *The Clouds Remember*, Oliver Stewart recalled his 'perfect flying machine': 'It had the single Vickers gun, with mechanical interrupter gear, fired by a short horizontal lever or trigger which projected back from under the rear part of the gun and was pressed downwards by the pilot. Some Pups were flown by their pilots completely "stripped", without even a windscreen or an Aldis tube, the ring sight alone being used.' Concerning the standard Pup, as used by the RNAS and RFC after September 1916, it may be added that the Vickers gun was installed as on the $1\frac{1}{2}$ Strutter and in conjunction with the Sopwith padded screen and Sopwith–Kauper synchronising gear. Some later aircraft had the Scarff–Dibovsky or Constantinesco gear. Although the gun was generally mounted centrally, there was also an installation above the port top longeron, perhaps to protect the pilot's face. A panel on the starboard side, in line with the feed chute, gave access

Vickers-gun installation on Sopwith Pup, showing feed chute and access panel for belt box.

to the belt box. When the padded screen was discarded by some pilots, the back of the gun was occasionally padded.

The figure of 80 lb, generally quoted in official reports as the Pup's military load, would be accounted for by a Vickers gun, associated gear and 500 rounds of ammunition; the figure is, in fact, precisely half that quoted for the Westland Wagtail, with its twin Vickers guns, gear and 1,000 rounds.

There were several unofficial, and generally unsuccessful, installations of a Lewis gun above the centre-section. These were made both in France and, to obviate firing 'special' ammunition through the airscrew arc, in Home Defence units. McCudden made himself a 'rough sight of wire and rings and beads' for such an installation. The only standardised installation of a Lewis gun on a Pup appears to have been made on the Ships' Pup (Sopwith 9901), the gun in this instance being mounted on a tripod of steel tubes forward of the cockpit and firing above the airscrew at a shallow angle, with the barrel passing through a cut-out in the centre-section, and the rear of the gun accessible to the pilot. A Vickers gun was sometimes fitted in addition, and another load, additional to the Lewis gun, was eight Le Prieur rockets attached to the interplane struts. On some machines the rockets were the sole armament, and the cut-out for the Lewis gun was covered. Four 20-lb bombs were sometimes carried under the fuselage.

Triplane The second Sopwith fighter produced in 1916, the Triplane was armed, with only three known exceptions, in the manner of the standard Pup, the single Vickers gun lying on the centre line ahead of the cockpit and having Scarff–Dibovsky synchronising gear. Ammunition supply was 500 rounds, and the Sopwith padded screen was fitted. That the Triplane had the 'Scarff Patent Gun Mounting No.3 Made by The Sopwith Avia-

Standard Sopwith Triplane, with Sopwith padded screen at rear of Vickers gun.

Triplane (Hispano-Suiza); detail showing installation of Vickers gun with Sopwith–Kauper gear and padded rear end.

tion Co Ltd, Kingston-on-Thames', was attested by a plate on the instrument panel. Of the three exceptions mentioned, one was the installation of two Vickers guns in a small number of aircraft; another was the fitting of a Lewis gun (additional to the standard Vickers installation) at the root of the port middle wing; and the third was the elevating of the Vickers gun to fire upward at an angle of about five degrees. This last installation entailed fitting an Aldis sight with a special graticule and was intended for stern or underneath attack at relatively long range.

Bee   At one stage, a Vickers gun was fitted to this tiny biplane of 1916.

L.R.T.Tr.   This long-range, or anti-Zeppelin, fighter (1916) may be compared with the Armstrong Whitworth F.K.12. Contrasting with the ungainly masses of the airframe and undercarriage, was a carefully streamlined nacelle built into the top centre-section. Forward of the leading edge was a cockpit for a gunner, and just ahead of this was a socket for a pillar-mounted Lewis gun. The nacelle underwent at least one modification in shape. The pilot had no gun, but immediately behind him was a third cockpit for a second gunner who had a Lewis gun on a swivelling pillar mounting which carried the gun on a perforated arm.

Triplane (Hispano-Suiza)   Yet another Sopwith fighter dating from 1916, this type differed radically from the earlier rotary-engined machine. Two examples were built, one with 150-hp, the other with 200-hp engine. Both had a single Vickers gun, mounted much as on the earlier type and having

329

Sopwith–Kauper synchronising gear. The end of the gun was padded and there was a small metal screen forward of the feed block. As on the earlier Triplane, there were drag and anti-drag wires attached to the spars of the lower wing, but on the Hispano-Suiza machines there were two access panels outboard of each of the ribs to which these wires were attached. These panels somewhat resembled those on the later Sopwith triplane fighter, the Snark, and with which auxiliary outboard armament was associated. Definite conclusions, however, would not be warranted, especially so as the panels were at the anchorage points for the lower drag wires.

Camel F.1   The essential qualities of the Camel F.1, first constructed in 1917, were heavy firepower and compactness. These qualities are epitomised in one of the 'Points to Observe when Overhauling Machine' covered in the *Technical Notes* relating to the type. To quote:

> 'Examine cartridge drums and see that they are secure and do not foul the carburetter.'

The Camel got its hump and its name from the building up of the coaming round the breech casings of the two Vickers guns ahead of the cockpit. Allied with the qualities already named was a high performance, and it may be noted in this regard that certain of the early Camel prototypes and some production aircraft were the only known British fighters to have the front ends of their Vickers guns fitted with fairings.

On the first Camel, the top line of the 'hump' sloped upwards to meet the high-set front rim of the cockpit, but, possibly in the interests of pilot view, the rim was lowered and the top of the hump was flattened, leaving the upper surfaces of the breech casings exposed. On production aircraft, the forward coaming of the cockpit was sometimes cut away to clear these casings and the windscreen was shaped to fit the barrel jackets. At first the spent cartridge cases and links from both guns fell clear of the aircraft through a projecting chute well down on the starboard side of the cowling, and Norman Macmillan has described how 'spent cases mostly fell on the lower wing, but their drumming on the fabric was deadened by the chatter of the guns' firing'. Later, however, case and link chutes appeared on the port side also. In the standard installation, the link chutes were high in the fuselage sides, in line with the feed blocks of the guns, and the case chutes were much lower and further forward, to clear the belt boxes. They were let in to the large oval inspection panel on each side. Ring-and-bead sights were fitted to the port or starboard gun, or sometimes to both guns, with the ring at the forward end, either on a pedestal or attached directly to the barrel casing. The usual mounting for the Aldis sight was on the centre line, with the rear end projecting behind the windscreen. Hyland loading handles were fitted to the guns, and Norman Macmillan mentions 'Feroto' jam-clearers, adding that a hammer was more effective. Although the Sopwith–Kauper gun gear was installed, this was succeeded by the Constantinesco C.C. gear.

How the Camel's hump developed: *top*, first Camel with original form of fairing over breech casings of guns; *lower*, second Camel with revised fairings for guns.

The weight of the two Vickers guns as installed in the Camel was 70 lb, and the two ammunition belts, each holding 250 rounds in Prideaux disintegrating-link belts, weighed 31 lb.

A fairly common fitting on Camels was a carrier for four 20-lb bombs attached beneath the fuselage between the rear undercarriage struts. The carrier was secured to the bottom longerons, but, as it was narrower than the fuselage, the brackets were cranked accordingly. Other identified loads were one 112-lb and two 40-lb Phosphorus bombs.

As the firing of 'special' ammunition through the airscrew was hazardous, and the muzzle flash of the guns at night temporarily blinded the pilot, a similar remedy to that used on the 1½ Strutter was adopted: the Vickers guns were removed; the decking lowered; the cockpit moved aft, and two Lewis guns were fitted on parallel Foster mountings. The bottom ends of the tracks of these mountings were attached to a cross-bar carried on two rearward-sloping members fixed to the top longerons ahead of the

The third (tapered-wing) Camel, showing immaculate gun installation and fairings at front end of guns.

The Camel at war, with a gun installation that is hardly immaculate, since the addition of chutes, sights, screen and, in this instance, a camera gun to port.

cockpit. A Neame illuminated sight, with a large-diameter ring, was mounted on the centre line. In one such installation the starboard gun was fixed alongside the track of the Foster mounting to fire upwards at an angle corresponding with that at which a ring sight was set on the cross-bar. On the night of 25 January, 1918, a Gotha was shot down in flames by two night fighter Camels flown by Capt G. H. Hackwill and 2nd-Lieut C.C. Banks, who thus achieved the first victory with the Neame sight.

At least one Camel F.1, greatly modified and carried on a lighter, had a single Vickers gun, mounted to port as on the 2F.1, and was fitted with two Admiralty Top Plane mountings for Lewis guns above the centre-section.

Camel 2F.1 This was the 'ships'' version of the Camel and normally had only one Vickers gun (port) and one Lewis gun above the centre-section. The type was a derivative of a design known as the FS.1 which may actually have been constructed as the 'Camel Seaplane' and of which a landplane version was certainly built. Like the FS.1, this aircraft had a Vickers gun to port and a Lewis gun over the centre-section. This gun was

333

Armed to meet RNAS requirements: the Camel 2F.1 with Vickers gun to port, with ring-and-bead sight mounted on gun, and Lewis gun on Admiralty Top Plane mounting.

fixed and was installed in the inverted position, with the ammunition drum projecting through a trailing-edge cut-out so that it could be changed by the pilot without recourse to a movable mounting of Foster or Admiralty Top Plane type. The latter was, however, standardised. Two double drums were provided for the Lewis gun, and there were 250 rounds for the Vickers gun, which had a ring-and-bead sight mounted upon it. At least one aircraft was modified to have twin Vickers guns, and the most famous 2F.1 of all—used by Lieut S. D. Culley to shoot down Zeppelin L.53 on 10 August, 1918—had two Lewis guns above the centre-section. An experimental installation of eight strut-mounted Le Prieur rockets was made.

It has been stated that for the raid on the Tondern Zeppelin sheds on 19 July, 1918, the bombs used by the seven Camels engaged were of 50-lb type. Marshal of the RAF Sir William Dickson, who took part in the raid, has, however, described them as 'specially made 60-lb Coopers'. He has also recorded that before the raid the pilots experimented with various forms of sight to improve their aim.

Camel T.F.1 'trench fighter' with two downward-firing Lewis guns and one Lewis gun on Admiralty Top Plate mounting.

Installation of Lewis guns in cockpit of Camel T.F.1. A sheet of armour plate forms the fuselage bottom.

Camel T.F.1 Camels were extensively used for low-flying attacks and one experimental 'armoured trench fighter' version was produced early in 1918. This is said to have been built originally by Boulton & Paul, although its rudder proclaimed 'Clayton & Shuttleworth Ltd'; but the experimental installations were made by Sopwith. The armament was three Lewis guns, two firing downwards, with their barrels projecting through the floor at a steep angle and one on an Admiralty Top Plane mounting as on the Camel 2F.l. Like the upper gun, the fuselage guns had their spade grips removed, and the ammunition drums were of the smaller (47-round) type. A sheet of armour-plate, slightly wider than the fuselage, extended from the fire-wall to the area of the petrol tank behind the cockpit.

Bomber Laid out along the lines of the single-seat bomber version of the $1\frac{1}{2}$ Strutter, with internal bomb stowage behind the pilot, this larger aircraft of 1917 was at first unarmed. While undergoing operational trials, however, it had a synchronised Lewis gun on the centre line of the fuselage ahead of the cockpit. The bomb compartment had an access panel on each side and appears to have had provision for nine 50-lb bombs, carried nose-up as in the D.H.9. J. M. Bruce records a total load of 560 lb and a test-load of twenty 28-lb Analyte bombs.

Cuckoo The Cuckoo has the distinction of being the first torpedo-dropping aircraft designed to operate with a wheeled undercarriage from the deck of a ship. It was closely related to the B.1 Bomber and likewise dated from 1917, production being initiated by the Blackburn company in 1918. Distinctive features associated with the carrying of the torpedo (Mk.IX

Sopwith Bomber, showing access panel to bomb compartment in side of fuselage
aft of cockpit.

of nominal 1,000-lb weight) were the three-bay wings and split undercarriage. The torpedo gear was a Blackburn responsibility and led to
developments by that company already described. The torpedo was heated
either by warm air from long exhaust tail-pipes, ducted to the region of
the buoyancy chamber as on the later Blackburn Swift and Dart, or by
electrically heated mats. There appear to have been at least two types of
torpedo installation. A photograph on page 338 shows the torpedo
slung by a cable which is visible between the V-struts of the undercarriage.
A crutch is seen roughly in line with the wing trailing edge and there is a
massive pylon structure associated with the nose of the torpedo. This
appears to have the dual function of steadying the missile and of acting
as a pistol stop, but in most other known photographs of Cuckoos it is
absent. The same photograph shows the torpedo depth-setting gear, located to the left of the pilot's wicker seat.

Under the Blackburn heading, mention is made of the importance
attached during the early days of torpedoplane development to a silent
approach to the target, and it is known that silencers were fitted to some
Cuckoos. During 1920 it was notified that there was a diving hazard
since modifications had been made and the Viper engine installed: the
Cuckoo was to be dived only with tanks half empty.

The most notable design feature of the Cuckoo to be influenced by

Sopwith Cuckoo (Blackburn-built) showing installation of Mk.IX torpedo.

armament was the split-axle undercarriage which allowed the torpedo to be carried and dropped. The following is a verbatim official description:

'The Chassis consists of two Undercarriages which are identical. Each Undercarriage is formed of steel tubes welded and pinned together, and consists of two portions. One portion, which is in the shape of a V, is placed parallel to the fuselage, the End Lugs being bolted to the front and rear Spars of the Centre Section Lower Plane. The other portion has one End Lug bolted to the Bottom Longeron, and is bent so as to form the Axle for one wheel, the other end resting in the apex of the V. Shock Absorbers are formed by 28 feet of 15 mms. diam elastic, which is given ten complete turns round the Axle and the apex of the V. The Steel Struts are stream-lined by means of wood fairing attached by metal clips, the whole being wrapped with fabric and then doped.'

Dolphin From the standpoint of armament, as from other aspects, the Dolphin of 1917 was a fighter of exceptional interest. By reason of the fact that it carried two free Lewis guns in addition to two fixed Vickers guns, it has been correctly described as the world's first multi-gun single-seat fighter. Yet the first Dolphin, with its deep car-type frontal radiator, gave scant evidence of being armed at all. The Lewis guns were not, in fact, fitted on this machine, although the Vickers guns were present beneath the cowling, as proclaimed by the breech casings visible in the cockpit, ejection chutes, and two small ports in the nose cowling. The link chutes were above the cylinder-bank fairings and the case chutes behind the exhaust pipes. When lateral radiators were adopted, the cowling was lowered accordingly and the forward portions of the Vickers guns protruded. In the Dolphin Mk.II (300-hp Hispano-Suiza engine) the guns were again submerged.

The rear ends of the Vickers guns were padded and came far back in to the sides of the cockpit at the level of the pilot's shoulders. The windscreen was far ahead of the cockpit and the centrally-mounted Aldis sight passed through it, being bracket-mounted at a point behind the screen and to the cross-tube which carried the Lewis guns. A ring-and-bead sight was mounted to starboard. C.C. gear Type B was fitted, and the guns had Hyland Type A or B loading handles. A prominent feature of the C.C. gear installation was the gear ring attached to the rear flange of the airscrew boss and the smaller gear wheel meshing with it below. Beneath the smaller gear wheel were two apertures in the cowling each exposing part of the box-type generator used with the Hispano-Suiza engine and a short length of the hydraulic pipeline leading to the trigger motor.

The two Lewis guns were swivel-mounted on brackets attached to the ends of the cross member which was officially known as the 'front spar tube'.

Twin Vickers and twin Lewis guns on Sopwith Dolphin. The windscreen is perforated for an Aldis sight, but the sight is not installed. Note also gear ring behind propeller hub, smaller gear wheel below it and part of generator and pipeline for starboard Vickers gun.

They pointed upwards at about 45 degrees and were restrained from firing into the airscrew by two cams, which nevertheless permitted their being trained to some extent outboard. The spade grips were removed, and the guns were fired by Bowden cable. Norman vane sights were sometimes fitted. When the guns were trained parallel, they were clamped above the pistol grips by fittings attached to the upper wing roots. The Lewis gun installation was not popular among pilots by reason of the guns' intrusion into an already cramped cockpit, and inevitably they affected performance. To fly the Dolphin, keep observation, operate the radiator, and use the Lewis guns as well as the Vickers guns was a one-man-band operation that few could have mastered. One or both guns were frequently removed,

Sopwith Snipe, showing gun installation with chutes and ring sight. Compare the arrangement of the chutes with the picture opposite.

although a single Lewis gun was regarded as standard. In No. 87 Squadron the guns were transferred to fixed mountings on the lower wings, somewhat inboard of the inner pairs of interplane struts, where they fired outside the airscrew arc. There were probably other schemes, and certainly a fixed Lewis gun was fitted on the upper wing. Other non-standard installations were an Aldis sight attached to the front spar tube and a Lewis gun on the cross-bar of a crash pylon above the open centre-section. For night work, Hutton illuminated sights were fitted. Four 20-lb bombs could be carried under the fuselage.

Snipe   Although the Snipe's basic armament of two Vickers guns was the same as the Camel's, and was similarly disposed, there were several variations as between individual aircraft. The 'hump' fairing on the prototypes,

Sopwith Salamander, showing armoured portions, guns, ring sight and chutes.
Attachment points for a bomb-carrier are seen under the cockpit.

Another comparative view of the Salamander and Snipe, in production at Sopwith's Ham works in December 1918. Note staggered Vickers gun installation on Salamander (front row) and flat sides.

A third Salamander/Snipe comparison, with the Salamanders in the foreground exhibiting not only the armoured forward fuselage but the staggered gun-mountings.

dating from late 1917, sloped straight down from the cockpit coaming to the lip of the engine cowling, but on production aircraft the decking was asymmetrical, being carried further aft on the port side and giving a stronger impression of a hump. There were subtle differences in the location and shaping of the case and link chutes; on production aircraft the link chutes were located high in the cowling, in line with the feed blocks, and the case chutes were far lower down and further forward, in order to clear the belt boxes. Provision was made on production Snipes for both ring-and-bead and Aldis sights. The ring was stayed to the starboard gun, and the bead was immediately forward of the windscreen. As the screen was well forward of the cockpit, the sight base was very short. The Aldis sight was on the centre line and passed through an aperture in the windscreen. It was carried in brackets attached to a fore-and-aft tube running across the centre-section cut-out. Like contemporary and competitive types of fighter, the Snipe was at one time required to carry a Lewis gun as secondary armament. On the third prototype, this was mounted above the centre-section, offset to starboard. On the example called by the makers Snipe 7F.1/5, the tube on which the gun was carried above the wing was pivoted at its front end on the centre line, and built out from the front face of the rear spar was a quadrant on which the rear end of the gun could be swung to starboard. On the Snipe with the large experimental spinner and other cowling modifications, there was a fixed fitting on the rear spar, not outboard of the cut-out ahead of the spar, as on the 7F.1/5, but inside, somewhat offset to starboard. It is recorded that during official trials a total of 235 lb of ammunition was carried for the three guns on one of the Snipe prototypes, but this can hardly be credited, even if the guns, which would weigh about 90 lb, were included. In any case, the position of the Lewis gun was criticised as being too near the pilot's head, and the gun was discarded.

Snipes in squadron service could carry four 20-lb bombs, the carrier brackets being of the type fitted on the Camel. A single 112-lb bomb was another load.

Bulldog Designed as a high-performance fighter-reconnaissance aircraft, this two-seater of 1918 had an unusual and heavy armament. For the pilot there were two synchronised Vickers guns, with 600 rounds each, mounted Snipe-fashion, with their padded breech casings all but touching the pilot's face. The windscreen was perforated for an Aldis sight, and there were separate case and link chutes in the cowling flanks. For the gunner there were two Lewis guns, one on a pillar mounting at each end of the elongated cockpit. To extend the field of fire in the forward upper hemisphere, the front pillar was extensible, and, as it was projected upwards, it raised, by means of a connecting tube, a rectangular screen hinged to the rear spar of the upper centre-section. Jointly with a small windscreen, this afforded the gunner a measure of protection. The rear pillar could be traversed from side to side. Possibly in the interests of gun

343

The Sopwith Bulldog, two aspects of which are seen, had unusual and heavy armament. In addition to two fixed Vickers guns there were two Lewis guns on pillar mountings. The foremost pillar was extensible and operated jointly with a protective screen.

344

handling, the ammunition drums were of single (47-round) type. In the original armament scheme, which did not materialise, two Lewis guns were to be mounted between the cockpits, capable of firing, like the single gun actually fitted, above the airscrew. The second (two-bay) version of the first Bulldog was armed as the first, but the second machine (Dragonfly engine) was unarmed, although a Scarff ring-mounting had been intended for it.

An attachment noted on the forward Lewis gun may indicate an intention that this gun could be fired also by the pilot, but this is conjectural.

Rhino   A counterpart of the D.H.9, the Rhino single-engined bomber of 1917 had internal bomb stowage. This was located under the pilot's seat, and the bombs—four 112-lb or nine 50-lb or twenty 20-lb—were winched into place complete with release gear. The bombs being so placed, it was not possible to provide the pilot with a Negative Lens sight, as on the D.H.9. Between Rhinos Nos. 1 and 2, there were interesting variations in gun armament. On the first machine the pilot's Vickers gun was mounted on the centre line immediately ahead of the cockpit, with the feed block faired over, the fairing also affording some protection to the pilot. The gun retained its land-service handles. On the second example the gun was similarly mounted and was wholly forward of the windscreen (lacking on the first machine). There was a fairing ahead of the feed block. Rear armament on the first Rhino was a Lewis gun on a rocking pillar mounting at the rear of the cockpit, as on the Bulldog. The second machine had a redesigned cockpit with a Scarff ring-mounting on the top longerons, the gunner thus having a considerable depth of protective coaming ahead of him.

The second Sopwith Rhino differed from the first in the installation of the Vickers gun, seen above, and in having a Scarff ring-mounting, the base of which is just visible on the extreme left.

The fuselage of the Sopwith Hippo was so narrow that the Scarff ring-mounting of the second example, shown here, overhung the sides.

Hippo   The Hippo two-seat fighter (1917) was a counterpart of the Sala-mander, in having backward stagger, and a contemporary of the Rhino, with which it was analogous in rear armament, the first machine being fitted with a pair of rocking-pillar mountings for two Lewis guns and the second having a Scarff ring-mounting for a single Lewis gun. The installa-tion of the mounting was somewhat unusual, the ring being considerably greater in diameter than the width of the fuselage. The pilot had two Vickers guns in a remarkably neat installation and one which imperilled his frontal features less than in some other Sopwith types, the breech casings being located lower and further ahead. But although the familiar Sopwith padded windscreen was thus rendered unnecessary, the leading edge of the top centre-section was padded in the interests of head protec-tion. There were separate case and link chutes low in the cowling and a small fitting, possibly for a sight, ahead of the windscreen. The gun gear was of Sopwith–Kauper type, and 500 rounds per gun were provided. The total ammunition weight of 260 lb, which has been recorded for the first Hippo, seems somewhat excessive, even if the four guns were included, for the guns themselves would weigh no more than 100 lb and the ammu-nition not much over 130 lb.

Snail   The Snail Mk.II single-seat fighter, which appeared in 1918 earlier than the Mk.I version (monocoque fuselage), carried its two Vickers guns in an extremely neat installation. The relatively large fuselage diameter enabled the guns to be mounted in the sides of the cockpit, the only external evidence of their presence being the extreme muzzle ends projecting into short troughs and the separate case and link chutes in the flanks of the cockpit. A Lewis gun was mounted above the starboard edge of the centre-section cut-out, the rear end picking up a fitting seen in the photograph on page 348. In firing position, the gun was parallel with the centre line, but a pivoted arm attached to the rear face of the front spar allowed the gun to be swung inboard for reloading. This was, in effect, a reversal of the system used on the Snipe. The windscreen was perforated for an Aldis sight. The Snail Mk.I does not appear to have carried its intended armament of two Vickers guns.

Salamander   'The armour plating is painted in chocolate brown. On the wings is a forked-lightning camouflage design to render it comparatively invisible from above.' Thus ran an eye-witness account of a Salamander, to which it was added that the machine carried no roundels. Thus passive protection was visual as well as in the form of the armour-plate for which this 1918 'trench fighter' successor to the Camel T.F.1 is best known. The entire forward portion of the fuselage consisted of armour, and additional plating formed part of the top decking round and behind the cockpit, as well as the characteristic head-rest. The weight of all this armour (nearly 650 lb) was doubtless the cause of one officer describing the aeroplane as a 'heavily plated product of the Sopwith factories' which 'on account of its clumsiness and poor flying characteristics was found to be more lethal to its pilot than to the enemy'. This criticism may have been over-severe, although Martlesham Heath reported that lateral control was heavy and that the aircraft was tiring to fly.

The armour gave adequate protection against German armour-piercing bullets fired from short range but presented problems additional to that of weight. In January 1919 the RAF gave notice that in trueing-up the wings it was advisable first to adjust the upper wings until the dihedral was correct, and afterwards to adjust for stagger. It would then be found that any inaccuracy would be confined to the first bay from the fuselage on the lower wings. Such inaccuracy would occur at the lower-spar housings on the armour-plate, and would be due to the 'very considerable' amount of distortion inherent in these plates caused by the hardening

One of the neatest gun installations of the 1914–18 war was that of the two Vickers guns in the first Sopwith Snail, as shown. A fitting for a Lewis gun is seen on the centre-section.

The fuselage of the Sopwith Swallow was that of the Camel, but the gun installation differed and the guns were more widely spaced, as seen.

process. The makers' order of erection was: place armoured portion on trestles and attach undercarriage vees and axle; true-up undercarriage; attach rear end of fuselage by means of four bolts 'through the joint box'; true-up fuselage; fit main petrol tank and connect piping as far as V.P. cock and first rubber joints in pipe from Weyman pump at bottom of main tank; mount engine, fit oil tank and gravity tank and connect all piping; connect engine controls, revolution counter and C.C. gear; fit magazines; mount Vickers guns and connect pipe lines to trigger motors; fit rear decking; place top gun cowl in position; attach side cowls and front engine cowl; assemble tail unit; and connect controls. These facts may lend further interest to the details from superb manufacturers' photographs now reproduced, apparently, for the first time.

Although the Salamander was closely related to the Snipe and was similarly armed with two Vickers guns, there were many differences in the armament installation, stemming from the requirement that each gun should have 1,000 rounds of ammunition. This led to the staggering of the guns in plan on the production type (starboard gun foremost). Case and link chutes were close together near the feed blocks. Sights were arranged as on the Snipe. Experimental installations reported, but not confirmed by photographs, were eight downward-firing guns (presumably Lewis), and two downward-firing Lewis guns and two Lewis guns over the centre-section, additional to the two standard Vickers guns. It was doubtless in

The first Sopwith Buffalo, with rocking-pillar mounting for Lewis gun.

350

The second Buffalo, with Scarff ring-mounting. Note extent of armouring in this view and that on the opposite page.

connection with the Salamander that Sopwith designed a form of magazine comprising two telescopic belt boxes. This arrangement was such that when one box was completely emptied the adjacent box was moved into it with the new ammunition supply occupying the correct position relative to the gun.

Provision was made for four 20-lb bombs, as on the Snipe.

Swallow   Although the Swallow parasol monoplane fighter, which appeared just before the Armistice, had a Camel fuselage, the two Vickers guns were rearranged. The hump was no longer in evidence, and the guns were more widely spaced, lying exposed along the upper cowling and having combined large ejection chutes for cases and links immediately below them.

Buffalo   Among the several Sopwith prototypes of 1918 was the Buffalo armoured two-seater for 'contact patrol' duties. As was the case with the Rhino and Hippo, the first example had a rocking-pillar mounting for the rear Lewis gun, whereas the second had a Scarff ring-mounting. The pillar traversed in a transverse slot at the rear end of the cockpit. The pilot had

351

a Vickers gun mounted on top of the fuselage to port and with the breech casing faired in. The link chute was by the feed block and the case chute lower down. Ring-and-bead sights were stayed to the gun, and there were brackets for a central Aldis sight. The armouring was structural, as on the Salamander, and was extended on the second machine by one bay aft.

Installation of twin Vickers guns in a Sopwith Dragon. The trigger motors associated with the C.C. synchronising gear are not fitted to the guns, but clearly seen are the protective pads and loading handles at the rear of the guns, the feed chutes and the link chute for port gun, and the windscreen perforated for an Aldis sight.

Dragon   This Snipe development of 1918 retained the same armament, and this can be said to have fitted like a glove, for the muzzles of the guns barely cleared the valve gear on the top cylinder of the Dragonfly engine.

Snark   Designed in 1918 and flown in 1919, the Snark was the most heavily armed single-seat fighter of the 1914–18 war; but by the time the Gloster S.S.19 appeared in 1932 with a similar armament—two synchronised Vickers guns and four wing-mounted Lewis guns—its existence seems to have been entirely forgotten. That only one of the three specimens built appears to have been thus armed (the basic war load being the two Vickers guns) does not detract from the type's significance. The two Vickers guns were entirely 'buried' in the fuselage, almost at the level of the rudder bar, and the Lewis guns were in two close-set pairs, one pair under each bottom wing, in which were provided a pair of staggered access panels. There were brackets for an Aldis sight forward of the windscreen, offset to starboard, and a ring-and-bead sight a little further to starboard, the pedestals being canted outwards by the curved monocoque fuselage.

Although it might not be supposed that a rear view of a single-seat fighter could convey much information on armament the reverse is true in this instance. The subject is the Sopwith Snark, and in a frontal view the 'buried' Vickers guns would be invisible. In addition to showing the four panels in the bottom wing, denoting the locations of the outboard Lewis guns, this picture shows brackets for the Aldis sight, slightly to starboard, and mountings for the ring-and-bead sight, the pillar for the bead being canted outboard to the right of the windscreen.

353

In this view of the Sopwith Cobham the location of the bomb compartment is seen through the inverted-pyramid tubular structure which anchors the undercarriage. On the Scarff ring-mounting the lever for locking and unlocking the mechanism is seen.

Snapper   The two Vickers guns of the Snapper single-seat fighter of 1919 were set in the top fuselage decking, widely spaced, with their breech casings in the cockpit and their barrels lying in long deep troughs. The windscreen was perforated for an Aldis sight, and there were ring-and bead sights in addition. As on the Swallow, there were combined large ejection chutes for cases and links below the feed blocks.

Cobham   The Cobham triplane bomber was flown in 1920. This first and only twin-engined Sopwith carried its bombs internally in the fuselage between the roots of the main spar. A load of 750 lb has been mentioned, and this seems altogether reasonable. Two access panels were located in the side of the fuselage just below the centre wing. There was a Scarff ring-mounting for a Lewis gun in the nose and a similar installation on top of the fuselage just abaft the wings.

Sunbeam

Bomber   This single-seat bomber of 1917 appears to have been unique among aircraft of the 1914/18 War in having a remotely-fired fixed Vickers gun. This was mounted above the engine several feet ahead of the single cockpit, where stoppages could not be cleared. In having external bomb stowage, it contrasted with the Sopwith Bomber, which it somewhat resembled. J. M. Bruce states that a bomb load of three 100-lb bombs was apparently possible. This type of bomb was a specialised anti-submarine weapon. Tandem tubular carriers suggest that a greater number of bombs was provided for, if not actually carried.

Supermarine

Night Hawk Noel Pemberton-Billing's second quadruplane (the P.B.29 has already been mentioned under the designer's own name) was similarly intended for anti-Zeppelin operations and was a veritable 'giant battleplane'. It was built in 1916. The primary armament was a 2-pdr Davis recoilless gun, with ten rounds of ammunition. This gun was in a forward upper position above the topmost wing and built-in to the deep central structure, which had internal crew accommodation. The gun was on a special mounting, designed to permit traversing and described as carrying the gun on a 'double parallel sliding bed, permitting practically any arc of fire'. The target for the Davis gun was intended to be illuminated by a searchlight carried on the aircraft, gimbal-mounted in the nose, power being supplied by a separate A.B.C. engine and dynamo. The design included nine separate petrol tanks with 'quick-change' gear, enabling any number of tanks to be used or isolated in case of puncture by gunfire. In addition to the Davis gun there were two Lewis guns on Scarff ring-mountings. (The designer once claimed four guns, but two were actually fitted.) The mountings were emplaced one forward of the central structure, in the nose of the fuselage proper, and one in the rear of the central structure, behind the Davis gun. For the Lewis guns, six ammunition drums were specified. Another design feature mentioned in connection with this aeroplane was the carrying of all controls, pipes, etc, outside the fuselage in armour-plated casings and a 'special revolver' enabling 'incendiary flares' to be dropped in a stick of one every twenty feet, so that, in straddling a Zeppelin of 65-ft diameter, at least three would strike. The 'perpetual haze of escaped gas' just above the top surface of a Zeppelin was considered by Pemberton-Billing to make it very vulnerable to such attack. This same designer schemed in 1915 an 'incendiary and bomb dropper' which was manufactured by the H.M.V. Gramophone Company and which was claimed to have continued in use long after the designer's political attacks on the Government.

Patrol Seaplane A Lewis gun and two anti-submarine bombs of 65 lb or 100 lb was the designed armament of this pusher two-seater. The bombs were to be carried in tandem under the lower wing on the centre line.

Baby A makers' drawing indicates that a single Lewis gun was the armament (actual or intended) of this single-seat fighter flying-boat (1918).

Channel This was the name conferred by Supermarine on the A.D. Flying Boat constructed by them and offered for sale in 1919. A Scarff ring-mounting for a Lewis gun with 'single' ammunition drums was installed

Supermarine Channel, with Lewis gun manned in bow. The gun has a 'single' (47-round) ammunition drum, and there are bomb-carriers under the wings.

a short distance back from the bows as shown in a photograph herewith. This same picture suggests the presence of a four 20-lb bomb-carrier under the port wing, and the makers mentioned a possible load of two 50-lb or 100-lb bombs.

Seal There has been conjecture whether the fixed Vickers gun, shown in a makers' drawing of the Seal fleet-spotter amphibian of 1921, was ever fitted. It was indeed fitted, on the port side of the bow. Arrangements were made for the gun to be withdrawn for take-off and alighting and for the associated aperture to be closed. There was additionally a Scarff ring-mounting for a single Lewis gun atop the hull aft of the wings, to the rear of a built-up superstructure. At one development stage, when the makers themselves called the aircraft 'Seagull', this structure was very large indeed, as a picture on the next page shows.

Seagull The production-type Seagull had the same rear armament as the Seal/Seagull prototype, but the massive experimental superstructure was not fitted. No bow gun was installed.

Sea King and Sea Lion Intended for operation from gun-turret platform or deck, the Sea King 'fighting scout' amphibian flying-boat, completed at the end of 1921, was armed with a single Lewis gun, for which there were six double drums. Total installed weight was about 100 lb. The makers appear to have drawn no fine distinction between this aircraft and the Sea Lion, with which the Napier Lion engine is associated, and the Hispano-Suiza engined aircraft illustrated was called by them 'Sea Lion'. The Sea Lion was stated to carry 'guns and ammunition' to a weight of 140 lb. Two Vickers guns would weigh about half this figure, so it seems that the

Supermarine Seal/Seagull prototype with protective superstructure over rear crew stations.

armament, actual or intended, was two Vickers guns with 500 rounds per gun. The hump forward of the cockpit appears large enough to house such an armament; on the other hand a similar hump appeared on the Seamew which had no fixed guns.

Scarab The Scarab was a bomber/reconnaissance amphibian developed in 1924 from the Seagull and resembling the Sheldrake. The superstructure aft of the wings, with the Scarff ring-mounting at the rear, had disappeared, but there was provision for a mounting of this type immediately behind the pilot's cockpit, in the forward part of the hull. Bomb load (under-wing) was typically two 230/250-lb and two 112-lb, but a 1,000-lb load is said to have been possible. If this were so, the range would have been short, for the entire disposable load totalled only 1,775 lb.

Southampton This most famous of the Supermarine flying-boats was built in 1925 and entered RAF service in 1927. There were two principal

Production-type Supermarine Seagull with standard installation of Scarff ring-mounting.

versions (wood- and metal-hulled) and several variants of these, mainly respecting engines, but armament remained unaltered in essentials if only because the emplacements for the three Scarff ring-mountings were very carefully built as integral parts of the hull structure. The mountings themselves were initially of the No.2 and later of the No.7 (wind-balanced) pattern. A contemporary account read:

'In the extreme bow is a cockpit for the observer or bomber, which serves also for mooring and casting loose. Behind the wings are two other gun positions. These are not on the centre line of the hull but are offset one to each side, so that the gun on each may be used to fire at targets vertically below the hull. In addition, owing to the absence of any bracing on the tail more than 3 ft from the centre line, these guns can fire aft and inside of a line parallel to the centre line, so that the line of fire from these two guns can converge on a target directly behind and comparatively close up'.

359

A makers' caption to this photograph reads: 'Sea Lion, fastest flying boat in the world'. The hump ahead of the cockpit is referred to in the text.

The mountings carried one Lewis gun each. Bombs were carried on tandem tubular carriers under the lower wings just outboard of the hull/wing bracing struts, and themselves braced inboard. Possible loads were four 230/250-lb or two 520/550-lb. Marine markers or light bombs were carried outboard. The weight of armament and military equipment in Case A (bombing) was given as 2,130 lb; in Case B (reconnaissance) as 1,000 lb less. Concerning the Kestrel-engined version at least (1932) it was

Supermarine Scarab with a 230-lb and a 112-lb bomb under the starboard wing.

Supermarine Southampton prototype, showing tubular carriers for two 520/550-lb bombs under wings and Scarff ring-mounting in bow.

stated that the aircraft could carry two 18-in torpedoes, one on each side of the hull, winches being fitted for the purpose under the bottom centre-section.

Although in the original Southampton bomb installation (tubular carriers) the 230/250-lb bombs were carried in tandem, there is some evidence that in the early 1930s a Southampton was tested at Felixstowe

Metal-hulled Southamptons under construction, showing how the emplacements for the Scarff ring-mountings were built in to the hull.

with two bombs under each lower wing suspended side by side. This may indicate the fitting of Universal carriers.

Sheldrake The Sheldrake of 1926 was a development of, and intended replacement for, the RAF Seagull. It was similarly armed.

Solent It was announced in June 1926 that 'News has just been received by The Supermarine Aviation Works Ltd. from their Chief Designer Mr Mitchell, who is in Copenhagen, that a contract has been signed with the Danish Government for a large three-engined flying boat.' This craft was known as the Solent or Nanok (Ice Bear) and was a version of the wooden-hull Southampton, but with three Armstrong Siddeley Jaguar engines instead of the two Napier Lions specified for the RAF. Offensive armament, however, was a striking departure, being two Danish-type 18-in torpedoes, weighing some 1,500 lb each, carried with their release slips and crutches where the Southampton's bombs were slung. Special winching arrangements were provided so that the torpedoes could be shipped either ashore or afloat, and the torpedoes were carried slightly nose-down to the angle of incidence of the wings. In order to operate with the torpedoes, special petrol tanks of 210-gal capacity were fitted, the tanks designed for the reconnaissance condition holding 560 gal. For heating the torpedoes the exhaust tail-pipes of the centre engine were led down below the wing. The Scarff ring-mountings were of wind-balanced type.

Tests were made with the torpedoes in place, but the project was aban-

Supermarine Solent with Danish torpedo under starboard wing and handwheel for hoisting winch in place. The midships Scarff ring-mounting is of wind-balanced type.

doned owing, it was said, to the Solent's inadequate powers of manoeuvre. Stripped of armament, and with other modifications, the aircraft became an 'air yacht'.

Seamew This 'Baby Southampton' of 1928 was a three-seat reconnaissance amphibian and carried two-thirds of the Southampton's defensive armament, that is, two Lewis guns on two Scarff ring-mountings. These were disposed in an unusual manner. The first (as in the earlier Scarab) was behind the pilot's cockpit, forward of the wings. It was raised well above the top decking of the hull on a turret-like structure the side walls of which were cut away to improve field of vision for observation. The second was aft of the wings, again on a raised structure. Under the lower wings were strong-points for bomb-carriers, possibly for two 230/250-lb or four 112-lb bombs, with four 20-lb or marine markers inboard on the port side.

Southampton X Built in 1930, this three-engined flying-boat was a wholly different aircraft from the earlier Southamptons, and was more heavily armed. In the bow was the usual Scarff ring-mounting for a Lewis gun, but this was now arranged to slide aft for mooring. Aft of the wings were two staggered mountings of the same type, set as in the Southampton (port ring foremost), but these were now deeply recessed below the top decking of the fuselage. The most notable innovation was the Scarff ring-mounting in the extreme stern of the hull, carried on a structure similar to that introduced on the earlier Blackburn flying-boats. The main bomb load was probably two 520/550-lb or four 230/250-lb bombs, and a torpedo-carrying capability was mentioned (two 18-in).

Scapa Originally built as the Southampton IV in 1932, this much-developed Southampton was named Scapa in the following year, when ordered for RAF service. The basic Southampton arrangement of the three Scarff ring-mountings for single Lewis guns (five drums each) was retained, but the bow ring was arranged to slide aft for mooring. Beneath this mounting, in the inward-curving plating of the bluff bow, was a hinged watertight door for bombsighting, a feature lacking on the earlier Southamptons, which carried their bombsights externally, attached to the bow of the hull. In this bow position were electrical bomb switches and, as at the other gun stations, five double drums of ammunition for the Lewis gun. The projectile load was probably identical with that described in some detail under Saunders-Roe London, alternative to two 80-gal petrol tanks (carried at the main bomb stations and known as 'bomb tanks') for extended range. As part of the aerodynamic cleaning-up process, so apparent in the Scapa, arrangements were made to carry the light bombs or flares within the contour of the wing.

An installation of Vickers-Berthier guns was made, but this appears to have been for experimental and/or publicity purposes, and was certainly not standard.

Showing the disposition of Scarff ring-mountings on (*reading down*) the
Supermarine Seamew, Southampton and Southampton X.

More gun installations on Supermarine flying-boats: (*reading down*), Scapa, Stranraer, Walrus. On the Walrus the mountings are of Supermarine design. (Centre picture, *Flight International*.)

365

The guns on this Supermarine Scapa are of the Vickers-Berthier type, which was developed into the G.O., or Class K, type for the RAF. A 520-lb bomb is also seen.

Seagull V and Walrus   Sufficient here to remark that the Seagull V private-venture three-seater fleet-spotter amphibian flying-boat of 1933 was a vastly different aircraft from earlier machines bearing the same name, whereas the Walrus (name conferred 1935) may be considered here as the same aircraft as the Seagull V. The first examples had a Scarff ring-mounting for a single Lewis gun in the bow and a position for a second mounting on the hull aft of the wing, though this position was covered by a hinged (not sliding) panel. A makers' brochure describing the production aircraft reads:

'In the bow there is an open cockpit fitted with a Vickers-Supermarine gun mounting. This compartment contains stowages for anchor, anchor cable, boat hook etc. A detachable cover is provided. A cockpit aft of the main planes is equipped with a Vickers-Supermarine gun mount for rear defence. Alternative bomb loads can be carried as follows: eight 20-lb bombs and four 112-lb bombs or four 250-lb bombs.'

The following items were listed under 'Armament':

'Ammunition pegs, 10; bomb sight, 1; fusing gear, 1 set; guns, 2; Light Series bomb carriers, 2; releases, 1 set; Universal carriers, 4.'

It may be added to the foregoing notes that the rear gunner's cockpit was provided with a sliding hatch. When this was moved forward on the rails provided, the rear half could be folded upwards to form a windshield for the gunner. When the hatch was in place, the gun was stowed inside the hull. Contrary to general practice, the Light Series carriers were fitted between, and not outboard of, the Universal carriers.

The gun mountings mentioned were of simple pillar-on-ring type, and on each was carried a Lewis Mk.III or Vickers G.O. gun.

There were later armament developments, notably the carrying of Mk.VIII depth charges, and 40-lb and 100-lb bombs were added to the types listed above.

F.7/30 (Spitfire)   There were points of strong resemblance between this fighter of 1934 and its contemporary the Bristol 133; but whereas the Bristol machine had its two outboard guns mounted in the wing above the retractable undercarriage, the corresponding guns in the Supermarine machine (which had a fixed undercarriage) were mounted in the wheel fairings. The troughs for the guns were formed in the inboard sections of these structures. The two fuselage-mounted guns were low in the sides and were accessible to the pilot. They fired through troughs in the usual manner, the countersunk exhaust collector for the Goshawk engine being fashioned to little more than the diameter of the spinner to allow clear paths of fire. There were louvres behind the troughs. Beneath the starboard wing were attachments for a Light Series bomb-carrier.

Supermarine F.7/30 (Spitfire), showing disposition of guns in fuselage and wheel fairings and attachments for bomb-carrier under starboard wing.

Stranraer   Originally known as the Southampton Mk.V, the Stranraer was first produced in 1935. In the bow was a Hawker ring-mounting for which there was a sliding hatch-cover, and below this was a bomb-aimer's station with hinged watertight doors and the usual fitments. In the midships dorsal position, slightly recessed, was a Scarff ring-mounting, for which there was a folding windshield and hatch-cover. There was a similar installation in the extreme stern, behind the tail surfaces. Universal carriers were fitted for four 250-lb or two 500-lb bombs, and the Light Series carriers were recessed into the wing as on the Scapa.

Midships station in Supermarine Stranraer. The hatch-cover for the dorsal gun position is in place. Also seen are two spare ammunition drums (inverted) and port and starboard fire-steps.

Spitfire Sir Ralph Sorley once declared of the fighters before the Hurricane and Spitfire: 'The Vickers guns had always been installed in the fighter's cockpit, within reach of the pilot, so that, should the guns jam (as they frequently did), he could, by great dexterity and exertion with a wooden mallet, clear the jam and resume the battle.' This same officer's explanation of how the decision was taken to mount the guns outboard and to waive the ancient requirements for re-cocking and clearance of stoppages will be given in Volume 2; and respecting the Spitfire (1936) the term 'outboard' was no overstatement, for the guns most distant from the cockpit were, owing to structural considerations, almost as far out as the tip sections.

As originally laid out, with four wing-mounted guns and provision for four 20-lb bombs under the starboard wing, the new Spitfire was a fairly direct descendant of the F.7/30. J. Smith, who was responsible for the entire development of the aircraft from the original designs of R. J. Mitchell, has recorded:

'While the estimated performance of this machine (F.7/30) was achieved it was felt that a considerable improvement could be made by certain drastic alterations, and work was begun almost immediately on a further project, a design which ultimately became the Spitfire. This design was submitted to the Air Ministry and accepted, with certain modifications. A period of intensive work on this design followed, influenced by three major considerations, the necessity for retracting the undercarriage, the advent of the Rolls-Royce Merlin engine (known originally as the P.V.12), and the Air Ministry requirement for the machine to be fitted with eight machine guns. The advantages to be gained by the first two considerations were obvious, and the wisdom of the third was apparent even in those days. At the same time, investigations into various forms of main plane construction revealed advantages to be gained from the use of one main spar at 25 per cent of the chord, with a torsion box formed by the portion of the wing ahead of the spar.

The prototype Supermarine Spitfire after development to Mk.I standard. The gun ports are seen. (*Flight International.*)

The 14-gauge flush-riveted covering of this box gave a good form to the most important part of the aerofoil section, and the position of the main spar suited the new arrangement of the chassis and the radiator and gun installations.'

The positioning of the inboard pair of guns was dictated by the outward-retracting undercarriage. Some distance outboard on each side was a close-set staggered pair of guns, and much farther outboard, almost to the tips, the pair which made up the eight. The positions of the guns were marked on the upper wing surfaces by access panels and on the lower surfaces by case and link chutes. The earliest Spitfires were delivered with four guns

369

Supermarine Spitfire Is with blast tubes projecting from four outer gun ports, ring-and-bead sights but no reflector sights, and without bullet-proof windscreen.

only, and short lengths of blast tube protruded from the four outermost ports. The weight of the full complement of eight guns (195 lb) was slightly greater than that of the 2,400 rounds of ammunition (185 lb). The weight of fire per second was 4 lb. A reflector sight was standard, but some early aircraft had ring-and-bead sights, with the ring behind the windscreen. To ensure that the guns would operate in temperatures often as low as —40 deg C, the gun bays were heated by leading warm air from the rear of the radiator duct through pipes of pressed material running behind the gun bays and undercarriage. There was an alternative scheme using hot air from a heater pipe in the exhaust manifold. When the Spitfire was adapted for photographic reconnaissance the gun-heating system was used to warm the camera.

Mr Smith gave this note on early armouring schemes:

'The first requirement put forward very early in the production of the Mk.I was the provision of a bulletproof windscreen, made by fixing externally to the front of the windscreen a $1\frac{3}{4}$ in thick bulletproof panel. Some rearward protection for the pilot was the next requirement, also at a very early stage, and 6 mm plate was introduced behind the pilot's head.'

Thereafter there were extensive additions.

The present writer may, perhaps, be forgiven for reprinting here a report he made on a visit to a Spitfire station in Scotland during the opening months of the war of 1939. (The base was, in fact, Drem, but this could not be identified at the time for security reasons.) These few paragraphs, he hopes, may stir some memories and restore in some nostrils the armoury-smells not only of the late war, but of 1914 onwards. He wrote:

'To our mind of supreme interest was the armoury, where a Warrant Officer spared himself no trouble to explain his deadly charges.

'That its thin insect-like wings can house so unobtrusively such a destructive concentration as eight ·303 in Browning machine guns with their long ammunition belts, feeding, heating and firing arrangements, is but one of the remarkable points of the Spitfire. On both the Spitfire and Hurricane the eight guns, which are fired by compressed air, are housed entirely within the wings, although the grouping is different . . . The belt boxes (or "ammunition tanks" as they are sometimes called) are loaded into the wing from beneath, being held in place by spring clips, and the first round of each belt is pulled through with a piece of webbing, being loaded from the top surface of the wing, which has detachable panels. The webbing idea was first thought out in the squadron concerned, and is now standard throughout the Service. It is said to effect a considerable saving in time in rearming.

Armourers at work on a Spitfire at Drem, on the occasion of a visit described in the text. The access panels over the two port inboard guns are removed; a third is still in place. Also seen are the pilot's bullet-resisting screen and reflector sight. (*Flight International*.)

'The Warrant Officer told us that he is continually impressing upon his men the importance of their work. We watched them coating the Brownings with anti-freeze oil, cleaning the barrels and making up ammunition belts. Each round is a finger-tight fit into its link, but the final alignment to ensure correct feeding is done on an ingenious machine. Evenness of feed is absolutely essential, for the guns, being placed within the wings, are not accessible from the cockpit, and it is not considered worth-while to provide them with remotely controlled cocking handles.

The actual make-up of the belts (i.e., proportion of armour-piercing to tracer and "ordinary" ammunition) is secret, though it can, of course, be varied to suit the particular requirements of Fighter Command. Empty cases and links are ejected through apertures in the bottom of the wing. Contrary to what might have been thought, the empties do not damage the fabric-covered ailerons.

'Heating for the guns is provided by a hot-air duct from the engine. The gun compartments are made more-or-less airtight until the first burst is fired by patches of fabric which cover each port. These also improve the performance of the machine and decrease the chances of corrosion. After an action they are replaced, if time permits, before the next engagement. Fitters, riggers, and sometimes even pilots, assist in the rearming, which, together with refuelling, can be accomplished in less than ten minutes.

'We were also shown the standard reflector gun sight, in which the illuminated image of a ring sight is projected on to an oval mirror in front of the pilot's eyes and behind the armoured windscreen. If the pilot knows the span of his adversary he can adjust his sight to "fit" and knows immediately he is within range. Ordinary ring-and-bead sights are provided in case the electric supply should fail.

'Fighters are now going into action carrying their cine camera guns, which use 16 mm film and prove or refute a pilot's combat report. The camera gun works only while the machine guns are firing and secures an amazingly detailed record of a combat. Four practice films were screened. A circle is first projected to represent the gun-sight ring and a cross marks the centre. The first film recorded a mock attack on a Spitfire from astern; the second a similar attack on a Blenheim; and the third and fourth attacks by a section of Spitfires on another section from the beam (here the aiming off was well demonstrated) and from astern. The accuracy of aim was remarkable, despite the obvious effect of a quarry's slipstream in the stern attacks. Training with the camera gun does not alone, of course, reproduce faithfully actual conditions, for the recoil of the eight guns naturally causes a decrease in speed and a dropping of the nose.

'At the butts we saw and heard (standing just in line with the leading edge) three Brownings fired simultaneously. The shattering crackle was accompanied by cascades of cases and links, which danced about the tarmac, and the smell of cordite, as smoke poured from the apertures in the wings.'

Sea Otter This refined, tractor-engined development of the Walrus was flown in 1938, but was not initially armed. Vickers G.O. guns were later installed fore and aft and there were under-wing Universal carriers.

Tarrant

Tabor   This immense triplane of 1918/19 was designed to carry a total armament load of 5,030 lb. Bombs and associated gear accounted for 4,650 lb (one possible load was sixteen 250-lb bombs) and the specified guns and ammunition weighed 380 lb. No armament was ever installed.

Norman Thompson

N.T.4 and 4a   The first N.T.4 twin-engined pusher flying-boat (1917) had a 2-pdr Davis recoilless gun mounted above the enclosed cockpit in the nose. The mounting was braced by lateral struts running downward through the cockpit. Later a Lewis gun may have been carried by aircraft of this type. For anti-submarine work a maximum load of two 100-lb bombs appears likely.

N.1B   A two-seater, this fighter flying-boat was probably intended to carry a Lewis gun for the observer's use.

N.2C   Developed in 1918 primarily for patrol, this flying-boat probably carried a Lewis gun, and perhaps bombs also.

Vickers

Gun Bus   Late in 1912 the Vickers drawing office was laying out a large twin-engined biplane known as No.14B, to be armed with a 1½-pounder semi-automatic gun, possibly of the type later fitted to the Sopwith No.127 and Short No.126 pusher seaplanes. The Vickers machine never materialised, but an outgrowth of the technical studies made was the pusher gun-carrying aeroplane which appeared at the Olympia Aero Show in London during February 1913. This was named *Destroyer*, and mounted in the nose of the duralumin-covered steel-tube nacelle was a Vickers belt-fed 0·303-in machine-gun on a mounting which allowed the gun to swivel through 60 degrees in both elevation and azimuth. The ammunition box was stated to be stowed 'just over the centre of pressure of the planes', the intention being that it should be wound forward on wire rails to its action station. That this aeroplane is stated to have crashed on its first flight because of nose-heaviness occasioned by its armament is not altogether surprising.

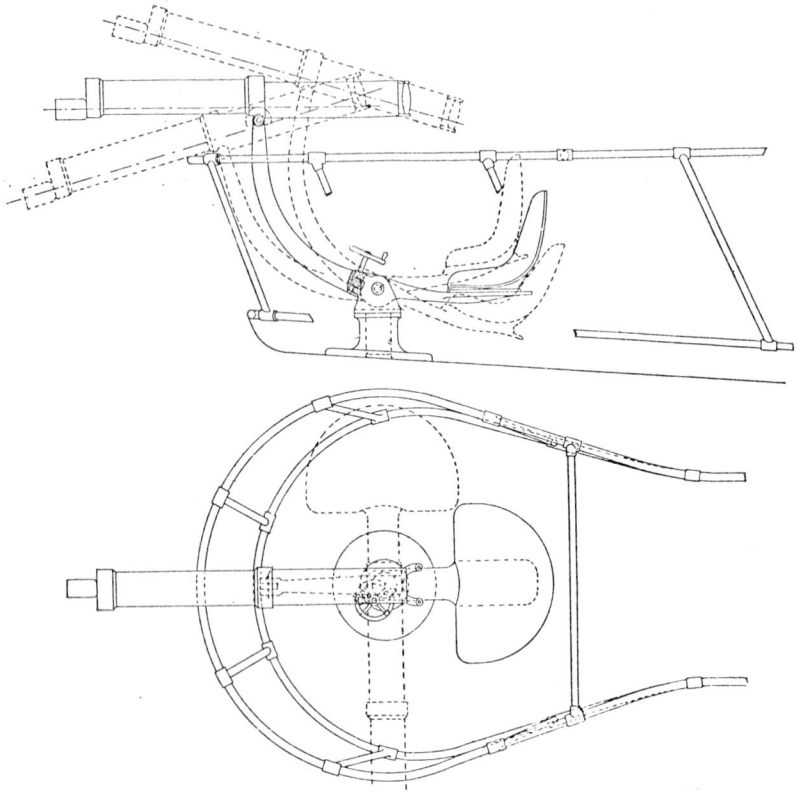

Mounting for Vickers gun designed by Lt C. J. L'Estrange Malone of the Admiralty's Air Department for the Vickers *Destroyer*, or E.F.B.1.

The *Destroyer*, or E.F.B.1, had been built to Admiralty order, and early in 1913 a gun mounting for a machine of the type (there can be no doubt of this, by reason of the raked nacelle-struts shown in an accompanying drawing) was designed by Lieut C. J. L'Estrange Malone of the Admiralty's Air Department. With this Department other notable developments in aircraft armament, notably the Scarff ring-mounting, were later to be associated.

The Admiralty mounting appears to have been designed after the appearance of the *Destroyer* at Olympia and may indicate the sponsor's dissatisfaction with the original Vickers installation, for the aircraft had been built to an Admiralty order placed in November 1912. Certainly the mounting suggests a closer association between the Admiralty and the Gun Bus than has hitherto been recognised.

The Admiralty mounting consisted of a cradle or frame which could rock in a vertical plane and also rotate in azimuth. At one end of this member, the gun was carried on a universal joint; at the other end was the gunner's seat. The cradle was curved in form and was mounted on a hori-

Nacelle of Vickers E.F.B.2 with Vickers mounting of the type illustrated in the accompanying drawing.

zontal pivot carried in a bracket which itself had a vertical swivelling pin stepped in a socket attached to the aircraft structure. A handwheel operating a worm gear was provided for traversing.

Whether this mounting was ever installed in an aircraft the present writer does not pretend to know; but the mounting identified with the next airframe development (E.F.B.2) was designed by Vickers themselves, and is likewise illustrated. In this installation the gun projected through the nose, somewhat as on the *Destroyer*, but the gap was closed by a shield of hemispherical form which moved with the gun both in elevation and traverse. This shield was primarily to protect the gunner from the airstream and to afford a good aerodynamic form for the nacelle nose, but the

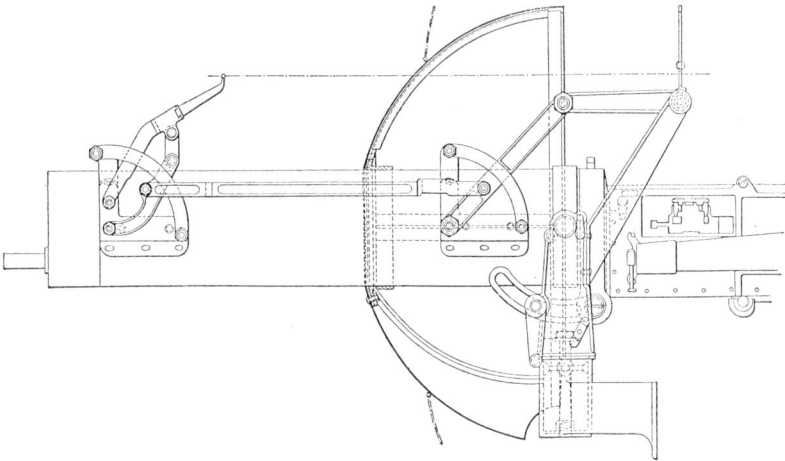

Vickers mounting for Vickers gun on E.F.B.2, a very advanced scheme which preceded far more primitive installations.

possibility of making it bullet-proof was considered. The mounting embodied a cross-head which carried the gun and was provided with a 'training pivot' mounted in a socket bolted to the forward portion of the fuselage. A plate having a curved slot concentric with the gun trunnions was attached to the gun and a clamp was provided by which the plate could be locked to the cross-head with the gun at any desired angle of elevation. The socket could also be fitted with a clamp for holding the cross-head rigid with the socket when the gun was not in use. Mention was made by Vickers of 'transparent sight openings in the hemispherical shield' and the form of the sight is shown in the drawing. The backsight was adjustable over a vertical scale.

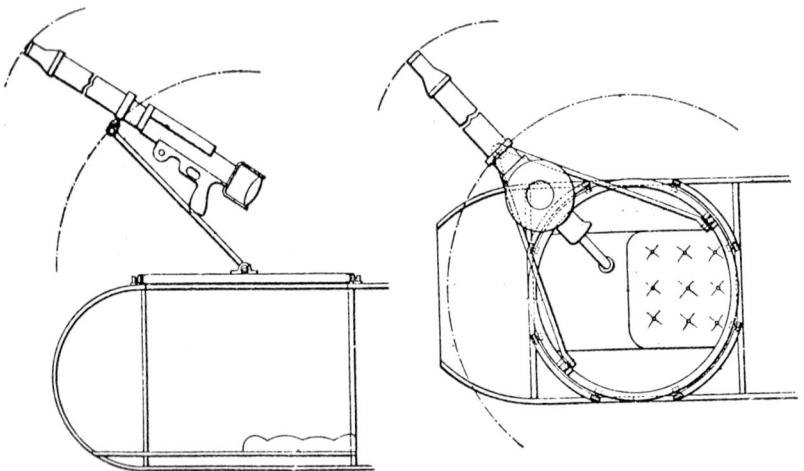

Though not to scale, this Vickers drawing shows salient features of the mounting designed for the Gun Bus by G. H. Challenger.

The possibility of armouring has already been mentioned, and armoured Gun Buses were actually built. In this context reference may be made to a paper read early in 1913 by Maj F. H. Sykes, Commander of the Military Wing of the RFC, calling for 'a two-seater fighting machine to carry a gun, ammunition, light armour and petrol for 200 miles'. Present on that occasion was Capt (later Maj) Herbert F. Wood, who was very closely connected with the development of the Gun Bus series and who remarked that, although Maj Sykes had stated that 'the armoured aeroplane could not lift as fast as the smaller machine', he was not sure that this were not possible if speed were sacrificed. 'Because such a machine would be used purely as a defensive factor against foreign flying machines,' he said, 'it ought to be possible to get sufficient speed for a short time by diving.' A similar practice was enforced upon Fury, Gauntlet and Gladiator pilots when the Blenheim bomber came in.

The 'transparent sight openings' mentioned by Vickers, in connection with the hemispherical shield-type mounting described, were in evidence on the E.F.B.3 when it appeared at Olympia in 1914. It was reported:

'In the nose of the *nacelle*, and mounted on a universal joint resting on the tubular framework, is a Vickers Automatic Rifle Calibre gun which had a range of action of 30 degrees in any direction from the line of flight. The gun projects through a circular opening, whilst a hemispherical shield is mounted on and moves with the gun barrel. This shield is fitted with mica windows, through which the gunner obtains his sights. This arrangement enables the gunner to operate the gun without the draught of wind interfering with the sighting of it.'

The ammunition supply was stated to be 300 rounds. Another report stated that the gunner was protected not only from the wind but from the gases from the gun when in action.

That this mounting constituted the first gun turret for aircraft can hardly be denied.

It will thus be seen that much ingenuity was applied to the earliest members of the family of aircraft which came to be known by the name 'Gun Bus' during 1914. Yet on the E.F.B.5 prototype, the gun mounting was of simple trunnion type, carried above a fairing built up from the shallow nose of the redesigned nacelle. Thereafter F.B.5s had various types of simple mounting, sometimes associated with variations in nacelle shape. The real significance of the reversion to a simple form of mounting may well have been an aerodynamic one, governed by considerations of side area rather than arcs of fire, for the pusher-type of biplane, with its tail carried on booms, must have been especially sensitive in this regard. Indeed, when the prototype E.F.B.5 arrived at Brooklands in July 1914 it was remarked that this 'latest Vickers gun-carrier, which may be regarded as the outcome of the experimental work carried out on the previous gun-carrier' embodied 'the modifications in side area dictated by those experiences'.

A small number of F.B.5s used by the RNAS were armed with a Vickers gun on a trunnion mounting and one machine so armed was captured intact by the Germans. Thereafter the Vickers gun was to suffer almost total eclipse as a free-mounted weapon, and the redesigned nacelle of the Gun Bus was an early factor in bringing this about, for the Lewis gun was far more easily handled in an exposed position.

Various forms of pillar or pylon mounting were fitted to Gun Buses in service, and with the four machines designated by C. F. Andrews (*Vickers Aircraft since 1908*, Putnam, 1969) as F.B.5A a new type of mounting was associated. This mounting was designed by G. H. Challenger, and for the first time the mounting was of ring form. The ring was rotatable and the gun was carried on a V-shaped frame, to which it was pivoted. The frame projected beyond the diameter of the ring to permit the gun to be fired vertically downward. Vickers made mention of 'counter-balancing springs', enabling the frame to be readily raised and lowered, and also of means for

Comparative views of Vickers F.B.5 Gun Bus with Lewis gun on simple spigot mounting (*top*), and F.B.5A, or F.B.9, with the form of mounting designed by G. H. Challenger.

locking it in any desired position. The gunner could raise and lower the frame with the hand he employed for firing the gun and training it round its pivotal connection on the arm, thus leaving his other hand free to rotate the ring.

It has been said of the Scarff ring-mounting that it was the first mounting which allowed for the gun to move round the gunner, instead of vice versa. This, however, was not the case, for the Vickers-Challenger mounting dated from the early summer of 1915, whereas the Scarff ring-mounting was developed in 1916. As events turned out, a number of F.B.5 Gun Buses were later converted as gunnery trainers, fitted with the Scarff ring-mounting.

Lewis gun on spigot mounting on Vickers F.B.5. The ammunition drum held 47 rounds.

For his original ring-mounting, Challenger developed early in 1916 a quite elaborate balancing system. Movement of the gun in elevation was compensated for the resultant moment due to air resistance and the weight of the gun, and movement of the gun in traverse was compensated for the moment due to air resistance. The elevation-compensating device was a spring-controlled chain arranged between the ring and an extension of one of the arms. The chain passed round one or other of a pair of pulleys, according to the position of the gun in elevation. The spring thus increasingly opposed motion on each side of a certain central position corresponding to the angle of gun elevation at which air resistance was exactly balanced by the weight of the gun. The traverse-compensating device comprised a spring-controlled chain and pulleys, arranged to give a central position when the gun was pointed ahead and increasingly opposed movement of the gun to the right or left of this position. Later in 1916 Vickers

379

developed the mounting by introducing a spring-controlled crank, moving synchronously with the gun.

The aircraft described by C. F. Andrews as the F.B.5A had an armour-plated nose, generally of the form shown in the Vickers diagrams reproduced. This same aeroplane is illustrated in an official publication as an F.B.9, and a drawing in this same publication shows a Vickers-Challenger ring-mounting with the arms of the gun frame slightly bowed.

E.S.1   Extremely neat installations of a single Vickers gun were made on single-seat 'scouts' of this type during 1915/16. The gun was recessed into the fuselage just inboard of the port centre-section struts, firing, in one type of installation at least, through a hole in the front of the engine cowling. The recessing of the gun is indicated in Vickers diagrammatic drawings which will be reproduced in Volume 2 in the context of the Vickers synchronising gear, and the E.S.1 undoubtedly played a part in the development of that gear. Certain it is that one machine was used at Farnborough for gunsight experiments, the sight apparently being of frame type.

F.B.7   To provide an all-round field of fire for its Vickers 1-pounder automatic gun, this two-seat fighter, which appeared in the summer of 1915, was given two engines. No details of the gun mounting have survived, though it is said to have been bolted to the thick duralumin floor of the cockpit and would thus have differed in principle from that later described in connection with the F.B.24E. Nevertheless, the gunner's seat is said to have traversed with the gun.

Installation of Lewis gun on Vickers F.B.8. The gun retains its land-service type cooling jacket, as on the standard Gun Buses.

F.B.8 Late in 1915 Vickers built this two-seat fighter, laid out generally along the lines of the F.B.7 but armed only with a Lewis gun. This was emplaced in the nose at the front of a narrow cockpit and appears to have had a restricted field of fire.

F.B.11 Apparently intended primarily for anti-airship duties, though having obvious potential as an escort fighter, this single-engined three-seater of 1916 had two Lewis guns on Scarff ring-mountings. The foremost of these installations was in the nose of a nacelle carried forward from the upper surface of the top wing; the other was immediately behind the pilot, just aft of the wing trailing edges.

F.B.12 The single Lewis gun of this pusher single-seater, which dated from mid-1916, was mounted on the centre line of the nacelle (viewed in plan) and far forward, with a short length of the barrel casing exposed. The position of the gun rendered the changing of ammunition drums difficult. Although in some installations the gun appears to have been fixed, there are strong indications in other instances of interlinking of the gun with the assembly ahead of the windscreen which carried the sights, suggesting that the gun could be elevated in conjunction with the sights. There is, too, some mystery attending the gun itself, as seen in at least two photographs, for this appears to be of neither standard Vickers nor Lewis type. Whether the 'gun' was a dummy, and whether a version of the Vickers rocket gun was fitted or intended, are matters for exciting speculation.

F.B.14 The basic armament of this two-seat fighter-reconnaissance biplane of 1916 was a fixed Vickers gun, having Vickers synchronising gear, for the pilot, and a Lewis gun on a Scarff ring-mounting for the gunner. There were variations in the installation of the Vickers gun, which was mounted ahead of the pilot, the breech casing being faired in some instances. The Scarff ring-mounting was attached to the top longerons, and in some examples the coaming was built up round it. By far the most interesting variant in respect of armament was the F.B.14D used at Orfordness for experimental work. On the occasion when this aircraft obtained an unconfirmed victory over a Gotha bomber in July 1917, the armament (according to C. F. Andrews, who adduces verification by Sir Vernon Brown, the pilot on that occasion) was a Vickers gun firing forwards and upwards at 45 degrees and two Lewis guns firing rearwards, one under the tail. The sighting arrangement had been devised by Melville Jones (later Sir), who acted as gunner. Mr Andrews records: 'The pilot laid the sight on the target for the gunner to fire the guns . . . allowance had been made for relative speeds of the aircraft and for wind velocity.' J. M. Bruce has further recorded that 'the experimental gunsights with which the machine was fitted proved to be useless', and these reports are in accord with a further statement that the sight was rendered useless by sun glare.

F.B.16 The original F.B.16 single-seat fighter (built mid-1916) had one Vickers gun mounted centrally ahead of the pilot, with the coaming rising sharply to fair-in the breech casing. Ejection chutes low in the flanks of the fuselage indicate that the system devised by G. H. Challenger, which will be described and illustrated in Volume 2, was incorporated. The F.B.16A likewise had a centrally mounted Vickers gun, but in this instance the gun was enclosed in a long fairing and was supplemented by a Lewis gun mounted above the centre-section. The F.B.16D had no Vickers gun, but in addition to a Lewis gun mounted above the top wing, offset to starboard, there was a second Lewis gun mounted between the cylinder banks of the Hispano-Suiza engine and firing through the hollow airscrew shaft. Sharply contrasting in armament was the F.B.16E, with its two Vickers guns in long fairings ahead of the cockpit and a bracket for a Lewis gun on the rear spar of the top wing, offset to starboard. Armament weight was given as 176 lb, suggesting that installation of the Lewis gun was a firm intention.

F.B.19 This derivative of the E.S.1 (1916) differed from its predecessor in respect of the Vickers gun installation. The gun was recessed as formerly but was mounted much lower in the fuselage side. The Vickers synchronising gear was retained.

F.B.24 This two-seater was built late in 1916 and was a counterpart of the Bristol Fighter. In all armed variants there was a Scarff ring-mounting for a Lewis gun, emplaced close behind the pilot under a large trailing-edge cut-out. Variants before the F.B.24D had, or were intended to have, a single fixed Vickers gun for the pilot, but the D variant had two Vickers guns, wholly cowled in and firing above the engine. This variant was perhaps the most formidably armed fighter of its time. Even greater interest attaches to the F.B.24E, which was a major redesign having the top wing attached directly to the upper longerons and flown from the rear seat. The occupant of the front seat sat high in the fuselage with his head protruding through a circular hole.

There has been speculation concerning the purpose of this aeroplane, but the present writer inclines to the belief that it was intended to carry a Vickers automatic 1-pounder gun on a Vickers mounting. There is clear evidence that during 1917 Vickers were working on the mounting illustrated in drawings herewith. This may have been a development of that installed on the F.B.7 and was certainly designed for an aeroplane and not an airship. Light weight and 'large angles of training and depression' were sought in this design. The mounting comprised a fixed ring which supported a carriage comprising two longitudinal plate girders, cross-braced, and provided with clips which, by contact with the ring, prevented the carriage from lifting when the gun was fired. The carriage was capable of all-round traverse, the training gear comprising a pinion, mounted on the carriage and driven through worm gearing through a hand wheel, meshing with rack teeth on the ring. At their forward ends the plate girders had upward

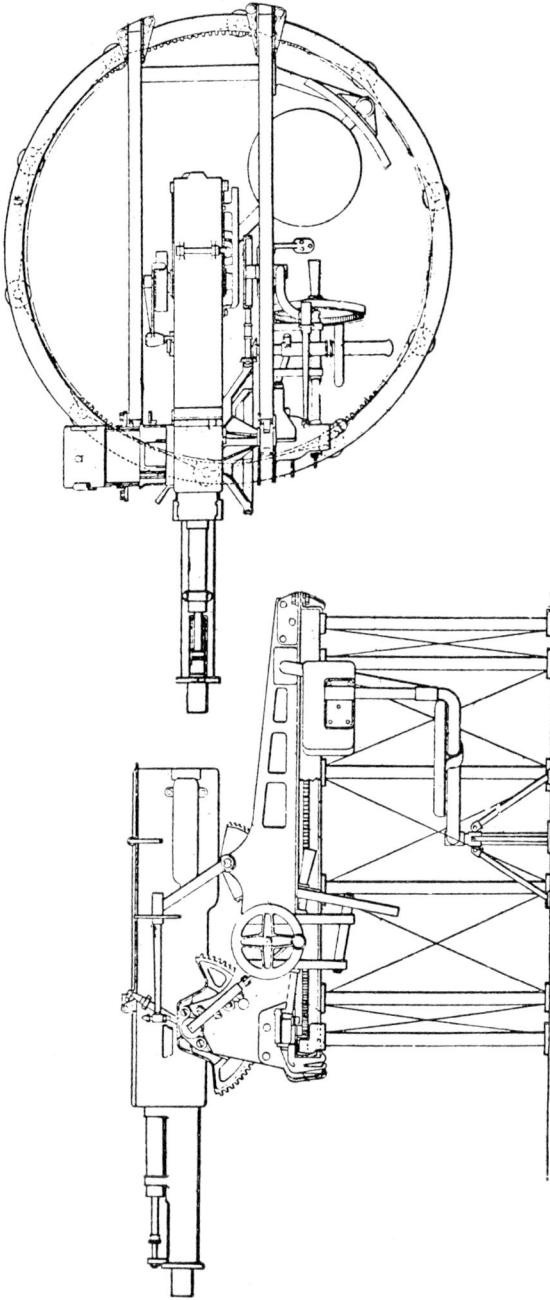

Vickers mounting for Vickers automatic 1-pounder gun. The author suggests that this mounting was intended for the Vickers F.B.24E and Martinsyde F.1.

extensions to receive the gun trunnions, and between one of these extensions and the gun was a worm-wheel segment gearing with a worm mounted on the carriage and driven by the elevating handwheel. The rear part of one of the girders carried a seat for the gunner, who therefore moved with the gun. It was suggested by Vickers that the ring, instead of being installed horizontally, could be disposed 'at an angle to the horizontal so that the weight of the parts moving in training can be utilised to assist in the training of the gun against the wind pressure'. The sight comprised a sight-bar pivoted to the gun carriage and moved by the elevating gear through an angle equal to that given to the gun.

The French-built F.B.24G had the top wing mounted as on the F.B.24E, but the gunner was in the rear cockpit, which had a Scarff ring-mounting for a Lewis gun. The pilot had two 'buried' Vickers guns.

F.B.25   Early in 1917 Vickers turned out a two-seat pusher anti-airship night fighter in the category of the Royal Aircraft Factory and similarly armed with a 'Crayford rocket gun'. Originally the gun was to have been supplemented by a searchlight in the nose, but this never materialised, although the gun, or a mock-up of it, was certainly installed. The two cockpits were side by side and staggered, that for the gunner being ahead and to starboard. The gun was trunnion-mounted ahead of the cockpit.

Vampire   Intended to have a single Lewis gun, the first F.B.26 (type later named Vampire) materialised in 1917 with two of these guns, set far forward in the nacelle well below the cockpit sill. As developed for Home Defence the Vampire was associated with some uncommonly interesting armament schemes. The Eeman mounting, with three Lewis guns, was fitted, at first as a fixed installation (raised higher in the nacelle on the third example) but with the intention that the mounting could eventually be elevated, in harmony with an Aldis sight, through 45 degrees. Eleven 97-round ammunition drums were specified. Adapted for ground attack, under the designation Vampire II, this aircraft had two Lewis guns set side by side in an armoured nacelle. The fitting of a B.R.2 rotary air-cooled engine in place of the earlier water-cooled types rendered this version less vulnerable to ground fire. Carrying 500 lb of armour-plate, the Vampire II weighed 1,870 lb.

Vimy   That the armament of the Vimy twin-engined bomber (1917) was given high priority during development is suggested by the melancholy fact that the third prototype was blown up by its own bombs at Martlesham Heath. Several alternative loadings appear to have been possible. For the Fiat-engined aircraft, declared obsolete by an Air Ministry Order of 1921, the following stowages appear to have been planned: eight 250-lb + four 112-lb internal (bombs nose-up); two 520-lb under lower longerons; four 230-lb under lower centre-section. The most common variant had Eagle engines, and this appears to have had provision for twelve 112-lb or 250-lb bombs internally; eight 112-lb under lower centre-section; four

Vickers Vimy, showing bombsight mounted on nose forward of Scarff ring-mounting, bomb-carriers and—glimpsed through the lower blades of the port airscrew—dorsal Scarff ring-mounting for twin Lewis guns.

112-lb under fuselage; two 230-lb under lower longerons. A loading of eighteen 112-lb + two 230-lb has been recorded and consideration appears to have been given to the carrying of two torpedoes.

The heaviest military load quoted by the makers was 3,410 lb, and in this condition the Eagle-Vimy had a petrol capacity of 1,670 gal, giving a range of 550 miles at 6,000 ft, cruising at 90 mph. The military load instanced probably corresponded to a bomb load of twelve 250-lb. Four Lewis guns and ammunition would account for only about 130 lb, so the rest of the military load would presumably be made up of gun mountings, bombing gear, flares, etc.

Although a load of two 520-lb bombs has been recorded for the Fiat-powered Vimy, similar provision appears to have been made, in post-war years at least, on Eagle-powered aircraft. The sight fitted to production Vimys was the Drift Bomb Sight, High Altitude, Mk.IA, bracket-mounted on the nose. Some post-war Vimys used for training had a modified bomb-aimer's station, in a lengthened nose.

Standard defensive armament of production Vimys comprised a Scarff ring-mounting in the nose, carrying a single Lewis gun; a similar installation on top of the fuselage, roughly in line with the trailing edges (an accompanying photograph confirms twin guns in this position); and a third station in the floor, lit by side windows. A single rear gunner manned the two last-named stations. For the nose gun(s) a $4\frac{1}{2}$-in Neame No.1 illuminated sight was specified, together with four spare ammunition

385

drums; for the ventral gun there was a 2-in Neame No.2 sight, and the two rear positions shared six spare drums between them. A contemporary account stated of the ventral gun:

'The gunner is able to fire through the bottom of the fuselage in a horizontal direction towards the rear. He can thus aim at a machine following at the same level without hitting the tail plane of his own machine.'

A notable experimental installation on one Vimy was made by the fixing of a trunnion-mounted 37-mm Coventry Ordnance Works gun to a pillar mounting, attached externally somewhat to starboard on a specially modified nose section.

Viking There were several variants of the Viking amphibian, first flown, in civil form, in 1919. Military versions had a Scarff ring-mounting for a Lewis gun on a built-up bow emplacement and a similar installation abaft the wings. The 'Service version' (presumably RAF Viking V) was said to be armed with two Lewis guns and two 100-lb bombs, which seems credible as the 100-lb bomb was an anti-submarine weapon and the aircraft was, as stated, amphibious.

Vulture The second Vulture (improved Viking) originally had provision for two Scarff ring-mountings, as on the Viking.

Vernon The 'bomber transport' class of aircraft was a British institution, and the Vernon, the first of the breed, made a distinct contribution to the RAF's effectiveness in bombing, as well as in the transport of men and stores. The bombing capability was not at first called for, the Vernon (1921) being a military counterpart of the Vimy Commercial and Vimy Ambulance, and officially classed as a troop-transport. C. F. Andrews records that as early as February 1922 a Vernon with bomb-release gear was sent to Martlesham, associating with this aeroplane an oleo-pneumatic undercarriage; and photographs of an early Eagle-engined Vernon, without markings, show what appear to be four bomb rails, two beneath each lower wing, inboard of the undercarriage. Thus, that it was officially intended that the Vernon should be used for bombing from the fairly early stages of its development appears probable. In April 1924 the editor of *The Aeroplane* wrote:

'Until comparatively recently bomb-dropping consisted chiefly in pulling the string and hoping for the best, largely because modern bomb-sights and bombing methods were unknown in Iraq. But of late the technique of bombing has improved thanks very largely to a Squadron Leader who happens to have made a hobby of bombing and navigation alike. It is said that after a course of systematic training his Vernons were able practically to obliterate any target on which they concentrated their attention. There is a story that one pitch black night he himself on a Roll-Royce-engined Vernon bulging with bombs of every kind took off from a landing ground whose total length was about equal to the length of run required by a fully loaded Vernon taking off. He found his target over fifty miles away by dead reckoning, located it accurately with half-a-dozen spotlights which he had rigged up on his machine, and then lit it up properly by Michelin flares; after which he proceeded to bomb it to the complete satisfaction of those on board the machine.'

That the Squadron Leader mentioned was 'Bert' Harris, later in his career to become Sir Arthur Travers Harris, AOC-in-C Bomber Command, 1942–45, will be known to students of RAF history; likewise that his senior Flight Commander was one 'Bob' Saundby. However, the familiar corollary that 'Bert' Harris invented the prone bomb-aiming position is wholly incorrect. Nevertheless, by adopting this position, in conjunction with a hole cut in the Vernon's nose, the young commander of No.45 Squadron was able to score triumphantly over his rivals in other squadrons, sighting 'over the side' from their Vernons, D.H.9As and Bristol Fighters. Using equipment illustrated in Mr Andrews's book, jointly with the 'Left, left. Right, right. Steady' technique, Vernon bomb-aimers were able to achieve an average error of 25 yards from 3,000 feet, about a quarter of that generally attained. At 3,000 feet the aircraft were outside the range of accurate rifle fire. Details of loads are lacking, but bombs of 112 lb and 20 lb were certainly carried.

Vickers Valentia, showing mounting for 37-mm Coventry Ordnance Works gun in bow and carrier beneath starboard wing for 520/550-lb bomb.

Valentia First flown in 1921, this twin-engined flying-boat was a counterpart of the Short Cromarty and was similarly armed with a 37-mm Coventry Ordnance Works gun, trunnion-mounted in the bow at the forward end of a cockpit oval-shaped in plan. There was a Scarff ring-mounting for one or more Lewis guns on top of the hull abaft the wings. Weight of guns, ammunition, etc., was given as 750 lb. Under-wing bomb carriers for two 520/550-lb or four 230/250-lb bombs were attached just outboard of the hull/wing bracing struts.

Virginia   In his foreword to *Vickers Aircraft since 1908* C. F. Andrews recalled the present writer's exhortation some years ago that he should sort out the complexities of Virginia development. This Mr Andrews did to his own and his readers' satisfaction, and the additional detail now offered is a tribute to his diligence.

'Fighting tops' on Vickers Virginia I. Scarff ring-mountings are installed in these positions but the nose mounting is absent.

As originally flown in 1922 the Virginia I carried nine 112-lb bombs internally and had Scarff ring-mountings for Lewis guns in the nose and just abaft the wings. The nose mounting was somewhat built-up from the fuselage decking on a low 'turret' and the rear ring was arranged to slide transversely on rails, having regard to the breadth of the fuselage. The Virginia II was similarly armed, except that the nose was lengthened in the interests of the bomb-aimer's comfort, and one of the bombs was deleted. The first production version, the Virginia Mk.III, had additional bomb capacity, under the inner portions of the lower wings, and a downward-firing gun in what Mr Andrews describes as the 'front fuselage'. Certain it is that the second Virginia III, which appeared at Hendon in 1923, had a projecting fairing under the fuselage in line with the trailing edges, and somewhat aft of this were side windows as on the Vimy. The fairing, though not the windows, appeared also on the Virginia Mk.V. On the Mks.VI and VII there was a longer and more angular fairing in this same region, and on the Mk.VII the bomb-aiming position was entirely revised to a form retained until the end of development. As for bombs, Mr Andrews states that on the Virginia Mk.IV there was an increase in the number of, and a repositioning of, the bombs carried in the fuselage.

This may indicate the restoration of the ninth internal 112-lb bomb. An increase in under-wing bomb load is also mentioned for the Mk.IV, and the external 'side groups' on subsequent marks are known to have been six 112-lb or four 230/250-lb or two 520/550-lb. Thus, with the 'central group' of nine 112-lb bombs, the maximum load was about 3,000 lb. An official publication confirms that on the Virginia Mks.X and XI there was

Comparative views of Vickers Virginia III (*top*) and Virginia IX, showing development of nose and gun installation. The earlier aircraft has carriers for four 520/550-lb bombs whereas the Mk.IX has two 'side groups' each of four 250-lb bombs.

provision for two Light Series carriers beneath the pilots' cockpit, the forward carrier for four 8½-lb practice bombs and the rear one for four H.E. (Aircraft) sighter bombs. A Mk.IIB course-setting bombsight is mentioned. With the Mks.IX and X a top-hinged bomb-aimer's window was associated, and the earliest installation for Service use of electrical bomb-releases appears to have been made in November 1930 (three aircraft of No.7 Squadron).

In the context of armament the Virginia's greatest interest relates to defensive, rather than offensive, arrangements. The earliest basic gun installations have already been mentioned, and to these may now be added an experimental scheme on the Virginia I. This involved the fitting of two

The elusive ventral gun position of the earlier marks of the Vickers Virginia is clearly seen in these comparative views of the Mk.VI (*top*) and Mk.VII. (Both pictures, *Flight International.*)

A picture having a double interest respecting armament, this shows in the foreground a Virginia VII, with ventral gun position in evidence, and a second Virginia (Mk.VIII?) with fighting tops at the upper trailing edges.

'fighting tops' on the upper wings, each having a Scarff ring-mounting for a Lewis gun at front and rear. Though aerodynamically clean, these structures, with armament and four gunners, increased the all-up weight by 1,033 lb. After conversion to Mk.VII standard (with redesigned front gunner's position) the same aircraft was fitted with fighting tops at the trailing edges only, the gunners having access to the fuselage along a track associated with an aperture in the top wing. There was no dorsal Scarff ring-mounting. Schemes such as this, which appears to have been applied to at least two Virginias (apparently designated Mk.VIII), had evident disadvantages, both aerodynamic and aeromedical, and Vickers' own inclination was towards a fuselage-tail position. A Virginia Mk.VII was

Lewis Mk.III machine-gun on Scarff No.7 ring-mounting in the tail of a Vickers Virginia X. The gunner's chest-pack parachute is stowed in the cockpit. (*Flight International.*)

391

Twin-gun installations on RAF bombers between the wars were relatively rare.
This one is on a Vickers Virginia X.

modified accordingly, setting the pattern for the Mks.IX and X. The gun
mounting was wholly behind the biplane tail, in line with a cut-out in the
trailing edge of the top elevator. There was a small windscreen, and, in at
least one instance, twin Lewis guns. Although the dorsal position was now
deleted, an official publication gave the armament as three Mk.III Lewis
guns (five drums each) on Scarff No.7 mountings. Of the Virginia tail
positions C. G. Grey once wrote:

> 'I have heard experienced RAF pilots say that the gunner in the tail
> of a big bomber has mighty little chance of hitting anything because the
> whole tail bobs up and down or from side to side as the pilot uses his
> elevators or rudder, and that the tail also twists rhythmically around
> the longitudinal axis of the machine because of spring in the fuselage

and the buffeting it gets from two airscrews lashing their slipstreams over and under the plane between the motor nacelle and the fuselage.'

But it was the Virginia that really established 'Tail-end Charlie' in business, and the type commands a final recognition in that one example—the Pegasus-engined Mk.X—was used for armament development at Martlesham Heath.

Victoria When the Victoria, first flown in 1922, was placed on the Air Ministry Open List in 1925 it was still described as a troop-carrier, but like the Vernon it was developed also for bombing. The first production version was the Victoria Mk.III, and an official publication concerning the Mk.V, but stated to be generally applicable to the Mks.III and IV as far as equipment was concerned, gave the following armament details:

'Bombs (side groups under centre planes) 6 × 112-lb or 4 × 230/ 250-lb or 2 × 520/550-lb. Two Light Series Mk I carriers, one under forward part of cabin for sighter bombs, one under starboard bottom centre plane. Course Setting Bomb Sight Mk IIG.'

This last-named sight was used in conjunction with a sighting aperture covered by a top-hinged panel under the nose—a legacy from Sqn Ldr Harris's Vernons.

Vixen The Vixen I of 1923 was a multi-purpose two-seater, having a fixed Vickers gun set to fire through a trough slightly above the port cylinder bank of the Lion engine and a Scarff ring-mounting for a Lewis gun on the top line of the fuselage immediately behind the pilot. The Vixen II had revised fuselage lines, and the Scarff mounting was below the top line. It was used for trials with the Vickers Class F gun. The Vixen III appears to have had the front gun removed or transferred to the starboard side, and on the Vixen V there was a gun on each side. This mark had under-wing carriers for eight 20-lb bombs. The Condor-engined Vixen IV and VI had no front gun, probably because the new and larger power unit made installation difficult.

Vanellus On this specialised fleet-spotter development of the Viking (1924) the forward Scarff ring-mounting was emplaced behind the pilot's cockpit, as on the contemporary Supermarine Scarab. The sides of the hull planking below the ring were cut away, as on the Supermarine Seamew of 1928. There was a second Scarff ring-mounting built up from the top decking abaft the wings. Each mounting carried one Lewis gun.

Venture This RAF Vixen derivative (1924) was armed as the Vixen II and was fitted with ring-and-bead and Aldis sights. When the Venture was placed on the Air Ministry Open List it was described as a two-seater fighter, and at Hendon in 1927 a Venture engaged Gamecocks in mock combat. The type had otherwise been associated with corps reconnaissance.

Vickers Venture two-seat fighter, showing Aldis sight forward of pilot's windscreen and sheltered position of Scarff ring-mounting. (*Flight International.*)

Valparaiso Another Vixen derivative, armed as the Vixen II.

Vespa The original Vespa I army co-operation biplane of 1925 had a Vickers gun for the pilot installed in, and firing directly from, a very prominent streamlined blister on the port side of the fuselage, with separate case and link chutes in the blister itself. On later marks the gun fired through a trough. For the Vickers gun there were 600 rounds, and for the Lewis gun five double drums. The latter gun was on a Scarff ring-mounting immediately behind the pilot. Two Light Series bomb carriers were attached on the centre line under the bottom wing.

Wibault Scout The two synchronised Vickers guns of this parasol monoplane single-seater (1926) were emplaced, with barrels exposed, immediately ahead of the pilot on top of the fuselage. Aldis and ring-and-bead sights were fitted.

This was the armament in the Vickers-built Scouts supplied to Chile, but French-built fighters of the type had two Darne guns in the wing additionally.

Type 123 In 1926 Vickers produced a new type of biplane single-seat fighter with the foregoing type number. The two Vickers guns were set low on the fuselage sides in large streamlined blister fairings, as on the original Vespa.

Vireo The Vireo (1928) was the first British fighter to have Vickers guns installed as free-firing weapons outside the airscrew arc. In a light, simple, low-powered naval fighter of its class (competitive with the Avro Avocet) the absence of synchronising gear was an obvious advantage, and the installation was rendered relatively simple by the very thick cantilever wing. The two guns were of the usual Vickers Class E type, and, although it has been stated that the 'cartridge chamber was of the undermounted revolver pattern' and was 'controlled remotely through a linkage system', the upper wing surfaces had transverse panels outboard in line with the feed blocks. Further, there was a case chute directly under each gun, and a link chute inboard, as might have been expected. Near the breech casing of each gun, on the upper surface of each wing, was a fairing, and these fairings were indeed associated with a remotely controlled linkage, as will be explained. A ring-and-bead sight was fitted on the centre line of the fuselage, the bead being set in way of the folding centre panel of the windscreen. An Aldis sight was carried on two brackets outboard of the windscreen to starboard.

The remotely controlled linkage system and fairings, just mentioned, were associated with the loading and cocking of the guns, a facility, it may be noted, which was dispensed with on the later eight-gun fighters such as the Spitfire and Hurricane. As Vickers put it, the system reproduced manually 'the movements of the barrel and the gun mechanism which occur

Vickers Vespa, showing close grouping of pilot and gunner and two Light Series bomb-carriers under lower wing.

395

during firing so as to load the guns initially and, in the case of a misfire, to eject the defective cartridge and cock and reload the guns'. Within reach of the pilot, on each side of the cockpit, was an operating handle, and this was interconnected by a transverse shaft with the Hyland loading handle on the gun. An alternative system of levers and links was schemed. The Vireo was a deck-landing fighter, with readily removable wings, and it was necessary to make the shafts in two parts, with a clutch between them to permit separation. In connection with the Vireo installation, Vickers also designed an auxiliary lever for 'co-operating with the crank handle of the gun in order to force an oversize cartridge into the cartridge chamber of the barrel'.

Valiant This contender in the 'general purpose' competition of the late 1920s had the pilot's Vickers gun mounted somewhat lower than on the Vixens and firing through a trough reaching almost to the nose. Bomb load (under-wing) was four 112-lb or two 230/250-lb with four 20-lb additional in each case. A ring-and-bead sight was fitted.

Vickers Vireo with full complement of two Vickers guns in the wing and Aldis and ring-and-bead sights.

396

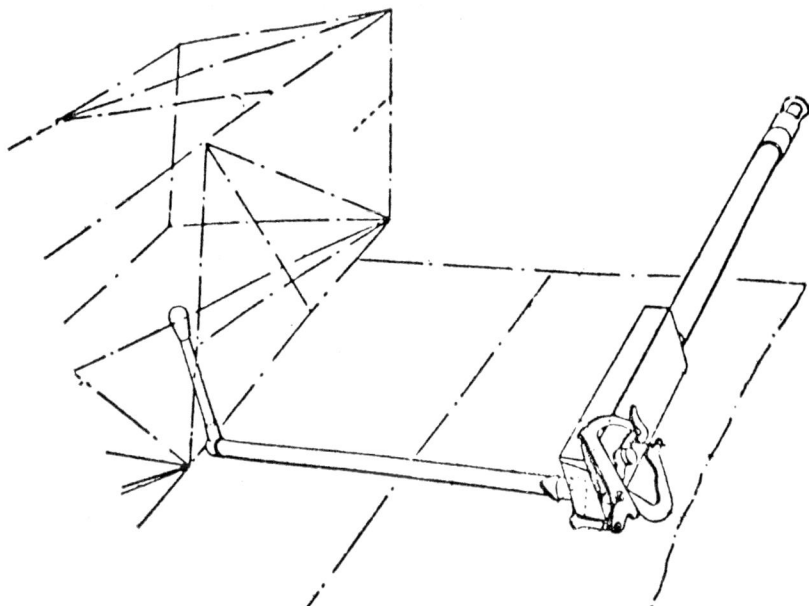

Makers' diagram showing gun installation of Vickers Vireo, with remotely controlled linkage system for loading handle.

Vivid   Two front Vickers guns, set as in the Valiant, were a feature of this Vixen derivative of 1927. The Scarff ring-mounting was of the wind-balanced type, for which Vickers held the rights, and one contemporary account mentioned a drum-fed Vickers gun for this mounting. This would be of the Class F pattern which was then being promoted by Vickers. There were strong-points in the wings (which were similar to those of the

The Vickers Vivid was one of comparatively few British two-seaters of the inter-war years to have two front guns. Under-wing provision was made for bombs.

397

Valiant) for bombs, and these were far enough outboard to clear the floats of the seaplane version. The intended bomb load was probably identical with the Valiant's, and Vickers drawings show two 112-lb bombs parallel under each wing. Another contemporary source gave the load as four 250-lb, which seems questionable not only because this was double the load of comparable types but because a supplementary load of four 40-lb was mentioned. A prone position was provided for the bomb-aimer.

Vildebeest   The original Vildebeest was one of the more modified aeroplanes. The type had been designed as a replacement for the Hawker Horsley torpedo-bomber in RAF service and the aircraft mentioned (N230) was first flown in 1928. The prototype carried its 18-in torpedo at only a shallow nose-down angle, but was later modified to have the more acutely angled installation later described. Bomb-carriers of the old tubular type were originally fitted, and with these the aircraft was tested at Martlesham Heath with four 250-lb bombs in two tandem pairs inboard. Production Vildebeests had Universal carriers. The pilot's fixed Vickers gun was installed generally in the manner of production machines, but the long ejection chutes, so characteristic of later Vildebeests, were not in evidence. A Scarff ring-mounting of wind-balanced type was fitted, as in early production aircraft. A feature of exceptional interest was the torpedo sight. As the pilot sat ahead of the wings, the usual sighting bars could not be attached to the struts, and the sight installed was of the Andrews type as made by Henry Hughes & Son Ltd and described in Volume 2. As it originally appeared, N230 had angular windows for the bomb-aimer's station, but later these were made round, as on the second prototype, and an additional window was let in at a higher level. Vildebeests after the Mk.I had angular windows (2 port, 1 starboard). The second prototype (Panther engine) was armed generally as the first and likewise had the Andrews torpedo sight. The Spanish Vildebeest (Hispano-Suiza engine) had brackets for an externally mounted Vickers gun, lower and further forward than on the radial-engined specimens. The following official description relates to the Vildebeest Mks.I and II in RAF service:

'A Vickers ·303 in. Mk. II gun is mounted on the port side of the fuselage and operated by synchronizing gear and a Mk. IIIA Lewis gun is mounted over the rear cockpit on a rotating mounting. The aeroplane may be employed either as a bomber, when bomb loads as described may be carried, or as a torpedo carrier when an 18 in. Mk. VIII* or 18 in. Type "K" torpedo is slung beneath the fuselage in a cradle attached to fittings on the bottom centre plane, sling adjusting gear for raising the torpedo into place being incorporated in the slip gear. The pilot is able to make adjustments for running depth from the cockpit and a separate torpedo heating installation is provided.
'The Vickers gun is carried on the port side of the fuselage and is aligned parallel to the datum line of the fuselage in plan view and 2°

up in elevation. The gun mounting brackets are carried on the fuselage top longeron, the front fork being free to swivel in the bracket and the rear fork being provided with vertical and lateral adjustment.

'A short cartridge chute is bolted between the bracket forks and conveys the empty cases into a second chute which is attached to the

Top, Vickers Vildebeest prototype with four 250-lb bombs on tubular carriers and Andrews torpedo sight. *Lower*, re-engined (Panther) prototype with torpedo (Mk.VIII) and Andrews torpedo sight. In the lower view the pistol stop is folded back behind the engine.

399

outside of the fixed cowling. A small link chute is attached by thumb screws to the side of the gun and the links are deflected downwards into the outer cartridge chute by a small hood in the large hinged door above the gun.

'The ammunition supply of 600 rounds ·303 in. S.A.A. for the Vickers gun is carried in an aluminium box placed transversely across the fuselage in front of the instrument board. The box is located in guides attached to fuselage cross member BB and locked in place by two spring bolts with knurled heads. The heads of these bolts are slotted and arranged so that for removal or insertion of the box they may be held withdrawn by partly rotating them. The box may be inserted or withdrawn through the lower hinged door on the starboard side of the fuselage and this operation will be facilitated by winding the rudder bar fully forward.

The first Vickers Vildebeest II, with armament as described in detail in the text.

'A neck through which the ammunition is conveyed to the gun fits over the upper port corner of the box and is attached to fuselage cross member BB by an adjusting screw so that its height may be exactly adjusted relative to the gun breech to which it is secured by ball headed screws. The box may be loaded in position through the large door above the gun, a hinged lid in the top of the box enabling stowage of the belt to be carried out.

'Ring and bead type sights are used for the Vickers gun. These are carried on a tube mounted at its rear end on a short socket bolted to the fixed cowling and at its front end on a vertical streamline section tube attached to the top of the engine mounting ring. The ring is mounted in a hole at the aft end of the tube approximately the regulation 36 in. from the pilot's eye. The bead is mounted at the forward end of the tube in a slot permitting transverse alignment. In plan view the sights are aligned parallel to and 2·55 in. to port of the fuselage centre line.

'The gear used is the Mk. II single. The firing trigger is placed in the control column handle. The reservoir is located in an inclined position on the starboard side of the fuselage. The generator on the starboard side of the engine is not required as only one fixed gun is fitted. It is connected to the outside of the aeroplane by an oil drain pipe. The timing position recommended for the gear is on the trailing edge of the airscrew blade.

'A Lewis ·303 in. aircraft gun, Mk. IIIA, fitted with a vane type sight is carried on a No. 10 mounting ring over the rear portion of the observer's cockpit. The mounting consists of a rotating ring carrying eight vertical and eight horizontal rollers which run on a second ring fixed to the cockpit decking. Both rings are aluminium silicon castings. The fixed ring is formed with an eccentric flange which provides a cam contour on which run two spring loaded rollers. The loading is applied to the rollers by a large compression coil spring mounted over the rotating ring between extensions of the levers on which the rollers are carried. The rollers are pressed to their maximum deflection inwards towards the mounting centre, and the spring consequently fully compressed, when the gun is in its aftermost position and the cam contour is so formed that as the gun ring is rotated either way from this position the rollers exert on it a progressively greater deflecting force which serves to balance the air forces on the gun due to the slipstream.

'The gun elevating gear consists of a tubular arch hinged to the rotating ring and located in the desired position by stop pins engaging with quadrant racks. The stop pins are actuated by the normal type of lever on the arch through wire cables which also connect to a tappet mechanism which operates the locking pins for the rotating ring. The weight of the gun is balanced by elastic cord loops. The ammunition is carried in seven Mk. II No. 2 magazines (97 rounds), six of the magazines being accommodated on pegs in the rear cockpit and the remaining one on the gun.

'The bomb loads are carried on the bottom main planes, the installation being the same for port and starboard; the following description is confined to the port plane. A group of four universal carriers is arranged as shown, the inboard carrier being a No. 2 type for 50–550 lb. bombs and the three outboard carriers No. 1 type for 50–250 lb. bombs. A light series Mk. I carrier is arranged outboard of the group. The alternative loadings on the four universal carriers are:—

   (i) 4 bombs, 100 lb., 112 lb., or 120 lb.
   (ii) 2 bombs, 230 lb., or 250 lb.
   (iii) 1 bomb, 500 lb., 520 lb., or 550 lb.

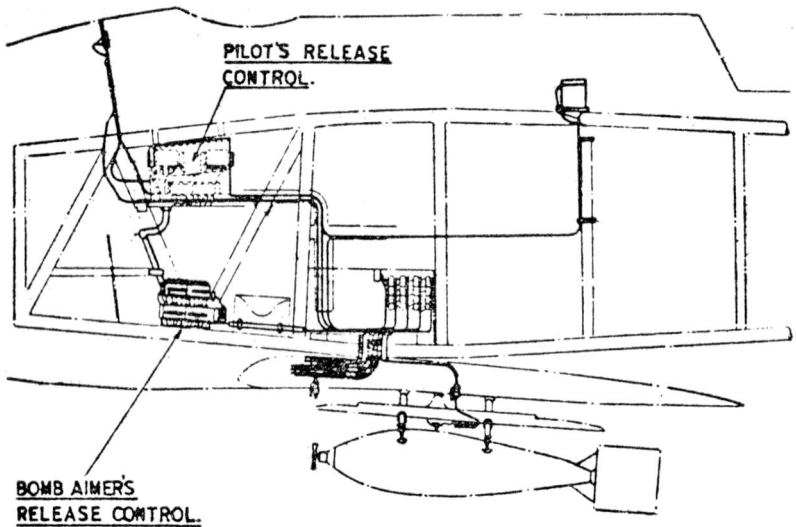

PILOT'S RELEASE CONTROL.

BOMB AIMER'S RELEASE CONTROL.

Makers' drawing of Vildebeest bomb installation, showing a 500-lb bomb on a Universal carrier.

'The light series carrier may be arranged to take 4–20 lb. Mk. I bombs or $8\frac{1}{2}$ lb. practice bombs alternatively. It can be loaded with 4 Mk. I smoke floats, or 4 Mk. I reconnaissance flares. All the above loadings apply also to the starboard plane. No bombs are carried when the aeroplane is used as a torpedo carrier.

'Cartridge fired release gear is fitted throughout the bomb and torpedo installation and control stations are provided in both the pilot's cockpit and the prone bomb aimer's position.

'Current for the operation of the system is supplied by a 12-volt 7 amp. hour accumulator mounted on a tray above fuselage cross member EE through a double pole switch on the pilot's instrument board and from thence to a fuse and terminal block on the electrical control panel in the forward end of the rear cockpit; from this point the wiring is taken to the selector switches in the two cockpits. The pilot's selector switches are connected in parallel with the bomb aimer's switches and the latter are wired to the cartridge connections at the bomb carriers and torpedo release gear . . .

'Each set of selector switches is numbered from 1 to 16, corresponding numbers in each set being in parallel. Switches 1 to 4 and 13 to 16 control the port and starboard light series carriers respectively, switches 8 and 9 the port and starboard No. 2 universal carriers and switches 5 to 7 and 10 to 12 the port and starboard No. 1 universal carriers. Switches 9 and 10, painted red for identification, are also wired respectively to the starboard and port torpedo release sockets. The jettison control and firing switches for the pilot are mounted on the instrument board and those for the bomb aimer close to the floor of the prone

402

station. The fusing lever is mounted on fuselage starboard side strut **BY** where it is accessible to both pilot and bomb aimer. The lever gives the usual three positions: "Safety," "Tail fuse," "Both fuses." After landing from a flight during which the fusing lever has been pulled over and then returned to "Safety" on account of abandonment of the dropping, the actual positions of the fusing pins on the carriers should be examined to see that they are clear before any attempt is made to remove the bombs.

'The bomb aimer is provided with a course setting bomb sight. The mounting which is of sheet duralumin construction is bolted to the port side of the bombing aperture and carries the three-bolt brass mounting plate behind its outer face, the bolts projecting through to take the bomb sight.

'The torpedo is carried in the cradle below the fuselage centre line. The cradle consists of a framework of steel tubes with welded joints, the front portion carrying the front crutch being assembled to the main cradle by four pins so that the cradle may be attached to the aeroplane round the upper ends of the axles which pass through the cradle. The two upper tubes of the cradle framework are attached to fittings on the front and rear spars of the bottom centre plane by quick release pins.

'The torpedo is held up in its crutches by a pair of slinging cables secured at one end to small sling adjusting winches attached to the lower longerons of the cradle and at the other end received in the jaws of a cartridge firing release gear attached to the opposite cradle longerons.

'An anti-aircraft drogue target apparatus, Type A, may be fitted to the Vildebeest.'

Spanish Vildebeest torpedo installation, showing also bracket mounting for Vickers gun behind engine, with feed chute above, ring sight, and window for bomb-aimer's prone station.

The bomb-aimer in the Vildebeest occupied a prone position in the extreme nose, in the floor of which was a metal door, the opening of which automatically allowed a windscreen to fall to protect the man from the slipstream being generated just ahead of him. Vickers claimed that the Vildebeest was a stable platform for bombing from 50 per cent top speed to top speed.

It has been noted that early Vildebeests had the Scarff ring-mounting, and this, it may be added, was associated with fire-steps to permit firing vertically downward. During 1933 the Air Ministry announced that the Vildebeest Mk.III then under construction had an 'altered rear cockpit and gun mounting'. The mounting was, in fact, of the Fairey 'High-Speed' type. When the original prototype was demonstrated in civil markings, Vickers announced that the torpedo was an '18 in Whitehead Weymouth', that the pilot's gun was of the E Class and that the rear gun (on a 'Vickers-Scarff' wind-balanced mounting) carried a Vickers-Berthier gun. A Vildebeest was used for firing trials of the Vickers Class J gun and was evaluated

Two forms of the Vickers Type 141: *top*, with guns low-set in fuselage, pear-shaped in cross section; *lower*, with guns raised.

404

as a specialised night bomber. At Martlesham Heath it appears to have been tested with six 250-lb bombs.

The Vildebeest Mk.IV was armed as the Mk.III, and an installation of an Aldis sight has been identified with this mark, though this was not standard. After a visit to a Vildebeest IV squadron in 1938 one observer recorded:

> 'The torpedo is carried at an angle of 9 degrees so that it enters the water more or less nose first, instead of doing what small boys call a "belly-flopper". A recent acquisition of No. 42 Squadron is a torpedo camera. From the photographs taken calculations can be made which show whether the torpedo would have hit its mark. This camera is a great saving in dummy torpedoes, for when they are dropped they have to be recovered.'

Type 141 As rebuilt with a Rolls-Royce F type (Kestrel) engine, the Type 123 was known as the Type 141 and had the two Vickers guns set very low in the broadest part of the fuselage, now pear-shaped in cross-section. The guns fired through long channels. Developed as a fleet fighter, competitive with the Hawker Nimrod and other types, it had a new gun installation, the guns being much higher in the fuselage, though the port

Gun arrangement on two Vickers fighters: *top*, Type 141 with raised installation, showing how the port gun was higher than that to starboard; *lower*, Type 143, with the gun troughs visible just below the tailplane level.

405

gun was higher than the starboard gun. A ring-and-bead sight was fitted forward of the windscreen.

Type 143 Otherwise known as the Bolivian Scout, this fighter (1929) was a Type 141 derivative. The gun installation was again somewhat revised to enable the guns to fire between the third and fourth cylinders (in side view) of the Jupiter radial engine. There were Aldis and ring-and-bead sights. Four 20-lb bombs could be carried under the lower centre-section.

Type 177 This Jupiter-engined fleet fighter of 1929 was the ultimate development of the Type 123 and displayed further armament changes. There were two distinct installations of the Vickers gun, one with the guns and troughs positioned as on the Type 143, the second with the guns set high to fire through troughs on each side of the topmost cylinder of the engine. In this instance there were combined case and link chutes lower down the cowling. Provision was made under the lower centre-section for

Vickers Type 177 with one of two gun installations mentioned in the text. Aldis and ring-and-bead sights are fitted and there are attachment points for a Light Series bomb-carrier beneath the lower centre-section.

Vickers Jockey in original form, showing trough, louvres and chutes for starboard
Vickers gun, Aldis sight and G.3 camera gun inverted on wing.

four 20-lb bombs. Aldis and ring-and-bead sights were fitted. C. F.
Andrews records some apparent difficulty in firing the guns properly when
a two-blade airscrew was substituted for the former four-blader, and this
can well be understood.

Jockey The French expression *Type Jockey* connoted a light fighter, and
when Vickers (who had close connections with France) built their Type
151 interceptor fighter in 1929 for the competition, eventually won by the
Hawker Fury, they dubbed it Jockey. The two Vickers guns (600 rpg)
were at roughly shoulder level and fired through troughs between the
cylinders of the Mercury engine. There were four louvres behind the
troughs and further aft, and lower in the cowling, combined case and link
chutes. An Aldis sight was mounted centrally, the forward bracket being
carried on a forward-curving arm, and it was evidently intended to fit a
ring-and-bead sight to starboard.

When the aircraft was shown at Olympia the Aldis sight had been transferred to starboard and a ring sight fitted centrally on an arm of the type
mentioned, the two arms being closely spaced. Maintenance was eased
by a hinged mounting for the engine and accessories, among them the
C.C. synchronising gear. A camera gun was mounted inverted above the
starboard wing.

In its revised form, with Jupiter engine and redesigned rear fuselage, the
Jockey had the same armament installation. As Vickers had a close

Vickers Jockey in developed form, with revised design of gun trough and with both Aldis and ring-and-bead sights.

association with the Colt company in America, the Jockey was offered for sale with either Vickers or Colt (Browning) guns.

C.O.W. Gun Fighter   This remarkable pusher single-seater should be studied jointly with the Westland machine to the same specification (F.29/27). This specification was written in the expectation that the 37-mm Coventry Ordnance Works gun, which Vickers themselves continued to promote well into the 1930s, would yet find operational status, though dating from the 1914–18 war. High performance was demanded, for, like the more familiar specification F.20/27, which brought the Hawker Fury into RAF service, the F.29/27 specification foresaw enemy bombers approaching at 150 mph at 20,000 ft. As the 37-mm gun, which weighed 200 lb, was to be fixed to fire upwards at an angle of at least 45 degrees from the horizontal, steadiness as a gun platform and dead-beat stability were required. A supply of 50 shells was called for, disposed, according to Mr Andrews, in 'special oversize clips'. As on the Westland machine the gun was set to starboard. The nacelle was specially strengthened to sustain the shock of discharge, and the pilot sat to port of the gun, with a periscopic sight before him. The gun is said to have been fired without much observed effect on structure or performance. Photographs show no partial fairing of the gun as on the Westland fighter mentioned.

Vickers C.O.W. Gun Fighter, showing details of gun. The gun handbook used in the design of this remarkable fighter is in the author's possession and excerpts and illustrations will appear in *British Aircraft Weapons*.

B.19/27 In the bomber built during 1929 to the specification named, Vickers sought to apply their Virginia experience to an aeroplane of higher performance. In particular they chose to retain the tail-gun position, as pioneered by their rivals Handley Page and in later years renounced by that same company. The central group of bombs was carried semi-internally, the bombs projecting half their diameter into the air-stream. The Light Series carrier was immediately below the pilots' cockpit, and, as the aircraft was tested at Martlesham Heath, this was followed aft by nine 250-lb bombs in three rows of three. Externally, under the bottom longerons, were Universal carriers for four bombs of 250 lb or 500 lb. The bomb-aimer's station was generally of Virginia form and was eventually modified to incorporate a deeper window. Retention of the tail-gun position drew the comment that the new aeroplane was of the *genus Amphisbæna*, defined as 'having a sting at both ends'. Curiously, although the

Twin Lewis guns were accommodated on the Scarff ring-mounting in the nose of the Vickers B.19/27 (*above*). The Universal bomb-carrier in evidence is flanking a group of bombs, semi-internally stowed. The C.16/28, seen in the comparative view at *top right*, likewise had semi-internal stowage. Below are a Virginia III, with ventral gun position (*uppermost*) and a Pegasus-engined Mk.X with tail gun station.

The tail units of the Vickers B.19/27 and C.16/28, shown in comparable views below, were designed to afford the rear gunner the widest possible field of fire. Just beneath the second of the two side-hatches in evidence on the C.16/28 are the tails of the three semi-internally stowed bombs forming the rearmost row of four such groups.

wind-balanced Scarff ring-mounting in the nose was adapted to carry two Lewis guns, the similar ring in the tail was apparently not so fitted. The rear gunner was sheltered in some degree by a built-up forward coaming and the arrangement of the tail surfaces was studied with special regard to field of fire.

C.16/28   Like its Gloster counterpart this private-venture transport aircraft and bomber, first flown in 1931, was four-engined, and it resembled in armament layout the Vickers B.19/27. It was test-flown with a load of twelve 250-lb bombs, arranged semi-internally in four rows of three, and there was the usual Light Series carrier at the forward end. There was a Scarff ring-mounting for a single Lewis gun in the nose and another behind the tail, and, as on the Gloster machine, there were two side guns at hatches.

Among proposals advanced by Vickers was the employment of the aircraft as a heavy escort fighter. The company was at the time endeavouring to regenerate interest in the Coventry Ordnance Works 37-mm gun (achieving a measure of success in connection with the Blackburn Perth) and it was suggested that three of these guns should be installed as well as machine-guns. The projected aircraft was known as the Battleplane, and recalled some of the early concepts in juvenile fiction to which allusion will be made in Volume 2.

Vickers Valentia bomber transport with Scarff wind-balanced ring-mounting in improvised dorsal position.

Valentia The Valentia bomber transport dated from 1933 and had the same basic armament as the Victoria. The Italian invasion of Abyssinia led to the makers being asked to scheme defensive gun positions, suitable for installation in the Middle East. This was done, and a number of aircraft appeared with a Scarff No.7 ring-mounting on a 'pulpit' in the nose and a similar mounting built up on the dorsal decking at the rear of the cabin. Each mounting carried a Lewis gun. There was, too, an alternative armament scheme, as witness this account by an eye witness:

'The Valentia was armed with three Lewis guns, one in a dorsal Scarff ring, another through a window opposite the door, and the third required the airman gunner to place one foot in a stirrup inside the door and the other foot in a stirrup on the wing and to lean his back against the door jamb. The door was, of course, taken off. The gun, mounted upon a "Y" tripod fixed to the floor inside the doorway, would swing outwards and upwards to a position midway between the inside and the outside of the aircraft. Needless to say, the position was pretty cold. So far as I can remember, the Valentias did only two raids—one over Rutbah Wells in the Iraqi campaign and the other over Sidi Barrani in daylight.'

Vickers M.1/30 with torpedo. The front-gun installation and bomb-aimer's window are also seen. (*Flight International.*)

M.1/30 Offensive and defensive armament of this torpedo-bomber (1933) was the same as that listed for the Blackburn machine built to the same specification. In some degree the angle at which the torpedo was carried was determined by the massive underslung radiator for the Buzzard engine, but the carrier was adjustable on the ground. For the bombs, provision was made for Universal carriers under the lower inner wings. A prone aiming station was associated with windows above the radiator. The pilot's Vickers gun was neatly installed in the port side of the cockpit and fired through a trough. For mounting the sights there was a fore-and-aft tube ahead of the windscreen, bracketed to the cowling frames. The fuselage decking round the rear cockpit strongly suggests that the gun mounting

413

Vickers-Armstrongs pillar-post mounting, as apparently installed in the Vickers M.1/30. The gun shown in this instance is of the Vickers-Berthier type.

was of the Vickers-Armstrongs pillar-post mounting, as now illustrated, apparently, for the first time. This being so, the gun would never be far outside the cockpit, and Mr Andrews relates how, when the machine broke up in the air while diving with a torpedo, the flight observer was 'suspended by his parachute back-strap from the machine-gun on the starboard side of his cockpit'.

G.4/31 This biplane prototype of 1934 was test-flown with two 500-lb bombs on Universal carriers beneath the wings outboard of the under-carriage. Intended bomb load was four bombs of this weight or combinations of 500-lb and 250-lb bombs, and provision was made for two Light Series carriers. The torpedo was carried beneath the fuselage at a steep nose-down angle. The pilot's Vickers gun was mounted, with the cooling jacket exposed to port, firing over the ring cowling of the Pegasus engine. The ring-and-bead sights were carried on a tube stayed to the upper cowling.

It was the installation of the rear gun, however, which was the principal feature of interest, and into the design of this B. N. Wallis (later Sir Barnes) put many man-hours and much ingenuity. To operate this mounting he devised a windmill drive, a feature which had been in the mind of F. W. Scarff during the 1914–18 war. Vickers, however, spoke of alternative possibilities—'an electric motor or a compressed air motor using the compressed air usually provided on the aircraft for other purposes.' They further explained:

'The reason for the mounting being in L-form is that when the upwardly extending arm is turned into a lateral (starboard or port) position and the seat is raised, a free space is left, fore and aft with respect to the fuselage, for the gunner to lie on the floor of the cockpit and operate a camera which passes through the floor beyond the gun or operate message pick-up gear.'

Vickers G.4/31, showing installation of pilot's Vickers gun and bracket under fuselage for windmill-driven rear gun mounting.

The L-shaped frame which carried the Lewis gun, as shown in drawings herewith, extended upwards near the side of the cockpit and extended transversely for attachment to a turntable. The mechanism for controlling the power transmission comprised a clutch and differential gearing and mechanism for selectively engaging the clutch at will to enable the direction and extent of rotation to be determined, the mechanism being operated by the turntable to disengage the clutch when the required amount of rotary movement had been imparted. The windmill was constantly driven by the slipstream when in flight and drove the driving member of the friction clutch through a flexible cable. The gunner controlled the drive by means of a dial mounted on the main gun-arm and having a series of holes into which he thrust a finger to rotate the dial clockwise or anti-clockwise.

415

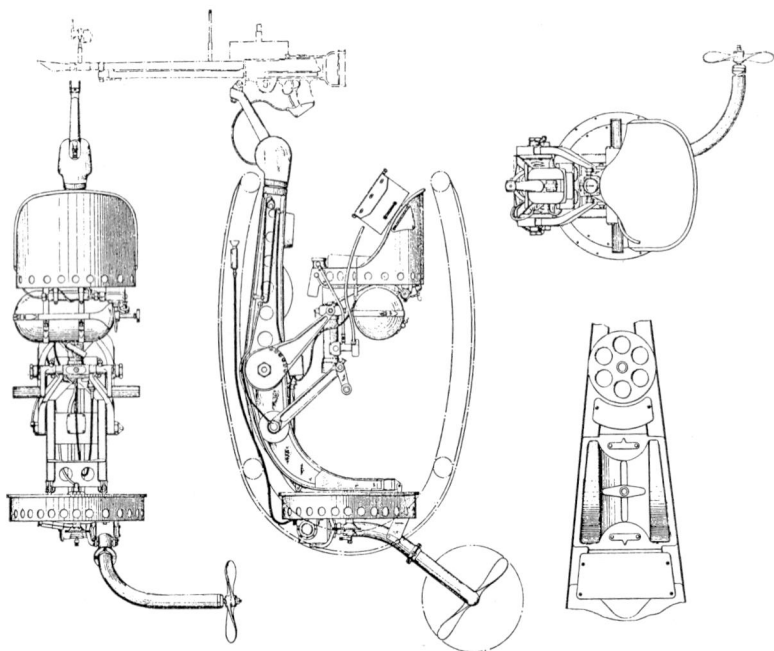

Designed by B. N. Wallis, this windmill-driven mounting for the Vickers G.4/31 was of a general type proposed by F. W. Scarff during the First World War.

Special means were devised to allow for electrical heating of the gun and of the gunner's clothing and for the supply of oxygen to the gunner, notwithstanding the rotation of the mounting. The supply conductors were carried through a plug and socket to terminals on brushes carried in a bridge-piece fixed to a stationary ring, the brushes being spring-pressed into contact with slip-rings on a flange fixed to the turntable.

Although the Vickers G.4/31 was selected for production from among eight competing types of aircraft it was eventually rejected in favour of the Wellesley, for which another form of Vickers mounting was devised, as later described.

Vellox The Vellox twin-engined transport of 1934 was offered also as a bomber and torpedo dropper (two 18-in). There were strong-points under the fuselage and a sliding metal panel under the nose for sighting from a prone position.

Vincent Being a general purpose development of the Vildebeest, the Vincent carried the same armament except that there was no torpedo installation.

Wellesley The Wellesley (1935) was one of the classic private ventures; a triumph of sheer technical merit over 'operation requirements', for it carried a distinctly greater load than demanded by the G.4/31 specification.

416

Vickers Vellox, showing nose panel for bomb sighting. There are strong points under the fuselage for bomb-carriers.

Gun armament was the specified pilot's Vickers (starboard wing, ring-and-bead sights), and rear Lewis, for which a folding protective screen was provided in conformity with growing practice. The gunner's cockpit communicated with the bomb-aimer's position in the nose of the fuselage by means of a passageway under the floorboards of the pilot's cockpit.

The Lewis gun was on a specially designed Vickers/Wallis mounting,

Vickers Vincent, showing Vickers gun installation and Lewis gun on Fairey 'High-Speed' mounting.

the gun being carried on a spring-balanced arm by means of which it could be raised or lowered. The arm was mounted, for angular displacement to port or starboard, about the axis of a barrel-shaped member located fore-and-aft and housing the balancing spring. The gun was stowed in a fairing with a slotted roof which allowed it to be raised to firing position. The arm was hinged to a fork on the barrel which could turn in fore-and-aft bearings on the fuselage. It was further connected by a crank-pin and connecting rod to a member feathered on the fuselage and pressing against a spring, the ends of which were anchored to the barrel and another member. When lowered, the arm was locked by a pin entering a recess; when raised, the arm engaged a catch on a bracket which could rock on an axle to disengage a tooth from notches on a sector-plate that served to retain the arm when adjusted laterally against the torsional restraint of the spring. The spring also served to retain the teeth in engagement with the notches and to assist in raising the arm.

Vickers Wellesley, showing port bomb nacelle, Lewis gun stowed and protective screen raised, and pillar for bead sight.

Internal bomb stowage was rendered impracticable by the novel form of geodetic construction employed. The prototype was flown with two 500-lb bombs attached externally, one beneath each wing, but clearly, if the full bomb potential was to be realised without undue drag penalty some form of fairing would have to be evolved, so under-wing 'bomb nacelles' were designed. On the prototype they were suspended from the wing by two tubular structures braced by cross-wires and lateral oblique wires. On production aircraft they were much enlarged and were cantilevered on two quite massive faired members. They were hinged at the edges and the doors hung vertically down to permit bomb-release. These nacelles were made by Heston Aircraft.

It has already been noted that the Wellesley's bomb installation was influenced by structural considerations, but the additional reasons for the remarkable scheme adopted do not appear to be generally appreciated. One of these reasons was that the distribution of the load relieved the stresses on the wing; another was the avoidance of aerodynamic interference, which could be considerable when groups of bombs were attached near the lower surface of a wing in the time-honoured manner.

When it was found that diving with the bomb doors open caused vibration, they were cut back at the leading edge and later deleted entirely. Maximum bomb load was 2,000 lb (four 500-lb or eight 250-lb). The bomb slips were hydraulically operated, and the bombs were sighted from a prone position. A torpedo was ultimately carried, though this was no part of the standard Service load of the Wellesley 'medium bomber', as the type was classed, notwithstanding its 'general purpose' parentage.

Venom   The first flight of the Venom eight-gun fighter was made in 1936, and although the Hurricane and Spitfire had been flown earlier they did not initially carry their guns, as did the compact little Venom. With the Jockey the Browning gun has already been indirectly associated, and the Venom was in reality a Jockey development with the eight guns of this type mounted in the wing. These were unequally spaced, as in the Spitfire, but more compactly grouped, one on each side just outboard of the airscrew arc, then one pair very closely set, and the fourth spaced as the first. Among the services supplied by a 12-volt generator were gun heating and illumination of the reflector sight.

Wellington   The Vickers B.9/32 twin-engined medium bomber (1936), from which the production-type Wellingtons were extensively developed, was remarkable not only for its geodetic structure but for the excellence of its aerodynamic form. Design provision was made for single manually trained guns at the nose, mid-upper and tail positions, and, although these were not actually installed, the type of installation designed for the nose and tail would not greatly have broken the fine aerodynamic lines conferred by the temporary transparent fairings. The dorsal cupola was intended to be retractable.

The nose and tail installations (the latter associated with characteristic 'pinching' of the fuselage under the rudder post) were described by Vickers as 'windscreens' and, except for the 'pinching' mentioned, continued the lines of the fuselage unbroken. They were rotatably mounted for angular adjustment about their axes, the inboard ends being on annular bearings. They were glazed with Perspex, and Vickers said:

> 'The screen is formed with a slot which may be adjusted in position longitudinally, which adjustment, combined with the angular adjustment of the screen as a whole about its longitudinal axis, enables the slot to be moved to any desired position.'

A seat, permanently fixed to the fuselage structure, projected into the cupola. This was adjustable fore and aft and laterally, could be raised or lowered, and carried a grid for the gunner's feet. Thus the gunner's weight

was carried within the cupola without his weight being supported by it, the seat enabling him to secure a firm purchase and enabling him thereby to rotate the cupola about its longitudinal axis. The slot for the gun was closed by an articulated band which was stored on a reel, as indicated in drawings herewith.

These mountings were designed by B. N. Wallis.

The nose and tail turrets of the Wellington Mk.I were likewise of Vickers design, but at the Air Ministry's request embodied Frazer-Nash power-control units. In designing these turrets, B. N. Wallis had again been much concerned with aerodynamic drag, remarking of the 'windscreens' as they were still termed:

'The necessity for the screen to move with the gun about the fixed training axis has hitherto necessitated the provision of a windscreen of circular form, which, when a wide training angle of the order of +90

Transition in Wellington development: the three aircraft nearest the camera have Vickers turrets, whereas the most distant machine has Nash and Thompson turrets.
(*Flight International.*)

421

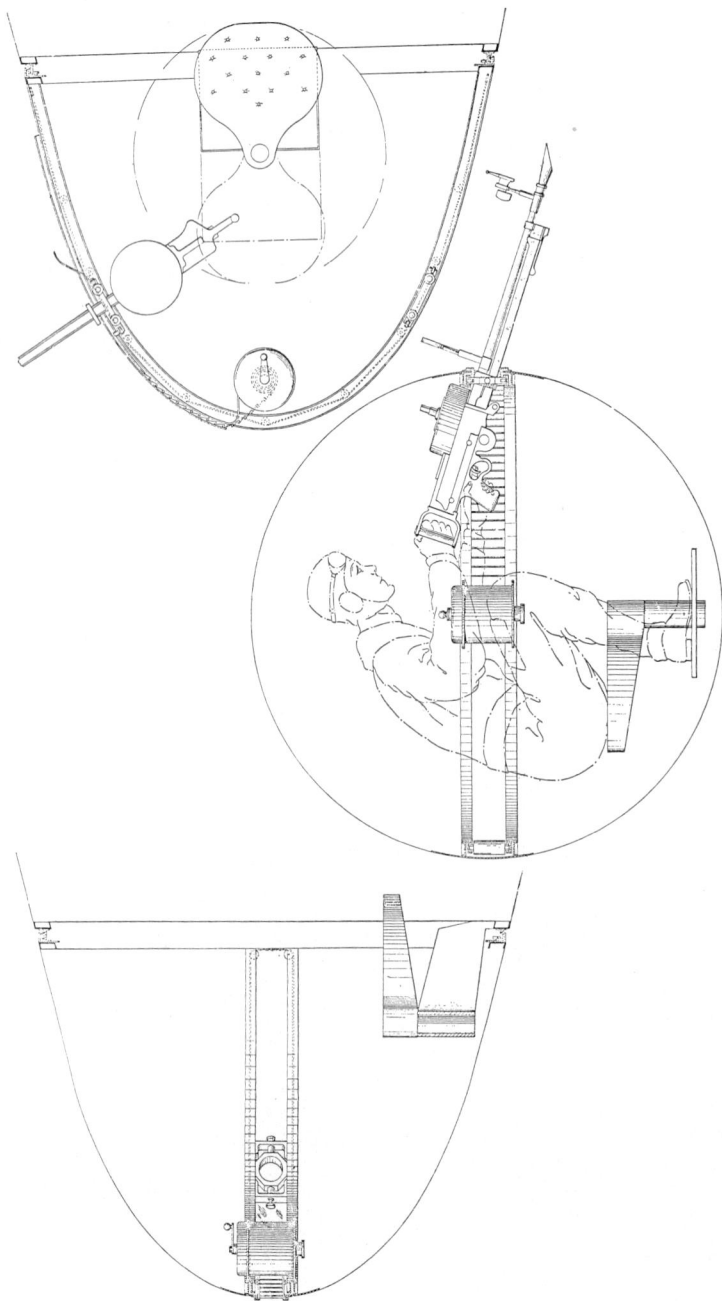

Vickers drawings showing the type of Vickers 'windscreen', or rotatable cupola, designed for the nose and tail positions of the Wellington prototype (**B.9/32**).

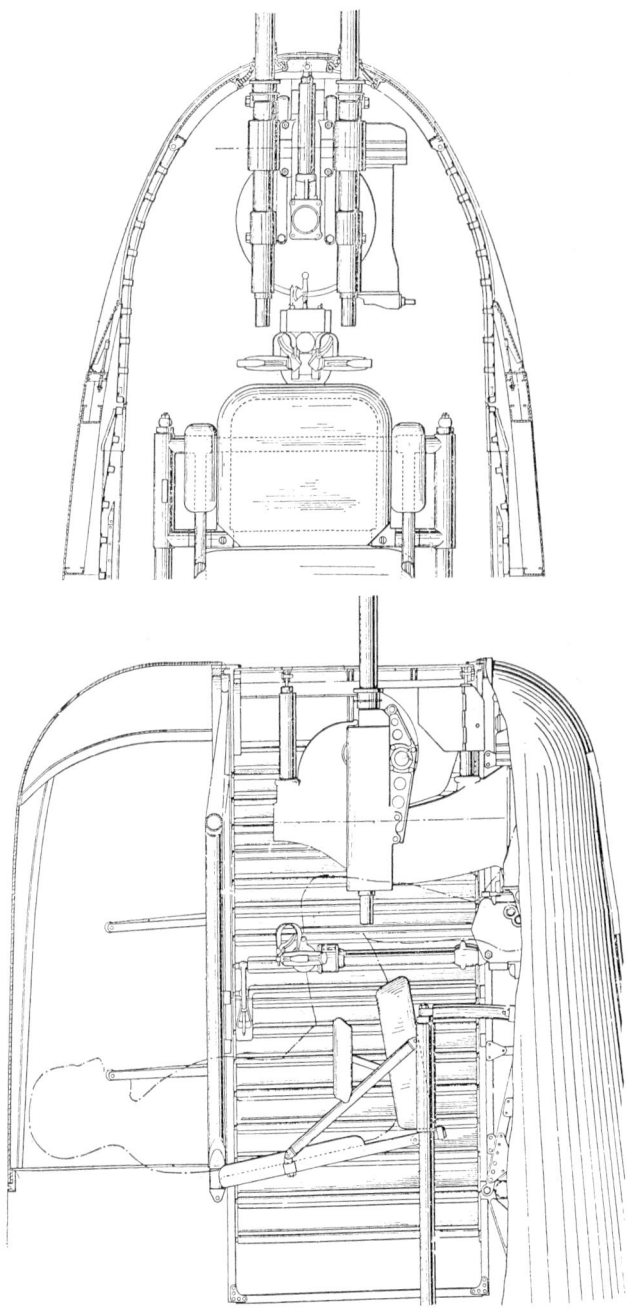

Makers' drawings of Vickers turret for Wellington I, showing installation of twin Browning guns.

degrees is required, prevents the best streamline form of the aircraft body being obtained, and thus involves considerable drag.'

To avoid imposing a circular form he adapted the windscreen to accommodate itself to changes in curvature and distance from the training axis as it moved round the nose or tail. The fixed upper part of the turret was transparent, and between this and the fixed lower part was a flexible band running on tracks and having vertical openings for two Browning guns. The flexible band was formed of a central part and two end panels and means were provided for automatically engaging and disengaging the end panels from the centre part. Rubber strips closed the vertical slots for the guns. The transparent fixed hoods were of good aerodynamic form and were made of I.C.I. Perspex.

These Vickers turrets proved troublesome and were replaced by Nash and Thompson types. A third (ventral) turret, initially of Vickers design, later F.N., was installed but was eventually abandoned, and armament modifications were very numerous thereafter, as outlined in Mr Andrews's book. Like the Vimy before it, the Wellington was fitted experimentally with a heavy gun, in this instance a 40-mm Vickers Class S.

The designed bomb load of the original Wellington was nine 250-lb for long-range operations, or nine 500-lb (maximum).

Warwick   Like the Wellington, the Warwick (first flown 1939) had an exceptionally interesting history respecting armament, culminating in the experimental installation of remotely controlled nacelle-mounted guns. Like the Wellington again, it was originally schemed to have Vickers turrets, but by 1938 the decision had been taken to replace these by Nash and Thompson products and the first prototype was initially flown with an F.N.5 (nose) and F.N.10 (tail). Each of these turrets housed two Browning guns, and a third twin-Browning turret (F.N.9) was later fitted in the mid-upper position.

Westland

N.16 and N.17   In common with other naval fighter bombers of their class these single-seater floatplanes of 1918 carried an offensive load of two 65-lb bombs. These were attached to tandem tubular carriers beneath the fuselage, falling when released between the cross-ties of the floats. A fixed synchronised Vickers gun was mounted on the fuselage centre line and was entirely enclosed in a 'hump' fairing. On the top centre-section was provision for a swivel-mounted Lewis gun, and running across the centre-section near the leading edge was a cross-bar which appears to have had the dual purpose of preventing the gun from being fired through the airscrew arc and of serving as a forward anchorage for the gun, pointing either slightly to port or to starboard. When bombs were carried, this gun

Westland N.16, with two 65-lb bombs, 'hump' for Vickers gun, and Lewis gun over centre-section. The pistol grip and spade grip of the Lewis gun are seen above the cockpit.

was not mounted. Westland gave the weight of 'bombs and gear' as 150 lb and of 'gun and 250 rounds' as 60 lb.

Wagtail A light single-seat fighter of 1918, the Wagtail carried its two Vickers guns externally immediately forward of the cockpit sides. The case chutes were very low in the fuselage in metal panels let in to the fabric covering and were canted down at an angle of about 45 degrees to the line of flight. The windscreen had a hole on the starboard side to receive the eyepiece of the Aldis sight. On the centre line was a ring-and-bead sight, with the bead immediately ahead of the windscreen. Westland gave the weight of 'two guns, gear and 1,000 rounds' as 160 lb.

Westland Wagtail, showing installation of twin Vickers guns, ring-and-bead sight, brackets and perforated windscreen for Aldis sight, and case chute in side panel.

Weasel The Weasel was built in 1918 as a specialised two-seat fighter. It had much in common with the Wagtail, including the mounting of the two Vickers guns, though these were somewhat recessed and fired through short troughs. When a Jupiter engine was installed the guns were faired in to the fuselage and fired through longer, deeper troughs. The case chutes were some distance down the fuselage sides. There were Aldis and ring-and-bead sights. The gunner was close behind the pilot and had a Scarff ring-mounting for twin Lewis guns. Below the ring on each side of the fuselage was a 'window', or uncovered fuselage section.

426

Westland Weasel two-seat fighter, showing pilot's fixed Vickers guns and installation of Scarff ring-mounting.

Walrus This three-seat fleet spotter of 1921 was a development of the D.H.9A and carried a similar gun armament except that there was no Vickers gun. The Scarff ring-mounting overlapped the fuselage sides and there were windows beneath it. The gunner had a protective screen.

The curious underslung gondola did not contain a ventral gun but was for the use of the observer, who lay prone. The object was to afford him a clear field of view, but as his windows often became obscured by oil he looked over the fuselage side.

Yeovil The Yeovil two-seat day bomber of 1925 was designed to carry a single bomb of 520 lb under the fuselage or two of 230 lb or four of 112 lb under the wings, in line with the inboard bracing struts. The bombs were sighted from a prone position beneath the pilot's cockpit, lit by side windows. The pilot's Vickers gun was mounted wholly externally on the port top fuselage decking, with an ejection chute in the fuselage side a short distance below. Provision was made for ring-and-bead and Aldis sights, the latter being attached to the centre-section. The Scarff ring-mounting, for a single Lewis gun, was a few inches to the rear of the pilot, with the coaming at a somewhat lower level. Provision was made for a downward- and rearward-firing Lewis gun.

Westland Yeovil, with 230-lb bomb under port wing. The exposed Vickers gun
and Scarff ring-mounting are also seen.

Westbury A cross-reference to the Boulton & Paul Bugle, the most
advanced twin-engined bomber of its day, will not be out of place in
connection with this 'heavy fighter' of 1927; the aerodynamic and structural
affinities are obvious, although in terms of armament the only comparison
is with the Bristol Bagshot, built to the same formula for the attack of
heavy bombers. The official classification of this class of aircraft was 'three-
seater fighter'; there was a gunner in the extreme nose (the shape of which
differed as between the two Westbury prototypes), the pilot sat high just
ahead of the upper leading edge, and there was a position for a second
gunner aft of the wings. At each of the two gun stations was provision for
a 37-mm Coventry Ordnance Works gun, the gun in the nose being on a
special Westland (later Vickers–Westland) rotating mounting which
allowed all-round training. The gun was mounted at the apex of a pyramidal structure formed of tubes comprising a tetrahedron, the base tubes
of which were connected at their apices to a central pivot by radial
members, the apices being constrained to rotate about the pivot by shoes
guided on a fixed base-ring. The mounting could be fixed in any position
of training by a brake pad which was urged into engagement with the ring
by a spring operating to rotate an eccentric shaft carrying the brake pad.
The pad was released to free the mounting by depressing a pedal. The
sight was carried on a crank which was mounted on a shaft passing through
a tube and geared by a chain with a fixed central sprocket which kept the
direction of the crank fixed, notwithstanding the rotation of the mounting.

428

Training was effected by a hand-gear operating on a pinion engaging internal teeth on a base-ring. The mounting was provided with a rotary platform for the gunner and a fixed cylindrical shield carried by the ring. The front nose section, with gun and mounting, was built on a spruce frame covered with three-ply and attached to the centre portion of the fuselage at three points, permitting easy replacement.

The gun station behind the wings was in reality a complex of positions. The main armament here was a second 37-mm C.O.W. gun, but this was on a simple trunnion mounting, the gun being used as a fixed weapon, though having a 'limited arc of training'. The gunner was to engage his target from a defined lower level, the gun being sighted by the pilot with a special sight mounted ahead of his windscreen. Aft of the cockpit which carried the gun at its forward end was a wind-balanced Scarff ring-mount-

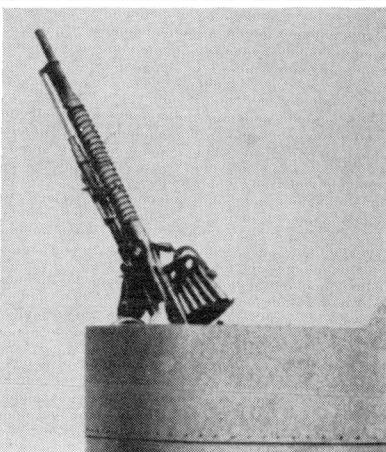

Westland mounting for 37-mm gun in the nose of the Westbury. The rights for this mounting were taken up by Vickers.

429

On this Westland Westbury ballast weights are seen in place of the two 37-mm Coventry Ordnance Works guns. Just visible behind the trunnion mounting in the nose is the rim of the wheel for traversing.

ing for a single Lewis gun. A special decking could be clipped on when the Lewis gun only was required. There was provision for a second Lewis gun to fire downward through the entrance hatch in the floor.

So powerful was the muzzle blast of the rear C.O.W. gun that several ribs were broken during the first firing trials and a special rubber-sprung sheet-metal protective shield was fitted over part of the upper wing. The nose gun is also said to have been fired in flight, up to an angle broadside to the line of flight, this despite the gun's recoil force of some 2,000 lb.

Wizard   A private-venture single-seat fighter to no official specification, the Wizard first appeared in 1927 and was quite extensively modified during development. As at first flown with Rolls-Royce Falcon engine the aircraft does not appear to have been armed, but when the unsupercharged Rolls-Royce F (Kestrel) engine was fitted the guns were fitted low in the cockpit sides, with small link chutes in line with the feed blocks and large case chutes near the bottom of the fuselage. Beneath these were attachment points for a four 20-lb bomb-carrier. The gun-troughs deepened and flattened very noticeably as they led out to the spinner, as they did on the similarly powered and contemporary Parnall Pipit. In this form the Wizard's parasol wing was carried on two pylons on the fuselage centre line, and no sights appear to have been fitted at this time. When conventional centre-section struts were fitted, in conjunction with a large trailing edge cut-out and a supercharged engine, both Aldis and ring-and-bead

The two Vickers guns of the Westland Wizard fired through long deep troughs, low in the fuselage. Beneath the case and link chutes are attachment points for a bomb-carrier.

sights were installed, respectively on the centre line and to port, though the positions were interchangeable.

Wapiti   The Wapiti was the successful entry in the competition of the late 1920s organised to find a two-seat general purpose aircraft to replace the D.H.9A. The type underwent considerable development after its first appearance in 1927, but basic armament varied little. As on the D.H.9A, the pilot's gun (Vickers Mk.II) was carried externally to port on an adjustable mounting, in line with the main longerons, though the appearance of the installation was considerably different owing to the building up of the fuselage coaming above the gun. The gun mounting was braced by a rectangular tubular framing, with a case chute, deeper at the front than at the rear (as on the D.H.9A) between the struts. The inelegance of the installation was worsened by the adjacent generator, which had its own triangulated tubular mounting below the gun barrel. The belt box held 600 rounds and was accessible through a door in the side panelling below the gun mounting. A ring-and-bead sight on the centre line was normal, but an Aldis sight was sometimes mounted to port. The ring-and-bead sight was used in conjunction with a flat vertical panel built out from the main body of the windscreen.

The prototype Wapiti had three sets of parallel rails for bomb-carriers arranged as on the D.H.9A; that is, one set under the fuselage and two sets under the inner lower mainplanes. Some early production aircraft also had this arrangement, but the standard scheme was for four 112-lb or

431

The Westland Wapiti prototype (*top*) is seen with two 250-lb bombs under the inner wings. The other Wapiti is the long-fuselage GP/AC version, with main bomb-carriers in tandem in line with the inner interplane struts. The Light Series carrier under the fuselage is also seen.

432

two 230/250-lb or four or eight 20-lb bombs at outboard positions near the attachments of the inner interplane struts and four of 20 lb under the fuselage. The 112-lb bombs were carried either side by side or in tandem, the latter disposition being standardised. Wapiti J9084 was tested as a landplane with the bombs side by side and as a seaplane with the tandem arrangement. Universal carriers were later fitted at the wing stations of

Points to observe on this Wapiti are the emplacement of the Scarff No.7 ring-mounting, with its horizontal coil spring; folding windscreen for bomb-aimer's station; Aldis sight and bracket for ring sight; G.3 camera gun inverted on top wing; offset message pick-up hook to clear fuselage bombs; and Light Series bomb-carrier just discernible under the starboard interplane struts.

RAF Wapitis. Westland quoted a bomb load of 'up to 580 lb', signifying two 250-lb and four 20-lb bombs. There was a prone bomb-aimer's position, having a separate oxygen supply and with a folding windscreen ahead of it, in the bottom of the gunner's cockpit, around the upper rim of which was fixed a Scarff No.7 wind-balanced ring-mounting. There were six 97-round drums for the Mk.III Lewis gun fitted to this mounting. Numerous loading conditions of the Wapiti resulted from its 'G.P.' functions, and one official schedule listed one 230/250-lb bomb, 300 rounds for the pilot's gun, six magazines for the Lewis gun, G.3 camera, P.7 camera and oxygen.

The relatively few Wapitis equipped for army co-operation had their message pick-up hooks offset to port to enable the bombs from the fuselage carrier to fall clear.

On the single long-fuselage GP/AC Wapiti supplied to the Air Ministry, a massive fairing, enclosing the complete area normally occupied by the Vickers gun, appears at one stage to have been fitted.

Witch   Built in 1928 as a high-altitude bomber, the Witch parasol monoplane had internal bomb stowage. A single 520-lb bomb could be carried as an alternative to smaller bombs (doubtless two 230/250-lb or four 112-lb). In the floor of the bomb compartment, which occupied the main fuselage bay forward of the pilot, were four 'flap doors' which were opened by the weight of the falling bombs, or, alternatively, could be operated mechanically from the prone bomb-aiming station. The pilot's Vickers gun was in the port upper position, with the breech casing under a prominent fairing, having the link chute in the side and the case chute below. The barrel lay in a short trough. A ring-and-bead sight was fitted on the centre line and the windscreen was of the type used on the Wapiti. The wind-balanced Scarff ring-mounting carried a single Lewis gun and was set well below the top decking of the fuselage, which it slightly overhung at each side.

An internal bomb-bay forward of the pilot's cockpit was a feature of the Westland Witch. Note housing and chutes for pilot's Vickers gun and countersunk Scarff ring-mounting.

F.20/27   The Westland monoplane interceptor fighter to the specification so numbered was built in 1929. An exhaust-heating system was provided for the two Vickers guns. These were set low in the cockpit and were totally enclosed, except for the usual case and link chutes, a series of louvres along the line of the blast tubes and two ports in the tapering cowling over the reduction gear of the Mercury engine. When a Jupiter engine was substituted, the ports were let in to the bluff front of the fuse-

The two Vickers guns of the Westland F.20/27 were installed with particular neatness. The Aldis and ring-and-bead sights are fitted in this picture.

lage immediately behind the engine and there was a corresponding 'nick' out of the nose-cowling ahead of the cylinders. Ring-and-bead sights were fitted on the centre line and an Aldis sight to starboard.

C.O.W. Gun Fighter   To Specification F.29/27 Westland produced in 1931 this derivative of the F.20/27. Requirements of this specification have already been noted under Vickers C.O.W. Gun Fighter. The sole armament was a 37-mm Coventry Ordnance Works gun, mounted with the breech casing in the starboard side of the pilot's cockpit and firing forward and upward at an angle of 55 degrees. A deep-chord fairing covered more than half the barrel. Ahead of the cockpit was a fairing for a periscopic sight, at the front end of which was a hole which 'looked' upwards at the same angle as the gun.

Having developed a special hand-trained mounting for the C.O.W. gun on the Westbury, for the C.O.W. Gun Fighter the Westland company produced a special device for feeding the fixed upward-firing gun (more strictly, dispensing them to the pilot, enabling him to recharge the magazine). This device took the form of a cylindrical stationary casing mounted rigidly ahead of the instrument board and extending almost the entire width of the cockpit. The casing was made of welded aluminium plate, and to its rearmost end was rigidly attached an internal drum having an inclined depression forming part of a chute. Mounted on a front end-plate was a drum adapted to rotate between the fixed drum and the casing. This rotary drum carried on its outer periphery fourteen lengths of U-section metal, and a similar number at its inner surface. With its U-section pieces the drum constituted a rotary carriage, charged with two concentric rows of shells. This carriage was rotated intermittently by a sprocket coupled to a smaller sprocket on a hand-operated spindle mounted alongside the casing. There were 26 rounds in the outer row of ammunition and 13 in the inner row, and these were loaded through a pair of filling necks on the rear of the casing in register with the outer and the inner row of ammunition respectively, the arrangement being such that when a filling neck was in register with a carriage compartment a round of ammunition was placed in the neck and moved forward by means of plug members pushed by hand. A depression in the inner drum registered with an external chute which enabled ammunition to be delivered to the pilot, and the casing was also provided with a chute whereby ammunition from the outer row could be similarly delivered. The shaft, carrying the small sprocket mentioned, was fitted at its rear end with a four-spoked handwheel, close to which was a thumb lever. At its end remote from the handwheel, the thumb lever was adapted to engage the periphery of a locking plate, rigidly mounted on the handwheel shaft, the periphery of the locking plate being so formed that the disc was normally locked in a position bringing one or more of the ammunition compartments into register with the filling necks and dis-

Installation of 37-mm Coventry Ordnance Works gun on Westland C.O.W. Gun Fighter, showing also housing for special sight. This view affords an excellent comparison with that of the corresponding Vickers machine on page 409.

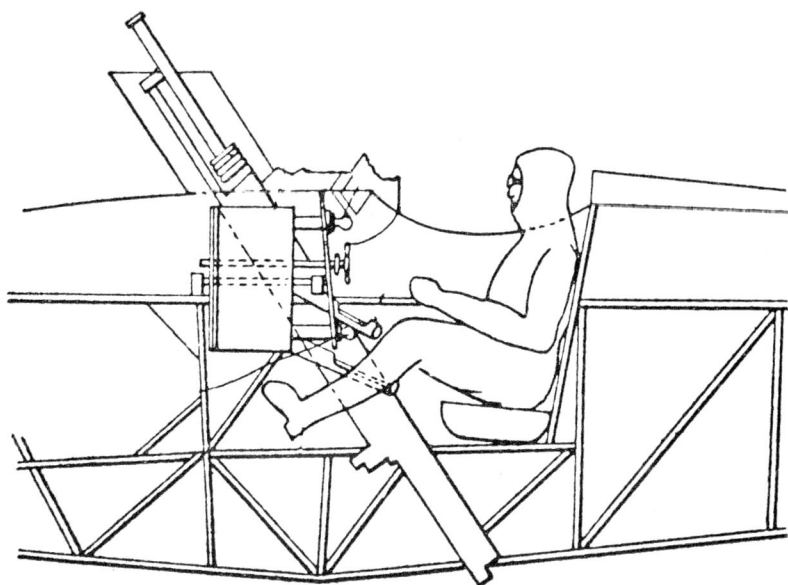

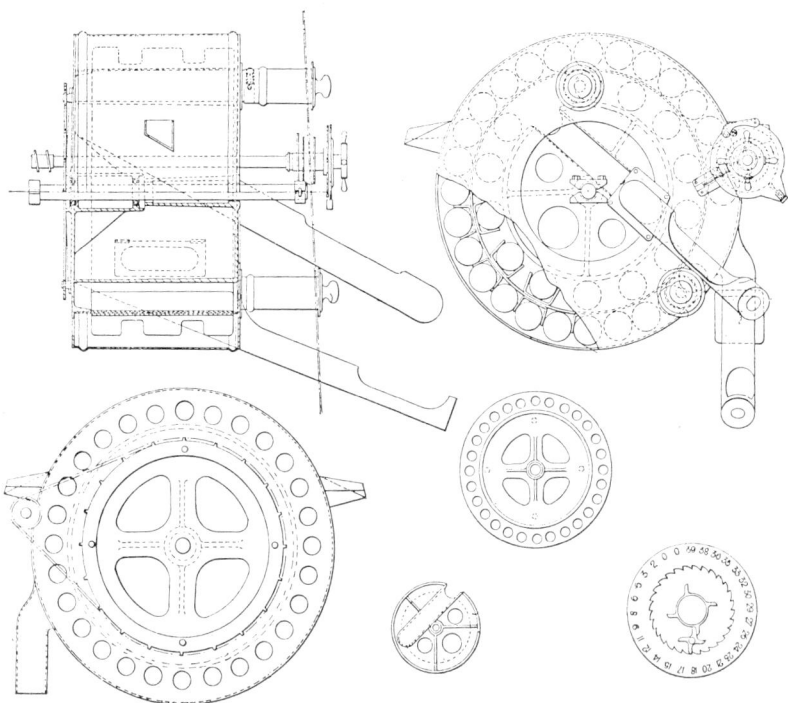

Westland drawings showing installation of gun in C.O.W. Gun Fighter, together
with the special 'ammunition dispenser'.

charge chutes. A ratio of 7 to 1 was provided between the rotation of the handwheel and that of the carriage, and the periphery of the locking plate was so formed that in order that the handwheel could be moved 'from a given locked position to the next the thumb lever had to be depressed. To show the pilot how many rounds remained at any given time, an indicator dial bearing numbers was rotated in steps by gearing as the handwheel spindle was rotated.

Of this ingenious rotary dispenser and the Westland mounting developed for the Westbury, V. S. Gaunt, who was in charge of Westland's experimental department at the time of their construction remarked some years ago: 'It has always seemed to me a great pity that these experiments were not further developed. Like many other devices they were fostered by a limited school of thought and allowed to lapse when changes in personnel removed a "leading light" from a position where he influenced such progress.'

P.V.3   Constructed in 1931, this biplane was intended to meet not only the normal RAF general purpose requirements but to serve alternatively for army co-operation or as a deck-landing torpedo-bomber. The installation of the pilot's Vickers gun was quite different from that on the Wallace, to which the P.V.3 bore a strong resemblance. The gun was mounted high in the port side of the cockpit and fired through a short trough in the upper cowling, beginning in line with the forward centre-section struts and having a series of louvres behind it. The link chute emerged near the gun, but the case chute was far down the fuselage side. The Scarff ring-mounting was well below the fuselage top line, and the gunner was sheltered accordingly. The bomb load could be two 550-lb, four 250 or 112-lb, or sixteen 20-lb bombs, or combinations. Four Universal carriers were fitted beneath the wings outboard of the undercarriage. Alternatively a torpedo of 1,000 lb could be carried under the fuselage. There was a prone bomb-aimer's station, lit by two windows low in the fuselage sides below the pilot's cockpit.

P.V.6 and Wallace I   Formerly known as the Wapiti VII, and later as the Wallace I, the P.V.6 (1932) was a development of the 'long-fuselage' GP/AC Wapiti, re-engined and aerodynamically improved. Not least among the improvements was the 'bulging' of the fuselage sides, enabling the Vickers gun—now set much lower in the cockpit—to be wholly enclosed except for the case and link chutes, a series of louvres and a short trough. In order to clear the path of the bullets, the Townend ring cowling round the Pegasus engine was given a very noticeable bulge on the port side, and at one stage of development there was a corresponding 'dent' in the upper segment of the cowling, slightly to port, to give an uninterrupted line of sight to the repositioned ring and bead. The earlier Wapiti-type screen, with its central sighting panel, was now abandoned in favour of a more conventional screen. The bulging of the fuselage sides had the further

Top, Wallace prototype, showing ring-cowling of engine bulged to clear line of fire of enclosed Vickers gun; ring sight; installation of Scarff ring-mounting; and parallel bomb-carriers under wings. (*Lower*), the same aircraft with 'dented' cowling for sighting Vickers gun.

effect of eliminating the cylindrical sub-structure below the Scarff ring-mounting, though there was still a pronounced lip. In production aircraft the indentation in the upper part of the engine cowling was eliminated in favour of a modified contour in the same area. Provision was made for Universal bomb-carriers instead of the old skeleton tubular type. Although the normal main bomb load was two 250-lb or four 112-lb a load of 1,000-lb was carried 'under special category'.

Westland Wallace II, showing final form of engine cowling, cockpit enclosures and fairing for bombsight.

Flying in a Wallace, the present writer took part in a mock front-gun attack on a drogue target towed by another Wallace over the Sutton Bridge ranges.

'At the bottom of each dive the drogue came fluttering out from under our nose in somewhat alarming proximity', he wrote, adding: 'Stern attacks are made possible by a small auxiliary drogue which deflects the main drogue out of the line of flight of the towing aircraft. At night, a searchlight on the range is used to illuminate the drogue.'

Pterodactyl V   Field of fire being of prime importance in the design of any two-seater fighter armed with movable guns, the Westland-Hill Pterodactyl 'tailless' layout had obvious appeal, and in 1932 a fighter of this description was built. In terms of armament this machine was intended to be more formidable than the Hawker Demon. The pilot had two Vickers guns mounted with their breeches mid-way down the cockpit sides under bulged fairings and firing through long troughs in the fuselage sides. For these guns there was a ring-and-bead sight. At the rear of the fuselage was provision for an electrically operated two-gun turret, but this was never installed. Close inboard under the port wing were lugs for the attachment of a Light Series bomb-carrier (four 20-lb). A projected development was to have had a similar turret installed in the nose.

Like the aircraft themselves, the electrically operated turret designed for the Pterodactyls was closely associated with the name of Prof G.T.R. Hill, Not only the turret indeed, for jointly with it was developed a special inter-connected sight, the axes of freedom of which were substantially those of the gunner's head and upper body in taking aim.

440

The foundation of the turret proper was a stationary ring, with an inner ring revolving inside it on ball-bearings and carrying an adjustable seat, gun mountings, sight-carrying mechanism, driving mechanism, ammunition containers and protective shield. Westland stated:

'The seat is associated with a rest for the gunner's feet and is capable of release by a trigger to permit it to tilt downwards in front to admit of rapid exit of the occupant in emergency. Hinged knee rests are provided to assist the gunner to retain his position, e.g. when the aircraft is climbing steeply or diving vertically.'

Two Lewis guns were installed, these being mounted on their sides with the drums inboard, thereby conserving space and permitting ready access for drum-changing. The guns were themselves mounted on what Westland termed 'drums', and it was explained:

'Rotation of the drums to effect elevation and depression of the guns is performed by shafts carrying worms engaging worm wheels, whilst rotation of the turret in azimuth is performed by a pinion engaging internal teeth on the fixed ring. The shafts and pinion are adapted to be rotated by a continuously running electric motor through suitable gearing including two infinitely variable disc and roller friction gear mechanisms, the drive to the shafts being conveyed by way of a worm and bevel wheels. Current for the motor is obtained through a telescopic pick-up device from an electric generator driven by the aircraft engine or by a windmill with a small battery as a voltage steadier, this battery also providing an emergency reserve when necessary.

Westland Pterodactyl V, showing ballasted rear fuselage with provision for turret and starboard trough and case chute for Vickers gun.

'The gear box conveys drive to the gun elevating and sight operating mechanism and the gear box conveys drive to the pinion referred to above engaging the teeth for rotating the turret, controlling means being provided operable from a point remote from the gear boxes.

'Conveniently variable speed gears may be employed for the gear boxes. With this arrangement if sudden acceleration is required it can be obtained by reason of the store of kinetic energy in the rotating system for less expenditure of electrical power than would be required by a direct coupled motor for example which would have to accelerate from rest.'

'The hand grip is held in the right hand and can be moved forwards or backwards and sideways or a combination of both motions (relative to the gunner) and the component motions of the hand grip transmit through the bellows chambers and hydraulic tubes similar motions, to the controls of the gear mechanisms in such a way that a transverse pressure to the right of the observer brings about traverse of the turret (and the gun and sight) at a corresponding rate to the right. Similarly, the component motions of the hand grip forwards or backwards relative to the gunner bring about depressions or elevations of the gun and the sight carrying arm at corresponding rates. The effect of this when operating the turret is that the gunner feels that he is actually pushing the sight in the direction required.

Details of the Pterodactyl V visible here include ring-and-bead sight for Vickers guns (bead on pillar behind spinner); mounting and trough for the port gun; and attachment points for bomb-carrier under port lower wing.

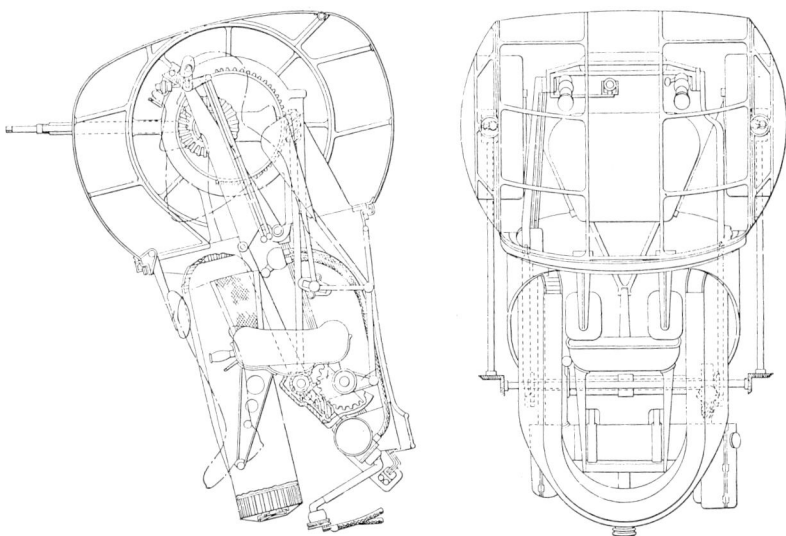

Westland drawings of the electrically operated turret designed for the Pterodactyl fighters. Two Lewis guns are installed on their sides.

'The control is spring loaded in order that, when the grip is released, the gear boxes automatically return to neutral. Firing the guns may be by remote control either at the grip or by means of foot pedals which are fitted to the foot rest forming part of the seat structure.

'The guns are easily accessible for reloading and can be taken out of their mounting drums readily for clearing jams or other purposes by the gunner from inside the turret.

'Spare ammunition drums are carried in a U-shaped chute supported by the movable ring. This chute contains eight ammunition drums which are automatically locked in position, four further drums being mounted on pegs in the body of the aircraft just behind the turret so that the gunner may exchange the four empty drums in his chute for the four full ones on the pegs. As each drum is emptied after firing it may be placed on top of one side of the chute and the operation of stowing it will automatically unlock the drums contained in the chute and will cause a full drum to rise to the opposite leg of the chute where it will be in a handy position when the next gun is to be reloaded.'

F.7/30 Among the unusual types of aircraft built to the requirements of this 'four-gun' specification, the Westland machine (built 1934) was the most distinctive by reason of the shaft-driven airscrew and the placing of the pilot ahead of the wings. The installation of the four Vickers guns was also of uncommon interest. These guns were in two staggered pairs in the fuselage sides, the uppermost pair being so far forward that the tips of the

Westland F.7/30 four-gun fighter, showing staggered guns, ejection chutes and ring-and-bead sight on brackets ahead of windscreen. The cockpit enclosure is not here installed.

flash eliminators coincided with the narrow gap between the spinner and the fuselage. The cooling jackets of these upper guns lay exposed in troughs, and their ejection chutes were close above the upper edges of the lower troughs, wherein only short lengths of gun barrel jackets were exposed. Behind these lower troughs were louvres and case and link chutes. Forward of the enclosed cockpit, the nose sloped away very sharply, and it was necessary to support the ring-and-bead sight on a special structure. This took the form of a forwardly raked inverted-V pylon supporting the forward end of a cranked fore-and-aft tube attached to the fuselage just forward of the windscreen and carrying a bead (front) and ring.

An installation of a multiple-barrelled gun firing through the hollow airscrew shaft of this fighter (in modified form) was suggested by Maj H. S. V. Thompson of the Martlesham Heath experimental establishment. The gun considered was of the Accles type, apparently deriving from the application in much earlier years of the 'Accles feed' to the famous Gatling gun. This feed possessed the important advantages in that its action was positive, and independent of gravity, enabling the gun to be fired at all angles. The Gatling gun had a cluster of barrels, automatically loaded and fired by the working of a crank.

The F.7/30 had provision for four 20-lb bombs under the port wing.

Westland P.V.7, showing form and disposition of the rear cockpit enclosure.
(*Flight International.*)

P.V.7 This two-seat high-wing monoplane was built in 1934 as a private venture to the G.4/31 specification and was designed for dive-bombing and for operation with a Mk.VIII torpedo. Intended maximum bomb load was probably two 500-lb + two 250-lb bombs, sighted prone through a sliding panel in the floor. This position was below the pilot, and was accessible from the rear cockpit through the cabin. The pilot's Vickers gun was installed much in the manner of the lower guns on the F.7/30. There was a ring-and-bead sight, the ring being mounted just forward of the enclosed cockpit, and the bead on a prominent pylon on the Townend ring round the Pegasus engine. Of the rear-gun installation Westland declared:

'The gunner, who is immediately aft of the wing, is provided with the Westland Patented Shielding Device which completely encloses him when not in action, and when open still shields him and enables him to use his gun comfortably at the top speed of the machine.'

The installation and mounting, in fact, resembled those described in

Demonstrating operation of rear gun mounting of Westland P.V.7 and the degree of protection afforded by the Westland Patented Shielding Device.

445

Torpedo installation (the weapon is a dummy) on Westland P.V.7, showing also the installation of the pilot's Vickers gun.

connection with the Wallace II, though the segmented sections were continued forward to complete the enclosure, there being no pilot's cockpit immediately ahead.

Wallace II As a corollary to the improved performance achieved in the Wallace I, Westland introduced during 1934 a development having a completely redesigned, and totally enclosed, rear-gunner's position, matched with an enclosure for the pilot. The pilot's enclosure was made up of a three-piece sliding canopy, the fixed windscreen and the fixed portion of the gunner's enclosure. This last-named portion was of roughly cylindrical section, with the axis running parallel to that of the fuselage. Within this portion folded a number of hinged segments which, when extended, completely covered the cockpit. These segments were metal-framed and covered with Rhodoid non-discolourable aircraft celluloid. To operate the gun, the observer folded the segments upwards within the cylindrical portion, which, together with the pilot's canopy, provided him, in effect, with a large windscreen. It was claimed that he could use the gun in comfort at top speed. Jointly with these innovations, the waist line of the rear cockpit was lowered to the level of the upper longeron, and with it the ring mounting. This ring was of special type, operating on the basic Scarff principle, but the toothed quadrant was attached below the bow which carried the single Lewis gun. The elastic cords were disposed horizontally, but otherwise the mounting strongly resembled (though was certainly not identical with) two versions of the Scarff ring-mounting, one of which was installed in the Boulton & Paul Bourges. Both these mountings, wherein the quadrant

446

was below the level of the ring when the gun was at rest, will be illustrated in Volume 2. When the folding segments were lowered the gun barrel lay in a trough, though with the drum exposed. The prone bombing position was now associated with a fairing beneath the fuselage for the bombsight. Cockpit heating was a further aid to crew efficiency. Performance was little affected whether the cockpits were open or closed.

Comparative views of Wallace II cockpit-protection arrangements, showing details of Westland Patented Shielding Device, gun mounting and stowage and pilot's ring sight.

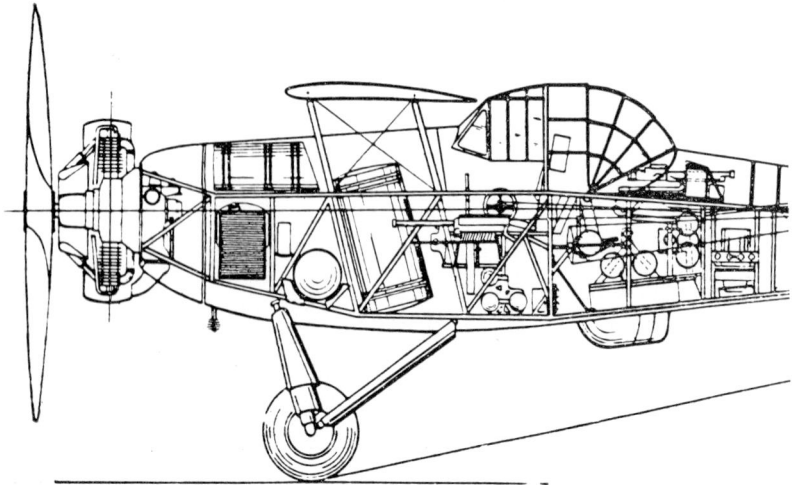

Westland drawing showing cockpit arrangements and disposition of military equipment in Wallace II.

Lysander A makers' description declared of this two-seat army co-operation aircraft, the prototype of which appeared in 1936:

'The aircraft is armed with three guns, two fixed and firing forward and one operated by the observer, and is capable of swift and easy manoeuvre for aerial combat tactics. Exploitation of its slow-flying qualities against attacking fighter aircraft with superior speed might enable the Lysander easily to out-manoeuvre them . . . The two fixed guns are fitted to the undercarriage beam and are completely enclosed within the wheel fairings. This position facilitates maintenance, and as it is outside the disc of rotation of the airscrew, interrupter gear is not needed. The guns are fired pneumatically and are aimed with the help of a reflector sight clamped to the windscreen framework on a level with the pilot's eye. Bosses are provided above the wheels for attachment of stub wings carrying bomb racks. One Light Series carrier may be fitted beneath the fuselage.'

The fitting of two front guns on an army co-operation aircraft was a new departure: the Bristol Fighter, Atlas, Audax and Hector had a single Vickers gun; but the Lysander had two Browning guns with 500 rounds of ammunition each. These guns were regarded primarily as offensive (ground-attack) weapons. They were fed from two ammunition boxes, one on each side of the fuselage, through chutes in the undercarriage fairings. In the pilot's cockpit were an air-pressure gauge for the wheel-brake and gun-firing systems; a gun-firing button high on the left-hand segment of the ring-type handgrip at the top of the control column; and reflector gun-sight master-switch and dimmer-switch. As an alternative to the reflector sight a ring sight could be fitted behind the windscreen for use in conjunction with a bead mounted on a pillar, braced to the engine exhaust-collector ring.

The observer had a Lewis Mk.IIIG or IIIE, or a Vickers G.O. gun on a Fairey pillar mounting, as fitted to the Fairey Battle and Blackburn Skua. For the Lewis gun there were eight 97-round drums and a Mk.I reflector sight. The gunner's seat was adjustable for height and traverse through a Bowden cable, and the ammunition drums lay flat on a magnesium turntable beneath the fuselage decking. This turntable was developed by Westland in the recognition that it was becoming increasingly difficult to locate ammunition drums for easy access, especially in an army co-operation aircraft which carried a wide variety of equipment and made exacting demands on the gunner. A spring-urged latch co-operated with a cam track and slots in the turntable under button control.

Bombs were carried on the stub wings attached to the undercarriage beams and far aft beneath the fuselage. They were fused and released electrically from either crew position. Hinged panels in the wooden floor gave access to the bombsight, bomb switches, tail drift-sight and message hook. The fuselage bomb-carrier was for four 20-lb H.E. Mk.I bombs, and another twelve of these bombs could be carried beneath the

Westland Lysander, showing stub wings for carrying bombs (carriers for practice bombs are installed), ports in wheel fairings for Browning guns, ring sight behind pilot's windscreen and bead on pillar above engine cowling.

In this side view of a Lysander the Lewis gun, with its reflector sight, is seen in its stowed position. The ring-and-bead sight for the pilot's guns is also seen.

stub wings, as alternatives to Mk.II practice smoke bombs or Mk.I reconnaissance flares. Other alternatives were four Mk.VII 112-lb or 120-lb G.P. bombs, or two 250-lb bombs, or two smoke canisters, or Mk.Vb supply-droppers or 25-lb incendiary bomb canisters.

As a result of war-time experience, twin Browning guns were installed in the dorsal position instead of a single gun, and a number of trial installations of armament were made which fall beyond the scope of this review.

Grouping of four 20-mm Hispano guns in the nose of the second prototype of the Westland Whirlwind. A pillar for a bead sight is just visible above the nose.

Whirlwind The first Whirlwind single-seat twin-engined fighter, to Specification F.37/35, flew late in 1938. Although of notable slenderness, the nose of the fuselage housed the concentrated armament of four 20-mm Hispano Mk.I guns, each with a 60-round ammunition drum. Not only did this allow a very high density of fire, but the pilot's line of sight was very close to the line of fire.

A now-familiar photograph of a Whirlwind, stated to be armed experimentally with a 37-mm gun (a caption endorsed by Westland themselves) appears to show, in reality, a 20-mm Hispano gun associated with a prominent lateral bulge. Other bulges of the same kind are in evidence and the lengthened and redesigned nose with which this installation was associated may well have been occasioned by revised feeding arrangements. For Whirlwind L6844, an installation of twelve Browning machine-guns has been recorded.

White & Thompson

No.3 This little flying-boat was acquired by the Admiralty in 1914 and was probably the first of its class in British service to carry armament. A Lewis gun was fitted to a pillar mounting on the port side of the cockpit.

Wight

Type 840 Like its counterpart the Short 184, this twin-float seaplane was designed to carry a 14-inch torpedo. On the first few machines the bracing-ties between the floats were arched accordingly, but these members were later made straight, and a bomb load of considerably less than the torpedo's weight was carried. A Wight seaplane of unspecified type was used in 1915 for bombing experiments at Calshot.

Bomber Four 112-lb bombs could be carried under the lower wings of this three-bay single-engined bomber of 1916. There was a Lewis gun on a Scarff ring-mounting over the rear cockpit.

'Converted' Seaplane This type of twin-float seaplane was developed from the Wight Bomber in 1917. Anti-submarine operations were undertaken with 100-lb bombs (specialised anti-submarine weapons) and one machine, operating from Cherbourg on 18 August, 1917, sank *UB-32* by dropping a bomb of this type just forward of the periscope. Up to four such bombs could probably be carried, and a load of two 100-lb and two 112-lb has been reported.

Twin Seaplane   This type of very large torpedo-carrying seaplane appeared in 1915. Drops were actually made, and photographed. The torpedo was of the 18-in Mk.IX pattern.

Baby Seaplane   Like its counterpart the Sopwith Baby, this little float-plane was intended to carry two 65-lb bombs. No gun installation has been identified.

Index

Admiralty Air Department A.D. Flying
 Boat, 2
A.D. Navyplane, 2
A.D. Scout (Sparrow), 1
A.D. Type 1000, 1
Aircraft Disposal Company A.D.C.1, 2,
 3
Airspeed Convertible Envoy, 3
 Oxford I, 3
Alcock A-1, 4
Armstrong Whitworth Ajax, 12
 Ara, 6
 Aries, 15
 Armadillo, 6
 Atlas, 12–15
 Awana, 7
 Scimitar, 17, 18
 Sinaia, 6
 Siskin, 7–12
 Starling, 15, 16
 Whitley, 21–26
 Wolf, 7
 A.W.XVI, 15
 A.W.19, 5
 A.W.23, 19
 A.W.29, 19–20
 F.K.3, 5
 F.K.8, 5–6
 F.K.10, 6
 F.K.12, 6
Arrow Active, 26
Austin Austin-Ball A.F.B.1, 26
 Greyhound, 27
 Osprey, 26
Avro Aldershot, 30–32
 Anson I, 40, 41
 Antelope, 36–37
 Ava, 33, 34
 Avenger, 35
 Avocet, 36
 Bison, 33, 34
 Buffalo, 35
 Manchester (biplane), 30
 Manchester, 42
 Pike, 29
 Spider, 30
 503 (Type H), 27
 504—27–29
 508—27
 510—29
 519—29
 521—29
 527—29
 528—29

Avro 529 and 529A, 29–30
 530—30
 626—37–38
 636—40
 637—38–40

Beardmore W.B.I, 42
 W.B.II, 42–43
 W.B.III, 43
 W.B.IV, 43–44
 W.B.V, 44
 W.B.26, 44
Blackburn Airedale, 53–54
 B-2, 61
 B-7, 69
 Baffin, 63
 Beagle, 58–59
 Blackburd, 46–48
 Blackburn, 51–52
 Botha, 72
 Cubaroo, 52–53
 Dart, 49, 50–51
 F.7/30, 63–64
 G.P. and S.P., 45
 Iris, 56–57
 Kangaroo, 45–46
 Lincock, 57
 M.1/30 and M.1/30A, 60–61
 Nautilus, 59
 Perth, 62–63
 Ripon, 54–56
 Roc, 71–72
 Seaplane Type L, 44–45
 Shark, 64–69
 Skua, 69–71
 Swift, 48–50
 Sydney, 59–60
 T.B., 45
 Triplane, 45
 Turcock, 58
 Velos, 54
 3MR4, 61
Boulton & Paul (later Boulton Paul)
 Bittern, 81, 82
 Bobolink, 73
 Bodmin, 77
 Bolton, 77
 Bourges, 73–77
 Bugle, 77–79
 Defiant, 86–89
 Overstrand, 83–85
 Partridge, 73, 81–82
 P.32, 82–83
 Sidestrand, 79–81

453

Bristol Badger, 95–96
  Bagshot, 99, 101
  Beaufighter, 121–122
  Beaufort, 120–121
  Berkeley, 98
  Blenheim, 114–119
  Blenheim Fighter, 119–20
  Bloodhound, 97–98
  Boarhound and Beaver, 98–99
  Bombay, 111–113
  Braemar, 96–97
  Bristol-Coanda Biplanes, 89
  Bulldog, 101–108
  Bullfinch, 97
  Bullpup, 108
  Fighter, 91–95
  M.1A, B, C, 95
  M.R.1, 95
  S.2A, 91
  S.S.A., 89
  Scout, 89–91
  Scout F, 95
  T.T.A., 91
  Type 101, 101
  Type 118, 108
  Type 120, 109–111
  Type 123, 111
  Type 133, 111
  Type 146, 113–114
  Type 148, 114
British Aerial Transport Bantam, 122–123

de Havilland Comet, 143
  Don, 144–145
  Dragon (Military Type), 143
  Puss Moth, 143
  Tiger Moth, 140–143
  D.H.1, 123
  D.H.2, 123–4
  D.H.3, 124
  D.H.4, 124–129
  D.H.5, 128–130
  D.H.6, 130
  D.H.9, 130–132
  D.H.9A, 132–135
  D.H.9AJ Stag, 137
  D.H.9b, 135
  D.H.10, 135
  D.H.11 Oxford, 136
  D.H.14 Okapi, 136
  D.H.15 Gazelle, 136
  D.H.27 Derby, 136
  D.H.29 Doncaster, 136
  D.H.42 Dormouse, 136
  D.H.42A and B Dingo, 136
  D.H.56 Hyena, 136–137
  D.H.60T Moth Trainer, 137
  D.H.65 Hound, 137, 140
  D.H.72, 140
  D.H.77, 140
  D.H.89M, 144
Dyott Bomber, 146

Fairey Atalanta and Titania, 153–154
  Albacore, 179–180
  Battle, 175–177
  Campania, 147
  F.2, 147
  Fantôme (Féroce), 170
  Fawn, 152–153
  Ferret, 156–157
  Firefly I, 158
  Firefly II, 159
  Firefly III, 161
  Fleetwing, 161
  Flycatcher, 151–152
  Flycatcher II, 158
  Fox I, 154–156
  Fox II–VII, 161
  Fulmar, 180
  G.4/31, 169–170
  Gordon, 163–166
  Hamble Baby, 147–148
  Hendon I and II, 167
  N.9, 148
  N.10 (Type III) and IIIA, 148
  P.4/34, 178–179
  Pintail, 149–150
  S.9/30, 170
  Seafox, 177
  Seal, 166–167
  Swordfish, 171–175
  IIIB, 148–149
  IIIC, 149
  IIID, 150
  IIIF, 158–159
Felixstowe Fury, 183
  Porte Baby, 180–181
  F.2A, 181–182
  F.2C, 182–183
  F.3 and F.5, 183

Gloster C.16/28, 195
  F.5/34, 199
  F.7/30, 196–197
  F.9/37, 199–200
  Gambet, 191
  Gamecock, 186–191
  Gauntlet, 195
  Gladiator, 198
  Gnatsnapper, 193–194
  Goldfinch, 193
  Goral, 193
  Gorcock and Guan, 191
  Goring, 192–193
  Grebe, 184–185
  Jupiter-Nighthawk and Jaguar-Nighthawk, 184
  Nightjar, 183
  S.15/33, 197–198
  Sparrowhawk, 184
  S.S.18, 194
  S.S.19 ('Multi-Gun'), 194–195
Grahame-White Ganymede, 202
  Scout Type Pusher (Type II), 201

Grahame-White Type 18, 202
1913 War Plane (Type 6), 201

Handley Page Anzani Biplane, 202
Clive, 216–217
Halifax, 226
Hampden, 224–226
Handcross, 213
Hanley, 209
Hare, 214–216
Harrow, 213–214
Harrow (monoplane), 222–223
Hendon, 212–213
Hereford, 226
Heyford, 217–220
Hinaidi, 214
Hyderabad, 209–212
H.P.21, 212
H.P.43, 220
H.P.46, 220
H.P.47, 220–221
H.P.51, 221
O/100 and O/400, 202–207
R/200, 207
V/1500, 207–209
Hawker Audax, 252–254
Danecock, 228
Dantorp, 255
Duiker, 226
F.20/27, 233
Hardy, 255
Harrier, 232–233
Hart and Hart (Special), 235–245
Hart Fighter and Demon, 247–252
Hartbees, 258–259
Hawfinch, 232
Hector, 259–261
Hedgehog, 228
Henley, 263
Heron, 228
Hind, 256–257
Hoopoe, 233–234
Hornbill, 231–232
Hornet, 245
Horsley, 229–231
Hotspur, 263
Hurricane, 261–263
Nimrod, 245–247
Osprey, 245
P.V.3 (F.7/30), 255–256
P.V.4, 257–258
Tornado and Typhoon, 264
Woodcock, 226–228

Kennedy Giant, 264

Mann, Egerton Type B, 265
Type H, 265
Mann & Grimmer M.1, 265
Martin-Baker M.B.2, 265–267
Martinsyde F.1, 268
F.2, 268
F.3, 268–269

Martinsyde F.4, 269–270
G.100 and G.102, 267–268
R.G., 268
S.1, 267
Miles Master I, 270

Nieuport B.N.1, 271
London, 272
Nighthawk, 271–272

Parnall G.4/31, 274–276
Heck, 276
Panther, 273
Pike, 274
Pipit, 274
Plover, 273
Possum, 273
Puffin, 273
Zeppelin Scout, 272–273
Pemberton-Billing P.B.23E and P.B.25, 276
P.B.29, 276
Phoenix (English Electric) Ayr, 277
Cork, 276
Kingston, 276–277
Port Victoria Grain Griffin, 278
P.V.1, 277
P.V.2 and P.V.2bis, 277
P.V.4, 277
P.V.5 and P.V.5a, 278
P.V.7 (Grain Kitten), 278
P.V.8 (Eastchurch Kitten), 278
P.V.9, 278

Robey Robey-Peters Gun Carrier, 278
Royal Aircraft Factory A.E.3 (Ram), 280
B.E.2, 2a and 2b, 280
B.E.2c, d and e, 281–284
B.E.8 and 8a, 28
B.E.9, 284
B.E.12, 284–286
B.E.12b, 286
C.E.1, 286
F.E.2, 286–288
F.E.2a, 288
F.E.2b, 288–289
F.E.2d, 289–292
F.E.3, 292
F.E.4, 292–293
F.E.6, 293
F.E.8, 293
F.E.9, 293
N.E.1, 293–294
R.E.5, 294
R.E.7, 294
R.E.8, 295–296
R.E.9, 296
S.E.2, 296
S.E.4a, 296
S.E.5, 296–297
S.E.5a and b, 297–298

Sage Type 2, 298
  Type 3, 298
  Type 4, 298
Saunders T.1, 299
Saunders-Roe (formerly S.E. Saunders)
  A.10, 300–301
  A.33, 305
  Cloud, 305
  Cutty Sark, 305
  Lerwick, 305
  London, 301–305
  Severn, 299–300
  Valkyrie, 299
Short Bomber, 309–310
  Chamois, 312
  Cromarty, 311–312
  F.5 (Metal Hull), 312
  Gurnard, 313–314
  K.F.1, 315
  N.2B, 311
  R.24/31, 316
  Rangoon, 314
  S.38, 306
  S.81 Gun-carrier, 306
  Sarafand, 315–316
  Shirl, 311
  Singapore, 312
  Singapore II, 315
  Singapore III, 316—317
  Springbok, 312
  Stirling, 319
  Sturgeon, 312–313
  Sunderland, 317–318
  Tractor Seaplanes, 307
  Type 184, 308–309
  Type 320, 310–11
  310-hp Seaplane, Type B, 311
Siddeley R.T.1, 319
  (For other Siddeley types see Armstrong
    Whitworth)
Sopwith Bat Boat, 320
  Bee, 329
  Bomber, 336
  Buffalo, 351–352
  Bulldog, 343–345
  Camel F.1, 330–335
  Camel T.F.1, 336
  Cobham, 354–355
  Cuckoo, 336–338
  Dolphin, 338–341
  Dragon, 352
  Gordon Bennett Racer, 321
  Gun Bus, 321–323
  Hippo, 346–347
  L.R.T.Tr., 329
  Pup, 327–328
  Pusher Seaplane Gun-carrier No. 127,
    320
  Rhino, 345
  Salamander, 347–351
  Schneider and Baby, 323–4
  Snail, 347–348
  Snipe, 341–343

Sopwith Snapper, 355
  Snark, 352–353
  1½ Strutter, 324–327
  Swallow, 351
  Tabloid, 321
  Two-seater Scout, 323
  Tractor Biplanes, 320
  Triplane, 328–329
  Triplane (Hispano-Suiza), 329–330
  Type C, 321
  Type 807, 323
  Type 860, 323
Sunbeam Bomber, 355
Supermarine Baby, 356
  Channel, 356–357
  F.7/30 (Spitfire), 367
  Night Hawk, 356
  Patrol Seaplane, 356
  Scapa, 363–364
  Scarab, 358
  Seagull, 357
  Seagull V and Walrus, 366–367
  Sea King and Sea Lion, 357–358
  Seal, 357
  Seamew, 363
  Sea Otter, 372
  Sheldrake, 362
  Solent, 362–363
  Southampton, 358–362
  Southampton X, 363
  Spitfire, 368–372
  Stranraer, 367

Tarrant Tabor, 373
Norman Thompson N.1B, 373
  N.2C, 373
  N.T4 and 4a, 373

Vickers B.19/27, 409–10
  C.16/28, 412
  C.O.W. Gun Fighter, 408–409
  E.S.1, 380
  F.B.7, 380
  F.B.8, 380–1
  F.B.11, 381
  F.B.12, 381
  F.B.14, 381
  F.B.16, 382
  F.B.19, 382
  F.B.24, 382–384
  F.B.25, 384
  G.4/31, 414–416
  Gun Bus, 373–380
  Jockey, 407–408
  M.1/30, 413–414
  Type 123, 394
  Type 141, 405–406
  Type 143, 406
  Type 177, 406–407
  Valentia, 413
  Valentia (flying-boat), 387–388
  Valiant, 396
  Valparaiso, 394

Vickers Vampire, 384
  Vanellus, 393
  Vellox, 416
  Venom, 419
  Venture, 393
  Vernon, 386–387
  Vespa, 394
  Victoria, 393
  Viking, 386
  Vildebeest, 398–405
  Vimy, 384–386
  Vincent, 416
  Vireo, 395–397
  Virginia, 388–393
  Vivid, 397–398
  Vixen, 393
  Vulture, 386
  Warwick, 424
  Wellesley, 416–419
  Wellington, 419–424
  Wibault Scout, 394

Westland C.O.W. Gun Fighter, 435–438
  F.7/30, 443–444

Westland F.20/27, 434–435
  Lysander, 448–450
  N.16 and N.17, 424–425
  Pterodactyl V, 440–443
  P.V.3, 438
  P.V.6 and Wallace I, 438–440
  P.V.7, 445–446
  Wagtail, 425–426
  Wallace II, 446–448
  Walrus, 427
  Wapiti, 431–434
  Weasel, 426
  Westbury, 428–430
  Whirlwind, 451
  Witch, 434
  Wizard, 430–431
  Yeovil, 427–428
White & Thompson No. 3, 451
Wight Baby Seaplane, 452
  Bomber, 451
  'Converted' Seaplane, 451
  Twin Seaplane, 452
  Type 840, 451